AMERICANS VS DEMOCRATS

BLACK EXPLOITATION: FUEL OF THE NEW CIVIL WAR

Written by: W Holliday

ISBN 978-0-578-49486-9

Website: www.wlholliday.com

To contact this author: hollidaw@gmail.com

Dedication

In memory of Jackie Cavanaugh, who was one of my dearest friends and staunchest supporters, I dedicate this book to all my wonderful friends and family, especially my wife, who questioned whether I would ever finish this project. With that said, in all sincerity, I want to thank everyone for their patience. And, knowing that this book may ruffle some feathers among certain groups, perhaps, I'll now add somewhat of a disclaimer:

Although I wrote this text in what I call simplese, it may contain some scenarios, and upsetting language, along with a heaping dollop of brutal truth, and bluntness that is not for the thin of skin or the political correctness crowd.

For some blacks, and white Democrats, and perhaps some conservatives, this writing may be particularly upsetting. This book is meant entirely for those adults with open minds and possessing enough intellect to grasp the fact-based, highly opinionated and no holds barred content inside, so please read at your discretion.

You have been warned.

Contents

Introduction and Purpose

In the year 1861, our nation became embroiled in a bitter civil war where a fight to the death was waged between Democrats and Republicans in brutal and bloody battles for the soul of our nation and the preservation of our newly written Constitution. This historic and defining clash of values and principles would ultimately result in victory for the Republican Party, and the subsequent freeing of black slaves from centuries of captivity.

However, the painful sacrifice and tremendous loss of life by Republicans for the freedom of Africans in the 1800s stands in stark contrast to the incredible shift today by unappreciative blacks, who now shun their rescuers and willingly embrace their former enslavers who fought to keep them in bondage permanently.

Over the last fifty years in America, blacks have faithfully voted over 90% democrat every election without fail. What had happened to blacks from the 1800s to present day for them to overwhelmingly support and vote for the party that had brutally enslaved their ancestors? What is it that has allowed the Democrat Party to continue, even to this day, to have such political dominance over blacks?

Furthermore, how can we explain the black community's continual manipulation, ignorance of our nation's political history, and immovable loyalty to their former-enslavers? And why have blacks today unwittingly assumed the most significant role in this country's moral decline and gradual acceptance of socialism?

With this writing, I will attempt to answer these questions and show how remnants of the Civil Rights Movement of the 1950s and 1960s underpins the progression of the cancerous and weaponized political correctness ideology that is now so pervasive within our society.

It is my fervent hope that readers understand the quite bizarre juxtaposition between Africans who were once captives of the 1800s Democrat Party, as opposed to liberal blacks today who is now the Democrats' most rabid supporters and potent weapon in their ongoing war against almost everything American.

As we examine the political history of both political parties, we will see that it was quite evident, even from the very beginning of these "United" States, that Democrats would always be against this country and anyone seeking what our Declaration of Independence promised; an unfettered life, liberty, and pursuit of happiness. I intend to, hopefully, show with some clarity the deception and methods by which white liberals have kept most blacks confused and unbalanced.

Think about this; most people don't have a clue as to what to call blacks nowadays, mainly because our "branding" has gone through a constant metamorphosis since the time Africans were bought onto America's shores. Blacks have been called Niggers, Negroes, Coloreds and now today, the absurd and exceedingly divisive and anti-assimilation misnomer of "African-Americans."

For the purpose of this book, and my sanity as a black man, I'll just stick with the simple branding of "blacks," because it is nondescript in nationality and presents little to misconstrue and twist into emotional knots by black and white liberals.

Of course, when I speak about the black community in this book, I do not mean all, that would be foolish, because there are many terrific blacks in this nation that have achieved much success and are great individuals who see in this country what a lot of other races see, a land of opportunity. This group of successful blacks have broken away from the mental prisons of Democrat plantations and have removed their racially-tempered shackles of victimization and entitlement inertia by which they were earlier impeded.

These independent blacks are not my main area of concern. Instead, my observations in this text will seek to highlight and focus on that rather large segment of black malcontents in America that is ruled mainly by animalistic emotion; eschewing intellect, morality, and personal accountability in favor of violence as a means to an end.

This rather large contingent of dishonest, self-enrichment by-any -means-necessary blacks are always seeking ways to cause division and racial discord. But like I said, these disrupters do not represent all blacks. So, as you are reading my thoughts, please bear in mind that we blacks are not an entirely monolithic race in this country, it just seems so when it comes to voting.

On that note, I will say that my primary intent here is to shake and awaken blacks and all Americans before our now unbalanced and teetering nation go entirely over the edge of identity politics and into the abyss of political correctness. As you can probably guess by now, there were many ways for me to broach the topic about which I am writing. However, I decided to direct my focus on the black community in particular. I do so because I firmly believe that the vast majority of power the Democrat Party wields today is derived, to a great extent, from the black community and their ever-present, racially-induced anger.

I know now that it is the black community's unseemly and unholy allegiance which has provided the means and conduit by which Democrats, with the help of their liberal mainstream media and tabloids, have been able to shape and mold erroneous racial perceptions and narratives in their ongoing attempt to gain permanent political power in this country.

In this context, I intend to detail how the Democrat Party has never, ever "switched," and is the very same party from the time of its creation in the 1800s to today's party, which still possesses a mob-like mentality and a belief in violence as a means to an end. As a result, our nation is now faced with an overly hostile environment of anti-American political correctness and groupthink, forcing everyone to walk around on "not-offending-anyone eggshells."

Even while writing this book, I see unprecedented assaults on our rights, freedoms, and livelihoods, along with frequent attempts to suppress the free speech of those not in alignment with the left's ideology. Today, there is an endless barrage of coordinated social media attacks, aimed squarely at conservatives, being carried out by radical leftists in an attempt to remove their voices from that space.

With that being said, this book is most decidedly anti-leftist and therefore not written in the vein of being politically correct, as was my intention. More to the point, this writing is about the unvarnished and unmitigated truth, which brings us to an old political adage: *"If you want to make any conservative mad, tell them a lie, and If you want to make any liberal mad, tell them the truth."*

However, before we wade into the beginning chapter of this book, there are some fundamental questions which I think all Americans should be asking themselves right about now: *Do we really want to live in a country without God and religious freedom? And can we truly exist as a nation without our constitution interpreted as framed and intended by the founders? Also, can we thrive in a country without free speech? And are we safe with our gun rights suppressed? Whatever happened to civility and respect in our nation? Lastly, who, or what is most responsible for the fear that most of us have of losing our freedoms and rights in this country?*

To each one of us, we need to answer the above questions with thoughtful and honest introspection. In writing this book, there are many other questions, pertaining to blacks, that I have asked continuously of Democrats, black and white, and have never gotten any satisfactory answers. So, at this point, I would like to pose these same fundamental questions to the readers of this text.

We know that the Nazi Party and Hitler tortured and exterminated millions of white Jews in Germany in the 1930s and 1940s, and because of the atrocities they committed against these Jews, today this party no longer exists in Germany and the name itself is stricken from their society. Now, here in the United States, no one, not even historians, disputes that leading up to the Civil War that it was Democrats alone that owned millions of black slaves. So, it is shocking to me that, although they were the ones who whipped and hung blacks from trees and imposed Jim Crow Laws in the south for decades, no such banning of the Democrat name has ever occurred or even been proffered by anyone in this country; why hasn't it?

What gives, why does the Democrat name still exist in America today? Why isn't this name, which is fully attached to the atrocities of the enslavement, lynching, and torture of millions of blacks in this country, stricken from our political arena just as the Nazi name is banned from Germany's politics?

Are blacks lower than Jews in this regard; to not have their former enslavers' name banned from ever being used again in this nation? And are today's white and black liberals, proudly strutting about and wearing the Democrat badging, openly racist?

And finally, why are most blacks today so eager to call themselves Democrats and angrily defend the party that enslaved their people?

These questions should give each one of us, black and white or whatever, some pause and reflection as to who and what we have aligned ourselves with out of our political ignorance. Hopefully together, and with the knowledge I have gleaned from my perusal of the history of both political parties in this nation, we can find the truth and answers somewhere in this text for future guidance in our political alliances.

But before we go any further, I must confess that, as a black man, I am humiliated and humbled that I didn't always have a full understanding of the subject matter which I am now writing about.

Although it took quite some time for me to get to this point in my journey, I wanna share with you now, through the eyes of a black man, the things which I have learned from my research. So, come along with me on the emotional rollercoaster upon which I rode some years ago to find myself and the truth. Shall we begin?

Chapter One

Introducing the Democrat Party

The Democrat Party's name officially became a part of our nation's political landscape in 1829 and... Ok, stop right there for a minute, now what images come to mind, and what do you think of when you think of this party? Do you think of what the Democrat Party now supposedly espouses: *"Tolerance, equality, diversity, love, strong unions, warm cookies and milk, sunny days on the beach, flowers, creampuffs and helping the little man?"*

Or do you think about what the Democrat Party represents today?: *"Illegal immigration advocacy, anti-God, anti-prayer, anti-Christianity, radical Muslims, violent groups like Black Lives Matter and Antifa, promoting campus violence, rioting, transgenders, MS-13 gangs, violent protests, free speech suppression, political smear tactics, flag burnings, abortions, anti-law enforcement, open borders, welfare dependency, and voter fraud?"*

Tough to reconcile this duality, huh? Well, let's see if we can sift and sort the truth from fiction, shall we? Just for a moment, I want you to come along with me on a quick and eye-opening journey into the past. This won't take long, I promise.

Let's imagine, if you will, that it's the summer of 1832 and a stiflingly hot afternoon in late July, with nary a cloud lingering overhead to provide even a modicum of relief from the radiant heat of the scorching southern sun. In this setting, we'll now sneak a peek at a scene in the deep south that exemplified this era in our nation:

"In a densely wooded area, intrusive rays of bright sunlight penetrated the leaves of outstretched maple and oak trees, illuminating patches of dried out and broken branch limbs strewn haphazardly about the forest floor like the defleshed and bony arms of the long

dead. All was eerily quiet as if the usually rummaging about small animals had suddenly suspended their foraging for food, wary of predators. And under an old Oak tree, sitting astride his steed and hunched forward in his saddle, the haggard looking, craggy-faced massa quietly watched as two paddy rollers dutifully knotted a noose at the end of a rope. With this task completed, an exhausted and sweat-drenched runaway was hoisted up onto one of their horses, hands tightly tied and resigned to his fate.

The African slave stared intensely into his master's eyes and stiffened his back with a steely resolve, erect in his seat as one of the men quickly slipped the noose around his neck. With bloodshot eyes and lips drawn tight, the angry and grim-faced slave owner wiped at his brow with the rim of his tattered felt hat as he spat a gob of tobacco juice onto the ground in disgust and muttered: "This'll teach you boy, and the rest of you niggers not to run."

Glaring at the defiant runaway slave with cold and soulless eyes devoid of mercy, the plantation massa pulled out a leather encased whiskey flask from his bosom and took a quick sip. Recapping the container and returning it to his breast, he wiped at his mouth with a sweat-stain discolored shirt sleeve and slowly dismounted his horse. Moving painfully and with a slight limp, the gimpy old massa breathed heavily, grunting as he approached the paddy roller's horse upon which the somber and stoic slave sat.

With a callous indifference and laser-like focus, the slave owner reached over, unhesitant, and gave a sharp tug on the rope of the horse's bridle, leaving the runaway dangling in midair. As the noose grew taut about his neck, slowly crushing his windpipe, the slave gasped for air as his flailing feet, seeking purchase but not finding anything of substance to alight onto, stabbed into nothingness.

Slowly rocking in a back and forth motion, neck bones cracking under his weight and lungs straining for air, the runaway's legs performed a slow dance of death, a jig, for his white audience who stood solemnly, impassively watching the silent and futile struggle of their prey's desperate attempt at survival.

After a short while and in a submission to the inevitable, the fran-

*tic and jerky movements ceased as the slave succumbed to the em-
brace of death, his battle lost and the once elusive and everlasting
freedom he forever sought, finally gained.*

*Still glistening with sweat, eyes now staring lifelessly at the white
plantation massa, the slave's body twirled slowly like a marionette
on a string, swaying gently in the hot July air until one of the paddy
rollers produced a knife and sliced through the rope, releasing his
remains.*

*And like big game hunters who'd just bought down a buck, the
paddy rollers casually tied the deceased slave onto the back of one of
their horses, much as they would a potato filled sack. The body would
be taken back to the plantation and momentarily displayed as a stark
warning and brutal deterrent for any of the other slaves on the plantation that might suddenly develop an itch to run.*

Although the punishment for this runaway had been swift and
harsh, his lynching had also come at a significant cost for the white
slave owner as well. The rebellious slave had been a prized buck and
in purely economic terms, with proper breeding, would have made
more little black slaves, livestock, to be sold on the market or to restock the fields.

However, the plantation would survive this loss, and the massa
would go on to continue with the control and dominance of his slaves
for a few more decades. The subjugation of the remaining black captives would be achieved by violence and mental conditioning; tools
necessary for keeping the enslaved in fear of retribution and dependent upon their captors for survival.

**Of note; because of Fugitive Slave laws passed in 1793, which
provided for the return of escaped slaves from any state in the country
back to their original owner, runaways had little refuge anywhere in
the country. During the 1800s, a slave's capture and subsequent return to the plantation of which he belonged was then seen as merely
the dutiful returning of property to its rightful owner.*

Scenes like the one depicted above probably played out numerous
times somewhere in the antebellum south during the dark period of
slavery in our nation's history when African slaves were being bought,

bred, and sold like cattle. This type of farming wasn't unusual; at the time it was quite routine for enslaved black families to be torn apart and redistributed to various plantations across the southern regions of this country, as most was viewed as just property.

However, it is most crucial for us to grasp fully, and understand the distinction which must be drawn here, that the white men and plantation owners carrying out these lynchings of blacks during this period were all Democrats. Our nation's real history shows us that none of these perpetrators were Republicans.

In my previous ill-informed and uneducated state of mind, I didn't know that it was white Democrats, like the ones depicted in the above story, from both the northern and southern states, who had tried to permanently install an oppressive system of black enslavement within this nation in the 1800s. And I was entirely unaware that it had taken a brutal war and the Republican Party to stop'em.

Upon research, not only did I find out about this bit of history, I also found out that it was mostly white southern Democrats who had used captive African slaves as forced labor to engineer a robust economic engine to drive generational wealth to plantations scattered all across the southern regions of this country during the pre-civil war era.

Today, this period of black enslavement in our nation's history is in the process of being sanitized, distorted, and rewritten by white liberal Democrats, liberal colleges and universities, Hollywood elites, and mainstream media outlets. There has been a concerted and ongoing effort to obfuscate, diminish, and in some cases, even erase the Democrat Party's culpability and role in the enslavement, exploitation, and destruction of black families and communities in America during the slavery era and even today.

In fact, whenever a movie or documentary is produced today regarding this subject, the opposing sides of the civil war are always referred to as the Union and the Confederate, generic terms to whitewash and blur history and falsely assign blame onto both parties. But to be clear, the 1800s Civil War was a battle in which the rebellious northern and southern Democrats wanted slavery and a breaking away from America and the Constitution, versus Republicans, who abhorred slavery, cherished our Constitution, and wanted a united country.

Because of the decades-long, continual blurring of our nation's history, I didn't have any real knowledge of the well-oiled, divisive, and racist inner workings of today's Democrat Party of which I had been politically affiliated. Our fully liberalized schools and higher learning institutions have been teaching us for decades that it had been whites within both parties who had owned slaves. There had purposely been no distinction, whatsoever, drawn between Democrats and Republicans.

However, after some more researching, what I learned was fascinating and quite revelatory. And during this process of being enlightened, it would be the absolute stunning duplicity of Democrats which would really shock and anger me to no end. With my newfound knowledge, I realized that I had been hoodwinked, duped, betrayed, and used for quite some time by white and black liberals. I had been nothing more than a pawn in their grand scheme of political power and dominance.

My anger would only grow when it dawned upon me that I had been fully supporting a party against my own best interests and one, over centuries, which had successfully conditioned generations of blacks like me and producing the pitiful political sheep which now passes for "African Americans."

I wanted to warn the world, but after speaking with some blacks about my "enlightenment" regarding the real history of both political parties, I quickly found out that it was gonna take a helluva lot more than historical facts to wake most of my people up to the real truth. I know now, with some degree of certainty, that you just cannot shake the majority of blacks loose from four hundred years of conditioning, manipulation, and deception in a ten minute conversation. It's an almost impossible task to get some blacks to even come to grips with being told that they have been living a lie and have been used for decades.

I should know, I was there at the very same point where most of them are right now, and can recall the times that I didn't want to see or hear anything contrary to beliefs which I had been taught early on, nor did I want to know about any adverse information concerning "my Democrats."

Eventually, though, this black ostrich pulled his head out of the liberal indoctrination sand and woke up, and I wanna tell you all about it.

Chapter Two

My Awakening

Ibecame aware of the truth about Democrats years ago, in 2008 to be exact, and I want to expand upon the knowledge I gained. But first, let's go back to when I was just a small child; a southern bred, barefooted young'un with milk stains still around his mouth.

I now want to give you a snippet, a taste, of my upbringing for context and background.

Third from the youngest of eleven brothers and sisters, my siblings and I were all naïve to politics in our youth, probably because, at the time, we had other more pressing issues besieging our family which had taken priority. We were destitute and in need; the bunch of us pretty much crammed together like sardines in a rather small and nondescript ramshackle house that, to me, always seemed to be in some state of disrepair.

This was the first house I can recall living in, and it wasn't much to look at. It was a real eyesore and craphole, but it was home. I still remember that when it rained, we would place buckets strategically inside the old, dilapidated clapboard home in areas where drips would often occur. Leaks were just about everywhere because the old patchwork roof was so much like a sieve that every time there was a storm, it was as if our entire family was camping outside and under Niagara Falls.

Even though we had been in dire economic straits back then and didn't have much, we never sought, nor did we get welfare or any other form of assistance from the government. Those were our lean salad days, and more often than not it wasn't even the whole salad we ate. Some days it was just wilted lettuce we nibbled on. So early on, most everyone in the family started taking any odd jobs that they could find to help out in the household.

I always think about the times when my younger brother and I would do our part and go out on certain days, picking up discarded bottles and returning them for the deposit at one of the local country stores. After a long and exhausting day of scooping up bottles and cans in the hot midday sun, one of our favorite rewards was to grab a sweet honey bun and wash it down with an ice-cold bottle of coke.

Yes, those were the days; my brother and I sitting under the cooling embrace of tree shade, enjoying our hard-earned treat as the wind dried the sweat from our brows, all the while laughing and joking about the strange people we had encountered that day. We really relished these times together and the good feelings that came along with it, knowing that it had been by our own hands and hard work that we had earned enough money to not only make those moments possible, but to also have enough pocket change left over for other snacks like two-for-a-penny cookies, which was another favorite of ours.

My brother and I were quite the hustlers back then and did many small jobs for our neighbors such as mow and rake yards, clean windows, and help scrap removers. We did whatever it took to make some honest money, which we mostly contributed to our struggling household.

Our pinch-every-penny mother always made good use of any funds coming into her hands, buying most foods in bulk to keep thirteen hungry bellies fed. So, even though the honey bun and coke had been an occasional treat for us in those days, in our southern household we had mainly subsisted on cheap but filling fare like rice, grits, bread, and other healthy foods like peas, beans, and collard greens, *until you put the fatback in 'em of course.*

I laugh about it now but our family, just as a lot of southern blacks and whites did back then, and still do today, ate just about everything from the pig. In those days, the seemingly ubiquitous swine didn't stand a chance with blacks, nor whites, in the south. I can still fondly recall the old southern saying among the elders regarding the pig's usage, *"from the rooter to the tooter."*

Our family eagerly munched and gnawed on pigtails, hog maws, pig knuckles, pig snout, pickled and unpickled pig's feet, chitterlings, fried pork chops, smothered pork chops, hogshead cheese, crackling bread, etc. I mean, nothing was wasted or spared from those little porcine fellas when we got a hold of'em. In fact, whenever a pig in the south saw a black man walking toward his pen in those days, he would fall onto his knees and into prayer.

Pork aside, I will always remember that even under some of the most adverse conditions and trying times we faced, one of the most important things giving us the strength to persevere was the religious foundation instilled in us by our mother, who believed in prayer and more prayer. With her guidance, our Bible and belief in God served as an anchor for us and would be mostly at the root of everything we did, producing the togetherness and bond we all shared.

As it was for us, most blacks back then were much more religious and God-fearing then they are today. This spirituality among blacks was no coincidence, going all the way back to slavery, the church has always been a central part of just about every black community across the nation, especially in the south.

The majority of blacks within our neighborhood relied mostly on religion-infused, Bible-based guidance seeing them through the hard times and keeping them on the straight and narrow. As a result, and unlike most impoverished and violence-prone black communities nowadays, circumstances we endured back then never produced criminal activities like what we see today among a lot of poor blacks.

In those days, no one in our neighborhood ever thought about slinging drugs on street corners or shooting other blacks just because they were impoverished and frustrated. Instead, most sought work and pulled together to make ends meet. Furthermore, most blacks back then could not be moved to harm their communities or one another in such a fashion as a lot of blacks do to each other today. My generation was also much more appreciative of hard work, were more respectful of our elders, the authorities, of each other, and valued life far more back then.

I must also note that in those days our family, and the black community at large, thought of survival and progress in terms of family unity, faith, education, and hard work. We never thought about relying on the self-defeating crutches of entitlement and victimization that cripples so many blacks today.

As to the political leanings of my family members, no one really talked politics, and I don't believe that my parents or any of my siblings ever voted back then either, to tell the truth. You know, I also do not recall there ever being any sort of overt political persuasion by either the Democrat or Republican Party during my teenage years. Not that it mattered, our family was seemingly unaware of politics, not really caring who was elected to office, because we had each other and that was all we seemed to need back then.

As such, and nearing my teens, our family managed to climb out of our economic predicament with the sacrifice and hard work of my older brothers and sisters, who had gotten factory and manufacturing jobs. Being good stewards, they had all saved and pooled their money together to purchase a better home and living quarters for us. Along with mine and my younger brother's after snack contributions, of course, this financial blessing enabled us to move into a brand spanking new and just-built home that had excellent indoor plumbing and a rain resistant roof.

Today, I can still fondly recall a few of my older siblings being employed in manufacturing and factory jobs, eagerly working as machinists and in other blue-collar positions, happy to be earning an income. I can also remember the many times when one of my older sisters, after a hard day's work at Campbell Soup, would come home smelling of tomatoes, tired but thankful. In those days, blue-collar jobs were plentiful, well-paying, and a Godsend for our family, pulling us up and out of abject poverty.

There is much more to be said about my early days growing up in the south, such as the time when, *as a small child, I had walked twelve miles to school...with just one shoe...without shoelaces...in the snow. Ok, ok...perhaps some other time.*

Seriously though, even though there is a lot of tantalizing tidbits about the days of my youth to be told, I am not gonna be too expansive on my childhood in this book. *I would suppose that some of my friends are probably breathing a sigh of relief about this and that's ok. I'll deal with them later.*

With that aside, I will tell you that in my youth I had been quite the voracious reader and curling up with a good book was the one thing that had been a constant for me, a welcome respite from my sometimes not so happy reality in my early days. Back then, my almost obsessive literary indulgence allowed me to take many enjoyable escapades from daily life. And on many occasions, it would be these imaginary adventures which transported me from mundane and dreary surroundings to sunny and fictional places of contentment.

Out of all my siblings, it seemed that I had always been the curious and fanciful one, endowed with a strong proclivity for seeking knowledge that would sometimes lead me into unfortunate situations as a child. I always wanted to know the how and why of things and wasn't one to let things be as they were just for the sake of being.

In my youth, I consumed a lot of novels, comic books, and newspapers, along with any other printed material I found stimulating. Curiously, somehow, I seemed to always gravitate towards just about any literature portraying a theme of good versus evil. I loved watching fictional detective shows and mystery programs, along with shoot'em up westerns like Bonanza, The Virginian, and High Chaparral, where the good guys always won.

However, it would take some time for my interest to develop on the subject of politics and how things really worked in our nation's capital. In those days, I had been deliberately ignorant regarding this particular subject, blissfully unaware of most of our nation's political history. Except for historical fluff like how George Washington Carver invented peanut butter or how that other George Washington had crossed Valley Forge and chopped down some cherry tree or something and didn't lie about it, I knew very little of any our nation's complex and brutal political history.

I guess my apathy regarding our nation's history came about because, at the time, I found the mechanics of political theater and history too cumbersome and tedious to really engage in as a teenager. But my political interest would begin to stir in the 1990s after I had gotten a chance to really watch politicians campaigning.

It was in that moment that I somehow felt strangely connected and drawn, in an inexplicable way, to Democrats and the warmth they seemingly exuded. To me, back then, these candidates just had a way with words that made you feel that everything was going to be alright if you just voted for their party.

My seemingly innately imbued emotional tether to the Democrat Party was strong and inviting and had caught me completely off guard. I soon learned from other blacks that this feeling I had experienced was something never to be questioned because, in our community, it was the right thing to feel and was as natural as being black and breathing. Like a lot of other blacks on the peripheral of politics, exposed to decades of subtle manipulation by white liberals, it had been a given that if I was ever gonna vote, I was to cast my ballot for Democrats and with no questions asked.

Looking back, I suppose that it was just to be assumed by most in the black community, and among white liberals, that my undying loyalty to the party was baked in just by virtue of me being born with black skin. And although I had accepted this sort of rite-of-passage and blindly followed liberals as other blacks, I was still deliberately lazy and apathetic towards all things politics in those days.

Ironically, the campaign and election of a "brother" to the Whitehouse in 2008 would not only serve to be my initial foray into politics but would also be the turning point and catalyst for my metamorphosis and journey into sanity and away from the plantation.

 Before awakening, I had been fully enclosed in my own bubble, not engaging in political conversations much, nor having any real interest in the political arena. You see, I had always thought that politics was something far removed from reality, and to me, all of the candidates jostling for attention and campaigning during election time was the same as watching a fictional movie; entertaining, but nothing that would really impact my own personal, social, economic or financial well-being. Well later, much later on, I would indeed find out just how wrong I was.

Knowing what I know now about Democrats and how they work today to disseminate false information to control the masses, I wanna tell you about my come to Jesus moment as a black man and confess the error of my ways to you.

I found out that I had been foolishly embracing a party and an ideology which wholly contradicted my core values and principles. So, as I look about me today in my newfound political sobriety, I now realize with startling clarity that most of our populace, especially blacks, have been dumbed down to accept just about anything from white liberals.

This brainwashing has allowed our country's destruction to be systematically and stealthily eased upon us bit by bit for decades, and with our very own complicity to boot. Today our country's self-induced downfall via the continual stripping away of morality, along with the erosion of our societal boundaries and norms, is the direct result of our nation's gradual acceptance of deleterious rules, behaviors, and laws totally incongruent with our Constitution and Bill of Rights.

We are, in no uncertain terms, slowly losing the foundation of Christian values and principles which has sustained us and made ours the greatest nation on earth. And make no mistake about it, there is anti-American sentiment being openly advocated for and promoted by the left that is undermining everything our country stands for. Right now, most Americans are unwittingly entangled in a new and much more nuanced Civil War, one which has been brewing and simmering since the end of the last Civil War of 1865.

What bought this revelation to the forefront for me was the election of Obama in 2008 and the sudden, accelerated push to divide the nation even more with identity politics and racial discord. Opening my eyes, even more, was the 2016 election of President Trump, a political outsider and unlikely working man's hero who emphasized America first. His ascension to the Whitehouse caused the inner workings of the Democrat Party to manifest itself and its apparent animus towards hard-working Americans and our nation.

The Democrat Party's carefully cultivated layers of deception, developed over decades and perhaps centuries, have now been peeled back, exposing the depth of violence and corruption within the dark recesses of our governmental agencies, academia, and media entities. The misdeeds of this morally bankrupt and traitorous party are now being made manifest, laid bare and in plain sight for those without emotional blinders to see.

However, there are still many in America, among all races and political leanings, that will not or cannot discern the actual battle lines which have been so sharply drawn between Americans and Democrats. *"Luke Chapter 12, Verse 56: Ye hypocrites, ye can discern the face of the sky and of the earth; but how is it that ye do not discern this time?"*

I know now that this pervasive ignorance among the citizens of this country is being driven by liberals embedded in our media and academia and tasked with running interference for the left. These anti-American operatives are hard at work, continually pumping out lies, innuendos, and mistruths, all to mislead, misdirect, and obfuscate.

These not so covert media plants ensure that all of the left's nefarious deeds and blatant acts of corruption are omitted, suppressed or buried daily in their "news" cycles, while gleefully vilifying everything Republican or Conservative.

In this regard, I firmly believe that news sites like NBC, CBS, ABC, CNN, and the NY Times, Washington Post, MSNBC, Facebook, Google, and most liberal universities and colleges are all adversaries of the American people and pose quite an existential threat to our country and way of life. These progressive media entities and their journalists are now the muskets and cannons in the new civil war Democrats are waging.

To ignore this ever-growing danger to our country would be to do so at our peril. I genuinely believe that liberals must be viewed as enemy combatants against our nation and its citizens and treated as such. Just as it was during the run-up to the Civil War of 1861, I do believe that we are at a juncture in our history where once again it's the *Union versus the Confederacy* in a fight for our constitution, our rights, our liberty, and our very lives.

Today, anti-American white liberals have use of much more stealthy and devious weaponry such as their inclusiveness, equality, tolerance, and diversity ideology, which they deftly wield with impunity. These enemy combatants use these innocuous sounding words in attempts to suppress our gun rights, freedom of speech and religion, and also to force our children into acceptance of Islamic doctrine, transgenderism, and gender fluidity.

With that said, you will find *inclusiveness, equality, tolerance, and diversity,* repeatedly in this text because they are at the epicenter of the political correctness scourge our nation faces and now being used as a trojan horse to destroy America's societal norms and boundaries. In a history repeats itself moment, and eerily reminiscent of its inception in 1829, there is neither diplomacy nor common ground to be found with today's liberal Democrat Party. Just as it was in the 1800s, Democrats still employ intimidation and violent tactics against their adversaries when they are failing politically.

Strangely, within this "inclusive" party there is an eclectic mashup of anti-American groups, adamantly opposed to each other, that share a kinship in their hatred for our country's values. These groups are comprised of the violent MS-13 gang members, illegal aliens, atheists, Satanists, Hollywood pedophiles, radical feminists, Black Panthers, Black Lives Matter, Antifa, radical Muslims, militant homosexuals, and transgenders.

And only under the Democrat banner do you find radical Muslims running for elected office in this country, even though they believe in sharia law, which contradicts our constitution and laws entirely. Also, it should come as no surprise that these Islamic Jihadists, seeking to infiltrate our government, are being backed by left-leaning, anti-American Muslim organizations right here within our country.

Just recently, a judge was sworn onto the bench in New York using the Quran to take her oath, forsaking the Bible and its teachings. As Americans take these developments in with eyes wide shut, there are Muslims that have been elected to Congress, as Democrats, who are adamantly opposed to Jews and Israel, our country's allies. In this Islamic invasion of our government, other Muslims are slithering into office in Minnesota and Michigan, as well as in other parts of the country, each taking their oath on the Quran.

What does it portend for our nation to have Muslims who are diametrically opposed to our Christian values elected to office as public servants to serve the American people? How can these people ever dutifully serve our country, uphold our laws and ideals, and protect our way of life when they view our Constitution and Bill of Rights as an impediment to the sharia laws that they so desperately desire to impose on the citizenry of this nation?

And if you haven't noticed yet, most of the Muslims running for office are confused plantation blacks. This is by design of course, because white liberals find that it's so much easier for them to sneak conditioned and brainwashed, hijab-wearing, anti-American blacks into office under their inclusiveness, diversity, equality and tolerance tag, then to try'n promote an Arab-looking candidate who looked like he had just flown a plane into the twin towers.

There's more, Democrats today are encouraging and embracing the flood of illegal aliens crossing our southern borders, often heaping praise upon these criminals for their "courage" in making such a long trek to break our laws. Liberals also greatly admire the misguided, and wealthy, black anti-American sports-playing dissidents who are kneeling on our national anthem and flag, celebrating and supporting these malcontents in their "cause."

Furthermore, leftist social media sites are banning conservative speech, prayers are being taken out of schools, and radical liberals are advocating for male transgenders to be in women's restrooms. Meanwhile, Cuba-like socialists, sensing that our populace has been dumbed down enough and the social fabric of our nation torn wide enough for them to crawl through, are unabashedly running for office in our country, again, as open borders and anti-law enforcement Democrats.

Given these things I've recently learned, I am now quite aware and convinced that just about everything wrong within our government and society, and detrimental to our nation, stems from Democrats and the destructive anti-American social policies they advocate for and promote. Their party has been the bane of every citizen in this country, especially blacks, ever since their inception in 1829.

So how can we, as rational and sane people, go for so long and not recognize the most apparent and present danger to our country? What is the reason for this suicidal blindness?

To answer any and all of these questions, I point you again back to the weaponized ideology of inclusiveness, tolerance, diversity, equality. Which makes me think about a quite prophetic quote attributed to Abraham Lincoln, perhaps our greatest president ever, who once said: *"America will never be destroyed from the outside, if we falter and lose our freedoms, it will be because we destroyed ourselves."*

Our nation's actual history shows, which you will see in later chapters, that right from the very beginning, the Democrat Party have always sought to undermine our Republic system of governance and way of life. And over the last five decades or so, one of the most successful ways they have done so is by utilizing the seemingly inherent and explosive anger within the black community. White liberals have been very effective at using deceptive and manipulative tactics to suppress and control blacks, their most crucial and reliable voting bloc today. Without this community fueling them politically, their party would quickly falter and have no standing in our political system, not now, or ever.

And to that end, the Democrat Party, along with the help of liberal colleges, universities and liberal media, have been cleverly disguising and covering up their past actions against blacks by reworking, contorting, and distorting their own slave-owning history to recast the Republican Party in the role of past enslavers and current oppressors of blacks in this nation.

I find that a lot of people today, strutting around and proudly calling themselves Democrats, especially blacks, unwittingly and ignorantly accept this patently false narrative as fact. The black community has, over decades, been continuously conditioned and brainwashed with fictitious documentaries and twisted retellings of our nation's history by leftist institutions and white liberals.

The parties' "switched" myth, which we will examine in multiple chapters throughout this book, is one of the biggest lies and hoaxes ever perpetrated in the annals of political history, and one of the many convenient fabrications that have kept many blacks mentally imprisoned and on the Democrat plantation for decades.

I believe that one cannot be intelligent and well-read and actually buy into this fairy tale. Yet, I was one of those blacks who ignorantly bought into this nonsense and for quite some time. It would take some researching on my part, but I eventually found out that this "switched parties" myth was one of the best conditioning tools for blacks, ever. I have since come to the realization that I had been nothing more than another one of the Democrat Party's brainwashed black zombies, emotionally and racially manipulated into unconditionally adhering to their ideology, platform, and agenda.

There is this brilliant conservative, Dinesh D'Souza, whom I once watched in a fascinating video on the real racists in this nation, who stated that at the start of the Civil War in 1861, no Republicans owned slaves. Because of what I had been led to believe all my life, this was an out of the blue revelation that, at the time, came as quite stunning news to me. Nevertheless, it appears that Mr. D'souza was correct in his assertion because I could find nothing in my research showing anything to the contrary.

Now, most blacks, still on the plantation, will get in an emotional huff over this historical fact and instead of listening with an open mind and some intellect, will automatically assume a defensive posture to try to explain away the Democrat Party's atrocities against blacks. If you watch'em closely, the majority of these blacks will never accept this truth and, just like their deceptive white liberal masters, will endeavor to conflate the two political parties as a deflection away from their slave-masters' past transgressions and violence towards blacks.

Unfortunately, I used to be one of these ignorant plantation blacks as well, defending Democrats at the drop of a hat, even getting angry at the messenger who was only delivering this truth. With my awakening, I am now clearly seeing how things really work in the political arena; the power broker influences, lobbyists, kickbacks, distortions, smears and outright lies, all bolstered by the liberal mainstream media which fabricates and promotes false stories to their viewers, all the while colluding with Democrats to subvert the will of the people.

Most startling to me; although blacks are the ones being hurt the most by their policies, we are the only race in America that is almost always in total lockstep with Democrats every election and on every issue. And even after being told of their real history, there are far too many blacks who are still quite content to stay trapped in the party's web of deceit and manipulation.

Furthermore, the majority of blacks, for decades, have been demonstrating an outright unwillingness to acquire the necessary and enlightening tools of education, rationale, and common sense to pry themselves away from their liberal assisted suicides.

What I find most remarkable, and sad, is that today a lot of blacks do not ever want to remove themselves from their plantations and will instead seek to justify why the Democrat Party is the best political avenue for blacks by throwing out the false equivalency of: *"Republicans won't do anything for us," "Both parties are the same anyways."*

This is quite odd because the majority of these blacks have never ever voted Republican in their lives, so how would they know what Republicans would do if they've never even tried voting for the party? *It was the equivalent of blacks expressing an extreme dislike of chocolate ice cream, although they never tasted it, because someone told them that it was awful.*

Also, if blacks truly believed that both parties were the same and equal in every respect, how come their voting for the last five decades have never been equally split between the two parties to reflect this thinking? Voting stats show that blacks have unconditionally and faithfully voted over 90% for Democrats, consistently and like forever. I know now that the root cause of this unflinching black loyalty is produced by the same mental conditioning which I had been subjected. You see, I had been told repeatedly by liberals that the Republican Party was cold and unfriendly, just a bunch of rich white men who didn't care about minorities. I was told that Republicans were unlike the warm, caring, and seemingly inclusive and multiracial-thinking Democrats who were always repeating their misleading and untruthful working-class mantra of "helping the little guy."

This messaging has caused most blacks today to be quite enamored with liberal crusaders who advocate for strong social welfare safety nets for minorities such as welfare, Affirmative Action, and Head Start to, uh, "help" the perpetually "disadvantaged and underprivileged" black community. In my previous state of mind, I used to think that if Republicans were elected to office, they would take away this assistance from blacks, leaving them to die on the streets. My severely misguided thinking had been reinforced by slick and deceptive messaging techniques and television ads by liberal candidates running for office, tactics often repeated in just about every election cycle to stoke black passions.

For decades, Democrats have extensively used weapons like the black "reverends," along with other black individuals and organizations, to issue dire warnings and urgings to the black community, in every election cycle, to get to the polls to prevent the impending catastrophe of Republican candidates getting into office. Later, I found out that all of these disaster "warnings" and doomsday scenarios by our black "leaders" and white liberals were just alarmist ploys to steer highly emotional and sensitive blacks like me toward their party.

My awakening would bring about another startling revelation, that the negative views and opinions I once held of Republicans were not thoughts independently formed by me. My thinking and unwarranted dislike for their party had not been based on anything factual but had been instead shaped for me by those within our community who had long ago pre-ordained my political allegiance for me.

The Democrat Party's false mantra of "Republicans don't care about you" had been purposely ingrained into my psyche during my formative years as an impressionable black youth. This mental conditioning had not come about as a sudden jolt, but as a gradual campaign by campaign, election by election, gentle and soothing messages of: *"Republicans are bad, but we'll be there for you because we care about you."*

As with most blacks, I had been fully immersed in the Democrat Party's ideology and platform, and because of this liberal cocoon, I did not seek to gain any knowledge, nor did I seek to find any other political alternatives. So, it is my sad confession that there had been little to no research on my part regarding the sordid and racist history of "my party" and the horrific acts they had committed against blacks, my people, during slavery.

To reinforce my decades of brainwashing, conditioning, and ignorance, I had been emotionally whipped by the well-paid black "civil rights reverends," overseers, who shilled for the party like highly paid political prostitutes.

I must admit that these traitorous black mercenaries had done a helluva job on me, and for a long time, I didn't even want to know or care about, whom or what was on the other side of the political aisle, Democrat was my party, period. Against my own best interests and judgment, for far too long I had relied solely on these traitorous overseers and the movement of brainless zombie-like plantation blacks to determine my allegiance and the political path upon which I would traverse.

Some time ago, I was watching a comedy program where a black comedian made a joke that when a black sees another black running, he doesn't ask why, he just starts running also. Although this joke was hilarious when he said it back then, today I think about this comedian's insight and how it aptly encapsulates the herd-like mentality of most in the black community. In this regard, I had been no different from the rest of the black community back then; misguided and led into my default political position and unto the Democrat plantation.

Before my awakening, I had been trapped like a paralyzed fly, entangled in a spider's web and locked in a liberal agenda-driven echo chamber that reverberated endlessly with the sounds of victimhood and entitlement. It was this constant deluge of falsehoods and lies from liberals which kept me enthralled with their ideology and mentally-imprisoned on their plantation for many years.

As a result, early on, I was one of those emotional blacks who would blindly and fiercely defend their party and, on many occasions, could be found vociferously voicing my stance and allegiance for all those within earshot to hear. At the time, in my state of mind, it had been nearly impossible for me to perceive the full import of the deception which I had been subjected.

It wouldn't be until after I had discovered the truth and extricated myself from the cesspool of lies and deceit and washed the filth and liberal stench from my being, that I could feel totally free. My long overdue journey to freedom from the plantation and my subsequent revocation of allegiance to the Democrat Party would give me a heightened sense of political awareness and newfound knowledge of both parties. *I found that to learn the truth that you must be willing to seek it and when found, face it head on, regardless of the revelations it may bring or the damage it may cause to your pride.*

With my newly acquired knowledge, it was as if I had been politically reborn, like a Phoenix rising from the ashes. I had been rejuvenated, cleansed like a drug addict who had finally gained sobriety and saw for the very first time the ravages of his addiction. And just like the recovering drug addict, with my vision now unclouded I could see with startling clarity, the unfiltered and complete devastation of liberal policies on the black community and our nation.

To me it was and still is quite something to behold; emotionally driven, mentally unbalanced and misled blacks all around me, still languishing in the same quagmire of liberal deceit and lies which I had escaped. Today, these blacks are now trapped in an illusionary progressive realm, believing in socialist driven prosperity that will never materialize, still in the throes of their addiction to empty promises by their white slave masters.

I realize now with some certainty that I, along with many others within the black community, had been nothing more than emotionally and racially exploited cogs in the Democrats' political machinery. We were just lowly pawns in their decades-long attempt to complete a socialist takeover of this nation by utilizing identity politics and victimhood to energize select minority groups.

Before coming to my senses, there was an incident which I can still vividly recall, and will always remember, that illustrates this blindness and the soft spot I once had for Democrats.

In the 1990s, while employed at this well-known financial institution as an underwriter, I had gotten into a heated, and one-sided, conversation with a white coworker over politics and Bill Clinton, who was president at the time. He had been very calm and soft-spoken as he attempted to gently explain to me why he was a conservative Republican and why I, as a black man, and all Americans should be too. At the time, he wanted me to understand the ideology and platform which I was unconditionally supporting.

Even though I knew little about the history of the Democrats Party at the time, I blindly forged on, getting all emotional and worked up as we blacks are prone to do whenever we receive information in conflict with the misinformation disseminated by white liberals into our communities. So, of course, I angrily defended "my party," reflexively rattling off one of my liberal-ingrained talking points: *"Republicans are racist and don't care about blacks, they are just for the rich."*

I remember going on this long diatribe about how Democrats always looked out for the working man and minorities, and that they genuinely cared about our well-being and the future of this country. While I was still on my soapbox of righteous indignation and in the middle of an all-out rant, my coworker just stood there silent, with a serene expression on his face, not saying a word and I'll never forget the look in his eyes.

My former co-worker seemed to be staring not at me, but through me and into my future. There had been this sense of sadness in his gaze that made me feel so uneasy that I had just stopped talking in mid-sentence, which is quite hard for me to do, and just silently stared back at him. Even though I had been seemingly immutable in my position at the time, adamantly opposed to anything Republican, I had felt the sincerity in his words that day.

Something about the calmness and confidence my former co-worker exuded that day caused a flicker of doubt to stir within me about my full-throated support of the Democrat Party. And it was at this very moment that I would entertain, for the first time, the thought that maybe there was a kernel of truth to what he was saying to me. His words had somehow pierced my seemingly resolute conviction and loyalty to Democrats, resulting in a brief moment of clarity.

However, this spark of sanity would be quickly snuffed out by the emotional, liberal black pit into which it had fallen. This fleeting glimpse of reality, errantly intruding into my bubble of darkness and ignorance, had been abruptly expelled like the blotting out of an unwanted ray of light by hastily drawn curtains on a bright and sunny afternoon.

Knowing what I know now, I wish I could go back in time and talk to that former coworker and apologize, tell him that I now realize that I had been duped and used. I know now, with some degree of certainty, that he had seen that my emotions back then negated any rational thought, or civil discourse, to be had between us that day. I believe, to this day, that he had known then that any of his salient points or facts about the real history of the Democrat Party, which I refused to entertain, would have been ignored and wasted and had politely ceased all dialogue that day, giving me up for a lost cause.

I wish that I could tell this former coworker that I now understand and that I am sorry for being such an uncompromising and unyielding fool. I want to say to him that at the time I had been so caught up in being so emotional and angry at anything outside of the Democrat plantation and liberal ideology, that this had been the reason why I had not been open to any reasoning or facts that didn't comport with my thinking or belief at the time.

My behavior back then was no anomaly, as with the majority of blacks, there is a highly passionate and entrenched belief that white and black liberal Democrats are like "family looking out for family and will make sure blacks are "helped," in their supposed four-hundred-year-old and counting "struggles. Because of this illusionary familial construct, the vast majority of blacks today are loyal to a fault to the Democrat Party.

As repayment for this loyalty, a lot of blacks are given taxpayer-funded welfare table scraps and provided access to other handout programs like section eight or additional government assistance. After relying on the government decade after decade, most blacks feel an indebtedness and gratitude, almost an obligation, to white liberals and will do just about anything to keep their handouts going. Nowadays, the majority of the black community are like crackheads willing to do just about anything for a welfare hit, even falling to their knees in supplication to their dealer.

This mostly one-sided quid-pro-quo is, inarguably, borne out by the fact that blacks vote over 90% for Democrats, no matter the candidate or platform, and have been doing so every election for the last fifty years with virtually nothing of substance to show for it except crime-infested, poverty-stricken, and economically stagnant communities.

To note, we are the only race in America, with our population percentage, to vote like this for any one party with no meaningful change to be found.

The problematic and systemic issues plaguing black communities, such as high black on black homicides, poor schools, drug dealing, and gangs, have been going on for decades in Democrat inner cities without so much as a whimper from black "civil rights" leaders and "helpful" white liberals. But as a deflection away from the devastating impact of their policies, white liberals have taught the black community to believe that their elected officials are working hard on their issues and that more liberal Democrats needed to be elected to office to combat the "racist" Republicans. This narrative causes highly emotional plantation blacks to foolishly reject anything conservative.

The majority of blacks have been conditioned to be more like trained attack dogs rather than human beings, which causes most to respond to a specific racial whistle, readily obeying any and all commands to attack anything that can be construed and twisted into a racial "incident."

With that said, most blacks will faithfully follow the orders of liberals, disregarding and ignoring their trappings of violence, poverty, and crime while hanging onto the hope that someday their baseless animus and violence toward white Republicans will somehow resolve their internal issues.

It is also most unsettling to me that the majority of blacks will, in no uncertain terms, unconditionally abide by whatever another Democrat black "brother" says without flinching. Blacks will also gravitate like a school of fish to white liberals who will play to their skin color, sell them the promise of another minority handout "program," or give reassurances that they will keep the current one in place.

You will notice that whenever these whites desire credibility within the black community, they often will look for "endorsements" from black "leaders" to serve as a dog whistle to let blacks in the inner cities know that it was ok to vote for'em.

As a child and teenager, I never viewed anything, or anyone, through this ever-present racial prism that most blacks now see through, and I never did develop the entitlement and victimization mentality that seems to be so prevalent within our community today. I guess this thinking goes to my upbringing; I was taught at a young age by my mother not to worry about skin pigmentation, but to instead worry about the character of the person because evil can come in just about any color. She always said that people are people, no matter who they are or where they come from, and they can all do you harm or do you good.

A very religious woman living by what she taught, my mother would entertain anyone at our home regardless of race and without any second thoughts. And even though we didn't have much at certain times, she would always cheerfully and selflessly share whatever we had with others less fortunate.

I remember as a teenager that there was this white couple, I believe their names were Johnny and Sue, who would come over to our house some early mornings for breakfast and would also, sometimes, stop by for dinner later on in the evenings. On occasion, I would get upset that they were eating our food, but I never focused on their skin tone, I just saw people gobbling up our grits, biscuits, ham, and eggs with impunity and reckless abandon. These friendly, free-loading and always hungry folks slurped our coffee, tea, and just about anything else they could get their grubby paws on, but this was all good though because, as I remember, they were pretty good people to be around.

In those days, I was quite naïve and totally unaware of identity politics and the racial division that is so often exhibited in our society today and now, seemingly, almost to the point of combustion. The Christian-based principles and core values I had been raised with never really allowed me to think along these divisive lines, or to see things in this manner. Truth is, I wasn't even aware of the contradictory nature of my political association and my core values and beliefs until much later in adulthood.

A lot of blacks today probably hold some of the same conservative values as I do but are now the emotional and violent enforcers that blindly serve and protect the Democrats' platform and ideology, even to the detriment of their community. I learned that with most blacks today, any discussion regarding Conservativism or Republican as an alternative to Democrats and their policies is taboo and will quickly get you side glances, scowls, and foul language.

To be black and publicly supporting the Republican Party today is considered egregious conduct and will make you an instant outcast and adversary. In our climate today, even speaking about anything conservative will cause the majority of blacks to become visibly upset and emotionally charged, almost to the point of getting physical. I finally realized, with the black community, that I had been laboring under the mistaken assumption that I had independent thought and, thus, able to freely express my ideas and opinions in this country without being belittled and threatened.

But after breaking away from the Democrat plantation, I found that my freedom-loving, free-thinking attitude would be quickly shot down and dismissed by many blacks that see my support for the Republican Party as a personal insult and threat to the community. To me, this groupthink mindset, embedded within the majority of blacks, is not one of a civilized people where intelligent, dissenting discourse can take place to foster creative ideas and solutions. Instead, the black community's behavior is more like that of a gang or tribe with dictatorial chieftains and black leaders directing their lowly and obedient underlings to follow their lead, unquestioningly and bereft of independent thought.

More to the point, most blacks today will viciously attack those blacks who have freed themselves and successfully fled the liberal inner-city welfare strongholds. Upon command, these conditioned plantation blacks will hurl demeaning labels of sellout, self-hater, Uncle Tom or my old favorite, coon, at their newly emancipated brothers and sisters.

This behavior is eerily similar to that of the KKK of the 1950s, also an emotional and violent enforcement arm of Democrats that *attacked, intimidated, and killed freed southern blacks and white Republicans as punishment for their opposition to their party. *We will undoubtedly dig more in-depth on this one later.*

When talking to many blacks today and pointing out the problematic issues plaguing our community and how their sorely misplaced loyalty to the Democrat Party has been the underlying cause for all of their problems, they just ignore this quite obvious observation, along with any other facts that do not align with what they were programmed to think. And further attempts at thoughtful dialogue with these low-info blacks are tossed about and dismissed like so much debris in an emotional tsunami of indoctrinated talking points given them by the liberal media and their black leaders.

Emotionalism has always been a weakness for blacks and, coupled with their unwillingness to actually pick up a book and read, their quick anger and lack of fundamentals prevents most from ever developing enough intellect to get even a rudimentary understanding of what has indeed really transpired in our nation's history regarding our race and community.

Most blacks, because of their blind allegiance and belief in the "parties switch" foolishness, today, have anger, not at the perpetrators who enslaved their ancestors for centuries, but at the ones the perpetrators have pointed to, Republicans, the ones that freed their ancestors.

The most noticeable and glaring hypocrisy at present; Democrats utilizes their faux equality, tolerance, diversity, and inclusiveness ideology to generate the emotionalism needed to manipulate the populace, especially blacks, and to beat their adversaries into submission. However, they themselves do not abide by their own words, or beliefs, in any shape, form, or fashion whatsoever.

For proof of this, we need to look no further than just about any liberal college or university campus where our nation's future liberal congressmen or congresswomen will eventually, and unfortunately, emerge. Indoctrinated liberal students, who adamantly preach inclusiveness, tolerance, equality, and diversity, are the very same intolerant students that riot, destroy property, and advocate violence to shut down and stop conservatives, or anyone else, with a different viewpoint from theirs from speaking out or expressing themselves on their campuses.

And just like the oppressive segregation of the 1950s and 1960s, these leftist students today often set up separate black areas or clubs on many school grounds, where Christians, straight white males and conservatives are not wanted, blatantly ignoring their own "caring for the people" ideology.

Furthermore, a lot of young blacks on college campuses are being used extensively by white "social justice warriors" in social engineering experiments to lend legitimacy to whatever agenda they are promoting. These students are the "exploited" pack mules and emotional whips for any and all social causes on the left, and the bedrock upon which most of their movements are built upon.

Black youths today are being used to advocate for policies and ide-ologies promoting welfare dependency, illegal immigration, Godless-ness, pedophilia, open borders, abortion, sanctuary cities, free speech suppression, gender fluidity, gun rights suppression, anti-constitution views, Antifa and Black Lives Matter riots, flag burning, high taxa-tion, national anthem disrespect, anti-military, anti-police, socialism, transgenderism, Islamic doctrine and the abolishment of law & order.

There is a stealthy undercurrent of deliberately fomented cultural chaos being developed and driven by white liberals in the hopes of one day creating enough division and lawlessness to topple our politi-cal structure, and then to rebuild into one in which we no longer have the Republic system of governance that our framers put in place.

Fortunately, at this writing, more Americans are gaining aware-ness as to the state of our country. Surprisingly, there are even some blacks waking up to the truth as well and finding out that Russia, North Korea, Iran, and China are not our nation's greatest enemies, nor are these countries the black community's greatest threats either. They now realize that most black "leaders" in their communities, along with the white and black Democrats in Washington, are their greatest enemies and not an outside entity as liberals and their media cohorts would have them believe.

*Citizens of this nation would be wise to heed the wisdom of an old African proverb: *"If there is no enemy within, the enemy outside can do you no harm."*

I was recently watching a few YouTube videos spotlighting people who were suddenly "woke" and walking away from the Democrat Party. Many were expressing their anger and frustration at being unwitting pawns and accomplices of liberals for so long. Unsurprisingly, when the Walkaway Movement, founded by Brandon Straka, a homosexual, and former liberal Democrat, went viral it was immediately denounced and attacked by liberals looking to tamp down this quite damming indictment of their party by former members.

Enter the mainstream media, which quickly went into hyperbolic overdrive to try and minimize and spin the devastating political optics of tens of thousands of now wide-eyed, disillusioned, former captives walking away from their deceptive party.

Suddenly, as if on cue and in unison, all of the biased liberal networks, social media sites, and liberal newspapers started calling the walkaways "Russian bots." *Which made me wonder at this point, what is it with Democrats and Russia? Is there no other damn country they can try to blame for their own corruption?*

I knew, like so many other sane and rational Americans that the videos weren't being made by any so-called Russian "bots." These informative and explosive rejections of liberalism depicted people; black, white, Asian, straight, gay, etc., emphatically denouncing the insanity of the left and proclaiming their departure, and sweet freedom, from the Democrat Party.

The viral testimonials of these walkaways were moments of raw, sometimes angry, and unfiltered confessions being publicly shared by ordinary folks detailing their sudden enlightenment and subsequent journey away from the liberal plantation. Thousands of once-duped American citizens had finally arisen, as I had, from their media-driven slumber and their displeasure was now on display for all to see.

The one thing I can vividly remember is that the walkaways eyes all had that same look of newfound clarity. You know, the look when someone told you, or you had found out, an unbelievable dark secret about someone you had looked up to for a long time. And after being told this truth, it shatters everything you knew about them, making you feel like a fool for believing and trusting in them for so long. They had somehow come to realize that they had been nothing more than lowly pawns in a political shell game where they were all stooges, marionettes on emotional strings pulled by liberal Democrats.

The walkaways had all been unwitting bit players, foot soldiers in the liberals' insidious war on our nation's principles and values. These former dupes had all shared but a bit part in the rainbow cabaret of political correctness where the enchanting and lilting tunes of inclusiveness, tolerance, equality, and diversity helped hasten the demise of our nation and way of life.

The walkaways found out that the Democrat Party was not promoters of harmony and peace as they so often proclaimed but instead, through violence and misinformation, were seeking the complete annihilation of our once civilized melting pot we so proudly call the "United States." The scales had fallen from their eyes, exposing the dark underbelly and wanton ravages of the leftists' corrupt socialist doctrine now permeating our country.

The former Democrats were now awakened to a nation divided into tension-filled, opposing chunks of cultures, races, genders, myriad "sexual identities" and nationalities that were now all made to be at each other's throats. This dramatic increase of incivility within our society has led to a sizeable contingent of indoctrinated and violent liberals refusing to assimilate into American culture and abide by our laws and societal norms.

Social justice warriors on the left no longer wish to adhere to our Bill of Rights, nor our Constitution, and now view these cornerstones of our Republic and society as just unwanted remnants of a bygone past. For these anti-Americans, the values we hold dear and ones that have produced the greatest nation on earth, are but an imposition and hindrance to the furtherance of their progressivism, and not seen as the societal glue which has held this nation together since its inception.

Most leftists are cult-like followers, thoroughly brainwashed to view our pledge of allegiance, national anthem, and flag as the hallmark of a "racist" and "white supremacy" system that must be done away with. It is the Democrat Party's firm belief, for their political gain, that our nation must now become "browned" to atone for European Whites taking over and resettling, or "colonizing," our country. *We are gonna go over this again in much more detail later in our illegal immigration chapter, so stay tuned.*

Upon their awakening, the tens of thousands, and growing, former diehard Democrats figured out that the erosion of our principles, the identity politics scourge, and the rising incivility and lawlessness they were now witnessing in this country, had not come about because of some natural occurrence. They now fully understood that the violence occurring in our country wasn't the result of some inevitable cultural decline over the years, but one which had been systematically orchestrated for decades by leftist political mechanisms; academia, Hollywood, and activist judicial intrusiveness.

I implore everyone to watch some of these riveting walkaway testimonials in which former steadfast and loyal Democrats of ten, twenty, and thirty years or more, are walking away from their party and experiencing true freedom of thought, perhaps for the first time in their lives. As you watch them, listen very carefully to what these people are saying, and it will become quite evident that they have found the enemy in our midst.

With that being said, the most significant impact on our nation and one where Democrats are doing the most damage is within our judicial system. It is in this area which liberal activist judges, and their rulings, are gradually wearing away and removing our Christian principles and values, the very foundation of our civilized nation, and pillars which constructs and informs our societal norm.

The polarization, divide, and contrasts of the values and principles between Americans and Democrats in this nation, along with the blatant exploitation of blacks, couldn't be any more significant than it is today. And it must be understood that the tumultuous times we are living in today really harkens back to the founding of this country and the beginning of our system of governance when there had been an initial jostling for political power, influence, and dominance.

The poisonous political climate, divisiveness, and lawlessness we are seeing on display today all stem from one party's deep hatred of our constitution and way of life. And what we see now with white liberals, their intimidation and violent tactics, is nothing new to those who have studied history.

So, to fully grasp what is occurring today, I wanna take this time to backtrack a little to the infamous origins of the Democrat Party. I want to show you how their anti-American ideology came to be and how this party managed over time to harness and exploit the deadly black fuel called "African-Americans."

I hope that you don't find the next few chapters too dull, if so, take a break, grab a cup of coffee and come back because it's essential for contextualization.

Now, I am not gonna delve too deeply into our nation's history, I just wanna go down memory lane far enough to set up the framework of what is happening today with blacks and Democrats and to show just what is at stake for our country.

So, have patience and indulge me, if you will, as we travel back in time to the beginning of this nation, the establishment of the initial thirteen colonies, and the start of the political exploitation of blacks.

Turn the page, you dig?

Chapter Three

A Country Being born

So, as you can see, the previous section really set the stage for me to go ahead and further explain my moving away from the Democrat Party, and to solidify my awakening by providing "evidence" for my departure. Now, I am by no means any heavyweight historian or leading authority on all things history, such as Thomas Sowell. But I do like to refer to myself, most of the time, as a *"Commonsensorian,"* an ordinary, rational person of reasonable intelligence rooted in reality.

What you are about to read in the next few chapters is basically bullet points of history that will establish a factual and logical thread for you to follow, one which most likely will prompt further discussions on the matter I am writing about. In that vein, let's see how the sausage, the founding of America, was made.

I think that we all can agree that America's capitalist system, as constructed today, is the greatest wealth-generating engine in the world, and one that is also vastly multiracial and multicultural. This unique system has, over many decades, produced quite a few successful black doctors, black lawyers, black millionaires, black billionaires, black CEOs, black sports stars, and many other black entrepreneurs, along with many other millionaires and billionaires in just about every other ethnic group who have adapted to capitalism and have bought into the promises and opportunities of this country.

As you can see, all of the individuals mentioned above, regardless of race, are today reaping the rewards from the initiative and foresight of White Europeans who landed on our shores in the early 1600s. So,

I would be more than remiss in omitting the fact that this country was indeed founded by whites, they were the ones that, while struggling to do so, would create the environment for the financial opportunities we see today, there's just no way around this fact.

So yes, much to the chagrin and discontent of today's deranged white liberals, militant blacks, and illegal Hispanics, all of the forefathers of this nation were pearly white males and, yes, some even owned African Slaves. You see, slavery was the trend back in the 1600s and prior, all across the globe and was quite chic and fashionable. I mean, this institution of bondage and servitude was all the rage during this era, sorta like today's iPhone.

White European settlers would come over to this new land we now call America and establish the first permanent settlement in Jamestown, Virginia in 1607. However, these early settlers would soon find out that surviving in the new land was no cakewalk and many would die from the harsh conditions they encountered early on such as hunger, diseases, the lack of fresh drinking water and, oh, also from fighting with the indigenous Indians who wanted to sorta hold onto their land.

So, out of the hundreds of settlers who first arrived, only a few dozen were able to survive their foray into the new land, but the remaining survivors would persevere and eventually overcome their obstacles and dire circumstances to make a go of it. These whites would go on to further develop the existing European capitalist system and create the beginning of what we now see today, an economy currently unrivaled anywhere in the world, making this the most unique and prosperous nation on earth.

With that said, the freedom and right to accumulate wealth and build a successful life in America wasn't always the case with blacks and other minorities because the institution of slavery in the 1600s was still an impediment to their progress and an immoral blemish and stain on our nation.

But to set the record straight, contrary to the belief of many in this country today, slavery wasn't systemic racism as the majority of today's uneducated blacks and manipulative white liberals erroneously and continually proclaim. No, the slave trade was just the forcing of servitude of the captured or conquered by the conqueror and was practiced worldwide by many countries and cultures for quite some time before America existed, or was even thought of.

Enslaved captives of all races, including Africans, were just commodities to be sold, bartered and bred, and to be worked in the fields like cattle or any other livestock, nothing more. One group enslaving another was a fairly common practice dating back to, oh say, thousands of years to ancient Egypt and almost to the beginning of mankind. You can even find the enslaved in Exodus of the Bible when Moses led the Israelites out of bondage, and into the Promised Land; took'em forty years to do it, but he did it!

Can you just imagine how many pairs of sandals Moses went through in delivering these slaves from bondage?

Anyways, during the slavery era, capturing the enemy and making them subservient laborers was not a form of "racism," but was merely the spoils of conquest. The victors were the ones in the position of power, and they were the ones to lord over the conquered by force until when, or if, the conquered could rise up to free themselves by force, or by whatever means, from captivity. Throughout history, whenever invaders of any race or nationality captured land and the people upon it, they had either killed or enslaved the men and women whom they had defeated and, in a lot of cases, even forced some of these women, and men, into becoming their sex slaves.

So, no, I don't believe that these conquerors back then really cared about or put too much thought into the skin color or ethnicities of the inhabitants they were fighting and enslaving, nor did they have any remorse for forcibly taking their land from them. Can you imagine any of those Spanish or Arab marauders back then saying, *"Oops, these are crispy Negroes, we cannot take or enslave these jungle fellas, sorry, they are just off limits!"*

Also, I don't think African warlords ever said this about other blacks they had conquered either, it wasn't like pigmentation was a prerequisite or something for the captured to qualify for enslavement. If the defeated could haul bricks, build temples, pick cotton, plow a field and perform whatever labor was needed, they were qualified regardless of color.

Really, the slave institution was probably the first real equal opportunity employer ever; the hours were long and grueling, the work backbreaking, and the pay was lousy or nonexistent. But on the brighter side, just about everyone was equal in the loss of their freedom while enslaved and, I imagine, no one ever protested over a $15 an hour minimum wage, I can just about guarantee that.

Prior to pure capitalism, most land and wealth acquired and amassed by any one group, anywhere around the world, were obtained mostly through conquest, which usually involved violence and bloodshed in brutal battles that sometimes killed hundreds of thousands. So, since the enslavement of other races had been done by Africans, Spaniards, the Europeans and just about every culture in the world for thousands of years, no one group today can ever really lay claim to a special carve out, or privilege, as to which group had been most victimized by their enslavers.

In the early 1600s, White Europeans from America, having little success with indigenous Indians and the Irish as slaves in the New World, traveled to the African continent after they had gotten wind of a rumor, probably from the Spaniards, that the black-skinned inhabitants there would be a little sturdier in their southern heat and could pick cotton like nobody's business. Unlike the liberalized movie Roots and other misleading recountings of slavery, whites wouldn't just land on the shores of African Nations and start casually scooping up unarmed-and-minding-their-own-business blacks that were busy frolicking around in the jungle wearing sagging loincloths, eating bananas, and picking coconuts from trees.

No sir, before Europeans from America ever arrived on the continent, warring African chiefs were already engaging in the original daily black on black violence and homicides against other African tribes and had amassed an impressive inventory of black slaves of their own that were marked, tagged, and ready for sale, much like today's flea markets. These African chieftains, *and future NAACP leaders,* gladly and willingly bartered away their captured black brethren to whites in exchange for guns, cloth, gunpowder, cotton, and brass, along with other household trinkets such as pots, pans, and copper.

And flying in the face of the false revisionist history often touted by white liberals today, over 90% of African slaves were procured in this manner.

For most of these white Europeans, it was as easy as pulling their ships up to a fast food restaurant and ordering a value meal:

"How can I help you today sir?"

"Yes, I'll have 400 Negroes please, sturdy ones too, a lot died on me last time before I got 'em home."

"Ok sir, we do apologize, with the new order, do you want leg irons with that?"

"Yes please, and can you make sure that about a quarter of them are breeding age female Negroes, last time you guys shorted me."

"My apologies sir, perhaps you should just order the number one, our extra crispy value package, it comes with 410 Negroes and includes 150 female Negroes of breeding age, matching tempered steel leg irons, and 25 whips."

"Hmm, ok, I guess I'll take that. Do you guys take American Express?"

"Uh, sorry sir, we do not take any credit cards at this time."

'Okay, what's the charge?"

"Let's see, that'll be 20 copper pots, ten guns, 50 cotton t-shirts, 30 yards of fine linen and 20 kegs of gunpowder."

"Whoa, wait a minute, last time the value package was only 15 copper pots, 25 yards of fine linen, five guns and 10 kegs of gunpowder, what gives?"

"Supply and demand sir, seems that the Arabs and Spanish have an insatiable appetite and demand for our Negroes as well, and that's driving up costs across the board. Our warlords are exhausted, they are out fighting and capturing these hard to catch Negroes day and night just to keep plenty of stock available for you guys, and most of them are working 18-hour days."

"Well, hmmm, ok, I'll take the extra crispy value package then, thank you."

"Will that be all sir?"

"Yes, thank you."

"Ok, can you pull your ship around over there? Your order will be out shortly, have a good day."

This initial and quite fruitful trip onto the African continent would see white Europeans from America finally engage in the centuries-long Transatlantic Slave Trade and Africans enslaved not only to the Spaniards, Arabs, and other tribes on the continent but for the first time also in bondage and servitude to white southerners in the new land called America.

During the 1500s and beyond, between 10 million and 12 million slaves would be removed from Africa's shores with about fifteen percent dying en route to their destination. Surprisingly, only about five percent of these Africans were ever bought over to America. It seems that during this same period, there were other countries in great need of forced labor and as a result, about 48% of blacks ever taken from Africa were shipped off to the Caribbean, while another 41% was spirited off to Brazil, mostly to cultivate sugar, tobacco, and coffee crops.

*And if you think white Europeans were brutal on blacks during slavery, just research and check out what kind of treatment they endured in Brazil and the Caribbean. The way those countries abused African slaves made plantations in America look like luxury resorts by comparison.

Now, the many trips over to the African continent to procure plantation "help" was dangerous, and sometimes deadly for the white Europeans, and was certainly no picnic for their African captives either. Slaves were squeezed and fitted as many as possible, like sardines, into each compartment of the ship's hold to maximize the inventory that could be transported back to the New World. Because these vessels weren't equipped with many amenities, so to speak, these long voyages were quite agonizing and discomforting.

But white Europeans didn't worry too much about their own comfort, nor the well-being of their "property." The frequent journeys across the North Atlantic were never intended to be Carnival Cruise Lines excursions for them, nor their black captives.

And certainly, Europeans didn't go through all the trouble of bringing blacks back from the jungles of Africa, and over to America on their dime, just so that they could sit around all day drinking 40ozs, eating fried chicken, playing video games and watching the NFL on 72-inch flat screen TVs.

This country was never intended to be a land of milk and honey for African slaves, who had been bought over to work the fields, pick cotton and tobacco, and perform any other back-breaking chores southern whites saw fit. Slavery was a business, cold and harsh, and the lengthy and arduous trips onto the Africa continent would play a significant and integral role in America's economy of the 1600s, 1700s, and most of the 1800s.

African slaves were an indispensable workforce, particularly in the south, for the required labor necessary to meet production demands in a booming economy dependent on cotton and other crops being grown in our nation's tropical and fertile southern regions.

Enslavement of blacks was brutal but was no different than, say, the Pharaoh enslaving Israelites and not allowing them to sit around all day under cool tree shade in yarmulkes eating hummus and drinking goat milk. They too were whipped and forced to make bricks, sometimes without straw, and build statues and temples and such. Furthermore, it would take the involvement of the Lord himself to free the Israelites from the obstinate, and probably liberal Democrat, Pharaoh: **Exodus Chapter 6 and Verse 6** *"Wherefore say unto the children of Israel, I am the LORD, and I will bring you out from under the burdens of the Egyptians, and I will rid you out of their bondage, and I will redeem you with a stretched-out arm, and with great judgments."*

Before we continue, I must note that it's not like the nation we now live in was some peaceful utopia of harmony and tranquility before whites came over. Some, but not all, indigenous Indians were in constant tribal warfare over territory or resources and native tribes like the Apaches, Navajos, Sioux, etc., fought each other quite often before the white man even landed on America's shores. These Indians captured, scalped, and killed each other regularly. So, most of these tribes weren't just innocent victims of whites, nor did they have all this unity that today's white liberals like to romanticize about today in their twisted retelling of this nation's history.

*Also, *Courtesy of truenews.org (American Minute April 22nd, 2019)*, to quickly draw some distinction here of who actually abused Indians on America's shores, look no further than Andrew Jackson, the father of the Democrat Party. His "Jacksonian Democrats" were the ones that demonized and vilified the Indians, calling them savages and signing the 1830s Indian Removal Act, which was enacted by a Democrat-controlled Congress and then carried out by Democrat President Martin Van Buren.

This law came about because of a gold strike in Georgia, forcing the relocation of about 46,000 Christian Cherokees from their land by 1837, with the last 17,000 being forcibly removed by the Federal Government from Georgia, Tennessee, Alabama, and South Carolina, and relocated to Oklahoma. The abrupt removal of Cherokees led to the loss of their ancestral lands, and the Trail of Tears where over 4000 would perish. These actions were vehemently opposed by Republicans and Whigs such as Abraham Lincoln, Henry Clay, Daniel Webster, and Davy Crockett.

Of note here, Supreme Court Justice John Marshall ruled in favor of Cherokees in the case of Worcester v. Georgia, but Democrat President Andrew Johnson, noting that the Supreme Court could not enforce their ruling responded, "John Marshall has made his decision; now let him enforce it."

*There is a lot more to flesh out and understand on this subject, and if you seek further knowledge I suggest, by all means, to do more research on these tragic events.

Now, even though every race on earth has endured some form of slavery at some point in history, it is most important to note that our country, one of the last to enslave blacks, would also be one of the first to abolish this inhumane institution. Afterward, a lot of other countries would follow suit as well and put an end to slavery, although, in some countries like Saudi Arabia, Mali, and other Muslim nations, tens of thousands of African slaves still exist today.

With that said, there's a lot more to be told on who enslaved who, who invaded who, and who conquered who throughout world history, but I won't go into that here, I just wanted to provide a little perspective on the main subject of these writings and set the framework for what I'm about to lay down.

Let's now get on board and go into detail a little bit more about the founding of our country, and we will do this by picking things up with the original thirteen colonies, which was first formed in this country by, you guessed it, our pearly white forefathers. During the 1600s, and for most of the 1700s, colonists in the new land were under the auspices and rule of Great Britain's laws and were practically in bondage themselves to King George, who continually levied all kinds of taxes and duties and straining their resources.

However, after some time of enduring this wealth redistribution abuse, the colonists got fed up with being taxed up the wazoo and their breaking point would come about soon after the 1754 French and Indian war. Seems like Great Britain had accumulated massive debt fighting in that conflict and old King George had sorta maxed out his credit cards and now wanted the colonists to make the monthly payments on the balance due, with interest, much like our government today.

To make matters worse, the Stamp Act of 1765 would be one of the most troublesome burdens imposed by Great Britain upon the colonists, and probably the proverbial last straw that broke the camel's back. This levy required a tax on almost all printed material in the colonies and to compound this directive, most of the paper to be used in the production of this material was to be produced in London.

This severe financial imposition on the colonists would serve as the catalyst for them to finally seek their freedom from Great Britain. So, soon after this decree by King George, some now-famous guy named Patrick Henry proclaimed, *"Give me liberty, or give me death!"* And in a relatively short period after that, the colonists would declare their independence from Great Britain and old King George. Their insatiable thirst for freedom would soon lead to the beginning of the Revolutionary War in 1775.

This Declaration of Independence, which would be written by Thomas Jefferson and voted on by the Second Continental Congress on July 4th, 1776, still stands today as the guiding principle for all Americans: *"We hold these truths to be self-evident, that all men are created equal, that they are endowed by their Creator with certain unalienable Rights, that among these are Life, Liberty and the pursuit of Happiness."*

However, to be brutally honest here, regarding blacks and other minorities, the original intent of the Declaration of Independence, especially the part about *"all men are created equal,"* did not pertain to blacks, Indians, Mexicans, Muslims, Japanese, or any other race or group except white Europeans at the time of its creation. The founders' original intent was for this country, once established, to be for whites only. This footnote in history would serve to, undoubtedly, debunk the notion that this country was supposed to be some sort of multiracial or multicultural melting pot from the very beginning.

In fact, Thomas Jefferson himself, writer of the Declaration of Independence, had over two hundred black slaves and had never really wanted blacks to be on par with whites in this new land, but would rather see them back in Africa before that happened. **I suppose that, even then, Jefferson had seen the propensity for violence that these blacks exhibited in their own land, and how badly they treated their own people by selling them off to strangers for peanuts and wanted no part of 'em. I believe that he probably felt that freed blacks wouldn't mix well with white culture.*

Considering the attitudes of a lot of today's blacks regarding whites in this country, there may indeed be a kernel of truth to this observation by Jefferson in the 1700s.

So, to clarify, when the Declaration of Independence was formally written and signed by our forefathers, blacks were enslaved, and Indians branded as savages and most killed off in battle, with the survivors relegated to designated areas such as reservations. Therefore, it is quite impossible that the well-known and oft-repeated phrase that *"all men are created equal,"* could have ever pertained to anyone other than white Europeans.

This exclusion of minorities wasn't about racism or "white supremacy," at all. The subjugation of Africans and Indians in this country was merely what many other conquerors have done to the vanquished since the beginning of time; fighting and taking land by force for themselves and their families and establishing their way of life by setting their own societal boundaries, rules, and laws by which they were to abide.

In this respect, whites founding this country was no different from any other race around the world that had forcibly taken land or wealth from another. You see, just about every piece of land on earth has been subjected to some sort of invasion at some point in history.

To make clear, the Declaration of Independence was merely a powerful missive to King George that the colonists were now emphatically asserting that they were fed up with his damn taxes and would no longer be subservient to British rule. They had served notice that they were to be seen as equals, as men and women who would now stand on their own two feet in their own country, and not be ruled by the British Monarchy or anyone else abroad.

Of course, to old King George this meant war, so he quickly dispatched his army of Redcoats to get the defiant and rebellious colonists back in line. This would indeed turn out to be a pretty bad decision on his part, because history shows us that the fired-up colonists of the newly formed Continental Army, led by General George Washington, soundly whipped his troops' asses and sent what was left of'em back across the ocean.

Soon thereafter, the Treaty of Paris, which officially ended the war in 1783, would be signed in Paris by King George's defeated and deflated representatives. With their resounding victory, the jubilant colonists were now freed from the tentacles of Great Britain's oppressive regime of taxation and laws that had created an undue burden on the citizenry of the new land.

*As an aside, I believe that Crispus Attucks, a free black and patriot, understood the full promise of his new land early on. He realized just what he was fighting for when he was one of the first persons to sacrifice his life in 1770 during the Boston Massacre, one of the early skirmishes with the British leading up to the Revolutionary War.

During those unsettling and turbulent times, I also have come to believe that Crispus Attucks grasped the big picture back then that even though blacks were bought to America as the property of whites, one day they would have a chance, much like today, to be free men and women with equal and full God-given rights. I sincerely believe that he envisioned his descendants one day having an opportunity to participate in the future wealth of this new nation, despite some of the founding fathers, like Thomas Jefferson, owning slaves.

Even before the Revolutionary War began, Crispus Attucks had been aware of the ever-growing anti-slavery sentiment of a lot of white "radicals," or future Republicans, who believed that their newly created Declaration of Independence should mean freedom and equality for every man and woman in their new country, regardless of color. I genuinely believe he had also known that these white "Radical Republicans" would just need a little more time to prevail in their argument of equality for blacks to have a chance at a better life in this country.

Today, I am quite sure the descendants of Crispus Attucks are proud and quite pleased that he possessed the foresight back then to recognize the potential of this great nation early on. They must know by now, that by giving his all, he had played a vital role in establishing this great nation that they are now a part of.

Unlike a lot of blacks today, Crispus Attucks exhibited loyalty for America and its ideals, even in those troublesome times of slavery. And because of his faith in the white radicals who would later come to be known as Republicans, the change he had envisioned for blacks would start to come to fruition soon after the Revolutionary War ended.

How is this possible you say? Blacks started getting independence after the Revolutionary War?! Really?

Well, let me explain, right after being freed from British oversight, our founders quickly set about establishing a new set of laws based on low taxation and a limited government of the people, for the people, and by the people, supported by a foundation of religious freedom and God-given rights.

Our Constitution was then drawn up and ratified or agreed upon in 1787 and was signed by thirty nine representatives of the thirteen colonies at the Constitutional Convention held in Philadelphia, the city of brotherly love. This defining moment in our nation's history would usher in our first real system of governance, a newly-minted United States, and a country unlike any other before it:

"We the People of the United States, in Order to form a more perfect Union, establish Justice, insure domestic Tranquility, provide for the common defence, promote the general welfare, and secure the Blessings of Liberty to ourselves and our Posterity, do ordain and establish this Constitution for the United States of America."

Benjamin Franklin, one of the framers in attendance, was asked a simple but crucial question after the convention had ended: *"What kind of government do we have sir?"*

He succinctly retorted, *"A Republic, if you can keep it."*

By his brief answer, we know now that Franklin was referring to this clause which came as a result of their gathering: Article 4…section 4 of the constitution:

"The United States shall guarantee to every state in this union a Republican form of government, and shall protect each of them against invasion; and on application of the legislature, or of the executive, when the legislature cannot be convened, against domestic violence."

By their actions, our founders had unequivocally established a Republic with limited power by which we were to be governed, and Franklin's response would seem to be a definitive answer, in and of itself, to today's supposedly learned pundits and politicians who are wont to exclaim every chance they get that we have a democracy.

We rarely hear the term "Republic" nowadays. If we've lost this rule of government our forefathers intended, we will have lost our nation because democracy, or mob rule, is nowhere to be found in any of our nation's founding documents and was left out purposefully by the framers of our constitution. Therefore, anyone disputing this historical fact and still calling our system of governance a democracy would have to show me where it is written in our Bill of Rights, Constitution, or Declaration of Independence.

Now, as I stated earlier, this land was intended for white Europeans only but soon after the Revolutionary War ended, and our new government established, a dramatic shift would occur when most of the northern colonists reconsidered the plight of southern blacks and quickly passed laws abolishing the institution of slavery in their states. These God-fearing white Republicans, and Northerners, of the 1700s, saw the need to address the oppression of enslaved blacks and the inhumane treatment they were suffering under Democrats.

So, even though all whites may look alike to most blacks these days, they are most certainly not all the same and are vastly different in a lot of respects, and have always been. And it is this remarkable difference of ideologies, principles, and divergent views on slavery among whites during the 1700s, as noted here, that would ultimately be the impetus for the freedom that blacks in this nation enjoy today. So, it stands to reason that if all whites were the same in the 1700s and 1800s, there would have never been an end to slavery.

With the abolishment of slavery completed in the north, blacks residing in these newly created "free states" were suddenly free men and women who were now to be included in the meaning of the creed that "all men are created equal," as guaranteed by the Declaration of Independence.

However, the ending of slavery in the newly created free states certainly didn't end all discrimination in the north or slavery in the south for blacks. This initial action by anti-slavery northerners would only be the start of a long and painful journey for our nation, and blacks, but would prove to be the spark needed for slaves in the deep south to one day obtain freedom.

In this regard, because of the actions of white radical Republicans in the 1700s, blacks today absolutely should celebrate the Fourth of July because this moment in history, the end of the Revolutionary War and abolishment of slavery in the Northern States, clearly marked the beginning of their independence in this country as well.

So, by the authority vested in me as a duly sworn black man, and one possessing this tidbit of historical knowledge, all blacks in this country now have my permission to celebrate the Fourth of

July, and with reckless abandon. So, break out the grills and the coolers!

The ending of slavery in the north was enthusiastically welcomed by most colonists and was seen as a monumental shift away from the suppression of blacks, and the cultural dynamics that had existed before the Revolutionary War. Black and white abolitionists in northern states also applauded this long-anticipated move but were fearful and concerned about the problems this would cause among others within the nation, especially the southern Democrat slaveholders.

This antislavery move by Northerners created a paradigm, a whole new ideological shift, whereby each individual in these newly created "free states," including blacks, would now be able to craft their destiny in this land of opportunity as free persons. But by their actions, the Northerners had unwittingly created quite an economic and political dilemma between the now "free states" and remaining southern "slave states." Opposing values and principles between the two sides would result in an insurmountable chasm where white southern slaveholders saw blacks as property and unequal to whites, while northern abolitionists, comprised of anti-slavery whites and free blacks, "radically" viewed all men as equal regardless of color.

Southern Democrats were petrified at the prospect of their African captives gaining freedom, realizing that if they were ever to abolish slavery as the Northerners wanted that their "property" would be on par with whites in the south and the immediate effect would be the devastating loss of all forced labor and slave-driven wealth in the deep south.

In the 1700s, the initial thirteen colonies primarily consisted of Maryland, Rhode Island, Delaware, Connecticut, New York, New Jersey, Pennsylvania, Georgia, Virginia, North Carolina, South Carolina, Massachusetts, and New Hampshire. As previously noted, much of the economy of the deep south was dependent on the cotton industry and other crops that relied heavily on slave labor. So, to maintain their economic stability and viability, Democrats in southern states like Virginia and South Carolina opted to keep the enslavement of blacks in place.

Now at this point, white southerners could have done as the northern states and released their African slaves from bondage and actually started paying them a decent wage to work the fields and such. But this was about much more than economics, this move by slave-owning Democrats was about the subjugation and control of an entire race of people, and there would be no freedom, nor $15 an hour for their black slaves.

These whites saw their black captives as their rightful property, vastly inferior, and not as men and women with equal rights. African slaves were their bread and butter and weren't going anywhere. And to make matters worse, the divide between the sides would become even more pronounced as the demand for slaves actually grew with the introduction of the cotton gin in 1793. This mechanical device, invented by Eli Whitney, significantly sped up the separation of seeds from cotton, thereby increasing production capabilities and requiring even more slave labor.

Because of the diametrically opposed positions between Republicans, and Democrats, in the north and south, the country became polarized and, thus, the Mason Dixon lines were formed, demarcated by the borders of Pennsylvania, a free State, and Maryland, a slave state. Much like today, most citizens in the 1700s became divided over positions denoting freedom for blacks on one side and bondage for blacks on the other.

So here we have, in the late 1700s, white slave owners in southern states attempting to hold onto blacks as their property, their economic cash cow, against the will of the majority in our new nation and things were starting to heat up between the two sides. It was at this point in history that Democrats had a choice; they could do as the Republicans had done in the northern states, abolish slavery, or they could just dig in their heels and prolong the enslavement of blacks for almost another half-century more. Of course, history tells us that these white southerners opted for the latter, choosing to continue the enslavement of blacks and the inhumane treatment that went along with it.

Also, if I may add here, that if Democrats had decided to do away with slavery at this time, this horrific institution could've been eradicated from our nation and all blacks released from captivity before the 1800s had even begun. Just think, this divide in our nation between slave states and "free states" happened in 1787 and the Civil War would not occur until 1865, a whole nother 68 years.

Do you know how many more blacks could have avoided being born into slavery? And how many more blacks could have avoided being tortured, lynched, and sold during this period? All of this misery could have been avoided with the simple act of Democrats releasing their slaves in the 1700s. And if they had done so at this time, the economic trajectory of blacks in this nation would have played out much differently than it did over the last 200 years.

Nonetheless, in the 1700s, white southern slave-owners were recalcitrant in their stance, a stone wall of unity in their subjugation and usage of blacks, much like today's Democrat Party. Furthermore, they were not only stubbornly opposed to giving up their well-controlled "labor" and African property, but the sneaky devils had other plans up their sleeves for a much more prominent role for their black underlings.

And, in this regard, the slave owners' next diabolical move would signal how the future Democrat Party planned to exploit blacks politically for the next two hundred years and beyond in their quest for wealth, dominance, and political power. During the establishing of our new Congress in 1789, white southerners demanded to have their slave population fully counted, even though these oppressed blacks were still to be enslaved on their plantations in the south with no rights or representation whatsoever.

This was a bold and outlandish move because, in these white slave-owners' eyes, their slaves weren't even considered humans, much less citizens, and were viewed in much the same way as cattle and other property. But now, all of a sudden, and for political gain and expediency, these future Democrats were forcefully expressing the need that their slaves be counted as full persons. *This type of abusive and exploitive behavior towards blacks has never really ended with Democrats and, today they still look upon the majority of blacks as their property and subservient.*

These southerners would press on with their demand to have their slaves fully accepted as part of the census count to gain additional seats in the new Congress. This action would be one of many attempts by Democrats to use blacks politically in order to control our government and install policies favorable to them and their plantations. However, God-fearing and freedom-loving Northerners saw through this deception and pushed back, quickly denying the slave owners bid for political power and exploitation of blacks. After many heated and contentious back and forth discussions between the two sides, an agreement was finally reached to count a portion of the slave population towards the representation of seats in the new Congress.

This was how the Three Fifths Compromise in our Constitution came about; not because blacks were seen as three-fifths humans by our government, but rather how the slave population was to be counted to determine how representatives from slave states and "free states" would be apportioned in the new Congress, which would then establish how much political power each side would have. Thus, the Three-Fifths Compromise:

Article 1...Section 2 of the constitution: "Representatives and direct taxes shall be apportioned among the several states which may be included within this union, according to their respective numbers, which shall be determined by adding to the whole of free persons, including those bound to service for a term of years, and excluding Indians not taxed, three fifths of all other persons."

Now, putting the attempted exploitation of African slaves into perspective, before the start of the Civil War in 1861 there were about four million black slaves in southern states that future Democrats wanted to have fully counted towards their representation in Congress. Just think, if black slaves were fully counted in the 1700s as their slave masters demanded, they would've helped facilitate the entrenchment of their own enslavement by delivering to southern white Democrats undue political power in which they were still not to be a part of. With that, we must be ever thankful that the framers of the Constitution, and courageous abolitionists, wisely decided to unite the two sides, somewhat temporarily, without going to war.

Without the Three-Fifths compromise, our country probably would've ended up with a civil war much earlier than 1861. I would surmise that the reason our nation had not gone to war then was due, in large part, to timing. You see, it was not too long after the Revolutionary War and Americans were battle-weary at this point and wanted to avoid more bloodshed.

Today, we have a most striking parallel where history is repeating itself. The Democrat Party is now attempting to have illegal aliens from Central America and Mexico counted in our nation's census by utilizing the 14th amendment, even though these aliens have no legal standing or citizenship in our country.

At this writing, Democrats are feverishly searching for ways to have illegal aliens voting in our elections to swing power to liberal states and eventually give their party permanent political dominance in our nation, just like they sought in the 1700s.

* We will dig a little deeper into this illegal aliens matter in a later chapter, of course.

So, now at this point in history, the 1700s, we have the two opposing sides deeply entrenched in their positions; southern white Democrats, dependent on slave labor and holding onto their captive Africans for dear life, against white northern Republicans, who abolished slavery in their states and now viewed the institution as inhumane and immoral. *The rhetoric was beginning to get much more heated between the two sides. Boy, something terrible was about to happen, I bet.*

*Before we continue, I just wanna interject here that the Three-Fifths Compromise was agreed upon in 1787, but the Democrat Party wasn't officially founded until 1829. During this period, some black notables would be born and among them were black heroes and heroines such as Frederick Douglas, who was born in 1818, Harriet Tubman, born in 1820, Nat Turner, born in 1800, and Sojourner Truth, born in 1797.

*Just think, if Democrats in the south had followed Republicans in the north and released their slaves in the 1700s, none of these aforementioned black pioneers would have been born into slavery. Let that sink in. Undoubtedly, it would stand to reason that these blacks, along with many other black abolitionists and freedom fighters during this era were all Republicans because they were all against the southern white slave owners who would later create the Democrat Party.

Some runaways, such as Harriet Tubman, seeking freedom and independence, would be successful in escaping the plantations of the 1800s, much like today's black conservatives who have fled the Democrat-run inner cities. However, during slavery, most African captives were reluctant to try to escape from their plantations, and one of the primary reasons that a lot of them stayed put was that most couldn't read or write and wouldn't know where they were going or how they would get there if they were ever to escape.

These plantation blacks, even with persistent prodding from former slaves who had made it to freedom and would show them the way, still refused to budge. Here is one of the famous quotes attributed to Harriet Tubman that is still being debated today: *"I freed a thousand slaves and could have freed a thousand more if only they knew they were slaves."*

I believe that there is a kernel of truth to this quote, of course, borne out by today's blacks and the Democrat Party's mental hold on the majority of'em. See in the 1800s, the slave population was about four million strong and captive blacks vastly outnumbered their white enslavers, which was reported to be between ten and twenty thousand. But a revolution by these blacks was not to be, the continuous physical torture and mental abuse by their white masters, over time, had turned most of these once fierce African warriors into docile, subservient sheep that was timid and afraid of their captors.

In this regard, most slaves back then were not only physically enslaved but also mentally imprisoned as well. As a result, a lot of them not only became used to the plantation's culture but had also come to depend on their white Democrat masters for their any and every need and would eventually view their enslavement as a way of life.

This daily conditioning created passive slaves that wouldn't even entertain the thought of running away themselves and didn't want others to try out of fear of upsetting their violent massas. Most blacks had been trained to the point that even when their cage doors had been mistakenly left ajar by their white abusers, they still refused to seek freedom for fear of retribution if caught.

In fact, some slaves, who enjoyed their relatively comfy and exalted status as house Negroes, in order to curry favor from their master, would get upset that other black slaves or field Negroes had attempted to run, or had actually escaped and would snitch and do whatever they could to assist their masters in trying to get'em back onto the plantation.

I believe that House Negroes of the 1600s, 1700s, and 1800s were the forerunners of today's black civil rights leaders, black news anchors, black pundits, the Black Caucus, NAACP, Black Lives Matter, and black celebrities who will viciously attack any black conservative who attempts to leave or have fled the plantation. Today, these well-off house Negroes are receiving staggering sums of money, in the millions in some cases, from white liberals to turn against conservative blacks who have escaped the plantation.

So, we know now that most black slaves in the 1800s were mentally imprisoned and unable to break away from their plantation mindset and would rather live as frighten captives than to die as men fighting for their freedom. These "Africans" would just assume their roles as property, subservient to white southern Democrats without so much as a whimper.

But not all slaves in the 1800s were weak and in fear of their oppressors. There were to be a few exceptions like Nat Turner, a rebellious black slave who broke free of his plantation in 1831 and led a group of about fifty slaves in a revolt. Turner and his group of freedom fighters would go about the Virginia countryside gleefully cracking a few of the slave owners' heads before they were finally caught and subsequently hanged or shot.

Of course, southern Democrats were so pissed at this insurrection that they sorta went off the rails and resorted to what they did best, perpetrate violence against innocents. So, they promptly rounded up and killed a few hundred other black slaves in retribution and as a reminder that they were so much better at killing than their slaves could ever be.

Although Nat Turner was caught and killed, it is essential to note that before he died, he got the chance to taste real freedom and had gone out on his own terms as a man standing on his own two feet and not on his knees in obedience to his Democrat master. Now, it must be noted that there were a lot of other Nat Turners during this same period, just not in this country.

Not too far removed from this point in history and over in Saint Domingue, which is now the nation of Haiti, the French had enslaved black Haitians as well. But these fellas, in 1791, were a little more gangster than the black slaves in America and rebelled, eventually defeating their French oppressors in 1804 and gaining their freedom. These Haitians had been willing to die rather than suffer for generations in captivity and groveling on their knees at the feet of these little Frenchmen.

Now I'm not saying that African slaves in America were without courage because I don't really know how I would react under those circumstances myself, but I do know that I love my freedom and hate being under anyone's control.

Anyways, the rebellion by the Haitians and their subsequent victory over their French oppressors is a glaring example of what blacks in this country could have accomplished with unity, some do or die bravery, and an unquenchable thirst for freedom. I would suppose a revolution didn't happen in this country because most slaves in this country during the 1800s just didn't have the gumption to go through the bloody process it would have taken to do what their black brethren in Haiti had done.

Don't get me wrong, I am not trying to beat down my peoples for not standing up like the Haitians to their oppressors in the 1800s; maybe the white southern Democrats were much more intimidating and violent than their little French tyrant counterparts in Haiti, who knows? In my romanticized hypothesis, I would like to believe that the Haitians defeated their enslavers in Saint Domingue, not by an army of fierce and determined freedom seekers, but had been victorious because Frenchmen were weak, wine sipping lovers and not skilled fighters, but this may skew history a bit.

*Speaking of black overseers, I just wanna interject a little-known and quite surprising historical fact here. It appears that some free blacks during this same period of slavery had gotten into the business themselves, resulting in over 3700 blacks owning about 13,000 slaves right here in our country. *And I am betting that some of their descendants are seated as Democrats in Congress right now today.*

By now, in the late 1700s, black slaves were resigned to their fate; they were mostly uneducated and living in dilapidated housing in communities beset by violence and having to depend soley on their Democrat masters for their clothing, food, and shelter, along with medical care and any other necessities. *No, I'm not talking about today's south side of Chicago here, or Detroit, pay attention we're still in the 1800s, sheesh.*

So, in the early 1800s, the full import of the problematic divide over slavery began to dawn on slave-owners in the south, who were now deathly afraid of losing the wealth derived from the backs of their black captives. Sensing that their money-makers could be taken away at any moment because of the ever-growing, anti-slavery sentiment among Northerners, white southern slave owners figured that it was now or never for them to make a move to install the institution of slavery in the south, permanently.

Of course, this bold undertaking would require a full and complete breaking away from the United States of America. It would also require the gall to create a whole new slave-friendly government, along with amassing an army to defy our nation and our Constitution as written. This overwhelming desire by white slave owners to cement black enslavement in America will undoubtedly take us to the next chapter, and the official formation of the Democrat Party, indeed.

Would you know more? Go ahead, turn the page, if you dare.

Chapter Four

Democrats and The Civil War

To recap, in the previous chapter, we talked about the slave trade and touched on Indian abuse and genocide by the Jacksonian Democrats. We went over the formation of our Constitution and government after the Revolutionary War ended.

*Then we reviewed how our nation became divided, pitting southern slave-states against northern free-states. And, we also reviewed how white slave owners who wanted their way of life to continue, was pitted against abolitionists, who wanted an end to slavery. With that being said, we're on to the creation of the official Democrat Party. Yippee!

Fearing the growing anti-slavery sentiment in the north, white southern slave owners made a shrewd and decisive move to protect their lucrative slave trade interests once and for all. This bold decision would set the stage for a climactic and defining showdown between two vastly opposed and ideologically different political parties that would forever change the course of our nation's history.

So, in 1829, and many decades after the Three-Fifths Compromise was enacted, white southern slave owners, to protect their way of life and to expand slavery into all of the other states in our union, banded together and officially formed the Democrat Party. Once their party was up and running, these southern slave owners went about creating laws that would be more in line with their ideology and principles and made plans to secede from the rest of the United States. Requiring a leader, Jefferson Davies was quickly elected as their new president, effectively creating the Southern Confederacy and separate nation right here on our soil and serving notice that they would no longer be a part of any "United States."

Democrats now had their own official party and felt more emboldened than ever. The formation of the Confederacy was not only a way for white southern plantation owners to ensure a continuation of the wealth the enslavement of blacks generated but would also produce a legacy and inheritance for their offspring for generations to come.

Now, there was to be some opposition against the new Democrat Party when northern abolitionists and Whigs, a political group formed in the 1830s, would rise up in resistance. However, these groups were much too fractured and weak to make any inroads to stop the now unified, powerful, and very violent southerners.

So now here we were, at a point in history where the rebellious Confederate Democrats, unwilling to abide by our Constitution and Republic principles, still unmovable, believing that blacks were their property, always to be underfoot and subservient to whites. With their own government and power cemented in the deep south, Democrats would continue, with impunity, in the enslavement and harsh treatment of black slaves and wouldn't encounter any real opposition or repercussions for decades more.

In fact, a real challenge wouldn't emerge until 1854; when anti-slavery Northerners concluded that the political impasse and dangerous division between the North and South were untenable and that the ever-widening political chasm could potentially collapse the entire nation. These God-fearing men were of the same ilk as those patriots who had bravely fought in the Revolutionary War for this country's freedom from Great Britain's monarch. They had endured too much and worked too long and hard to bring about a united nation just to lose it all.

The political power play by the newly formed Democrat Party and their dangerous southern confederacy had served to reinforce their steadfast belief that the country must be united and that the institution of slavery, unjust and inhumane as it was, must come to an end. And steadfastly believing that all men were created equal, these patriots made up their minds that they would never let the enslavement of others expand in this nation or this new party to continue to go unchecked and unchallenged.

It was imperative for these men that our new country be unlike any that had gone before it. It was then that these angered, anti-slavery Northerners decided that they would have to step up and do something to finally rid our country of the immoral and inhumane institution of slavery and the permanent underclass status it produced for an entire race of people. These Americans also realized that, for the restoration of our "United States" to happen, there would be a strong possibility of bloodshed among their brethren but were undeterred.

So, in 1854, this group of God-fearing men would officially form the Republican Party to oppose the expansion of slavery and to stop the secession of southern slave states from our young country's union. By taking on the daunting task of confronting the violent Democrat Party, the new Republican Party were declaring once again, and un-equivocally, that this was the United States and that all men were created equal.

*Ok, ok. I just wanna interject here. This was probably the most crucial inflection point in our history, the fate of four million black slaves, and their futures, hung in the balance, their freedom now resting solely on the shoulders of white Republicans.

Here, it must also be stated that these Christian white men could have easily done nothing and let the Democrat Party just have their own country and their black slaves. Republicans, in the 1800s, could have also compromised and divide the land up to accommodate the southern white slave owners and avoid war.

This would have been the easy way out and more importantly, prevent the bloodshed of their fellow countrymen. After all, both of these opposing sides were all white men, weren't they? But there was something about these God-fearing Republicans in the 1800s that brings to mind a quote by Edmund Burke: *"The only thing necessary for the triumph of evil is for good men to do nothing."*

Today, I always hear pundits and everyday folks running around saying that Democrats and Republicans need to find common ground.

But what if there is no common ground to be found as it was in the 1800s? Imagine if common ground had been found between Democrats and Republicans at this juncture in history, what would have happened to the millions of black slaves in the 1800s for a compromise to be had between the two sides?

Would Republicans have worked a deal with violent Democrats to leave some kind of slavery in place as appeasement? Should Republicans today try to find common ground with violent, mob-like Democrat adversaries that even now in 2019 seek to rewrite our constitution and deny the rights of the citizens of this country?

Since the 1800s, nothing has changed as to the dynamics of the Democrat Party except for the mainstream media and social networks that are now deployed to cover up their corruption and misdeeds. No, the 1800s didn't have the technology we have today so there would be no whitewashing of the crimes and corruption of Democrats during this period. Back then, they couldn't benefit from the dizzying array of technological misinformation contrivances that the liberal media employs today to brainwash the masses. *So, there was to be no lying, leftist pundits on CNN screaming: "Republicans are tearing the country apart."*

In the 1800s and during the run-up to the Civil War, the truth was made manifest and laid bare for all to see, uncloaked and unobscured. With that being said, onward we go.

Looking to avoid conflict at all costs, Republicans searched for an influential and diplomatic leader to steer them through this high stake impasse. Abraham Lincoln, a gangly statesman, and once a Whig Party leader, fit the bill perfectly and was elected president of the Party in 1860.

Once aboard, Lincoln immediately sought to unite the country with diplomacy and some sort of compromise with Democrats to avoid war and bloodshed. However, as history tells us, the unification of the nation wouldn't be so simple and that it would be inevitable that the two sides would soon come to blows. The most significant sticking point for Lincoln was that Democrats was not about to give up their slaves for anyone, not then, not ever. Much like today, these southern plantation owners didn't care about any diplomacy or dialogue in the 1800s, they were fully entrenched in their positions and would give no quarter to their adversaries.

Like gangsters, Democrats had already determined that there would be no adherence to any rules or laws that did not include the institution of slavery. These bloodthirsty and defiant slave owners wanted to take it to the streets and battle it out, shunning diplomacy and opting for violence and force, taking what they wanted when they wanted.

From the beginning, these southerners realized that their principles, values, and way of life did not align with the new attitudes of most Americans and just didn't give a damn. As noted earlier, there was no common ground to be had, and they were willing to kill their fellow citizens to maintain their tight grip and control on their black slaves, their valuable investment and property.

* I wanna interject here again if I could. Surprisingly, at the time of the Democrat Party's formation in 1829, there were no black supporters with their chests puffed out, strutting about and proudly proclaiming that they were Democrats. I mean, there was not one proud black Democrat to be found anywhere within the Democrat Party. *Why weren't blacks beating down the doors and defending these plantation owners in the 1800s? Well, just where were they you ask?*

Oh, I guess they would've joined, I suppose; however, at this particular time in history, they were, er, just a tad too busy getting their black asses whipped, lynched, bred, sold, and worked in the fields by their white Democrat masters to do so.

But hold on there sonny, today's steadfast and loyal blacks needn't fret none too much about this little oversight because, after about three hundred or so years of their white enslavers whipping their black asses unmercifully, liberals within the Democrat Party would eventually see fit to let'em join... *about a hundred years after the end of the Civil War.*

I mean, blacks would be thoroughly broken in by then and would actually be able to read just a little. Of course, the "blacks" in today's Democrat Party couldn't be too smart, you know. To qualify, they can only possess just enough intellect to be able to make out the names of other Democrats in Congress and to say that white Republicans are all racists and black Republicans coons. From the start, Democrats never wanted any independent thinking, rational blacks anywhere near'em. It would be much later on, and many decades after Republicans had blacks in Congress, that the Democrat Party would welcome dumb, aggressive and emotional, banana-eating, minstrel-show jungle blacks who did exactly as they were told to do, just like during slavery. For evidence of this, just listen to today's Black Congressional Caucus speak and you'll be quickly convinced that not one of them could ever be considered a Mensa candidate, not by any stretch of the imagination.

These congressional Democrat blacks today have got to be some of the most ignorant and dumbest people on earth. And to test my assertion about the first blacks in Congress, just go ahead and try to research, on any internet browser: *"first black Democrat elected to Congress."* If you do, you will always see liberal websites referring back to 1870 and the first *"Black Republican"* Congressman. *Yeah, just try to find that first Democrat Congressman or Congresswoman on liberal websites. Grab some coffee though, it's gonna take a minute or so, because I can absolutely guarantee that you will not find any black Democrats in Congress until after the party lost power, briefly, over blacks in the 1960s.*

Anyways, I digress, let's now go back to the troublesome 1800s. One of the most remarkable catalysts leading up to the Civil War of 1861 was the Dred Scott Vs. Sandford case in 1857 in which a black slave, Dred Scott of course, took his case for freedom up to the Supreme Court, the highest court in the land.

The problem with old Dred's timing, though, was the lopsided makeup of the court during this period; dominated by pro-slavery Democrats and not really conducive to racial equality or adherence to fairness for blacks. There, on the bench, Chief Justice Robert Brooke Taney, an old, pearly white Democrat, along with six other racist white justices quickly ruled that Dred Scott was still the property of John Sandford, his master, and owner, and would remain his slave like forever, or until he died, whichever came first.

And just like that, Dred Scott's decade-long battle for freedom culminated, and ended, with seven Supreme Court Justices ruling against his fundamental right as a human being to be free, just because of the color of his skin. These pro-slavery Democrats had invalidated Dred's God-given right to freedom while simultaneously reaffirming the rights of their slave-owning brethren to travel with their African captives into free states and then bring them back to slave states without losing rights to their "property," sorta like tagged luggage.

The Supreme Court's majority saw, in their opinion, that blacks were indeed just property and not citizens of the United States, and therefore undeserving of rights as citizens. More profoundly, old Chief Justice Taney really showed out and wanted everyone to understand his position and feelings he harbored toward black slaves with his opinion : *"They are so far inferior, that the Negro might justly and lawfully be reduced to slavery for their own benefit."*

However, Republican Justices John Mclean and Benjamin Robert Curtis dissented, of course, and expressed the reasonable and heartfelt opinion that since blacks in five of the thirteen states did have voting rights at the time, that this did indeed give all blacks within the entire United States full rights. Therefore, they had reasoned, this would also allow Dred Scott to enjoy the same rights as every other citizen in America.

I am interjecting again here. In hindsight, why the hell did Republicans fight so hard for blacks back in the 1700s, and 1800s? They never wanted to have ownership of these fools, nor to use them as slaves and political pawns. They just wanted them to have the same liberty to partake of the many opportunities this land already provided for themselves and their own families.

Oh well, unfortunately for Republicans today, they now see that the old adage still rings true; that no good deed goes unpunished.

Anyway, after his case was ruled on, much to the delight of his Democrat owner, who probably whipped his ass some more for making him waste his time going to court, a disappointed Dred Scott went back to being a slave for a little while longer.

However, after this ruling, an infuriated President Lincoln would give a quite heated speech. I mean, he went off. Let me now present to you a few of the excerpts:

"Chief Justice Taney, in delivering the opinion of the majority of the Court, insists at great length that Negroes were no part of the people who made, or for whom was made, the Declaration of Independence, or the Constitution of the United States....."

"He finds the Republicans insisting that the Declaration of Independence includes ALL men, black as well as white; and forthwith he boldly denies that it includes negroes at all, and proceeds to argue gravely that all who contend it does, do so only because they want to vote, and eat, and sleep, and marry with negroes! ...."

"Now I protest against that counterfeit logic which concludes that, because I do not want a black woman for a slave I must necessarily want her for a wife. I need not have her for either, I can just leave her alone. In some respects she certainly is not my equal; but in her natural right to eat the bread she earns with her own hands without asking leave of anyone else, she is my equal, and the equal of all others...."

This profound speech didn't matter to Democrats, they were unmoved, Lincoln's condemnation of the outcome of the Dred Scott case was met with deaf ears. The defiant slave owners now considered themselves their own country, and had already declared their sovereignty, and nothing would make them believe that blacks were their equal. Tensions were running high, and for these wild-eyed southerners, it would soon be time to take it to the streets. So, they ramped up their saber-rattling and anti-American rhetoric, imploring Republicans to give them what they really desired, a conflict to determine the fate of the nation's political power.

Feeling that they now had a strong enough army to carry out their plans of toppling the antislavery Union in the North, Democrats craved war and violence and was salivating at the chance to test the mettle and underbelly of the supposedly "soft," polite, and diplomatic Republicans. *I mean, these violent slave-owners really thought that they were gonna be fighting Mitt "kittens" Romney and Jeb "low en-*

ergy" Bush or something.

So, the die was cast, and a confrontation to settle things once and for all would be needed to unite the country and eradicate the institution of slavery, which now hung like a dark, palpable cloud over the entire nation. This looming conflict would be a high stakes gambit by a diplomatically exhausted Lincoln and Republican Party to bring about law and order within the country and restore harmony among its citizenry. They knew what this would entail of course but were firm and resolute in their stance.

*I am interjecting again. To reiterate, at this juncture in our history, four million black "African Warriors" were depending on the supposedly "racist" and "white supremacists" Republicans for their freedom. And to really emphasize the point, it was these pearly white Republican men, willing to sacrifice their lives, who would be fighting pearly white Democrat slave owners to free crispy black African slaves from bondage. *Let that gnaw on your tittles for a moment.*

So again, to my earlier point; all whites were not the same in the 1800s and still isn't in 2019, no matter what ill-informed blacks believe today. In fact, if all white men were the same back then, blacks today would still be picking cotton and saying "yes suh" to any and all whites they encountered. *And to really drive the point home, and to make a most profound statement; if it had been left up to just the four million black slaves to fight and win their own freedom in the 1800s, they would probably still be in chains today.*

*Now wait a minute, hold on, just to be fair, I do wanna note that about 180,000 blacks fought alongside Republicans during the Civil War and about 30,000 of them died, mostly from diseases though. These blacks, like Crispus Attucks, understood the promise of Ameica, and the chance to be free from the shackles of enslavement.

Anyways, the Civil War would begin in earnest at Fort Sumter in April of 1861, and at the very start, smug, slave-owning whites actually invited their wives, dressed in their finery, to partake of the supposedly festive event. To them, it would be just like the gatherings they all enjoyed when they hanged blacks from oak trees back home; just a relaxing day and time of celebration with the family.

Out on the battlefield and just before the shooting started, these southerners had an air of arrogance, much like today's snobbish white liberal Democrats you see at celebrity red carpet affairs, where they can often be seen prancing about smirking and grinning in their supposed "superiority" over lowly commoners while patting themselves on the back and receiving awards for "pretending.

So, light-hearted and dismissive of their impending clash with determined Republicans in the 1800s, Democrat women arrived upon horse-drawn wagons and under umbrellas in bright floral sundresses and hats, bearing picnic baskets laden with bread and meats to watch the "event." In a festive mood, they were chatty and gossipy of course, tossing their hair about and making small talk with each other. Why it would be just like their husbands going out hunting and shooting coons and squirrels they were told. Their men would be back home by supper; they were assured. I guess these foolish, "resistance" Democrat white women didn't notice all the guns, bayonets, sabers, lances, cannons, and knives that were being readied for action on the other side of the field.

Today, the similarities are striking in that white liberals, news anchors, celebs and pundits are also lightheartedly brushing away the rising anger of Republicans as the Democrat Party is attempting once again to overthrow our government.

The Civil War of 1861 would be the first of many cases in which the Democrats' miscalculations and delusions about the will, determination and grit of Americans would prove to be their undoing.

The Democrats' hopes for a quick victory at the start of the Civil War would quickly turn into fiercely contested and protracted bloody clashes, such as the Battle of Antietam, and Bull Run, along with many other brutal battles in which hundreds of thousands of combatants would be killed. Many historians believe that Gettysburg, a clash between the two sides where over 50,000 men were killed in just three days of fighting, would be the decisive turning point in the war.

Along with the many deaths, these strongly contested and horrific conflicts during the Civil War also would cause many soldiers to be severely injured and maimed, resulting in a massive number of amputations, and arms and legs being stacked like so much human firewood on the battlefield. The gruesome injuries and causalities of this senseless war illuminated the enormous sacrifice extracted from white Republicans to free black slaves and unite the country and would also illustrate the overwhelming desire by the win-at-any-costs Democrat Party to defy our country and maintain the slave institution they so desperately wanted to hold onto.

Nonetheless, President Lincoln in 1863, amid the Civil War, still angry over the Dred Scott decision, doubled down by signing the Emancipation Proclamation and declaring that all slaves were free, not just in northern states but also in southern states as well and everywhere else in the nation. Of course, this move really, and I mean really, pissed off the Democrats in Congress who responded to Lincoln's action by declaring an overreach of powers.

The 1800s Democrats viewed the Emancipation Proclamation like how an abusive boyfriend sees a restraining order by the court to leave his ex-girlfriend alone, with laughter and contempt. And with Lincoln's proclamation, they would defiantly renew their efforts to retain their slaves and newly established Confederacy.

To these white Democrat slave-owners, it would take much, much more than a silly piece of paper by Lincoln, their hated nemeses, to free black slaves from the clutches of their party. To that end, the Civil War would rage on with over 700,000 casualties in four years of fighting and wouldn't come to an end until 1865, when Confederate General Robert E Lee would surrender to Union General Ulysses S Grant at the Appomattox courthouse in Virginia. This capitulation by southern slave owners marked their sound defeat and long over-due dismantling of the Confederacy. The rebellious Democrat Party had been subdued, and their anti-American ideology vanquished.

If I may interject again, I believe that it is here, at this moment in history, when the Democrats were soundly defeated, and their party obliterated, that their name should have been banned from our society for all time and stricken from our political arena.

The Democrat Party's hopes of seceding from the United States had been effectively crushed by Republicans. Their defeat would also signal freedom for millions of blacks and the eradication of the ruthless institution of slavery in America once and for all. And although the war had been costly, with a tremendous loss of life on both sides, Republicans had persevered, accomplishing what they had set out to do, preventing the Democrat Party's attempted destruction of our new Constitution and government, and in the process achieving freedom and equality for black slaves, all in one swell swoop. *Or had they?*

It is here where I will ask once more, at this point why wasn't the Democrat name banned from our society for the centuries of atrocities they had committed against blacks, or for the many lives lost in the Civil War?

The Germans did it with the Nazi name, wasn't centuries of cruel and inhumane treatment of black slaves deserving of the Democrat name being stricken from our society as well? These are questions I will keep asking throughout this writing.

Ok, to summarize; the Civil War was a bitter, hard-fought, and very bloody clash that took over 700,000 lives in a contest of wills between anti-slavery white Republicans in the north and slave-owning, white Democrats in the North and South. There couldn't be a much clearer distinction between the two parties, no matter who or what tries to spin this written-in-stone historical fact today.

The most chilling question to me and one that all blacks should be thinking about at this point is, what if Democrats had actually won the Civil War? What kind of nation and government would we have now? Would we still have filthy rich black superstar rappers, black sports stars, and other black celebs, who are proud Democrats today, whining about racist systemic oppression, or would they still be in a field somewhere under a hot sun toiling for white slave owners and picking cotton while getting their black asses whipped?

Whoaaaa, I got off track again, didn't I, where was I? *Oh, ok...* Now you would think that the end of the Civil War in 1865 would bring about a fairytale ending for the newly freed blacks, and you would be very, very wrong, of course. Because there would continue to be a fly in the ointment of freedom for these newly released slaves.

After the war was over, there remained a lingering, bottomless well of bitterness and anger among the beaten southern whites. In their defeat, they became consumed by a nearly unquenchable thirst for revenge and would soon set about finding ways to regain the black "property" they had lost.

In the aftermath of the Civil War, a broken and rudderless Democrat Party was left lying in ruins, directionless, and now depended on Republicans, their political adversaries, to piece everything back together for'em in the south. I mean, they were such a sad and pitiful group at this point. The gambit on their "superior" unified "resistance" against the polite and diplomatic Republicans had resulted in a nice ass whipping for the former slave owners, turning them into a discombobulated, vindictive, and much more dangerous bunch of serpents. *You know, sorta like how they are right now with Trump's presidency. Too bad Democrats didn't have their media cohorts around in the 1800s to spin their defeat. Can't you just see the fake headline? "Unfit Lincoln causes hundreds of thousands of lives in needless war!"*

Anyway, with the dismantling of their new "Confederacy" in the 1800s, the Democrat Party, sensing that they couldn't achieve what they wanted politically, would turn to corruption, sabotage, and violence as a means to an end, much like today's party, which is still adamantly opposed to our constitution as written. *Americans must understand by now that there can be no real common ground with a party such as this, not then, not now, and not ever.*

For the ever diplomacy-minded and freedom loving Republicans of the 1800s, the purpose of their bloody battles was not to establish political dominance but to bring the country and its people back together again as one. These gentlemen viewed the results of the Civil War as an opportunity to work together with the now beaten former slave owners to reaffirm our Christian values, principles, and rules, along with acknowledging the rights every citizen was entitled to, regardless of race.

Under their theory, constitutional rights were now supposedly cemented whereby each citizen of their own volition, including blacks, would be able to determine their own path and financial future by their own merit and ability. This sounded really beautiful because at the time the majority of people in the country desired healing and a coming together of the two war-weary sides. *How could it not be a win-win for all?*

Drinking their own Kool-Aid in the 1800s, naivety, and decency would get the best of God-fearing Republicans who wanted to do things in a gentlemanly manner and "work across the aisle" with the still devious and forever-plotting Democrats. With blind faith and tolerant blinders on, Republicans endeavored to put the past behind them and start anew and were more than willing to let bygones be bygones. They believed that everyone needed and wanted to get a fresh start, and that this change would come about by rebooting our principles and beginning a new chapter in a country that had now supposedly redeemed itself of its rocky and inglorious past.

President Lincoln honestly felt that the nation, and former black slaves, had suffered enough already and that the deep south could be rebuilt to accept our political structure and governance as written in the Constitution. *Well, alrighty then.*

This hopeful thinking, as history shows, would turn out to be quite the mistake for Lincoln and the Republican Party. They had greatly underestimated the determination and resourcefulness of the pro-slavery southerners, and this oversight would be their undoing. Republicans hadn't understood back then that it was quite difficult to fight in a bloody, protracted war with a treacherous and violent foe like the Democrats, and after defeating them, have expectations they would later become upstanding citizens and find other ways to accumulate wealth and political gain without the enslavement or manipulation of others.

*It was sorta like trying to get a long-time crackhead to give up the pipe cold turkey and, once you had succeeded in your mission, that the crackhead had learned his lesson and wouldn't ever attempt to smoke again.

You see, Democrats still harbored an insatiable hatred towards Republicans after their defeat and were, understandably, still quite bitter at losing control of their slaves and source of income. Their rage would grow like an uncontrollable and vengeful flame, burning even more intense with each passing day. Democrats were defiant and didn't care about the citizens of this nation, only power, and were now at the point where they would never entirely yield to the values, principles, and ideals upon which our Constitution was drawn.

I do believe that, at the time, President Lincoln had put aside the Democrat Party's moral turpitude for the sake of diplomacy and unity, mistakenly thinking that the former slave-owners were salvageable. And like Lincoln, most Americans were also tired of conflict and sought healing and unity and were holding out hope, with their arms wide open, to embrace their defeated southern brothers and sisters.

But how could they know that even in defeat that the former slave owners would still be plotting, covertly jostling for power while attempting to set up another shadow government and using any means necessary to obtain political dominance again? The violent and deceitful Democrats believed wholeheartedly that their path to power was not one of diplomacy or peaceful negotiations, but one of deception, chaos, and political sabotage. The broken party's theory in the 1800s was that if they could just take back power politically, or by any other means, they could then put the genie back into the bottle by shredding the constitution and enslaving blacks once again.

Meanwhile, over in the Republican camp, President Lincoln knew that it was going to take a lot of hard work and an enormous amount of sacrifice and effort to sort everything out and bring about a unified country. The most daunting task he faced was getting white Democrats to accept their former slaves as equals so that southern states could be integrated back into the union to once again complete these United States.

To achieve this goal, Lincoln realized there would need to be a complete restructuring of the entire southern region to reflect the principles, values, and laws of the rest of the nation. He had genuinely hoped for a peaceful transition and meaningful reconciliation between southern whites and their former black slaves. He truly believed that the two could coexist and strive together to create a much more harmonious relationship with each other in the south.

Oh boy, did Lincoln and the Republicans have a lot to learn in the 1800s. I mean, over centuries, these take-no-prisoners white southerners had honed their skills of violence and control on their black slaves and were now addicted to power and would never just roll over and concede that their livestock was their equal. To them, there would be neither peace nor equality for blacks in their world, not then, not now, not ever.

Again, I wanna interject here and submit that at this time; after Democrats had been soundly defeated in 1865, that if their broken and defeated party had just left their former slaves alone, the majority of blacks today would be independent, self-sufficient, and prospering in America just like every other race in this country.

If the Democrat Party had seen fit to just back the hell up and become peaceful and tolerant Americans like they fraudulently espouse today, the grief and pain that blacks would go through for the next one hundred years or so, and still going through today, would have never occurred.

Alas, history tells us that this was not to be the case; blacks being allowed to enjoy their new found freedoms would turn out to be the farthest thing from the truth of what really occurred in the aftermath of the Civil War.

This would bring us to Lincoln's last ditched, and futile attempts to sanely and rationally deal with the irrational and violent Democrats, and also illustrate his determination in trying to stop the former slave-owners' relentless and dogged pursuit of black suppression during Reconstruction. Well, good luck with that peace offering sir, because the long road to equality for blacks was just getting started and it was gonna be one helluva ride.

Turn the page, please.

Chapter Five

Reconstruction Destruction

Ok, so the last chapter detailed the formation of the Democrat Party by plantation owners, their attempt to secede after creating the Confederacy, and their efforts to install a permanent slave institution in this nation.

*We then saw the hatred of slave-owning Democrats produce a brutal civil war that took over 700,000 lives, all because of their party's refusal to abide by our Constitution and release their slaves. At this point, you would think the defeated anti-Americans would say, *"Look, we've had enough, blacks can have their freedom, we've lost enough lives already trying to keep 'em on lock-down."* But no, these Democrats were resilient and on a mission, and as history tells us, we would be oh, so wrong to believe anything else otherwise.

So as the commercial says, *"But wait, there's more!"*

After the Civil War ended in 1865, Lincoln drew up ambitious reconstruction plans that he believed would integrate the rebellious southern Democrats back into the union with the Africans they had formerly enslaved. On paper, this was great; however, in reality, this desire by Lincoln would prove much more daunting to implement because of Democrat "resistance" and "obstruction."

Nevertheless, old Honest Abe would still see reconciliation between former slave owners and former black slaves as a means to heal and unite the country. He longed for a peaceful and colorblind society where newly freed black men and women in the south could also partake of the American dream and pursuit of happiness, unhindered by any of the restrictions that had been previously placed upon them before the Civil War.

There was plenty of optimism at the beginning of Reconstruction, bringing fresh hope for newly emancipated blacks as political opportunities soon opened up for them, resulting in some becoming Republican Congressmen in the deep south, a first for the nation. And with blacks now eagerly taking advantage of their newfound freedoms, many started developing businesses such as hotels, dry cleaners, restaurants, banks, and other entities. These thriving and bustling communities would later come to be known as Black Wall Street.

However, it wouldn't be long before Democrats became highly incensed that their former slaves were becoming financially independent and gaining political power in the south. They were repulsed that blacks would now be on equal footing with southern whites. Meanwhile, Republicans still pressed forward, doing everything possible to make sure former slaves could gain access to all the opportunities they were entitled to in these United States, this time as free men and women with full God-given rights.

For perspective, we must remember that in the 1800s, during Reconstruction and the building of Black Wall Street, Republicans were actually thought of as "extremists" and "radicals" for viewing former black slaves as equals and encouraging their progress and political growth. To these God-fearing men, our nation was finally starting to live up to the essence and creed of the Declaration of Independence.

What had been initially intended for white colonists only, were now supposedly applicable to everyone in the nation. Looking back, it would seem that the equality Crispus Attucks had foreseen as he he fought in the Revolutionary War had finally come to fruition for blacks: *"We hold these truths to be self-evident: That all men are created equal; that they are endowed by their creator with certain unalienable rights that among these are life, liberty and the pursuit of happiness."*

However, to the now defeated, powerless, and frustrated white southern Democrats, these words were just the meaningless gibberish of Republican sympathizers, nigger lovers who had caused the destruction of their pro-slavery Confederacy. In their eyes, the "Radical Republicans" were using the Declaration of Independence as the means to facilitate the theft of their black "property" and were now daring to bestow rights upon these newly freed blacks as if they were their equals.

This was blasphemy of the highest order for Democrats and a slap in their faces because, as a result of their defeat in the Civil War, just like that their investment, their slave institution and cash cow had all gone up in smoke, erased like a fart in the wind. Everything was lost after centuries of building up a quite lucrative slave-dependent industry in the southern states, and now they were left wondering; *"Who were these Republicans to dictate to them what rights blacks would have in the south and what businesses they could run in this country?"*

Being pushed to the brink, Democrats realized that something had to be done, and quickly. So, it would soon come about that their plans to stop reconstruction in the south, and black progress, from ever being completed, would begin to materialize when their operative, John Wilkes Booth, stunned the nation by assassinating President Abraham Lincoln on April 14th, 1865.

This almost predictable and violent act of retribution would move one of their own into the president's chair as planned. Andrew Johnson, the Democrat vice president who had run on the Union ticket in 1864 with Lincoln in the hopes of unifying the nation, took office immediately upon his death.

Once seated, President Johnson quickly got to work and tried, as much as he could, to circumvent and stop all of Lincoln's reconstruction plans by appointing former slave owners as provisional governors all over the south and ordering them to establish new all-white, pro-slavery governments. This action by Johnson would serve to re-establish many elements of the Confederacy in the deep south, much to the delight and satisfaction of southern whites. Recent history shows that this would not be the last time a Democrat president would appoint activist judges and government officials all across our nation to circumvent our laws and rewrite our Constitution.

*To note, you can look at the election of 2008 where another president, surprisingly black, was installed to do the very same thing for the Democrat Party.

Wait a minute, a black Democrat president working against America, black progress, Republicans and the Constitution, who would have thunk it?

Hell, this foolish black socialist puppet even tried to rewrite specific laws all by himself, such as DACA, which we are now in the process of trying to untangle and undo today.

My, how times have changed, or have they?

In 1865, newly installed President Andrew Johnson, who believed that former slaves were still the property of southern whites and should never have any part in any reconstruction plans, looked for other creative ways to nullify the freedoms and rights blacks had gotten under Lincoln. So, the Democrat Party would, with the backing of their new president, quickly set about creating black codes in the deep south. These new, hastily enacted codes would be among many other draconian restrictions that were designed to impede and obstruct any and all progress of free blacks in the south.

One such example of these laws, which was vehemently opposed by Republicans, was passed in November of 1865 in Mississippi: *"No freedman, Negro, or mulatto shall carry or keep firearms or ammunition."*

*Freed blacks were four million strong and southern whites wanted to keep them disarmed and vulnerable to their subsequent KKK raids and lynchings

Today, this is similar to the Democrat Party's thinly-veiled attacks on our 2nd amendment rights, and the NRA, in a modern day attempt to disarm the citizenry of this nation, just as Hitler had done to Jews before exterminating a large swath of 'em in Germany in the 1930s and 1940s

Other black codes were thinly veiled attempts by former slave owners in the deep south to continue their control and suppression of blacks:

Sec.1...Be it ordained by the police jury of the parish of St. Landry, that no negro shall be allowed to pass within the limits of said parish without special permit in writing from his employer...

Sec.4...Every Negro is required to be in the regular service of some white person, or former owner, who shall be held reconcilable for the conduct of said Negro...

Sec.6...No Negro shall be permitted to preach, exhort, or otherwise declaim to congregations of colored people, without a special permission in writing from the president of the police jury.

*Note...If I may interject again, with the corrupt black preachers that we have today, I don't really mind that last code staying in place!

Not satisfied with just black codes though, southern Democrats doubled down and imposed harsh Jim Crow laws on blacks in the deep south, relegating them to underclass status once more. These laws would bring about segregation and the designation, by race, of separate water fountains and entrances and many other suppressive measures designed to force former slaves back into a plantation-like environment.

But even with these developments, Republicans were still fighting the good fight, bless their hearts, and trying to encourage black progress. This was evidenced in February of 1866 when Republican Congressman, Thaddeus Stevens, introduced a bill to give former slaves "40 acres and a mule" as a form of reparations. But once again the pro-slavery Democrat Party, led by President Andrew Jackson, would vehemently oppose the measure and it would quickly die in Congress after a contentious debate. *I am guessing here, but I can imagine that there may have been Democrats on the Senate floor at the time screaming: "People will die if we give blacks 40 acres and a mule!"*

You see, unlike today's Democrat Party gleefully doling out welfare handouts to blacks and Hispanics for votes, in the 1800s, Democrats knew that freed blacks were not gonna support the party they had just gained their freedom from, the memories of enslavement, whippings, and lynchings were too fresh in their former slaves' minds and would need some more time to dissipate.

So, there would be nothing given to blacks, not one dime or nickel, by white Democrats until their party could harness their former slaves' political power for themselves and was assured they had their votes well in hand. I would suppose that, in the 1800s, there were no inducements to offer former slaves. There was no welfare, no section eight and flat-screen TVs, nothing to lure them away from Republicans and sweet freedom. So, Democrats turned to what they did best, violence and intimidation tactics to prevent blacks from gaining financially and being politically active.

If I were living in the 1800s as a black man and going through the hellish nightmare Democrats were causing my people, it would be beneath me to even dignify with an answer the seemingly farfetched question of, would their party ever find a way to eventually turn descendants of their black African slaves into their most potent voting bloc in the ensuing decades in America?

I would've thunk that it would be quite absurd. I would never even begin to entertain the thought that future blacks would be that stupid. I mean, why would any sane black even think about voting for Democrats, their former enslavers? That would be like unfathomable and truly insane and really, really weird, wouldn't it? Well, just keep reading about our strong black African Queens and Warriors, the truth is stranger than fiction.

Now, even with the Democrats' denial of the 40 acres and a mule proposal, other developments and wealth-creating opportunities would open up for blacks when Republicans created the Freedmen Bureau. This agency, which lasted from 1865 until about 1870, was endowed with federal authority and power and tasked with dividing up and redistributing confiscated and abandoned property. These actions resulted in land and homes, once owned by white southerners, being given to former slaves.

The Freedman Bureau would also help create higher learning institutions for blacks such as Fiske and Howard Universities, and many other primary and secondary schools during Reconstruction. *So, in effect, it was the Republican Party which first established the historically black colleges we see in this nation today.*

With the Freedmen Bureau's work, blacks begin to enjoy land ownership which was, and is still, the key to building a vibrant community and accumulating wealth in America. However, this initiative, and financial windfall, for freed blacks would be very short-lived when President Johnson got wind of it and subsequently ordered that all land taken from the former slave-owning southerners be returned to them post haste.

This devastating order had the immediate effect of forcing many blacks to return to plantations throughout the south to sharecrop for their former masters, which was just slavery-lite, sans daily whippings of course. With sharecropping, the deal was that white landowners would provide housing to their former slaves who worked the fields, and in return, these blacks would get a share of the crops which was usually between a third and about a half, with the price being set by the landowners.

White southerners were pleased that they now had a reliable, low-cost workforce that was once again captive because many of these blacks could not readily acquire or accumulate enough money to leave the plantation and buy their own land and homes. In this regard, sharecropping created a suppressive situation where most of the southern blacks were now tied to land they didn't own. They were forced, once again, back into the servitude of their former slave masters.

To be fair, during this period, I must also note that there were actually a few white farmers who had fallen on hard times themselves and was sharecropping as well, but I am betting that they had fared a little better than their black counterparts as to pay for their services.

Republicans, realizing that Democrats in the south were at it again, were forced to step in once more to do something about the Black Codes and other crippling restrictions imposed upon southern blacks. To remedy this situation, and for the first time in our young nation's history, Republicans pushed through an expansion of governmental powers to facilitate the change they had envisioned for blacks. This action resulted in the first Civil Rights Bill being passed in 1866, which again declared that everyone in the United States was citizens and equal before the law, regardless of race.

The Democrat Party, along with President Johnson, would, of course, try to veto and prevent the bill from passing, while angrily declaring that it was a law that discriminated against whites. *Say what? Just think, the Democrat Party, the same party that today espouses tolerance, equality, and diversity, actually said that passing a bill in the 1800s to recognize blacks as men and women was a form of discrimination against white southerners? Wow, you just can't make this stuff up.*

*Of course, liberals today will just gloss over this tidbit of truth with the old" parties switched" myth.

Anyways, Democrat "resistance" and "obstruction" against the 1866 Civil Rights Bill would bring about the first ever veto in our nation's history as Republicans defied both the Democrat Party and President Andrew Johnson. There also would be other meaningful amendments passed by a Republican-dominated Congress, codifying constitutional rights for former black slaves, all against staunch Democrat opposition:

The 13th amendment, *which freed blacks from slavery altogether, was passed and adopted on December 6, 1865, by Republicans with Democrats vehemently opposing.*

The 14th amendment, *which granted citizenship rights for newly freed blacks and their offspring, was passed on May 10th, 1866 by Republicans, with 100 percent of Democrats opposing.*

Note: Although Democrats staunchly opposed this Amendment for blacks in the 1800s, the party is zealously using this amendment today to justify the citizenship of anchor babies born to Hispanic illegal aliens in this country. Let that sink into your noggin.

The 15th amendment, *which established voting rights for blacks, was passed February 3rd, 1870, by Republicans with 97 percent of Democrats opposing.*

Here, it must be noted that the primary reason Republicans were so successful in getting all of these amendments through and into law for blacks was that, at the time, there were more of them in Congress than Democrats. This majority came about as a direct result of Republicans refusing to seat the all-white, former slave-owning, southern activist appointees that President Andrew Johnson wanted as representatives in Congress after Lincoln was assassinated in 1865.

* So, there seems to be a thread developing here. It appears that anything that was done politically in the best interests of blacks always seemed to happen under a mostly Republican Congress. All of

the civil rights amendments of the 1800s favoring blacks were passed by Republicans, despite the Democrat Party's fierce opposition, obstruction, and resistance.

With that being said, blacks today owe every last one of their damn freedoms and rights, everything, to white Republicans who defied a Democrat president and Democrat Party that lacked the necessary political power to stop them at the time.

Boy, as a sane and self-sufficient black man, I sure wish we could go back to the days of a real Republican-dominated Congress. That is what I would call making America great again! Hey, I think I'll coin that phrase; Make America Great Again! I hope no one else thought of it yet, I really wanna use it.

The Reconstruction Act of 1867 would divide the deep south into five military districts and send federal troops to the region to protect blacks from southern Democrats. As with everything done for the progress of blacks, this act would be another law for blacks passed by Republicans over the "resistance" and "obstruction" of Democrats in Congress and the threat of President Johnson's veto. Fierce opposition from the Democrat Party would come about because the Reconstruction Act mandated, as a condition of being integrated back into the union, that southern states ratify their local governments to accept blacks as lawful and equal citizens.

With this new law in place, the prospects for southern blacks started to look promising once more and would get even better after the Republican Party got another political boost in 1868 when Republican General Ulysses S Grant was elected president. With Grant on board, Republicans soon pushed through the 15th Amendment, as previously noted, which gave blacks the right to vote. This Amendment was an essential and crucial "right" and was entirely necessary for blacks to achieve political power and bring about much-needed change for their community. Its passage made sense; voting was the mechanism by which freed blacks would become politically active and empowered.

The 15th amendment was intended to also help blacks determine their destiny and give them the necessary tools to fight back, collectively, against the Democrat Party, their former captors and oppressors. And it stood to reason that newly freed blacks would vote Republican, and their own best interest, to reward the party that had gone all in and shedding their blood in the Civil War for their freedom.

It was very, very clear to former slaves during the 1800s that it was Republicans fighting for and pushing through all of the rights they had gotten as new citizens of this country. Post-Civil-War, this alignment of blacks and the Republican Party had all come together like ham and eggs, completing a painstakingly beautiful portrait of black progress. Former slaves now had all the incentive in the world to vote for Republicans because their freedom, futures, and very lives all depended on these God-fearing white men who represented their best interests and continued to push through bills favorable to them and all Americans. It was a win-win situation.

Again, looking at unappreciative blacks today, you wouldn't be able to tell how much Republicans have done in the fight for them to have all the rights they now enjoy, the SOBS. Anyways…let's keep it moving, shall we?

Now, a problem would soon arise with the 1866 Voting Rights Act, as the law was based entirely on race and could be easily challenged in other areas. Seeing this, Democrats immediately searched for loopholes, probing for ways to obstruct or restrict blacks from voting, anything to circumvent the new voting law. Democrats would soon find the gaps they were seeking and would utilize gender, literacy, and familial constructs and just about anything else they could find, in many cases, to obstruct and deny southern blacks their right to vote.

Now, let's just pause, sit back a spell, and think about this moment in time: *During the 1800s, Republicans were known as extremists and "radicals" because they supported full equality for blacks. And had to enact many laws to force Democrats in the southern states to count newly freed blacks as citizens and to let them vote.*

In direct contrast, the opposing Democrats of the 1800s, which today is still a threat to our country and individual liberty for all Americans, did all they could to suppress and restrict the rights and freedoms of blacks in any way, shape, form, or fashion that they could, even if it meant violence.

*But, to really understand the Democrats Party' deviousness, let's rewind for a moment. If you will recall in the previous chapter, when Congressional seats were being apportioned in our newly formed Congress in 1789, it was these same white slave owners who were more than eager to have their then black slaves fully counted to gain a political advantage. But now, since blacks were no longer under their control and picking cotton and could freely choose the party they would vote for, Democrats were now all of a sudden adamantly opposed to these now free blacks being counted or having any voting rights.

See how this is playing out? Think long and hard about this one and let it sink in, slowly. Deceptive and sneaky of Democrats, isn't it? But it's to be expected, anything less from this party would be quite disappointing.

So, to counter "resistance" and "obstruction" by the Democrat Party and fortify the new voting law in the late 1800s, new governmental protections were put in place by Republicans. With this development, southern blacks were once again able to exercise their now unencumbered "right" to vote and soon went to the ballot box in droves, with some again seeking political office in the deep south.

Of course, since these blacks were all Republicans and voted as such, and because they were a large part of the population then, the Republican Party soon started to dominate politics in the deep south and it would be a time of renaissance and revival for blacks all across the nation. During this period of Reconstruction, over 1800 black Republicans held office in the south and things were starting to look look a little rosy. But all of this happiness and independence for the former slaves would turn out to be just another pot of fool's gold.

I can just imagine what the now pissed-off Democrats could've been saying about the political gains blacks were making in the south during this period: "You just wait until our leaders in the party find out about this nonsense of you uppity publican niggers holding office down here."

The leaders of the Democrat Party did "find out" about this revolution and quickly marshaled their forces to create a stop-gap measure for this black surge of political power in the south. *Oh well, it was good while it lasted!* So, to quash and put down the political gains and progress blacks were enjoying under Republican leadership during Reconstruction, in 1866 the Democrat Party created a not so lovely organization called the Klu Klux Klan as their enforcement arm to control and intimidate blacks and to discourage antislavery whites from helping out in the south.

*Just imagine, if the mainstream media we have today had existed during this time, they would most certainly have gone through hell and highwater defending this violent organization, just like they do with today's violent Democrat-sponsored and funded groups like Antifa and Black Lives Matter.

Anyways, the creation of the Klu Klux Klan in the late 1800s was merely a violent reaction, and direct response by the Democrat Party to the enactment of the 13th, 14th and 15th amendments, which gave former black slaves freedom, voting rights, and citizenship in America. Much more importantly though, the impetus to create this organization came about primarily because of the Democrat Party's impotence to stop the Republicans politically. They would now use members of their Klu Klux Klan organization to achieve by force what they couldn't accomplish politically, much like today's Democrats.

These former slave-owners had decided that they would do whatever it took to impede any black progress created during Reconstruction. They would resist and obstruct any and all laws that would establish freedom and equality for blacks in the south. The standing command Democrats gave to members of their KKK organization was to intimidate and harass blacks wherever they were, and if necessary, even kill to stop their progress. *Again, this action is eerily similar to today's Democrats who espouses violence, strong-arm tactics, and advocates for the "push back and confront Republicans, wherever they are" methodology.*

During Reconstruction, the Democrat Party's Klu Klux Klan earned their keep and burned black businesses and lynched blacks all across the south and other areas with impunity while also threatening and killing many white Republicans who were assisting southern blacks. One of the troubling incidents that would highlight the Klan's destructive tendencies and propensity for violence would occur on April 13, 1873, during the massacre in Colfax, Louisiana, where hundreds of blacks were murdered, and their businesses burned to the ground.

Another atrocity, omitted from the history books, happened between May and June of 1921 in Tulsa Oklahoma, at the time another mecca for black-owned businesses, where hundreds of blacks were killed, and many growing companies destroyed. Between 1882 and 1968 the Tuskegee Institute recorded over 4000 lynchings, including 3446 blacks being hanged, along with another 1297 white Republicans being murdered by Democrats.

At this point, I'm still trying to figure out when the parties "switched. "Please read the previous statement and timeline once more, so far, I've drawn a pretty straight line, but we'll continue.

With the systematic destruction of black businesses in the late 1800s, along with the frequent riots and killings, Democrats would achieve their goal of effectively destroying Black Wall Street, shutting down all black progress in the south, and arresting black economic development and growth all over the nation. After the resounding success of their intimidation and violent tactics against freed blacks and white Republicans, white Democrats in the south went about imposing voting restrictions on blacks once more, and this time they would have the full backing and enforcement of their brutal KKK organization.

These violent voter suppression tactics would ultimately result in much fewer blacks turning out at the polls during election time. Can you blame them? This precipitous drop in black voting would be the spark needed for Democrats to take back full control of governments in the south, resulting in the purging of all black Republicans from office and, thus, removing any and all black political power in the region. It would also, in effect, send delegations of former slave-owning southern whites back to Washington to comprise the Democrat Party in Congress once again.

These celebratory southern delegations sent to Washington during this period came to be known as "redeemers" because they had effectively restored former slave-owners back into their "rightful" positions. A now weary Republican Party, especially after the 1873 economic depression, started to lose interest in the fight for Reconstruction, which had begun in 1865. The Democrat Party had proven to be a resilient, obstinate, and energy-sapping obstacle; a determined foe in dogged pursuit of denying blacks equality in the south and it was just taking too much out of them to continue to do battle.

Republicans found that their pro-slavery adversaries was quite formidable, and tireless, in their quest for black rights suppression and was in it for the long haul. These wily southerners would not so easily give up in their mission to keep blacks underfoot in the south. The coerced steering of the black vote by the any-means-necessary Democrats provided the pathway by which future elections were to be evened out a bit for their party.

The suppression and manipulation of the black voter would also pay off bigly and almost immediately for the former slave owners as their egregious conduct, along with the violent tactics of their Klu Klux Klan, made the presidential race of 1876 a close and hotly contested race.

With this election, the issue of the popular vote would arise after Democrat nominee Samuel J Tilden beat former Union Soldier Rutherford B Hayes by more than 247,000 votes. The results of the election would be hotly contested when, although Tilden had won the majority of votes, Republican Hayes had been declared the winner of the contest by winning the bulk of the electoral votes. Amid the uproar by Democrats, it was found that their nominee's margin of victory in the popular vote came, suspiciously, from the southern states of South Carolina, Louisiana, and Florida where blacks were suppressed and forced to vote Democrat.

Nonetheless, because of this disparity in votes, an argument would ensue from pro-slavery Democrats, who believed that the majority of votes should rule. Soon, a very bitter and nasty disagreement would surface, forcing devious Democrats, and Republicans to come an agreement. Thus, the Hayes-Tilden Act of 1877, also known as The Bargain, would be agreed upon. This compromise gave full control of the south back to Democrats, with the stipulation that all federal troops be removed from the southern region as well. With this action, federal protection put in place to guarantee the rights of former slaves in the south were now gone, leaving these southern blacks to fend for themselves.

At this stunning development, victorious Democrats popped the champagne and celebrated as they once again reimposed crippling laws and restrictions against blacks in the south. And this time these harsh and draconian measures would remain in place for many more decades to come and would also effectively end the last chance for blacks to reap the benefits promised them by the Republican-enacted Reconstruction Act of 1867.

In other words, the freedoms, rights, and opportunities for blacks established during Reconstruction were now about as dead as a door-nail, and the former slaves would not have another bite of the apple of true freedom in the south until the 1960s and the Civil Rights Movement. *Ain't that some bull?*

So now, up to this point, we've seen that the problems and issues blacks endured before, during, and after Reconstruction were the results of "obstruction" and "resistance" by Democrats, who had opposed every freedom and right for blacks since they were bought to this country. Along with their KKK's intimidation tactics, segregation, and other restrictive laws, these former slave owners were once again entrenched as the base of political power in the south. Stymied and suppressed blacks, relegated to second-class citizens once more, now treaded lightly to avoid any confrontation or misunderstanding with volatile and violent white southern Democrats.

To put the finishing touch on their political comeback, the pro-slavery Democrat Party, after taking back control of Congress in 1892, quickly repealed the 1866 and 1875 Civil Rights Act. Sadly, these rights, *put in place by Republicans,* would not be revisited again until the Civil Rights Movement of the 1950s and 1960s.

*Of note, during this period, one of the black organizations estab-

lished by Republicans in 1909 was the NAACP, which was headed up by black Republican James Johnson, who would also write the "lift every voice and sing" theme song that is still sung today by blacks.

Surprisingly, throughout all of the racial turmoil and suffering they had endured, most blacks still remained steadfastly loyal to the Republican Party in the 1800s, realizing then that it was Democrats and Democrats alone who were their enemies and the stumbling blocks preventing them from thoroughly enjoying their freedoms and full rights as citizens of the United States.

However, in the early 1930s, all of this support would suddenly go out the window, and things would drastically change as the clarity of foe and friend would become blurred. There would be a seismic political shift that would astonish white Republicans who had gone to bat for blacks, even spilling their blood for their freedom.

It is my firm belief that it was at this point in history that the majority of southern blacks had just resigned themselves to their fate; to always be subservient and under the violent oppression of the Democrat Party. Sadly, not only would most of these former slaves begin to accept their second class status and being underfoot to southern whites, but surprisingly, many would also start to learn how to benefit from being kept and exploited by their former masters.

Up to this point, I've shown what Democrats, alone, have done to blacks. Now, I am going a step further and show how blacks empowered Democrats politically, and destroyed themselves in the process.

As with the Garden of Eden, when Adam had eaten of the fruit of the forbidden tree, the generation-altering and unholy alliance that blacks were about to enter into would doom our race to be a cursed people who would wind up in bed with the very same serpents that had caused their ancestors so much misery and grief in their new land for so many years.

Can you stand it? Go ahead, turn the page, will ya.

Chapter Six

Blacks and The New Deal?

TO recap, in the previous segment, we saw Democrats assassinate Lincoln and vote against the 13th, 14th, and 15th amendments, and against any and all other civil rights for blacks. We also saw the Republican Party, thank God, push through all of these amendments for blacks despite the "resist" and "obstruct" opposition by Democrats

*We briefly detailed the Jim Crow Laws and Black Codes put in place in the deep south by Democrats, and the how and why the KKK was created by the Democrat Party.

*We saw the 1800s Reconstruction and Black Wall Street started and black businesses booming until the KKK burned it all down, along with murdering hundreds of blacks in the process.

*We revealed that land given to blacks by Republicans during Reconstruction was subsequently taken away by Democrat President Andrew Johnson and given back to former slave-owners.

*We also detailed how it was Republicans who created the historically black colleges we see today, and the NAACP.

*We also saw Republicans trying to get "40 acres and a mule" as reparations off the ground for blacks in the 1800s, only to be stopped by Democrats, again.

*And sadly, we witnessed an exhausted Republican Party caving to the non-stop violence of Democrats and relinquishing their hold on the South. What happens next? You will be amazed and flabbergasted.

The New Deal would be a significant turning point for most blacks in America, but unfortunately into a direction from which they would

never truly recover. Regardless of the twisted and distorted narrative being bandied about by liberals today, the majority of blacks did not switch to the Democrats in the 1960s. All the conjecture surrounding the notion that blacks were somehow angry with Republicans in the 1960s and started voting for Democrats in large numbers would be patently false.

No, blacks switched in large numbers in the early 1930s because of the nationwide economic morass caused by the Great Depression of 1929, and after our nation's entire economy had gone bust. During this period, over half the banks in the country failed and, along with the crippling loss of over 15 million jobs, the majority of Americans were suffering mightily.

Seeking to alleviate the economic impact on the country's financial institutions and citizenry, Democrat president Franklin Delano Roosevelt signed the New Deal, the most massive expansion of government in our nation's history. This redistribution of wealth would ultimately change our nation's financial system from one of pure capitalism and limited government into a quasi-socialist economic system of big government, which was never intended by our founders.

Prior to the great depression, going back to Reconstruction, Republicans had held onto most of the political power in this nation, and rightfully so, winning the majority of elections with a focus on limited government and low taxation. But, since President Herbert Hoover and Republicans were in power when the Great Depression had begun in 1929, they were blamed by Democrats for the cause of our economy's collapse.

We must note here that a lot of historians credit spending by the U.S during World War I in 1914, along with other uncontrollable factors, as the primary underlying cause for the Great Depression.

Nonetheless, going back to Reconstruction, Democrats had always probed for any openings to get their former black slaves, their property, back onto their plantations and underfoot. So now, these power hungry ex-slave owners, upon realizing what had fallen into their laps, saw the New Deal as the opening needed to revitalize their party politically and immediately seized the opportunity. Democrats would begin exploiting this massive crisis by quickly proposing new programs to "help" struggling Americans with safety nets such as welfare and entities like the FDIC, or the Federal Deposit Insurance Company, established in 1933 by the Banking Act, which insures depositors in the event of bank defaults or failures.

Also formed in 1933 was the Conservation Act and Civilian Conservation Corps, a program which paid young people to help build parks, trails, and other such public works across the country. And to combat the housing crisis, the FHA, or Federal Housing Authority, was created in 1933 under the New Deal as well, and two years later the Social Security Act would also be passed in 1935 for retirees as an aid in helping them save for after-work life. *These were just some of the many "helpful" programs enacted under the New Deal, and ones today being exploited and gouged by Democrats for self-enrichment and political gain.*

To cement their party's newfound power in the 1930s, Democrats would also create powerful unions under the New Deal to "help" workers gain rights in the workplace. *These same unions today have morphed into nothing more than manipulative political organizations, money launderers for the Democrat Party, blackmailing and extorting rank and file members to fund the campaigns of Democrat candidates, who will then turn around and support the well-paid union heads.*

And in yet another savvy political move by Democrats during the 1930s, an unprecedented number of blacks were appointed to a new cabinet called The Federal Council of Negro Affairs. These puppet black cabinet members were policy "advisers" who worked alongside President Franklin Roosevelt on "black affairs" and they, along with other political leaders, would help facilitate the moving of black civic organizations from the Republican Party over to the Democrat Party during this time of national crisis.

*Of note, and curiously strange, in the 1930s, even though the New Deal Democrats were supposedly helping blacks by moving them over to their party, restrictions such as Jim Crow laws and Black Codes placed on blacks in 1865 during Reconstruction still remained fully entrenched in the south.

It would seem that southern Democrats, yet unsure if they had the black vote entirely in hand, made no attempts in the 1930s, whatsoever, to end segregation or any other impediment for blacks in the deep south. So, while the New Deal was being heralded by many as life-saving, southern blacks were still being segregated, suppressed, and lynched by the Democrat Party's Klu Klux Klan.

To clarify, even with the New Deal and welfare "help" in place, blacks were still without equal rights and representation, all while being exploited by Democrats for political gain. Nonetheless, undeterred by the small inconveniences of being hanged, beaten and killed by the Democrat-created KKK, most southern blacks were now almost entirely supporting the party that still viewed them as no more than property, like so much livestock.

The immediate effect of this surprising, traitorous move by the black community in the 1930s was that the Democrat Party would now have almost the entirety of the black vote in the south, and their political power, without having to give them the rights and freedoms other citizens in the country enjoyed. This wasn't just a New Deal for Democrats; this was a Fantastic Deal and life was good.

So, as it were, not only had the New Deal opened up an avenue by which the exodus of blacks from the Republican Party would begin but would also usher in the very first political usage of black overseers to control and direct the low-info black masses. With the New Deal and welfare handouts having been successfully implemented, the party of slavery and secession was now getting a whole new image makeover with their black political leaders. The primary mission given by Democrats to their willing black puppets was to mentally shackle former black slaves and herd them back onto the plantation, this time with economic inducements and other taxpayer-funded incentives as the leg irons.

For this newfound loyalty, the New deal provided about a ten percent allotment of its welfare handouts to blacks. To the Democrat Party, it was like slopping the hogs and fattening the calves for slaughter. Along with these handouts, the New Deal also created the Public Works Administration, which gave government-created jobs and other benefits to blacks.

This initiative would be the start of the public jobs bloat we now see in this country and the reason why a lot of blacks today view all things government as their savior. As a result, our government today is the world's largest employer with over two million employees and many redundant, made-up positions and services, all paid for by the heavily taxed citizens of this nation.

Members of Congress today make an astronomical $175,000 annual salary working just 138 to 162 days out of the year. The rest of their time is spent fund-raising, vacationing, and spending time with their families and friends. So, by using the high end of the scale of 162 days worked per year, a Congressman or Congresswoman today makes a whopping $1080 each day they are in the office, or about $135.00 an hour. Based on these salaries, Congress members, uh, servants of the people, can also retire with a generous $139,000 annual pension. Very nice, right? But wait there's more!

*The Government Ethics Reform Act of 1989, voted on and passed by legislators, called for an automatic increase in pay every year for congressional members and there has never been a call to repeal this act. I wonder why? In this regard, government employees' salaries, paid for by struggling taxpayers, have far outpaced the employees in the private sector over the last five decades. How did public servants of the people get to dip into the taxpayer-funded government till in this fashion and live so high on the hog?

Democrats and the New Deal of the 1930s would be your answer. Once opened, the Pandora's Box of big government unlocked the floodgates of unlimited till-dipping by federal employees we see today, making public sector jobs a magnet for corrupt hustlers. *Old tax'em-to-death King George of Great Britain would've been quite proud to see this development by his Democrat protégés.*

So just to recap, and get back on track, in the 1930s up to 70% of blacks who were once loyal to the Republican Party moved over to the Democrat Party because of the New Deal and welfare. And even though pro-slavery Democrats still had restrictive Jim Crow laws, black codes, segregation, along with the KKK to police and suppress the rights of blacks in the south, this stunning betrayal and willing migration back onto the plantation by their former slaves had still occurred.

This unconscionable move would be the start of the welfare hand-out dependency and entitlement conditioning we see nowadays that has stripped away independence, motivation, and self-worth from a lot of blacks in many black communities across the country. It would be this decades-long reliance on welfare and viewing government as a way to make it in America which would prove to be the downfall of the majority of blacks.

Looking at this thing side-eyed though, it must be said that even as most all other races struggled during the Great Depression and had partaken of the aid pro-offered by Democrats, they still warily viewed this "help" by the government as temporary, a band-aid, and would never be beholden to any social service agencies for their long-term sustenance.

As I ruminate on this period in which our entire nation was suffering, I hear from some folks, opining that blacks did whatever they had to do to survive back then. And, of course, I have taken this aspect into consideration in my thought process while writing this text. However, I would be, I feel, most derelict in my duty in being truthful, logical, and honest, not to point out the fallacy of these opinions.

You see, nationwide, the population of whites in the 1930s was much higher than that of the blacks and, by far, more of them were helped by the New Deal during the Great Depression. Yet, receiving government aid did not induce these whites then, nor today, to vote anywhere near the percentages as blacks have done for just one party.

No, the majority of whites in the 1930s believed strongly that our government, no matter which party was in control at the time, was doing what it was elected to do, and what was necessary to dutiful uphold our Constitution and look out for the welfare of its people when it had to, albeit, temporarily.

Unlike blacks, the white community, as a whole, did not see accepting welfare, this stop-gap aid, as a lien on their future votes and would not be beholden or obligated to any one political party because of any support given to them in a time of need. Also, most whites would not sign a forever-mortgage note on their votes, nor would they sell their souls to the Democrat Party for welfare table scraps and substandard housing.

In this regard, most whites never became single party or single-minded voters, and have always enjoyed their options and freedoms as to who or what party they would vote for during every election. It was quite simple, the majority of whites viewed the New Deal and its programs as what the government was supposed to do in times of crisis and acknowledged the Democrat Party for doing as expected, nothing more.

And because the majority of whites are not as politically gullible as most blacks, their vote in just about every election since the 1930s has been nearly split 50/50, with a slight nod to the Conservative Republican side. This is the reason why Democrats today so desperately seek to control blacks politically; their former slaves have always been the crucial tiebreaker vote needed to move their candidates over the finish line.

I must also note here, that if the majority of whites had felt the same way about government handouts as blacks in the 1930s, this nation would have had a one-party rule from the Great Depression on, and Democrats today would have the permanent political dominance they have craved since their party's inception in 1829. You know, I want to really emphasize a point that is not lost on me. Thankfully, the majority of whites were intelligent enough not to cast their entire lot with Democrats, even while in dire straits. It is this political awareness, this instinctive self-preservation, and rationality by most in the white community that, I believe, has prevented the total destruction of our nation as we know it.

Still yet, the most perplexing revelation I find personally distressing is what little it took for blacks to jettison the Republican Party in favor of Democrats. Let's just for a moment, compare both parties and black loyalty, shall we? Because with the Democrat Party, most blacks in the 1930s acted like $2 hos on a street corner, turning tricks for the next passing John.

Ok, so white Republicans had gone through hell, losing many lives in the Civil war to free blacks and making sure they had their freedoms, citizenship, and voting rights afforded them as other races in this country. However, when Democrats came along and offered welfare programs and table scraps, the majority of blacks quickly moved their affiliation over to the Democrat Party.

So, as a reward for freeing blacks from slavery, beatings, lynchings, Jim Crow laws, Black Codes, the separation of families and being treated like sub-humans, and for passing Civil Rights and voting bills for blacks while losing over 300,000 lives fighting in a civil war, Republicans received only 64 years of loyalty from former black slaves; from about 1865 to 1929.

Ok, that seems like a really long period there! But wait a minute, on the other hand, for just meager welfare scraps and the privilege of living on poverty-stricken plantations, amid drug-dealing, homicides and gang violence, blacks gave Democrats, the party that for centuries enslaved and whipped their asses, an astounding 88 years of loyalty from the 1930s to today, and continuing.

* With that, let's now check our scores in the Superbowl of black ignorance and stupidity:

God-fearing Republicans: *deliverers of blacks from centuries of captivity and the nightmare of slavery... 64 Points.*

Democrats: *enslavers, lynchers, and oppressors of blacks for centuries.. 88 Points.*

***Blacks:** perpetual victims...0*

Game over, the crowd of white liberal Democrats is going wild! Yayyyyy! Democrats won, black communities lost, what a game!

Looking at these scores, it would seem that the majority of blacks today have indeed placed a much higher value on a monthly welfare stipend and being "kept" by their former captors on inner city plantations, as opposed to standing on their own two feet as men and women and having true freedom.

With this tidbit in hand, we must surmise that this lack of character and integrity among most blacks is a most compelling and persuasive argument that the majority are not honor-bound and also lack any sense of loyalty. We must also conclude that most in the black community are easily manipulated by any financial enticements, even if that inducement serves to strip away their independence and hinder their ability to function as productive adults in society.

So, in this context, I ask these questions of you, the reader, how much money per month would it take for you to give up your freedoms and go to prison? And how do you quantify true liberty?

Can I perhaps persuade you to take a monthly stipend of say, $400 and an Obama phone in exchange for you being locked up and beaten for the next 88 years?

Will you make a deal with me to have you voluntarily give up your most valuable possession; your freedom?

With welfare dependency, starting with the New Deal of the 1930s, this is precisely what most blacks have done, willingly being broken all over again and placing themselves back onto the Democrat plantation and into the services of their former white masters. However, unlike during Reconstruction, with the 1930s migration, the black community this time would be recycled into an almost unbreakable and just about monolithic voting bloc that would last for decades, and still going strong today. This critical and defining moment in our nation's history defied all logic; former black slaves who had gone through hell to gain freedom from centuries of Democrat atrocities and servitude, were now running back to the very same party that had brutally enslaved them? How could it be that blacks were going back to the same party which had caused a civil war that took over 700,000 lives to set them free?

Here, I do want to point out something of great importance, we must also consider that in the 1930s, not all blacks went over to the Democrat Party for handouts and taxpayer-funded government jobs. There had been a segment of proud blacks who possessed integrity and remained loyal to the Republican Party, not forgetting what they and their ancestors had endured at the hands of violent Democrats and their Klu Klux Klan organization.

These blacks fully understood and appreciated the tremendous sacrifices made by God-fearing white men and would never forsake or turn their backs on Republicans, nor betray the party of Lincoln by going back to their former captors and their plantations.

Just like most Americans during the Great Depression, these blacks struggled economically but saw this as a small price to pay for the enormous and unpayable debt they felt were still owed the Republican Party, their deliverers. They were genuinely free and would remain so, regardless of any future hardships they would endure. They would stand as men and women, without depending upon welfare table scraps and aligning themselves with their former enslavers.

I firmly believe that it is the offspring of these blacks, the ones that didn't accept the thirty pieces of silver from Democrats, who now make up the small portion of blacks in this country that has continued to be steadfast conservative Republicans. This sliver of blacks has wholly assimilated into American culture, tapping into the most significant wealth accumulation system ever created on earth. They also understood then, as they do now, that the behavior of today's do-nothing plantation blacks still screaming "white supremacy" and howling at the so-called "racist" moon in the hopes of obtaining even more independence-stripping government aid, is almost hopelessly mentally imprisoned.

Sadly, because of Democrat control, many blacks today exhibits a moral weakness and lack of intestinal fortitude and are always seeking and taking the easy path of welfare handouts and any other government aid given to them. A large segment of blacks today is unwilling, as men and women, to put in the hard work and required labor necessary to overcome adversity and build a lasting and economically viable community based on the cornerstones of family, God, education and a strong work ethic.

It is this laziness and "being kept" attitude among many blacks, starting in the 1930s, that is so pervasive in our communities. This path of least-resistance mentality is evidenced by the majority of black youths living in inner-city single-parent homes, headed up by single black women, aspiring to be fast money rappers or sports stars, dismissing any vocation that honors hard work and the gradual building of wealth. Blacks relying on becoming stars, being high-paying athletes, banking on their physicality and brawn, and violence, has proven fatal for the community as a whole.

Unfortunately, these aspirations have long since supplanted intellect and strong work ethic among many blacks; ravaging black communities and creating poverty-stricken and violent drug dens, all while obliterating the potential of generations of black youths who might have been doctors, lawyers, engineers, etc.

One of the most glaring weaknesses within the black communities today, making it so susceptible to manipulation by white liberals, is that the majority of blacks, it seems, are always in need of a leader to tell them where to go and what to do. Most easily-led and low-info blacks are told what party to align themselves with, how to behave and what or who to get mad at, just like during slavery: *"Massa, we's sick?" "Massa, we's mad?"*

As previously noted, Democrats, recognizing this seemingly inherent weakness among blacks early on, seized upon it during the implementation of the New Deal and welfare, and promptly installed their own black leaders to shepherd these sheeple blacks back into their fold. These new house Negroes were made into well-paid overseers and recruiters who were tasked with tightly controlling the inner cities and leading the black masses, these now so-called "African Americans."

This black leadership, along with the scant welfare crumbs of the New Deal, would prove to be more than enough to entice most blacks to do whatever they were told to do by white liberals. It is this herding by black leaders, and acceptance of decades-long government assistance, which would do a number on the black community in the ensuing decades, turning most of our black youths into wards of the so-called "white supremacy" government system they supposedly detest.

But even under the spell of the New Deal programs and welfare, the black community would have one more shot to right the ship and become men and women of character, integrity, honor, and Godliness. These descendants of former slaves would have more crack at the chance to redeem themselves and recapture their dignity, which was given away for almost nothing to Democrats.

Southern blacks would have another shot at establishing true independence, regaining a strong family structure and buying into the value of faith, hard work, and education. This would be their last grasp for salvation, for economic viability, and a chance for political leverage like they had never seen before. It was to be the black community's last ditched attempt at redemption and opportunity for total political realignment.

With the 1950s and 1960s, there would come about a cataclysmic sea change which would see Jim Crow Laws and Black Codes being struck down, falling once and for all in the deep south. There would come about the eradication of all Democrat-imposed restrictions on southern blacks which would seemingly herald their unfettered ascension to their rightful position as equal citizens in this nation.

Of course, these events, of which I speak, will take us to a pivotal point in our nation's history which would illuminate the unity and empowerment that can happen when blacks truly strive together towards a common goal. With their newfound and hard fought solidarity, there would arise the chance for these now empowered blacks to obtain that which had eluded them during Reconstruction and Black Wall Street of the 1800s.

Now, it must be said that with all of this overcoming, equality getting, and sudden independent political clout, there would be a very steep price to pay, a pound of flesh extracted, if you will. Indeed, all of the black community's celebrations in the 1960s and being "free at last," would ultimately be laid to waste by one cruel and despicable act, resulting in most blacks being consumed entirely by the serpents in whose political bed they now permanently reside.

Let's now go to the Civil Rights Movement and the Honorable Dr. Martin Luther King Jr, to see how this all shakes out, shall we?

Go on, if you will, turn the page with ya bad self.

Chapter Seven

Dr. King, Democrats & Jim Crow

S o, in recapping the last segment, we saw that after all their struggles, and loss of lives Republicans suffered to help blacks get
the rights they were entitled to as rightful citizens of this nation,
most of them turned their backs on the party of Lincoln for welfare
scraps from their former enslavers....

Ok, I'm disgusted.....I just can't.... let's just continue, I don't
wanna recap a damn thing from that last chapter....don't even wanna
think about it...

The last chance for real equality and independence for blacks, and
the most significant threat to the Democrat Party's plans of controlling
and exploiting their community would come about in the 1950s with
the rise of Dr. Martin Luther King Jr and the beginning of the Civil
Rights Movement. King, a gifted orator, minister, and activist, had
risen from his Southern Baptist pulpit to urge blacks in the deep south
to break the stranglehold of Jim Crow Laws and the chains of oppression and welfare dependency. He admonished blacks to focus on
education, a stable family unit, faith in God and hard work, and to do
it with peace and love.

King's persuasive and emotional speeches lifted directionless and
dependent blacks to new heights, restoring a sense of brotherhood
and unity while fostering a can-do attitude and belonging back into
their communities. Under his leadership, many blacks in the 1950s
and 1960s now clearly realized where they had gone wrong in accepting welfare handouts from their former captors in the 1930s and
began to rejoice at the idea of gaining true liberty and independence.

Rejuvenated southern blacks now reveled in the exciting prospect of taking their rightful place in society alongside other races and finally tapping into the vast wealth and opportunities this nation offered, just as Republicans had promised during Reconstruction.

Dr. King's call to do away with segregation and Jim Crow Laws in the deep south resonated with most Americans and the Civil Rights Movement would swiftly grow into a massive campaign of compassion and equality where people of all stripes would join in. There would be marches, sit-ins, and peaceful protests, and in a flurry of activity, King orchestrated freedom rides and bus boycotts while he continued delivering speech after speech that stirred the hearts and tugged at the consciences of most Americans.

Now, of course, Democrats wasn't just gonna let the Civil Rights Movement or Dr. King go unchallenged and protesting blacks would soon become involved in violent confrontations, just like during Reconstruction. In June of 1963, George Wallace, the Democrat Governor of Alabama, would stand defiantly in the doorway of the University of Alabama in Tuscaloosa in an attempt to prevent two black students from attending classes there.

For these students to eventually gain access, President John F Kennedy, a Democrat with conservative leanings, would have to call out the National Guard to force their entry into the school, which would ultimately result in the subsequent integration of the university, along with other schools in the south. *I firmly believe that this action by Kennedy, along with him pushing the Civil Rights Bill for blacks in the 1950s, would be one of the unforgivable transgressions against the Democrat Party that would lead to his assassination later that same year while in Dallas, Texas.

There would be other Democrats against black progress, like Eugene "bull" Durham, in Birmingham, Alabama, who would turn dogs loose on blacks (like old John Lewis, who is now, strangely, a member of the all-black Democrat Black Caucus). There was also Georgia Democrat, Governor Lester Maddox, who wielded ax handles to stop blacks from entering his restaurant: *"No chicken or collards for you Negroes!"* And how can we overlook Robert Byrd, one of the Democrat Party's most lauded heroes, and exalted member of the KKK for decades, who hated blacks and was a lifelong Democrat in Congress until he passed away in 2010?

In 1964, old Grand Wizard Byrd would filibuster the Civil Rights Bill for over 14 hours in an attempt to block its passage. Nonetheless, he still had many Democrat friends, like Hillary and Obama, who bestowed numerous accolades upon him regarding his service to their party and would deeply mourn his death upon his passing.

There would be many more violent clashes between marching blacks and white southern Democrats in the 1950s and 1960s during the Civil Rights Movement, leading to many blacks being arrested, beaten and even killed. *Just to reiterate, one such black beaten the hell up is old frothing-at-the-mouth John Lewis who is now a proud Black Caucus member and, surprisingly enough, a very staunch advocate and overseer today for the Democrat Party.*

Now, you may have noticed at this point that I am still only mentioning Democrats here as the party opposing blacks and beating the hell out of'em during the 1950s and 1960s Civil Rights Movement.

Well, what about the Republicans you ask, just what were they doing during this same period? Just like during Reconstruction and the Civil War, white Republicans were still fighting for blacks and still getting killed by Democrats for their assistance during this tumultuous time. And even though the majority of blacks had defected to their former enslavers in the 1930s, the never-wavering Republicans were the ones still fighting, since the late 1800s and Reconstruction, to get Black Codes and Jim Crow laws removed from the south and was still paying the price, pretty much.

As previous stated, over 1200 white Republicans was killed while assisting blacks during this period. More importantly, since this violence by Democrats against blacks was happening in the 1950s and 1960s, you must ask yourself again, when did this mysterious switching between the parties occur? In this same vein, it must be noted that Republicans have never lifted one finger against blacks, you can scour history, and you won't find anything contrary to this statement.

So, as it were, throughout all the violence occurring in the deep south with the Civil Rights Movement, an undeterred King continued with his historical and soul-stirring journey, delivering thought-provoking messages of inequality and shaking this nation to its moral core and Christian foundation.

Dr. King's remarkable journey would culminate with his most emotional and uplifting "I Have a Dream" speech at the Lincoln Memorial on August 28th, 1963, where hundreds of thousands of people gathered, listening attentively in rapt silence to his impassioned pleas for equality and a colorblind society. This would be the speech to cement his legacy among blacks and whites as perhaps the greatest civil rights leader our nation has ever seen.

Under Dr. King's guidance, hardworking and spiritually-infused black families started gaining a renewed sense of pride, a can-do attitude, and self-sufficiency and were beginning to assimilate fully into American culture. The once-downtrodden black community was finally approaching an upward trajectory of economic and social power in this nation that would, if left unchecked, establish them as an independent political bloc to be reckoned with.

But at this development, Democrats became quite alarmed and began to panic, suddenly realizing that something would have to be done to thwart the removal of blacks from their control. So, they quickly got to work searching for ways to bring Dr. King down, and one of the things they would default to was the political smear playbook that they often use today against conservatives and Republicans.

Democrats would begin an FBI investigation, spearheaded by J. Edgar Hoover, head of the agency and a Democrat who personally hated King. Unsurprisingly, after this fake investigation had gotten started, Dr. King was suddenly accused of being a communist, probably from some fabricated dossier I suppose. *I'm betting that the Democrats probably even tossed the rumor around that King was colluding with Russians and was an anti-American spy. Does this sound familiar?*

In thinly veiled attempts by Democrats to block his messaging and cut off his access to the black community, Dr. King would be arrested on several occasions on fabricated and trumped-up charges and thrown in jail. One of the most memorable moments would come when he was jailed in 1963 right after the Montgomery bus boycott.

To reiterate, just what do you suppose was the reason for this suddenly aggressive stance by pro-slavery white southerners against Dr. King and the Civil Rights Movement?

Well, let me answer, Democrats was in full panic mode at the looming prospect of southern blacks no longer being under their nightmarish restrictions and political control. They begin to realize that there was a possibility that their "property" would do what they had done during Reconstruction after gaining real freedom; become Republicans in the south, leave the plantation, and develop a sense of self-worth.

Democrats greatly feared blacks becoming self-sufficient, independent, and no longer desiring or needing handouts or welfare. They were now quite aware that with Dr. King's leadership and messaging, their hold on the black community was becoming tenuous at best, and that any large-scale black defection from their party would significantly reduce their political clout and aspirations of dominance.
For the Democrat Party's future political ambitions, it would be catastrophic to lose this vital voting bloc they had so doggedly and painstakingly built over decades.

An ominous warning for King would occur in 1958 when he was stabbed by a crazed black woman, probably a brainwashed plantation black, in which the blade of the knife had come exceedingly close to slicing his aorta and killing him. After he recovered, Dr. King famously stated in a speech that if he had sneezed, he would have died. I believe that this stabbing had been the violent, win-at-all-cost Democrat Party's shot across the bow, a warning to King that he was playing with fire and that they needed him to back off his pursuit of equality for blacks in the south.

As a quick aside, Dr. King's stabbing by a black woman was eerily similar to the death in 1964 of Sam Cooke, at the time a giant in the music industry, who was shot and killed by a remorseless black woman, Bertha Franklin, just as he had finished writing and producing the black anthem, "A Change Is Gonna Come," against Democrat oppression of the 1950s and 1960s. With these two incidents, I want you to keep in mind the political role of the black woman as we wade through later chapters.

So, with his stabbing in the 1960s, King had been put on notice that the black community was Democrat property, bought and paid for, and there would be hell to pay for anyone trying to take what was rightfully theirs. Brushing aside and ignoring this warning, a determined King continued with the Civil Rights Movement, demanding equality and full rights for southern blacks until, finally, a Civil Rights Bill was bought to Washington and Capitol Hill. In Congress, a vigorous effort was launched by Democrats to "resist," "obstruct," and do whatever else necessary to prevent the bill from passing.

The heated rhetoric between the parties would soon devolve into a highly contentious battle on the Senate floor with even more Democrats attempting a filibuster to stop its passage.

* Now, remember, for all you "party switchers" this was happening in 1964 and the Democrat Party's thread of violence and opposing black rights, as I have detailed so far, hasn't been broken from the 1600s, 1700,1800s, and 1900s, yet.

So, after being vehemently opposed by Democrats, the Civil Rights Bill of 1964 was passed into law with strong Republican backing, effectively ending the Democrat Party's imposed segregation, oppressive Jim Crow, Black Code laws, and many other restrictions that had been placed upon blacks in the southern states.

*Of note here, at the time of the bill's passing, the black community had an almost 80% two-parent household, a strong work ethic, real spirituality and educational goals for their children. Also, during this time, there were low prison rates for the black community and little need for "prison reform." *Incarcerated black males in the 1960s were estimated to be in the low thousands nationwide, which is a far cry from the one million plus incarcerated in prisons today under Democrat conditioning and brainwashing.*

With King's leadership in the 1960s, blacks had overcome and were finally moving forward in society under the bright prospect of attaining generational wealth and progress just as other races were doing in America. Their path to prosperity, unity, and harmony, for the most part, was now clear; no black gangs were fighting over drugs and killing each other over turf in inner cities, and the welfare-state mentality had not yet entirely taken root in most black communities the way it has today.

It was, at this point in history to be a new beginning and joyous times for blacks in the deep south, they would finally be on par with southern whites and citizens of all stripes all over the nation. But overlooked in all this equality euphoria, though, was the ominous and quite prescient warning delivered by Lyndon B Johnson upon signing the Civil Rights Bill in 1964: *"With this bill, niggers will be voting Democrat for the next 200 years."*

*Well now, just hold on there skippy, what did this Democrat president know about the future of the black vote, and why would he say that? Wasn't this civil rights bill, which reaffirmed voting rights for blacks and ended discrimination of race, gender, etc., supposed to purposefully extend the same rights to blacks as with other races, making them whole and rendering their second-class citizen status obsolete?

Why would a Democrat president, in a supposedly moment of great joy for blacks, who had finally achieved equality and true freedom, say niggers would vote for his party for the next 200 years when he signed this bill? How was this goal of politically controlling blacks for the next 200 years to be accomplished, especially since this proclamation and warning was coming just after the black community had seemingly overcome?

Was this just an empty threat by a Democrat president angered by a Republican Party that had forced him to sign a bill to remove his party's imposed restrictions on blacks in the south?

I mean, these southern blacks had just obtained real independence and freedom and wouldn't be desiring or needing any welfare handouts anymore, and therefore wouldn't need the Democrat Party anymore either. Right?

But there was a thread developing here; just as it was when Democrat President Andrew Johnson adamantly opposed black rights during Reconstruction of the 1800s, here now was Lyndon B Johnson, another Democrat president, in the 1960s, seeking to put into motion plans to have blacks permanently underfoot to the same party, again.

So, even though the presidencies of Andrew Johnson and Lyndon B Johnson occurred almost a century apart, they were much alike in considering blacks to be nothing more than property, like cattle and other livestock, to be herded and controlled for whatever purposes they desired. Just maybe, these two Johnsons were of kin to each other, in thought and deed.

Nevertheless, after the Civil Rights Bill was enacted, this earlier prophesying by President Lyndon was largely ignored by jubilant blacks, who went on barbecuing and partying like it was 1999. I suppose the thinking by many of these southern blacks was, with King's leadership nothing could stop them, and as to President Johnson's statement, it was highly improbable that anything of the sort could ever occur.

It seemed as if nothing could derail the independence and equality train blacks were now riding high on, they were intoxicated with true freedom and wouldn't even entertain any thoughts otherwise. However, the cunning and violent Democrats would soon prove, as they had with Kennedy and Lincoln, that they meant business and wasn't to be trifled with in their quest to control blacks in the south.

You see, for centuries, Democrats viewed their former slaves as the key to their party's future political ambitions and nothing would stand in their way of controlling this voting bloc. They considered blacks as belonging to them, lock, stock and barrel, and no damn activist Negro preacher were gonna throw a monkey wrench into their grand scheme of political dominance or usurp their ownership to what they felt was their rightful property.

So, after Democrats in Congress failed to prevent the passing of the 1964 Civil Rights Bill, it had been determined by the party's leaders right then and there that this issue with King and his ever-rising influence on the black community would need to be resolved, and soon, and by any means necessary.

The urgency for the Democrat Party to rid themselves of Dr. King would be further stoked by the passage of the 1965 Voting Rights Act which reaffirmed the 15th amendment of the 1800s, preventing the suppression of the black vote in the south ever again. Democrats were now furious, King had been warned, there was just too much at stake to allow this siphoning of blacks away from their party to continue to go unchallenged.

True to their word, Democrats assassinated Dr. Martin Luther King Jr. on April 4th, 1968 on the balcony of the now infamous Lorraine Hotel while he was in Memphis Tennessee to give a speech for the embattled and striking black sanitation workers that were facing inequality in the workplace.

King, knowing that he had angered pro-slavery southern Democrats to no end, gave a quite prophetic speech the night before at the Mason Temple in Tennessee where he spoke of his impending demise at their hands.

Dr. King's death would shock the nation, causing many blacks and whites to be almost inconsolable at the loss of the benevolent black leader. The black community's uncontrollable rage spawned riots and wanton destruction of property, along with many other black deaths in cities across the nation.

Never ones to let a good crisis go to waste, Democrats feigned outrage as usual and slyly stepped in to channel the anger and frustration of blacks. Like with the New deal, this suffering by the black community would provide another political opening in the 1960s and a golden opportunity for Democrats to use this tragedy to recruit emotional blacks onto their party's nascent, and deceptive ideology of inclusiveness, tolerance, diversity, and equality.

Even though Democrats were responsible for King's assassination, because of the immediate confusion among blacks as to whom or what was to blame for his death, their emotional and sympathetic ploy worked like a charm with grieving blacks. Democrats then went on to the next phase of their plan, quickly installing their own black "Civil Rights Reverends" and other black leaders to shepherd rank and file blacks into their party, just as they had done with black puppet leaders during the New Deal.

At this development, President Lyndon B Johnson's prophecy of Democrats garnering the black vote for the next two hundred years was starting to come to fruition. With their newly installed black "leaders," along with taking control of most of the media, the Democrat Party's political dominance of black communities across the nation began to slowly take hold during the chaos in the aftermath of Dr. King's death.

Of note: when you think of black stars in the 1950s and 1960s like James Brown, Louis Armstrong and others of this era having to use back entrances and separate water fountains for "coloreds," few people ever associate this with the Democrat Party's imposed segregation and Jim Crow Laws in the deep south.

And today most people do not fully grasp that it was these Democrat restrictions in the 1950s and 1960s which resulted in the banning of black players in baseball, football, and basketball during this period in our nation's history. To go even further, every movie ever made about slavery, including Roots, 12 Years A slave, and Django is merely illustrating the brutality and oppression by the Democrat Party during their enslavement of blacks, and nothing more. Yes, every ill will against blacks, outside our race, in our nation's history, has been perpetrated by white Democrats, period.

Ok, I am gonna conclude this chapter; however, in the next segment we are gonna explore in detail the traitorous duplicity of the black overseers who were installed by Democrats to lead the black community. But before we do so, let's do some soul searching: *To me, it's a damn shame and indeed a pitiful disgrace, for politically abused blacks in this country to have been beaten down, spat upon, hoses turned on'em, and dogs sicced on'em by Democrats during the 1950s and 1960s Civil Rights Movement, and still today embrace the party like crispy fried chicken with waffles on a late Saturday night after the club.*

Now you may ask, at this point, what would it take to pry blacks away from the Democrat Party? Well nothing really, because the die was cast after Dr. King's death and most of the bereaved community wasn't going "N T" where. Everything was falling into place for

Democrats, and it was just too late for most blacks. So, all I can do at this point is detail the still ongoing Jim Jones-like mass suicide by the majority of blacks in this nation.

Keep reading, if you like sad and teary-eyed stories, because it's gonna get much more real, and tragic, for the black community from this point on y'all. So, grab a box of Kleenex and let's continue. Oh, turn the page will'ya?

Chapter Eight

"African Americans" and Crack

Ok, so if you been with me so far, up to this point, we've seen Democrats enslave blacks starting in the 1600s, which would continue until the late 1800s.

*We've seen Democrats fight to retain their African slaves during the Civil War, killing hundreds of thousands of Americans in their failed quest.

*We now know that Lincoln was murdered by Democrats while trying to help blacks gain freedom, and we know that the Democrat Party's KKK shut down Reconstruction and Black Wall Street in the late 1800s, stopping black progress in its tracks.

*We also know that most blacks moved over to the Democrat Party in the 1930s for welfare table scraps, and we know that murerous Democrats killed President Kennedy for trying to help blacks.

*We then detailed how Democrats murdered Dr. Martin Luther King Jr in 1968, the last and best hope for the black community. And lastly, we know that Democrats, in the aftermath of King's death, installed their own black leaders to guide the black community. Ok, then.

So now we pick things up when the leadership vacuum created by King's death in 1968 had been filled with the black "civil rights reverends" who, amid the subsequent riots and looting, were quickly installed by the Democrat Party to serve as community leaders. Black militant groups, such as the Black Panthers, would also spring up, gaining prominence within the chaotic black community, their "black power" rhetoric resonating with many angry and disillusioned blacks.

These Democrat-controlled militant black groups would immediately seek reparations and violent retaliation upon whites for generations of slavery and Dr. King's death.

The Black Panthers' stance, as designed, would serve to undo much of King's messages of peace and love, and sink the black community even further into chaos. Curiously, from the start, black groups such as these never ascribed blame to any one party or group, nor did they ever point out that it was solely Democrats who were the oppressors of blacks and responsible for their community's lack of progress from the 1600s to the 1960s and onward. Militant groups of the late 1960s and 1970s were instead coached to just angrily lash out at all whites, generic placeholders, as the reason for blacks being held back and the ones responsible for Dr. King's death.

Just stop for a moment and think; Republicans and Dr. King were the ones opposing and fighting Democrats all throughout the 1950s and 1960s and were largely responsible for the removal of the harsh and suppressive Jim Crow Laws and segregation in the south. So, it was very, very clear during this period what party and who was against blacks in the south. Yet somehow, after King's assassination in 1968, and not too far removed from violent clashes with Democrats, militant black groups and black" Reverends" were suddenly confused as to who did what to whom and declared that all "whites" were responsible for slavery and Dr. King's death.

If you can wrap your mind around this *"all whites"* narrative, which quickly gained traction among angry blacks, entirely ignored was the glaring fact that also during this same period that it was the Democrats' KKK lynching over three thousand southern blacks, along with killing another twelve hundred or so white Republicans assisting them. One would wonder then, why didn't groups like the Black Panthers just speak the truth in the 1970s and say that it was Democrats, only, who had enslaved and oppressed blacks?

This blurring of our nation's slave history and the recasting of the ones responsible was no coincidence, everything was coming together, these black militant groups, along with the newly installed black leaders, had been instructed by their Democrat masters to always use the generic term "whites" as their "oppressors." This command and the quickly created "Black Power" anthem of the 1970s was then used by the black "reverends" to incite the racial divide necessary to till the victimization soil within the black community and develop new inner city plantations for their Democrat masters.

Dr. King's death in 1968 and the ensuing chaotic aftermath would also usher in the beginning stages of the "parties switched" myth." This hoax would later help establish the Democrat Party's long-running emotional and mental stranglehold on the black community that we see today. We must also note that it was also during the 1970s when the branding of "African Americans" was suddenly introduced to the nation by the civil rights reverend "leaders," supposedly, to stoke passions among blacks and bond their community in solidarity and brotherhood.

The renaming of blacks by Democrats in the 1970s was purposefully designed to create even more of a chasm between the races, sending a clear and unmistakable signal that blacks born in this nation were not of this country and that their rightful land was Africa, the motherland. This ingenious ploy by white liberals and their black "reverends" would also send the message that there was to be no assimilation for blacks in this nation and that their community must now use the party of their former enslavers, supposedly as their new social justice defenders, to fight for equality in this nation.

Moreover, the changing of names of American blacks would also be just the beginning of the divisive wordplay of identity politics that we see today, which is now being used extensively by white and black liberal leaders for attacks on their conservative opponents and to keep blacks emotionally unbalanced and unhinged.

With that being said, I wanna go on a short rant: *"As a black man, it is for this very reason that I dislike being called African American. And I say this with no disrespect to Africans of course, but merely with an awareness of the truth of who I am, an American who happens to be black and have little knowledge of African culture.*

Blacks born here are not "African Americans, they are Americans, black Americans, period. I mean if blacks born here are "Af-

rican Americans," what would you call the ones just coming over? "African-African Americans?" How about "Really Real African Americans?" Or, "No Kidding African Americans?," or how about "No Preservatives African Americans?"

The new "African American" designation is a huge part of the nonsense that has, for many years, kept most blacks in this nation divided and locked in a confused and perpetual state of emotional instability. Beginning in the 1970s, this racial identity "crisis" that "Africanism" and "Black Power" birthed among blacks would prove, in the ensuing decades, to be politically invaluable for manipulation and exploitation by Democrats come every election.

There was more to come for the black community; during the same period that the installed black civil rights leaders were promoting "Africanism," Muslim leaders would also get in on the action, proclaiming that they were looking to secede from America and would be creating a separate black nation right here on our soil. This declaration was strikingly similar to southern white slave-owning Democrats of the 1800s who had also wanted to secede from the United States with blacks in tow. What was going on, and why was everyone after blacks?

I guess it was no secret then that most of the black community was seen as a violent, overly emotional, and easily exploited group. Without question, if you look at the enormous amount of inner-city violence across our nation today, you would have to conclude that a lot of Democrat-bred and conditioned blacks are indeed innately violent, often displaying traits of pre-industrialized incivility towards each other and just about every other race in this country.

And blacks are not just violent here in America, they are violent just about everywhere, even on the African continent, the "motherland." For a relatively recent example, during the Rwanda genocide in 1994, the Hutus murdered over 800,000 Tutsis in about 100 days. And keep in mind that both groups were "Africans," all crispy black folks, but they gleefully killed each other with spears, machetes, guns, axes, hatchets, trained crocodiles, icepicks, rocks, clubs, and whatever else they could get their hands on.

So, it seems, black Muslim leaders in America, just like their liberal white Democrat counterparts, wasn't too far off base in trying to recruit the one group in America that seemingly had little problem with killing another human being. With that said, the Muslims' plans of a separate all-black Islamic nation within America was still totally illogical of course, the white population at the time was about 150 million as opposed to the black community which stood at approximately 13 million.

To me, the most confounding part to all this seceding and whatnot, that if these Democrat Muslim leaders had so desperately wanted to be in an all-black nation back then, they had the entire African continent and many other Muslim dominated countries to migrate to. It escapes me as to why black Muslim leaders would ever want to build an Islamic nation in a white, mom-and-apple-pie, white-picket-fence, Christian, and capitalist-based country that they continually profess to loathe.

Really, it was so simple and straightforward, there were many all-black and ready-made nations already established in Africa, and there would be no need for Muslims to go through the quite violent and grueling political process to develop one in America. All that would be needed of these black leaders was just to pack the hell up and roll to any one of these all black and, uh, welcoming African countries. It's not like tolerant, and meek Christian whites in America were holding them here against their will or something. This is a free country, and they had the opportunity to leave, of their own volition, at any time they saw fit.

Ahhhh, but here's the rub; like most ranting, raving, and deranged liberal Democrat celebrities in this country today, these politically posturing black Muslims would never leave our soil. This nation is the land of milk and honey where blacks like them can enjoy the opportunity of exploiting other dumbed-down blacks, all while preying on white guilt to increase their political power base and in the process enriching themselves. All this demanding of a "black nation" by Muslim leaders was all hat and no cattle, a political sleight of hand and very effective "brotherhood" indoctrination tool used to recruit even more intellectually-challenged blacks into their fold.

For example, take the so-called "million man march," organized and held by Muslims some years ago. This racial incitement horse-and-buggy show was nothing more than the stoking of emotions and division to recruit even more misguided, delusional, and out of work black men. Nothing would come of this highly televised spectacle of course, except more media exposure. And as always, true to form, when this highly-touted march of "unity" had concluded, a lot of these "brotherly" and recently "unified" black males would go right back to welfare dependency and shooting each other in the streets over some drug turf or Air Jordans.

The common thread with all these Democrat "leaders," white, black, Muslims, etc., was that it was always about power and money and seldom about the real welfare of the easily-led rank and file low-info blacks they condescendingly view as their underlings. Uneducated and emotionally fired up blacks, for decades, have been the unwitting pawns in much of the political chess games played in this nation, just like they have been dupes of black Reverend leaders who would sell their mothers up the river for a buck.

Perched at the very tippy top of this political exploitation food chain are the devious white liberals, descendants of former slave owners, who are still in control of much of the black community today. These Democrats have farmed blacks for decades, carefully cultivating the political soil by planting "victimization" and "racism" seeds, then attentively watering their precious black fools with welfare and other government aid fertilizer.

Without a doubt, it is this tried and true method which has consistently produced perennially bumper crops of emotional and angry blacks since the 1970s. This sound, patented, and clinically proven black vote growing methodology has created a most reliable cottage industry of ready to consume votes that the Democrat Party just heat and serve every election.

During the 1970s and the black power movement, it seemed that there was no shortage of "black leaders" and black-centric groups jostling for political power. Publicly, they railed against the supposed "white supremacy system," while behind the scenes they were making plenty of bank from white liberals. So, it comes as no surprise that most blacks within today's radical militant groups do very well financially, getting richer and richer under the same "white supremacy" system that they so frequently proclaim is holding other blacks back.

In this regard, "racism" has become a multibillion-dollar industry in America, and today new groups like Black Lives Matter are having tens of millions poured into their coffers by wealthy liberal Democrats. This financial windfall allows this wholly misnamed organization's top leaders to live lavish lifestyles among liberal whites in safe, beautiful communities as a reward for their dirty work of creating havoc among rank and file blacks.

Today, it is easy for newbies like Black Lives Matter to control most blacks because the "reverend" leaders, starting in the 1970s, soon after King's death, would begin reversing his hard-fought messages of peaceful cohabitation and racial tolerance among blacks and whites. These black overseers also would go on to fully endorse and promote the qualifier of one's skin color to determine which social and political camp to be aligned.

Of course, if black, you were to adhere to the Democrat Party and their platform, no exclusions or exceptions. To cement the brainwashing of blacks in the 1970s, the "reverends" would give fiery speeches imbued with black power and "brotherhood" rhetoric, which reinforced their crippling messages of "victimization" and "entitlement." And to emotionally worked-up blacks, there would be no peace in this country until all reparations for slavery were fully satisfied, and some other vague demands met.

It was a farce of incredible proportions and a hoot that these "reverends," who were inciting poor blacks to demand reparations from "whites," were at the same time being paid large sums of money by white liberals to do so. This duplicity was quite the feat and a neat trick to try, much less pull off, but most blacks were stupid enough, so why not? Like everything else with low-info blacks, this racial dog whistle worked and as a result many blacks today run around shouting "reparations," touting it as the mechanism by which "whites" nowadays were to atone for the past sins of their supposed slave-owning ancestors.

The biggest problem with this, uh, polite demand is that the blacks doing all this calling for reparations are the same ones fiercely supporting and defending the Democrat Party, which enslaved their ancestors.

My head really and truly hurts trying to wrap my mind around this; anybody got an Advil? Tylenol? No?..ok, but just for my sake, I do need to go over this one once more, ok?

So today, blacks, who will fight to the death defending Democrats, the same people who beat, lynched their ancestors and denied their rights for centuries, are now running around shouting "reparations," while eagerly looking forward to the next election to get more Democrats elected to office?

About that Aspirin or Tylenol, the whole damn bottle, please.

Even though the demand for "reparations" by many blacks has been a rallying cry for decades, slick and devious black "leaders" know damn well that there will never be any payment of the sort to anyone, at any time. Nevertheless, black overseers, playing to emotional and racially-charged blacks and thereby increasing their political capital within the community, still give fiery and emotional speeches proclaiming their community have a right to some form of compensation for slavery.

The ironic thing here is that many of today's proud "African Warriors," who are constantly screaming "white oppression" and "systemic racism," actually receive benefits from our supposedly "white supremacy" and "racist" government and are dependent upon handouts from mostly whites for their basic needs.

So, even with all the yelling and yapping about a racist system, many blacks are still beholden to white liberal Democrats, their past and present enslavers, for their daily sustenance and survival and will gladly do their bidding every election.

Just to summarize, blacks who have lived ten, twenty and thirty years or more in broken down communities run by white liberal Democrats, will complain about the "white supremacy" system, yet will vote every chance they get for pearly white liberals. And after enthusiastically voting for these white Democrats, welfare-dependent blacks will then turn around and protest the very same "white supremacy system" they just voted for?

Ok, ok...I believe I've belabored this point enough; I think you get the picture, let's move on. So, after killing Dr. King and installing their own black puppet leaders, what more could liberals do to further break the black community?

Well now, I'm sorta glad ya asked. Democrats in the 1980s would continue on to the next phase of their crusade of destroying the black community by introducing drugs, mainly crack, into black neighborhoods, causing violence and poverty of epidemic proportions in the inner cities, which still remain today.

Now, some misguided blacks will say the CIA and federal government, again, generic placeholders, were the ones responsible for the drug epidemic and all the other ills associated with the introduction of crack into their neighborhoods. This may be true, to some extent, but the feds and CIA weren't the ones standing on street corners selling crack to blacks, that would be wack, wouldn't it?

Drug dealers in black neighborhoods were and still are, unemployed, criminal-minded, and opportunistic blacks selling to other blacks. There was just no way in hell a white man would, or could, stand on any corner in any black community and sell drugs without being maimed, severely wounded or killed. *Ok, ok, so you haven't drawn the connection between the Democrat Party and crack distribution in black communities in the 1980s yet, so let's continue, shall we?*

As with their modus operandi, black leaders, most who probably smoked crack or abused other drugs themselves, ala Obama and Marion Barry, today, often try to blur the lines to imply that maybe it was both parties involved in the drug trade so that blacks would believe that Democrats and Republicans were somehow equally responsible for the crack epidemic ravaging their communities.

This readily accepted narrative by most blacks proves that there's no lack of fools among them, most of whom have parroted this absolute baseless falsehood and nonsense within their communities for decades. Well, let's dispense with this foolishness right now and connect the dots by asking some basic questions: *What party has manipulated emotional blacks for decades, causing them to vote over 90% for their candidates every election without fail?*

What party have been running all these drug infested, homicidal cities in this country since the 1980s, when crack was first introduced into the black community?

What party do most blacks still fiercely defend today, even though the members of this party, running their cities for decades, blithely ignore the astronomical daily and weekly drug-related killings?

More importantly, another question to ask is, which party benefits the most politically from the drug epidemic in black communities? And lastly, which party do you think crackheads in the black community eagerly vote for?

Now don't blow a fuse, take your time and think deeply, because answering these simple questions should give everyone a clue and some insight as to who and what is responsible for placing crack in black neighborhoods and who and what stands to benefit by allowing this scourge to continue unabated, for decades, in these same communities.

Ok, time's up, the answer will always be Democrats, of course, because there aren't any Republicans heading up any of these violent drug dens called inner cities; haven't been for decades. I often tell mentally challenged blacks to forget the talking points they were taught from their black and white overseers and to use common sense because their false, rainbow-infused narratives do indeed go against reality and any critical thinking or rationale any sane person would possess. I also advise plantation blacks to stop being emotional fools and place the blame for the conditions of the inner city plantations they are living on where it squarely belongs.

Democrat politicians are at the helm of all these criminal black communities and have been allowing illegal drug activity to continue virtually unchecked and unchallenged for decades, completely ignoring the misery, destruction, and poverty that comes along with it.

Conditions have gotten so bad that in certain quarters within many black communities, drugs and gang violence have become an almost expected and accepted way of life for a lot of black youths. More often than not, young black children in Democrat inner cities can be seen casually shrugging their shoulders at the sight of another black body riddled with bullets and lying dead in the street.

You would think that if leadership, including black and white liberals, and the political power structure in the inner cities, truly cared about the plight of their black "constituents" and wanted to affect positive change within their dangerous drug-infested neighborhoods, they would have addressed this issue early on during their decades-long and still ongoing governance of these communities.

Nonetheless, liberal Democrat politicians presiding over the constant chaos in inner cities across the country, for decades, have remained politically unscathed and still beloved by welfare-dependent and brainwashed blacks. In this regard, these leaders will never address the drug issue and destruction their policies cause because their feet are never held to the fire by the black community. Besides producing over 250,000 black on black killings over the last five decades in the inner cities, the constant violence, and chaos created by drug-dealing serve yet another purpose in being one of the perpetual "crises" needed to condition poor blacks and foster a plantation-like environment. To white liberal Democrats, all crises are useful, even blacks killing themselves like cockroaches over drugs on their plantations, and can be used every election so that their candidates can give self-righteous speeches about "helping" the poor downtrodden, suffering, and forever "disadvantaged "blacks.

The Democrat Party ruling class can comfortably deceive and exploit low-info blacks without flinching and have no vested interest in cleaning up anything because most members are well-heeled and do not live among their black "constituents" in impoverished, drug-dealing communities.

No, instead, these wealthy liberals make gobs of money off the plight of their black "property," which affords them the luxury of living in affluent suburbs, some gated, among other "caring" wealthy liberals. In a scheme that has gone on since the 1930s New Deal, the Democrat Party's wealth redistribution to themselves is mostly done by taxing the working class and raping the government's coffers by skimming off the top of federally funded "programs" that they advocate for and supposedly implement to "help" disadvantaged minorities.

And while Democrats are abusing blacks and pilfering government aid intended for their communities, they deflect all blame for any fallout from their harmful policies by screeching, *"it's the fault of the Republican Party."*

But again, there are neither Republicans nor NRA members anywhere to be found in any of these violent inner city plantations, nor are there any of their influences to be seen. These predominately black, homicidal drug-dens have been Democrat strongholds for decades. With that being said, there are still low-info and brainwashed blacks blaming Republicans for the dire situation their communities are in. This is insanity at its finest and further illustrates just how intellectually challenged a lot of "African Americans" have become.

At this moment, I'm gonna try to piece this thing together and bring it home, so concentrate will ya?

Just think about this, most black communities have a drug and gang problem, right? And today, white and black liberal Democrats heading up these areas want open borders with Mexico, the hub for the trafficking of vast amounts of heroin, cocaine, and other drugs that come across our borders annually and into our country, right?

We all know, by now, that the bulk of drugs coming into this country ultimately find its way into our black communities, right? And we do know that about 90% or more of the drugs coming into this country arrives via our southern border with Mexico, right?

With these questions, we can now see that, logically, one of the primary ways in which to help the black community regain its footing is to stop the flow of illicit drugs from entering into their neighborhoods, seems so simple right?

Well no, really, it's not so simple when you have an entire party in this country not only backing illegals and the illicit drug trade but are actively and openly promoting this scourge. The Democrat Party is adamantly opposed to anything and everything that would slow, prevent, or stop the trafficking of illegal drugs across the southern border and into our nation.

Now, as a black, white, or whatever person reading this text, you gotta ask yourself, why is this? Why wouldn't Democrats, who professes to absolutely adore blacks and their community, want to stop the root cause of something that has killed over 250,000 blacks in the inner cities they have run for the past five decades? *Are you with me so far?*

Liberals, especially the black ones, are still staunchly unified against a wall or stopping the flow of drugs from Mexico, and are deeply entrenched in opposing the one thing that would stem the tide of the black community's decline and destruction. Democrats are against any and all border security, against any apprehension of drug mules coming across the border, and against stopping the increasing influx of illegals that are helping facilitate the distribution of drugs within the United States and into black communities.

To make this even more surreal, today, many hyped-up blacks are running around like neutered banshees screaming that building a wall to slow and prevent the massive flow of illegals and drugs into their communities is racist. *My people, my people, is there a brain cell among thee?*

I wanna recap and connect this Twilight Zone-like insanity for those thick in the noggin: * *So, there is a raging crack epidemic which has been going on for decades, fostering high homicide rates, poverty, and destruction in black communities all across the country, all with no outrage to be seen from the Democrat Party whatsoever. However, during this same period, the oh, so "caring-for-blacks," liberals have been eagerly encouraging and protecting illegal aliens, the ones mainly responsible for smuggling vast amounts of drugs across the Mexican border and into black community and causing untold violence and chaos.*

So, with this information, it would be logical to conclude that Democrats, for some time, have had full knowledge of crack being distributed into black neighborhoods and causing the destruction we have seen since the 1980s. And, it would also appear that most

Democrat millionaires in Congress are enjoying substantial financial gains from this decades-long drug trade.

The question now is, how is the dumping of drugs and illegals in black communities being done in plain sight with no political repercussions? Well, the Democrat Party's complicity and culpability in the continual flow of drugs into the black community is often downplayed and obscured by their deceptive ideology of inclusiveness, tolerance, equality, and diversity. Under this "caring" umbrella, the party's open borders stance is supposedly demonstrating "humanitarian" compassion for illegals who have supposedly fled "persecution" and violence in their countries.

Democrats, since the 1970s, have used black "victimization," supposedly shared oppression, and emotionalism to keep black and white social justice warriors off-balanced and distracted while they make millions from the drug trade and the chaos it causes in black communities. And to protect their illegal alien investment and drug profits, you often hear white and black Democrat leaders say: *"We don't need any wall; it's racist, we need the border open to help those fleeing oppression and violence."*

But strangely, these same liberals seem nonplussed and unconcerned when it comes to black on black genocide right here, in this country, within the same black communities that they, themselves, run. It's quite odd to me that the 6000 or so blacks killed annually in inner cities over drugs bought into their communities by illegals are never spoken about among Democrats with the same care and passion as with Hispanics supposedly fleeing drug-dealing and violence-prone areas in their native countries.

Nevertheless, with their black leaders installed in the 1970s and crack introduced into black communities in the 1980s, everything was going just as expected and the way Democrats envisioned after they had assassinated Dr. King. However, something was missing but sorely needed to finish the conditioning of their new black slaves.

Something else was required to put the final touches on their new inner city plantations. There was just one more piece of the puzzle that was needed. Democrats realized that to subjugate the majority of blacks entirely, they would need to obliterate the black family unit, which seemed to be still hanging on, albeit by a thread, and keeping blacks somewhat tethered to this notion of self-sufficiency bought on by the Civil Rights Movement of the 1960s.

So, liberal Democrats, along with their black "reverends," would enlist their most potent and devastating weapon yet to accomplish their goal of completely dismantling the black family. They deployed the nuclear option, the one sure thing that would turn out to be just the dynamite needed to finish blowing up the black community and scattering its pieces to the winds.

For this task, Democrats would reach out to the all-purpose, omnipotent, liberal black woman. Wait, how can this be, our black "African Queens" turning on their own community? Please, say it ain't so.

Wow, do you really wanna see what happened after white liberals got a hold of'em, really? Is there more to be said?

No? Well then, what are you waiting on? Turn the page, Negroes, and Negretts.

Chapter Nine

The Exploitation of "African Queens?"

So just to recap, blacks were brutally enslaved in the 1600s, and their horrific treatment on plantations in the deep south would continue, unabated, for centuries until Republicans soundly defeated the Democrats in 1865, thus, releasing blacks from slavery. However, shortly after Republicans freed blacks, Democrats would stop Reconstruction and the progress of former slaves by killing Lincoln. Afterward, they would create the KKK, whose members would burn black businesses and lynch thousands of blacks, along with killing many white Republicans assisting them in the south.

*Democrats would then double down and impose Jim Crow Laws and Black Codes on blacks in the deep south as a new form of enslavement.

*But during the 1930s, after the great depression had done a number on the country economically, Democrats ingeniously offered welfare as bait to blacks. And even though they were still under Jim Crow laws, segregation, and Black Codes in the south, there was an immediate jailbreak and all-out stampede by most of the black community in accepting these "inducements" to join their former captors.

*But hold on, the Democrats' plans for blacks would be rudely interrupted when, during the 1950s and 1960s, Dr. King and Republicans would pass the Civil Rights Bill of 1964 to remove the Jim Crow Laws, segregation, and all the other restrictions on blacks in the south. However, as a reward for his efforts, Democrats would promptly assassinate Dr. King and install their own black reverend "leaders."

* Then, in the 1980s, to further obliterate any notion of blacks ever again climbing back aboard the independence and self-sufficiency train, Democrats saturated their neighborhoods with crack, creating

poverty, gangs, and violence in the inner cities. With that being said, this brings us to the final nail in the black community's hide; the exploitation of the omnipotent "African Queens," the much-protected jewel of white liberal Democrats. Ok, got it so far?

I remember some moons ago when I had the displeasure of residing in a predominately black and "depressed" community among people of little means. There was constant loud music and yelling, barbecuing, trash being indiscriminately thrown about on the ground, and sometimes shootings…but for the most part it was an idyllic and tranquil community of…*ok, ok, so I was living in the projects, alright?*

Anyways, I can always vividly recall the dynamics in the projects that would occur on the first of each month when black women, who had been walking around the entire month with naps and curlers in their hair and looking dejected, would suddenly spring forth from their inner city section eight hovels like African violets in bloom.

These black women were like Lazaruses; they would arise from the dead every first of the month and come forth. And they didn't need Jesus to call'em either, just the anxiously anticipated sounds of the mailman. They would be all "done up" in nice jeans, and evening gowns during mid-day, frolicking about and celebrating in the festive air the first-of-the-month welfare check produced.

Now for full disclosure and to be fair, back in the day, I used to chase a lot these women in the club after they got all "done up" and caught a few too!

Anyways, with the hard-earned money of taxpayers, these black "queens" would get their nails done, hair weaved, toes painted and hit the club later that night after getting "auntie" to watch their litter of "chil'ren." At the time, I saw nothing untoward of this monthly ritual and thought it entirely necessary for these impoverished women to have something fun, besides myself of course, in their dreary lives to look forward to, even if it was just once a month. I was naïve then and didn't see any issue with what was going on and, to me, it was all good back then.

It was to be much later on when I would connect this routine first of the month behavior of these women to the ongoing devastation of the black family. You see, most were liberal Democrats and strong influences in the black community, so it was only natural that their black men would also align themselves with the party their "queens" supported.

However, this political alliance was about as far as most of these African "Warriors" would venture with their "African Queens." The majority of black women in the projects were single mothers, living in poverty, with too many fatherless kids to look after. Most were just living month to month on government assistance and never really going anywhere.

Now before we go any further, let's backtrack a little to get some background and context on welfare dependency among black women. As previously noted, to finish destroying the black community, Democrats had to first get rid of the intact family unit. For this to occur, they needed to get black women on board the entitlement express, the last piece of the puzzle for their dominance of the black community.

To put this plan into action, with Lyndon B Johnson's Great Society programs of 1964, the Democrat Party began offering section section eight and other welfare inducements to single black women who had children, or were in the process of having some, with the stipulation that the fathers be removed from the households to qualify for this government "aid."

This proposition was gladly agreed upon and accepted by many struggling inner-city black women, who quickly abandoned their independence and freedom for dependency on government scraps, and thus, trapping themselves and their offspring into a cycle of generational poverty. In the ensuing decades, more black women would hop aboard the welfare and section eight train, destroying the black family and shattering Dr. King's vision of self-sufficiency for the black community.

I was recently watching videos of black males who delighted in castigating and denigrating black women who had, for many years, gotten comfortable living off taxpayers and were now lamenting the loss of section eight benefits under President Trump's new get-tough administration.

129

These black males viewed this development as a comeuppance of sorts for lazy, entitled, and always angry black women who had all of their economic and financial eggs nestled in one basket and depending entirely on government assistance for survival. Indeed, on occasion, I, myself, have entertained the very same views as these brothers. However, I believe that this is a simplistic view of a more complicated and nuanced situation, and in that regard, I will revise my thoughts just a little here, but not much.

I don't think that the black woman's acceptance of welfare and section-eight was some evil and well thought out malicious act against the black community on their part because there are people, in just about every race in this country who has accepted government aid at some point. So, it wouldn't be fair to single out black women as the sole underlying reason for the black community's downfall and failure.

However, if I may say so, it is my thinking that it is the abuse of welfare which has directly and indirectly, caused much more damage to the black family than among families of any other race receiving assistance. With that said, I don't think the acceptance of government aid, in and of itself, is evil and isn't necessarily the main issue with blacks. But I do believe that it is fair game to examine the laziness and entitlement attitudes welfare dependency engenders among black women, and their foolish choice to stay on the government dole seemingly forever and not seek to better themselves at some point in their lives.

This crippling, generational dynamic has devastated the majority of once intact black families, resulting in white liberal Democrats being able to take complete control of most inner city households.

Looking back, I do not believe that most of these manipulated black women possessed the foresight at the time to be able to envision, by their selfish actions, the adverse outcome on their community. But where the rubber truly meets the road, so to speak, is that once the truth started coming out about the many issues welfare dependency was causing within the black community, instead of changing their mindset and seeking to reverse this destruction, many black women became Democrat operatives and took to working the welfare "system" like fish to water.

And to further enshrine this dependency within the black community, a lot of these black women took to passing their welfare system-working "skills" and entitlement attitudes along to their daughters and granddaughters. Dishonest actions such as these reflect poorly on black women and is a sad indictment of the black community as a whole. This lack of character among many blacks plays into the notion that most often think in selfish terms and will never give any thought to who or what they are hurting to obtain their "funds," just so long as they have satisfied their own needs.

I have long since concluded that the use of the black woman, along with welfare dependency, by white liberals is the most potent and deadliest weapon that the Democrat Party possesses in its arsenal today. You see, black women are also the emotional igniters and fire starters for all social causes on the left and, because of their selfishness and scheming, have been able to utterly decimate and rot out the black community to its foundation and core.

Because of the many incentives welfare programs provide, early on, a lot of black women became baby-making machines for economic reasons and today will do whatever it takes to maintain their status quo and level of importance to Democrats by eagerly supporting their candidates in whatever fashion they can, come hell or high water. The most crippling aspect of this damaging handout quid pro quo is that most of the single black women in inner cities who have fatherless and directionless children running amok within the community and creating havoc, are themselves directionless and uneducated high school dropouts.

It is my opinion that because of the lack of proper education, the majority of these women never developed the necessary intellect to discern the motives of the deceptive Democrat Party, whose primary aim was to change the dynamic of the black community fundamentally. It must be said that welfare dependency is just one of the many perpetual "crises" destroying the black family that white liberals have been forever riding in on their white horses to perpetually "fix."

The Democrat Party's overwhelmingly successful gambit of using black women, proved to be ingenious and has paid off in dividends in producing the desired results of a devastating shift away from two-parent households, and ending the foundational nuclear families in many black communities. In the end, the impact has been quite significant, and disastrous, for the black community as a whole.

As previously stated, before the passing of the Civil Rights Act in 1964, blacks enjoyed a robust 80% two parent household, which today, tragically, is now at a dismal 20% or less ratio. This steep, and troubling, decline of two-parent families over the last five decades was something not seen even during slavery.

More surprising, the Democrat Party have caused this annihilation of black families without any out-of-pocket cost to themselves, while in the process coming off as compassionate heroes to blacks in promoting welfare and section eight, the programs at the very center of the breakup of black families and the continued poverty which most blacks are now accustomed.

And, as with all of their socialist handout programs, white liberal Democrats have, since the 1930s New Deal, redistributed the funds of hardworking middle-class taxpayers to implement and fund their nefarious black vote engineering racket. With Democrats, it seems that it was always easier to steal from others and give to another, then to reach into their own pockets.

And with the Democrat Party's new inclusiveness, tolerance, equality and diversity ideology as cover, if there was any pushback from conservatives about taxing the middle-class and redistributing their hard earned money to generational welfare deadbeats, white liberals immediately went on the offensive and attacked, with the eager assistance of their liberal-controlled and complicit media.

Today, it is no secret that Democrats benefit significantly from having most of the mainstream media in their pocket, often getting plenty of airtime to accuse anyone questioning their welfare handouts of being heartless or "racist," and not caring about the "women" and "children." This offensive plays into the level of protection afforded black women receiving welfare and section eight, creating an entitlement mindset and attitude among them that is unrivaled in any other race.

One of the many videos I watched on this subject, included a black female in her late thirties or early forties, with fifteen sad-faced children, temporarily living in a cramped hotel room. She was staring into a camera and berating her harried and beleaguered-looking social worker for not being able to procure suitable housing promptly for her rather large litter of fatherless government dependents. This black woman swept her hands about the room, and over her somber looking children, in ripe indignation, while proclaiming in all sincerity: *"Somebody's gotta be held accountable for all these kids, somebody's gotta pay."*

The welfare moocher had uttered these words in such a matter-of-fact way that I was completely caught off guard. It was as if this woman, herself, hadn't been the one who had lain down with a man or men, and conceived and birthed each and every one of these little black Democrat voters and future Black Lives Matter members into this world.

The scene was surreal and quite bizarre, this heifer was crazy, it was as if someone had suddenly thrust this gaggle of children upon her to care for, and that she was the innocent victim of some cruel scam in which strangers had abandoned their undesired children upon her doorstep to look after. This woman's demeanor was one of a victim; she had been thoroughly conditioned and wholly disconnected from reality after years of being brainwashed by liberals. Reality long since departed, she now resided in an illusionary socialist world where self-sufficiency and accountability were but a passing thought.

To sum up this incredibly sad and delusional situation, this breeder had spent a total of about one hundred and thirty five months carrying these children in her womb and was now somehow confused as to whom or what entity was responsible for their care and welfare. When I first viewed this video, I was disgusted, then I became angry and questioned, why are hardworking taxpayers like myself footing the bill for people like this, white or black, or whatever?

But after having a few minutes to cool off, I realized that what I was seeing was tragic, like a train wreck, and would just put an exclamation point on how white and black liberals have masterminded and perfected the farming of inner city black women. Such despair, abject helplessness, and dependency among most of these women have given Democrats complete control of the black property they had lost as a result of their defeat in the Civil War in1865.

As I said before, I am not gonna lay all the blame for the destruction of the black community entirely at the feet of black females because there is a particular segment of impoverished black women living in inner cities that are decent, hardworking, and struggling to make it. Having been in the system for years, these black women have a sincere desire to find a way off welfare and are clawing and scratching their way off the government dole and finding financial independence.

However, the only fault I have with this group of self-sufficient "sisters" is that after moving away from welfare and freeing themselves from the nightmarish inner city plantations, most of them will still stupidly support and vote for Democrats. And shockingly, some will even go on to become black overseers and herding other misguided black women into the ideology of white liberals.

There is still yet another segment of decent black women on welfare and living in inner city hellholes who are seeking to better themselves and get out from around the other black serpents. These women are the real victims, not only of white liberals but also of black males, who are once again doing stud duty for their white Democrat masters, just like they were commanded to do in the 1800s during slavery.

These black pollinators and playboys drift from woman to woman, impregnating, and creating fatherless children and wreaking havoc throughout the black community. Most are usually unemployed, fried-chicken-eating, all-day-long video playing enthusiasts, and many of their sexual conquests in the inner cities often result in the government becoming the babies' daddies of the new voting livestock they are creating. These rampant hood "indiscretions" always leaves hard-working middle-class taxpayers to pick up the welfare tab, all while the Democrat Party receive the credit for "helping" the mothers of these illegitimate and "underprivileged" children.

There are many black, fatherless newborns entering life dependent on the government for their survival and are emotionally crippled and manipulated from the womb to the tomb. Most of these inner city children are programmed at birth to follow the Democrat Party's dog whistles of "racism," "entitlement," and "victimization," and will riot on command. At a disadvantage, most suppressed inner city blacks have never experienced anything other than liberalism because Democrats often beat back, and hold at bay, any conservative or self-sufficiency ideology that may intrude upon the political stranglehold they have on the black community.

As I noted earlier, not only have a lot of black women become breeders, but most are also the emotional whips for the Democrat Party and will come running whenever they are called upon, and will enthusiastically and unabashedly defend every social program and cause that white liberals advocate and promote.

We know that it's a scientific fact that women are more emotional wired than men, but some black women seem to have way more emotional wattage than women of any other race and are only too eager to let it be known. Within the Black Caucus, and on just about every news network, talk show, and any other liberal program, there are always loud-mouthed and angry, Asian-weave and wig-wearing, unintelligent-sounding liberal black women shilling for the Democrat Party.

These black females are encouraged by liberals to scream, pout, rant, and go into emotional and incoherent histrionics when confronted with facts contrary to the lies they are paid handsomely to defend. I mean, some of these "African Queens" are downright deranged and unhinged, often ignoring civil dialogue and rational discussion in favor of uneducated and fiery filibustering outbursts. And as a bonus for this display of their "attitude," these black women are heartily applauded by their white Democrat masters on liberal networks and talk shows while their like-minded audiences clap and bark like trained seals.

Social-justice-warrior black women are the prostituted swat team of the Democrat Party, their given mission is to kick down the doors of "civility," to swarm and dominate any conversation that goes against any of their party's narratives and "talking points." They are there to bust up any truth that may somehow get through to viewers. Having these emotionally unstable females entirely in their service, to facilitate the destruction of their own community without hesitation, has been quite the achievement for the same party that had enslaved blacks for centuries and opposed every civil rights bill, act, or law for their race since the 1600s.

With the manipulation of most black women complete, the Democrats' mission to destroy the family unit has indeed succeeded beyond their wildest dreams. And with the black woman's rabid defense of their platform and agenda, the party now owns the black community, it is all theirs to direct and command.

The fallout from the complete dominance of these women is readily apparent and can be seen today in a lot of black communities across the country today as fatherless black males commit over 51% of all violent crimes in America. So, it is no coincidence that the steep rise in violence we see among blacks nowadays has also resulted in similar incarceration rates for black males across the country as well. The decades-long, rising incivility and lawlessness among them has resulted in over one million black males being incarcerated in our prisons today, a far cry from the few thousand occupying jail cells before Dr. King's death in 1968.

We must also remember here, that we are only talking about a relatively short period of about twenty years, or so, for this drastic sea change of young black men being imprisoned at an unprecedented and alarming rate to occur.

This was all designed, of course, by white liberal Democrats who have always viewed blacks as dumb animals that were uneducated, violent, and highly sensitive. In this regard, our history tells us that during slavery, southern Democrats tried to prevent African slaves from gaining any education or knowledge and if the white "massa" ever caught a black reading anything, even if it were a grocery store receipt, they would hang a nigger that day.

But today, with every election cycle, liberals use sleight of hand on the black community by fostering the notion that education for their black children is a priority for them. However, back in Washington, these same politicians neglect inner city schools and oppose any voucher programs which would allow parents with kids in subpar schools to send their kids to schools of better quality outside of their community. This deception has been going on for decades, with the same disastrous results for decades. To many, it is common knowledge that schools in many black communities are just holding pens where the majority of unionized, "unfireable," and well-paid black and white liberal Democrat teachers are tasked with keeping as many black kids as dumb and emotionally unhinged as they possibly can.

Because of the lack of a father figure in the home, unfortunately, a lot of black youths in inner cities view corrupt black leaders such as the black Reverends, black Hollywood celebs, black sports stars, and black street thugs as role models and heroes to look up to and admire. Without an influential male figure of character and integrity present, most black youths in single-parent homes often take on their mother's emotions and attitudes, developing, early on, very aggressive feminine tendencies and inclinations which causes them to be easily triggered by the smallest of any perceived incident of "racism."

These highly sensitive and intolerant black youths will then respond to just about any real or imagined racial slight or "disrespect" with overly aggressive verbal language and even physical attacks which, in a lot of cases, lead to senseless homicides and incarceration. To add to this volatility, emotionally weaken black youths are then further damaged by their mothers, sisters, aunts and other females in being encouraged to align themselves with homosexuality, illegal immigration, transgenders, Muslim terrorists and any other "social cause" agenda foisted upon them. So, as you can clearly see, most of the black community goes as the black woman goes. They are the ones, at the behest of the Democrat Party, dictating its direction.

We can get a more accurate snapshot of just how important black women are to the Democrat Party by going to the 2016 presidential election, where they voted about 4% for Republicans, while black men voted about 10%. To contrast, this liberal-induced and self-defeating mental illness among the majority of black women, white women voted about 51% for Trump and the Republican Party. Hell, even Hispanics voted about 35% for Trump and Republicans. So, I think that we can deduce, from these percentages, which group of females have been prostituted and pimped out for decades by Democrats.

Need I say more on this? Uh.....I think I should.

Unlike the majority of black women in this nation, most white women think long-term, are mentally stronger, and are decidedly not single-issue voters. And during elections, these women will focus on issues that positively affect their communities and their households. Now don't get me wrong, there is a segment of sane, beautiful, and God-fearing black women in this country who are true queens, whom I cherish, that also think along the same lines as most conservative white women. But this is a rather small, continuously attacked, and shunned group within the black community and society at large.

To be entirely fair, there are far more nasty, Godless, and looney liberal white women, probably more so than the entire black race actually, that are emotional wrecks when it comes to anything conservative or Republican. These pussy-hat wearing, crotch-grabbing, profanity-spewing liberal harlots are really insane.

With that being said, thank God for decent, conservative white, Hispanic, and black women. Just think, if white women in this country were to ever vote in the same percentages as black women in any election, whatever party they supported would win and the black vote in its entirety would be null and void. We must be ever thankful that the majority of white women in America do not see the welfare "system," or any other government handouts, as a generational cash cow to be passed along to their daughters like entitlement heirlooms.

We must also be grateful that Republican white, black, and Hispanic women in the 2016 election voted for Americans, thus preserving our nation. These conservative and God-fearing women were focused on reality and kitchen table policies that genuinely affect their lives and futures, ones that revitalize the economy and their pocketbook.

More importantly, these women were also focused on jobs for themselves and their spouses; on business opportunities, real healthcare, secure borders, and neighborhoods where they can raise their children to be respectful and well-mannered adults who will have a healthy respect for the presence of law enforcement in their communities.

Now some can criticize me for saying that most of our black women don't want the same things as conservative white women; however, their voting record over the last fifty years bears out their self-destructive tendencies, and these stats don't lie. I can only go by the statistics as mentioned to establish the validity of my assertion that the overwhelming majority of black women who vote, do not share the same wants, nor rationale, as the majority of white women who vote. Because if the majority of black women really desired the upwardly mobile things most white women desires, voting Democrat, undoubtedly, over the last five decades, has proven the wrong way to go about achieving these goals.

More profoundly, if you really think about it, the 2016 presidential race really boiled down to white conservative women versus liberal black women. And as a patriotic black man, I just wanna take this moment right now to shout out a heartfelt thank you again to all of the conservative white, black, and Hispanic women who voted for America and Trump in the 2016 election because they helped prevent the complete annihilation of our country.

It's kind of ironic that it would take the votes of mostly white conservative women in this election to help get manufacturing and factory jobs back into this country for blacks, especially black males. Their votes would also get Trump, along with other members of his administration, talking about prison reform for black males and giving some a second chance at being productive members of society once again, which is a good thing.

Voting by mostly white conservatives also placed a white billionaire president in the Whitehouse that, with his policies, helped engineer a 400% increase in black business startups. Along with helping to elect our 45th president, these are but just a few of the many things for which I am extremely grateful to conservative white women. Their faith in Trump, who I believe will be the best president, since Lincoln, for blacks and our country, is being rewarded with the most explosive and booming economy in history and this bodes well for the black community, now with the lowest unemployment rate ever recorded.

As I am ending this chapter, I now realize that there is much more damage liberal Democrat black women have done to our communities than first thought. With the influence and guidance of white feminist Democrats, the majority of black women have lost their way, becoming Godless and sinful murderers, killers of their helpless unborn children. This wasn't any accident, the loosening of morals among blacks has been steadily on the rise ever since the end of the Civil Rights Movement of the 1960s, and has accelerated even more in recent days

Under Democrats, the destructive and immoral behavior of black females has drilled down to unprecedented and unfathomable levels and has contributed significantly to the ruination of the once religious and spiritual foundation of blacks as a whole.

Before the Civil Rights Movement of the 1960s, if an unmarried black woman happened to get impregnated, she was to be married to the one who did the deed, or there would be shame in the family. Well, not so much these days, there is no such disgrace anymore for most in the black community regarding out-of-wedlock pregnancies, nor is there any shame today of black women discarding their own flesh and blood like so much unwanted rubbish.

With that being said, let's now go into how liberal white women have taught our community's once God-fearing and spiritually-grounded black women, uh, African Queens, the fine art of killing their own children while still enjoying their own lives and liberty.

I take no delight in pointing out this little-noticed epidemic among black women, which has snuffed out the lives of too many of their unborn children. So, with a heavy heart, let's saunter on over to the next chapter.

Take a walk with me, if you will, and sadly turn the page.

Chapter Ten

Black Women and Abortions

To quickly recap; blacks were enslaved by Democrats from the 1600s to the 1800s until Republicans freed them in 1865. But in the ensuing decades, Democrats would oppose and stop the progress of blacks at every turn, gaining their former slaves' loyalty in the 1930s with welfare, and would later introduce their own black leaders, and crack, into black communities for political gain.

*White liberal Democrats then would grab ahold of black women and deploy them on the front lines of their social engineering agenda to destroy the black family unit and what was left of the black community. But liberals weren't done using black women, not just yet, there would arise another ungodly task for the "African Queens" to perform...

The issue I'm about to broach here is quite touchy for a lot of people, for many different reasons, and therefore deserving of some sensitivity, so I'll... Oh, never mind, I am not gonna be that sensitive, tiptoeing around baby-killing, because who else is gonna watch out for these little innocent fellas that will never get a shot at life because of some liberal agenda?

It simply amazes me just how a woman, endowed and blessed with the precious gift of giving birth, and life, can enjoy the time she had conceiving a child, yet ignore and suppress her natural, and innate, maternal and nourishing instincts by killing and disposing of her own flesh and blood as she would toilet tissue after its use.

This horrific and immoral act of infanticide, unbornacide, or whatever name you wanna call it, occurring quite frequently in our nation nowadays, isn't by accident but is merely the results of the decades-long loosening of our morals and our country moving away from God. In 1973, with the push of liberal white Democrats, abortions became mainstream and even normalized in our society after Roe vs. Wade was passed into law, legalizing the killing and butchering of the unborn. Today, abortion-on-demand is a booming cottage industry and all the rage among liberal white women who will go to the ends of the earth to keep this law in place, often holding protest marches and demonstrations to protect their rights to murder their unborn children.

To supposedly lessen the impact of their immorality and wickedness, and apparent lust for baby killing, the Democrat Party's argument in favor of abortion is that the procedure is nothing more than the removal of fetal tissue, no bigger than a pinhead, from the womb. To further defend their position, liberal Democrats today also toss about their "scientific" narrative and talking point that aborted fetal tissue is not yet in human form as we know it, and therefore not a living being.

Of course, this is patently false and misleading and illustrates the Democrat Party's deceptive and callous indifference regarding the value of an unborn's life, or anyone else's, that they want removed from this earth. To put this atrocity on full blast, I am going to go over one of these abortions with you, in graphic detail, and let you draw your own conclusions as to whether an abortion is the removal of non-living tissue, as Godless Democrats proclaim, or the wanton killing of a living human baby as we know it to be. There is a quite disturbing video that everyone needs to see, it is only about five minutes or so in length, but extremely educational and enlightening.

Doctor Anthony Levatino, a gynecologist who has performed over 1200 of these procedures, describes one of the many abortions he has completed during his career as he testified before the Congressional House Judiciary Committee some time ago. He went into horrific detail as he illustrated for Congress one of his many second-trimester abortions, which is usually between fourteen and twenty-four weeks of gestation:

"During this period in the pregnancy, the baby at this point, as he points out, is small and about the length of your hand.

He says that once the "patient" is asleep on the table, a catheter is entered into the uterus, and after suctioning out all of the life-sustaining amniotic fluid from around the baby, clawed forceps with serrated edges is then inserted into the patient's womb to grab whatever parts it can clamp onto. Once located, each tiny body part is then callously ripped out one at a time; the baby's legs, arms, and spine. Then the doctor proceeds to remove the organs, like the heart and lungs, which is also grasped and brutally yanked out in the same fashion.

As for the head, the good doctor says that he maneuvers the forceps around blindly within the womb, probing until he can feel the head, which is about the size of a plum at that point and once grasped, squeezes down until white liquid, which would be the baby's brains, runs out of the patient's cervix.

The doctor finishes up by searching for and removing any pieces of skull or other body parts he may have inadvertently left behind. Dr. Levatino morbidly points out that when he pulls the skull out that, sometimes, he sees a little lifeless face staring right back at him.

This procedure usually lasts until all of the extricated body parts have been stacked up on the table and adding up to a complete infant. Each "piece" must then be painstakingly inventoried and accounted for to avoid mistakenly leaving any pieces of the infant's body in the patient that would cause life-threatening complications later on.

Once it has been determined that all was clear and there weren't any infant parts left inside the Democrat woman's womb to "endanger" her, the "pinhead fetal tissue" abortion would be complete.

*Today, for whatever reasons, Dr. Levatino no longer performs these abortions.

As for the devious nature and deceptiveness of liberals, I can still remember that prior to this powerful testimony, an enraged and wild-eyed Democrat Congressman had pounded his podium forcefully while emphatically declaring that he was pro-choice and that having an abortion was a woman's choice and right. Well, what then does this "caring congressman" say about the rights of the murdered and dismembered infant lying on the medical table and tagged like auto parts? The "body parts" lying on the table was not a "woman's right," but an innocent being who didn't ask to be bought into this world. This unwanted child had not come about as the result of some accident or affliction that suddenly happened to a female just minding her own business.

I mean it's not like the woman was just walking down the street on a cold and windy day and suddenly caught a case of the pregnancies. No, the female has to lie down, perhaps get in a doggy position, or whatever position she desires, open her legs or toot her ass up and allow a male to penetrate her until he ejaculates his semen into her. Then that semen has to find an egg within the woman and sorta go about pollinating it and presto, baby time!

Now, the morning after, when both male and female wake up suffering from hangovers caused by their night before drinking, they look at each other, shrug, and go groggily about their separate ways. Then, about a couple of months later, finding out she has conceived, and a new life has been created, this liberal Democrat woman is at an abortion clinic executing her "rights" and discarding the child that she had so much fun creating with the long-gone male on their night of drunken lust.

So, just to clarify, two immoral and sinful liberal Democrats get together and lustfully have fun copulating, which results in an innocent child being produced. Finding this out, the Democrat woman then casually saunters into a clinic and kills the innocent child in her womb. And with the murderous deed now done, she calmly goes back to her ways of promiscuity as if she'd just only stopped in a restroom to empty her bladder.

To liberal Democrats today, abortions are a no fuss and no muss way to alleviate weight gain, just pull into the butcher shop and get' er done, chop, chop. *But, just hold the press for a minute there sonny.* Democrats have upped the ante in their thirst for baby slaughtering. In recent news, satanic and Godless Democrats in Virginia and New York doubled down and are now in the process of attempting to have bills passed that would actually abort a child after it's born.

Yes, you heard me, these oh so loving, inclusiveness, tolerance, equality, and diversity Democrats are saying that it is more than ok after a baby is born, through no fault of his own, to crush his skull like a walnut until he is dead, right there on the delivery table. Yet, these same Democrats are going absolutely batshit crazy over 700, 000 illegal alien DACA children: *"We must protect them, they are here through no fault of their own!"*

In this regard, it seems that disposable American-born children are the in-thing, chic, and fashionable among liberals. With this atrocity now in plain sight, Americans must realize by now that this party is pure evil and that there is nothing they won't do for power, even killing the defenseless innocent among us.

I believe, no, I know that the act of aborting any child is evil and unholy, and one of the absolute worst sins a woman can commit. And yes, I believe there is sin. I believe in God and the Bible, and I believe there's good and evil. And I also believe in redemption, forgiveness, and salvation. The Bible tells us that there are many sins, and the good book also says that if you commit one that you commit them all, which I believe as well.

Now, this may come as a startling revelation, *well, uh, maybe not to those of you who know m*e, but I am guilty myself of sinning and probably on many occasions, but I am trying to live upright.

At this point, my voluntary confession and admission of sinning may seem like a gotcha moment and an opportunity for those women who, after hearing this, would then say that I am a hypocrite because I have sinned and is no better than a woman who has had an abortion and killing her newborn. And I say, fair enough.

So, to dispel the notion of any contradiction of my seemingly hypocritical view on sinning, I wanna dig a little deeper into the issue of conscience, guilt, forgiveness, and redemption because all sins may be the same in God's eyes, but are they in ours?

The answer is that we, as humans, do not perceive all sins the same, and therefore, the way we view and feel about each one can be vastly different in many aspects. Most of us often tend to try to rationalize the sinful actions we have taken by searching, in our minds, for circumstances or situations that may justify what we have done. However, I want to talk about conscience because I believe that this is our moral compass and guide as to how each one of us responds to our wrongdoings and the subsequent actions we may take to correct these trespasses.

For example, if I had committed the sin of stealing or lying, and afterward had atoned for my transgressions by replacing that which I had taken or had come forth with the truth, can I then be genuinely at peace with myself after being fully forgiven by those whom I had transgressed against? I would think that most people would feel at peace with this cleansing of their guilt for these particular sins and would feel unburden going forward.

But in the same vein, after a woman murders her defenseless and unborn child in the womb, and after seeking atonement by asking for forgiveness for this transgression, will her conscience allow her to find true contentment and peace within her soul ever again?

And if she can easily find peace within herself after killing her unborn child, her own flesh and blood, what does this say about her conscience, morality, and character?

If I were to liken myself to this woman, can I just shoot and kill someone, and my conscience then allows me to be at peace with myself? And if I could so easily and comfortably take a life without having any second thoughts about my evil deed, what does this then say about *my* conscience, morality, and character? I believe that each sin we commit is a cross to bear, how big is your cross?

These questions are for us all to ponder as we go through this chapter. By now I believe that a lot of liberals, if reading this text, are indeed pissed at me and will begin asking the usual questions in defense of their murderous positions: *"What if a woman is raped, huh, what about that? What if a relative got a woman pregnant, what about that?*

My response to these questions? Well, just keep reading until you get to the abortion stats and everything will become much more apparent. It is not my intent in this text to address the many reasons why a woman may have or want to have an abortion; I am merely stating my opinion and views on the subject from a religious, moral, and conscience viewpoint.

Recently President Trump nominated a pro-life justice, Brett Kavanaugh, to serve on the Supreme Court and you would think that white liberal Democrats, the ones espousing love, inclusion, and tolerance, had just witnessed the second coming of Jesus, their hated nemeses, the way they had broken into mass hysteria. White and black liberal Democrat women went into full panic mode, frothing at the mouth over the prospect that this judge could be confirmed and somehow, possibly prevent them from killing their innocent unborn and helpless children in the womb.

Satanic Senate Democrats went into overdrive, pulling out all the stops in an attempt to derail Kavanaugh's confirmation; even turning to smear tactics by fabricating evidence of sexual assaults supposedly occurring thirty years ago. As with every attack on conservatives, there was this sudden parade of liberal Democrat activist white women in the media, all claiming they were "assaulted" by the judge somewhere but just couldn't remember the exact place or time. Lacking any validity to any of these claims, of course, these "victims" failed miserably in their social justice "cause" and disappeared just as quickly as they had appeared

With abortion being a critical mainstay for their party, even now, months after Judge Kavanaugh had been confirmed as a justice on the Supreme Court, blood-thirsty, baby-killing liberals are still plotting, trying to find a way to impeach and remove him from the bench so there wouldn't ever be a threat of ever preventing them from murdering their unborn.

At this point, the Democrat Party should go all in and just do away with their false narrative and pretense of "It's a woman's choice and right" and adopt a more befitting slogan for their wanton liberal women like, say: *"You spread'em, and we'll kill'em!"*

Yeah, I guess old Chuckie, Pelosi, Auntie Max and the rest of the baby-killing gang would get a real kick outta that one. I mean, if anyone just mentions anything about reducing or outlawing abortions today, Democrats quickly circle their media wagons, screaming and screeching: *"It's a woman right, and you cannot tell her what to do with her body!"*

"These abortions are for women who have been raped, what if they do not want to have the ill-conceived child?!"

But wait a minute, with all of this high octane rhetoric, let's dig into these ginned-up hysterics a bit shall we? Because all of these arguments ring hollow and false in the face of reality and facts. Our nation averages anywhere from *400,000 to 600,000 abortions a year, yeah that many,* and if what liberals are saying is true, these staggering numbers would make for an awful lot of rape and an epidemic of massive proportions taking place annually in this country.

The hypocrisy in all of this abortion brouhaha is the recent flap over rugged-assed, uh, I mean precious, little illegal alien border children that were somehow tough enough to travel thousands of miles over rough terrain, crawl through sharp barb wire, and swim through snake-filled lagoons to get to America's border. Remember when these now suddenly "tender" and "delicate" little illegal angels, according to their liberal Democrat benefactors and hyperbolic media henchmen, were being supposedly badly mistreated?: *"Some were even crying from being ripped, ripped I tell ya, just ripped from their mother's arms. They won't see 'em for a week or two, and this is not who we are."*

Democrats carried on ad-nauseum, for weeks, over these 2000 little non-English speaking, welfare-seeking criminals: *"Oh, the inhumanity and the horror these poor little defenseless children are going through, how can we sleep at night knowing they're not safe!"* The liberal media went into hyper-overdrive with nonsensical and overly compassionate pleas for the "safety" of these "innocent and defenseless" border children, all while splashing their humanitarian "crisis" all across their networks to stoke emotions in their viewers.

Meanwhile, with this media "air cover" as a distraction, Democrats on the ground were quietly going about business as usual, advocating and promoting the casual slaughtering and butchering of hundreds of thousands of unborn babies each year without any outrage or any media coverage. *What the hell?*

This callous attitude and indifference for the unborn exist primarily because the children Democrats are so eager to murder are American babies, disproportionately black, and seen as nothing more than disposable commodities. And the eye-opener in this mix is that Godless liberals have been practicing this form of demographic eugenics for decades, slowly culling the black population and cheering the gradual decline of white births, all while promoting foreign births, primarily Hispanic.

This brings me to the connection between black women and Planned Parenthood, and right now I want to speak to these women, these proud "African Queens: *"What has become of you? Why are you perfectly ok with following in the footsteps of satanic liberal Democrat white women in killing your unborn child? You black women used to be some of the most spiritual creatures on earth. You used to hate abortion and the killing of your own flesh, what has happened to you? What has happened to your morals and character?"*

You know, most black churches I have attended over the years are mostly filled with "holy" black women, yet black women have the most abortions, percentage-wise, than any other race in America. How is this so? How do we reconcile this? What in the hell has happened to our community? Is it church on Sunday and abortion on Monday for most black women?

Something is seriously wrong with a lot of our black women. Have they have lost their way? And have liberal Democrats succeeded in removing the true and living God from their lives. Oh, I seriously think so, blacks total about 13% of this nation's population, yet black women have about 36% of all abortions in the United States. Let's see, on the high end; 600,000 abortions in this nation annually, x 36% yields about 216,000 little black young' uns not ever seeing daylight, every year. *"No life, no future for you little Negroes! Why? Because your "caring" social justice warrior liberal Democrat black mother said so, that's why!"*

Again, let's backtrack and juxtapose these hundreds of thousands of abortions of black children with the recent firestorm over the 2000 "precious" illegal Hispanic children at the Mexican border for a moment. Let's recall the feigned outrage by liberal Democrats, not over these black abortions, but over the illegal alien children: *"One kid stuck at the border without his parents is one too many. Did you see the video of them crying?" "My God, they were in cages! What have we become.....monsters?!"*

The reaction by white liberals is also quite different when you contrast their illegal alien anger with their nonexistent outrage over thousands of black youths being killed annually on the streets of Democrat-run inner cities. As to black lives mattering to white liberals, it is crystal clear to blacks with any sense what the Democrat Party has been really saying to our community for centuries: *"Who gives a damn, these niggers are used to being killed and killing each other by now. They are only animals, livestock, just like when we bought'em over from Africa. So, don't ask about'em, don't tell us anything about 'em, and don't publicize anything about their deaths, oh, and tell'em that the parties switched, their black asses will never figure that one out!"*

So, with that being said, it would stand to reason that 2000 precious little Hispanic illegal alien kids' lives are worth far more to Democrats than the over 216,000 dead black children their party kills in the womb every year. Now, you may be wondering at this point, just where is the outrage from the NAACP, the Black Caucus and Black Lives Matter on this black infanticide? Uh, how about the angry, self-righteous, racism speech-giving black civil rights 'Reverends' or the racial incident seeking social justice warriors, such as frothy-mouthed black celebs and black sports stars...etc.?

No protests, and no fiery speeches about how white Democrats are just a hunting little black children down in the womb? When are these proud "African Americans" from the "motherland" the uh, cradle of mankind, gonna speak up and "weigh in" on the Democrat Party's annual ritual of killing hundreds of thousands of innocent and defenseless unborn black children? Ok, I am thinking here that these black overseers and traitorous bastards will probably "weigh in" oh say, like, the very first of Neveruary.

Like the African chieftains during the 1600s, who sold their own people to Democrats for pots and pans, today's black "leaders," wealthy puppet black celebs and sports stars are also selling out their communities. Black overseers like these, are deliberately ignoring the aborting and murdering of black children just as they've done, for decades, in overlooking the massive number of black on black killings on the streets of inner cities that their Democrat masters preside over.

On the flipside though, these same black leaders are emotionally invested and, oh, so concerned about poor, suffering Hispanic border children caught crossing illegally into the country, and just have to make sure that these young trespassers and criminals are not harmed in any way, shape or fashion and quickly reunited with their families! *Why? Because their white masters have commanded them to do so.* It's incredible what thirty pieces of silver will buy with these black Judases nowadays.

Really, has it come to the point in which our esteemed liberal Democrat black leaders really and genuinely prefer "good hair" Hispanic children over little "nappy headed" black children? It would also appear that it's no fluke that black "leaders in Congress are ignoring the astronomical number of black abortions conducted every year in this country because most are tied politically to the organization which performs the bulk of these abortions.

Planned Parenthood is a self-styled, federally funded butcher shop with franchises in just about every city, sorta like McDonald's, where liberal Democrats are continually killing black children; cutting, chopping, and dismembering and selling their body parts on the black market like little black McNuggets.

Margaret Sanger, the founder of Planned Parenthood, is a heroine to white liberal Democrats, of course, so much so that the party even took to annually bestowing an award in her name unto the liberal who best advocated for and promoted the killing of babies for the year. Special isn't it?

Old, weed-out-the-Negroes Sanger has had sainthood status conferred upon her by liberals and sanctimoniously praised by Hillary Clinton, the corrupt ice queen herself, who once said that her dear friend Margaret didn't go far enough in culling this nation's black population and that Democrats still have unfinished work to do.

You know, maybe, just maybe, one day white liberals can up the abortions to one million babies a year. Let's see, one million Americans aborted every year and two million Latinos added every year, yeah, that'll go a long way in "browning" the nation like liberalized and wild-eyed black pundits and CNN anchors breathlessly screech about on their telecasts.

Margaret Sanger was a eugenicist who believed, like the Nazis, that an ultimate and pure race could be created by weeding out from among us the weak and deficient, which is just code words for blacks and other undesirable minorities. In 1926, she gave a speech at a Klu Klux Klan rally in Silver Lake, New Jersey, and afterward joyously bragged that she had indeed won that segment of Democrats over and had been invited back to speak at functions of more than ten other KKK chapters in the future.

The Democrat Party and Margaret Sanger have been very successful in repackaging the extermination of blacks in the guise of *"a woman's choice"* and *"we are helping blacks with family planning."*

Sanger held many beliefs regarding minorities, and these are just a few of the many racist views she harbored:

She believed that it had been a colossal error even to have blacks in America in the first place and had considered them blight on the land.

She also believed that the best way to deal with Negroes is to remove them through abortions, slowly.

She believed that the black community should be the primary target to remove unwanteds from our society and that birth control facilities should be easily accessible for blacks.

She believed that predominately black schools should be targeted way more than white schools for 'family planning" education.

Today's Planned Parenthood, an organization used by liberals to control specific demographics, is mightily protected by Democrats, who have always voted to support and fund this human meat grinder with taxpayers' money every year. In a nice political setup and quid pro quo, federal funds are directed to Planned Parenthood, then this organization turns around and donates some of this taxpayer money back into the coffers of campaigning liberal Democrat candidates to help get them elected. Once in office, these baby-killing Democrats then opt to funnel even more taxpayer money back into Planned Parenthood, and the nefarious money laundering cycle continues.

You gotta admit that these cunning white liberal Democrats do have one of the most ingenious and creative ways of ripping off hard-working taxpayers to carry out their perpetually-funded killing of the unborn, sweet isn't it? In this regard, working Americans are being involuntarily forced into funding the wholesale slaughter of hundreds of thousands of innocents each year in this country.

So, to bring this full circle, working Americans are actually being forced to pay to bring illegal kids over to bolster their population, while at the same time paying to exterminate our own kids born here.

During the 2018 election cycle, Planned Parenthood donated over $310,000 to Democrats while, curiously, nothing was given to Republicans. *How strange is that?* Think about this, due to abortions disproportionately and routinely performed on black women, the black community have not only seen stagnated population growth in the last five decades but have also lost a lot of ground to most every other race, primarily Hispanics, who have seen their birthrates rise, remarkably unhindered by Democrats.

Let's go ahead and wrap up this chapter, because I believe everyone should have, by now, gotten the message on the staggering amount of abortions of American babies, backed and funded by Democrats, being performed annually in this nation.

But hold on, wait a minute, before we get to the end of this here chapter, I wanna dig a tad deeper into the "parties switched" myth in a little sidebar, and I'm gonna use the black community itself to dispel this myth, again.

As evidenced during the 2016 election, black women eagerly voted 96% Democrat, therefore proving they are overwhelmingly Democrats. These same black women also have over 36% of all abortions annually in this nation, which is an astronomical ratio for only 13% of the total population.

And, to think, there are many young and stupid black males running around today screaming that white cops are tough on'em and hunting them like deer. Well, readily available abortion stats show that law enforcement isn't the issue they need to be concerned with, they better worry about dey mommas, because most liberal black women will kill a little Negro quicker than the police ever will, and a lot more of'em too, probably while drinking some Hennessy to boot! With the police, at least a criminal black youth has a fighting chance to escape by running, sagging pants and all. But Democrat black women got their little black and whiny asses in the womb, all curled up and nowhere to run, and these females know it.

Anyways, since 1973, with the passage of Roe vs. Wade, liberal black women have joyfully murdered over 20 million of their unborn children who thought they were all snuggled up and safe in their mommas' wombs. *Y'all don't hear me, I said over 20 MILLION black chil'ren have been taken out by dey mommas. Surprise little Negroes!*

It's almost as if Democrat black women have excelled in liberal arts *"Kill a Negro 101"* classes or something. Just think, all of the millions upon millions of aborted black children owe their deaths to black women who support the Democrat Party's "inclusiveness, tolerance, diversity and equality" ideology and platform. So, this begs the question, if the "parties did indeed switch," what did today's liberal black women supposedly switched from now that they are dyed-in-the-wool Democrats and remorseless baby killers? *Just let that tidbit swirl around in your noggin for a minute. Is it connecting yet? No?...read on then with ya bad self.*

In contrast, true Conservative Republican women, black, white and Hispanic, believe in God and the sanctity of life and just don't have the same bloodlust for killing their unborn children as liberal women do, and never will. From the very inception of their party in 1854, Republicans have never advocated for abortions and absolutely abhors the thought of anyone killing their unborn. This reverence for life has always been one of the core tenets of real conservativism.

Looking back, prior to Roe V Wade being passed, black women didn't have the insane number of abortions we have seen in recent decades. It wasn't until black women were mostly liberal Democrats, and getting welfare benefits, did the dramatic rise in the systematic killing of their unborn started to occur. Listen, can you just hear old Democrat President Lyndon B Johnson's words of 1964 echoing here: *"When I sign this bill, I will have those niggers voting Democrat for the next 200 years." *Really, my man should have gone a bit further and included that he would also have those same niggers killing each other and their babies for the next 200 years as well.*

To sum up, unlike today's liberal black women, conservative and Republican black women wouldn't dream of having an abortion and have "remained" steadfast conservatives with Godly values during the 1950s, 1960s, 1970s, 1980s, and 1990s, and right on up to present. So, as these facts present themselves here, we must then conclude that once a black woman switches from being Republican and fully immerses herself in the liberal and Godless platform and ideology of the Democrat Party, the odds of her becoming an immoral baby killing machine goes through the roof.

So no, the parties haven't switched, nor have their ideologies, and I'll keep providing proof throughout this text if there isn't enough already.

Oh heck, let's do one more example; today in 2018, even when conservative women protest, they are polite and intelligent in their conversation, well-mannered in their behavior, and speak with intellect and rationale. Now juxtapose this behavior with liberal Democrat women; the Satan-worshiping, nasty, disrobing-in-public heathens you see parading about in our nation's streets wearing pussy hats and grabbing their crotches while screaming obscenities about the "right" to kill their unborn children.

So, in drawing upon my observations, and the inarguable and unassailable facts I have presented, black women who are Democrats today are predisposed to being mostly immoral and without conscience, much like their liberal Democrat white woman counterparts. Now, I do realize that there is probably gonna be some anger and blowback regarding these statements, but personally, I say to these black women, there is no need to get upset or agitated and attack me, the stats speak for themselves, and you are what you support.

By now, everyone with some sanity should be able to draw a straight line from the 1800s Godless Democrat Party to today's Godless Democrat Party, nothing has changed or "switched" at all, only blind fools would think so. You see, Democrat slave owners in the 1600s didn't value Africans much as humans when they bred and sold them back then, and today they still don't place too much value on blacks as humans, as evidenced by the massive black abortions they so eagerly promote.

Readers, I think that we are at the point in this book where you should absolutely get it by now, so I'm just gonna leave it right here. I wanna move on to Obama phones, Section Eight, ebt cards, Medicaid, etc. *You know, the handouts which create black dependency, wheeeeee?*

Yoooooooouu whoooooo, hello?... I'm talking to you, put down that chicken foot and focus. Uh, how's about just flipping the page, how else is ya gonna get to the next chapter?

Chapter Eleven

Democrats, Blacks & Welfare

Well now, we've certainly come a long way together haven't we? So, I feel that a short recap is in order: *Democrats enslaved blacks, created the KKK, killed Lincoln and King and stopped black progress whenever and wherever they could, for decades.

*Democrats then poured crack into black communities and exploited black women by enticing them with section eight and hair weaves.

*Finally, Democrats got black women, their most potent weapon, to kill their unborn unmercifully. And now, here we are with welfare handouts, the uh, ties that bind the black community.

We'll now take a gander at welfare, the root of the Democrat Party's hold on the majority of blacks, their political fuel. But first a quick listen to Booker T Washington and what he has to say about welfare: *"Among a large class, there seemed to be a dependence upon the government for every conceivable thing. The members of this class had little ambition to create a position for themselves but wanted the federal officials to create one for them.*

How many times I wished then and have often desired since, that by some power of magic, I might remove the great bulk of these people into the country districts and plant them upon the soil – upon the solid and never deceptive foundation of Mother Nature, where all nations and races that have ever succeeded have gotten their start – a start that at first may be slow and toilsome, but one that nevertheless is real." ...Booker T Washington

With generational welfare, it is tough for me to digest the insanity almost an entire race of people have been led to believe, that they could potentially "handout" their way to prosperity. Unfortunately, and stupidly, this is what a great many blacks have been betting on for the last fifty years, and more, all while shunning the notion that it takes an educational foundation, intact family, moral character, a strong work ethic, and the right mental attitude to achieve real economic viability in this nation.

White liberal Democrats and their black "Civil Rights" Reverends have the black community laboring under the decades-long false assumption that they can have broken families, poverty, Godlessness, drug-dealing, a lack of education, wanton violence towards each other and gangs in most of their neighborhoods, and all that would be needed to fix these ills is welfare, WIC, and section eight.

There is a small segment of intelligent, independent blacks in this country who know better and has figured it out. These escapees from inner city plantations are now living and thriving in black suburban enclaves and doing quite well for their families and themselves and have worked hard to get where they are, without the benefit of government aid.

However, the tragedy for the black community as a whole is that most blacks, even the successful ones as mentioned, are still voting Democrat. The reason these "freed" blacks vote in this manner, and will never speak out about what is really happening among our people, is they fear the backlash and retribution from the rest of the brainwashed black community for airing their "dirty laundry," so to speak. It is this climate of hush-hush among these middle-class blacks which has served to empower and enable Democrats to continue, unchecked, to implement devastating and crippling policies within the inner cities that these blacks have escaped.

Today, there are two types of blacks; those who have tapped into this nation's wealth-generating capitalism and ideals of Americanism and are enjoying all the opportunities available to them. Then there is the rather large segment of blacks, mentally conditioned and brainwashed by white liberal Democrats, who perceive capitalism and the wealthy in this country as evil.

The latter group of blacks view America as an oppressive and racist country, even though it is the monthly drippings from the table of mostly wealthy, white capitalists which sustains the majority of them. Just for a moment, let's review a few conversations I think probably could have occurred within each of these two very different groups, in their respective homes, at any given moment.

First, we'll take a look at an engineer who has a doctor for a wife, a prime example of a middle class, hard-working and successful black couple. They both struggled early on to make ends meet, studiously applying themselves in school and studying hard. They sacrificed time together, working long and grueling hours to become successful and to have the things they always wanted and are now enjoying the financial comfort they have.

And finally, this couple has produced two smart, articulate, and well-mannered children; one in high school and one in college. Let's eavesdrop a little and listen in on their conversation, shhhhh:

"Hey babe, the Lion King is playing at the amphitheater next week, want me to grab two tickets."

"Oh, I don't know dear, I have that medical symposium that I have to attend next week, depends on the day and time, I suppose."

"Uh, ok hun, I'll check and see which shows we can go to that won't conflict with your schedule. Oh, don't forget, we have that meeting with our financial advisor to go over our portfolio and investments tomorrow at 4:30 pm as well."

'Ok, think I can make it, I'll be there."

"No cooking for you tonight babe, I've already made reservations at the Ritz Restaurant for us."

"Thanks, hon, you are the best."

Ok, that was a nice, now let's go to the "entitlement and victimization" couple, or the flip side of today's black coin. We'll now saunter on over and drop in on a black mom in her early twenties who became pregnant at fifteen and dropped out of high school, never completing the ninth grade. Unfortunately, she has drifted from man to man ever since, relying on the Democrat Party's system of "helpful" welfare programs to survive.

Now with four kids, two acting out in school, one in a street gang and dealing drugs, her lone glimmer of hope is the one son, who is studying hard and staying off the streets and, because of his athletic ability, have a shot at possibly playing basketball in the NBA one day. However, her stay-at-home-all-day-long-video-playing boyfriend is also a dropout and 40oz drinking, weed-smoking, unemployed dependent. Let's listen in, shall we?:

"Taquando, I need some money to help out around here."

"Yo man, I already told you I got something coming in soon, so chill alright, you gets money every month."

"But you've been saying that for weeks now and I ain't gonna do this with you no mo. I am also tired of barely making it, and I ain't buying you yo weed no mo?"

"Damn man, you see what's been happening when I tries to get a good job, and I ain't working no damn McDonalds, they ain't paying shit, let me finish my game."

"We ain't making it, I'm gonna go back to school to try to get my GED, and you should think about it too."

"Man, you tripping, what the hell that gon do? White cracker mofos ain't gonna let you get nowhere, you'll see. We are the original Israelites and gotta take what's ours."

"Taquando , you gotta stop playing that damn game for a minute and listen to me, I'm serious, we have to get out of this neighborhood, I'm tired of living like this!"

"What the hell, bitch, you done made me mess up my game! I'm gonna go hang with my homies until you cool off, you tripping, I'm out."

Sadly, these two scenarios serve to illuminate the stark differences between those blacks who, early on, placed emphasis on hard work and education, versus those blacks who had, early on, bought into the entitlement and victimization policies of white liberal Democrats and are now struggling in the perpetual cycle of poverty that welfare dependency brings.

These are the all too real divergent paths and realities for the black community in this nation; one in which blacks have escaped the Democrat plantation's stranglehold and are now enjoying true freedom, opportunities, and fruits of their labor. And one where blacks today are still residing on Democrat plantations, on welfare and in despair and hopelessness, even though the door to their self-imposed imprisonment is wide open and they can leave at any time they choose.

By focusing on education, family, and sacrifice, the first couple did all the right things to succeed and is now reaping the rewards. But the patently unfair aspect to all of this is that, although this couple built a comfortable life by working hard, they are now being forced by Socialist Democrats to have exorbitant taxes taken out of their hard-earned paychecks to be redistributed to others on welfare.

So, even though the second couple hadn't done any of the things that would've been necessary to improve their situation and lot in life during this same period, they would now be able to partake of the first couple's hard work and sacrifice. This taxation and theft is grossly unfair to the first couple, to be penalized for pursuing their American dream, and also very unfortunate for the second couple, who lost a lot of time listening to the promises of liberal Democrats, squandering their opportunity to build a fruitful life like the first couple.

To their detriment, the second couple opted for the shortcut to nowhere and received welfare table scraps and the alluring appeal of long naps and care-free lounging every day. This seemingly easy way out has gotten a lot of blacks stuck on the liberal hamster wheel of generational dependency, fostering frustration and hopelessness among many uneducated blacks still trapped in poor communities. The lack of education, the eschewing of hard work and the viewing of our capitalist system as the adversary, has placed the second couple in an entirely untenable financial and economic position for theirs and their children's future.

And because a lot of inner-city residents are dropouts, it is well noted that most Hispanic, black, and white welfare recipients are of low intelligence, highly emotional, and easily manipulated. It is this lack of knowledge driving poverty among these groups, and also why it is so difficult to have any meaningful dialogue with a lot of blacks about the Democrat Party and their policies, which have kept many blacks forever impoverished and dependent on handouts.

Now, by no means are the second couple villains in the above scenario, they are merely the deliberately uneducated pawns of scheming white and black liberals, and of the black "civil rights" leaders who vigorously spew their "victimization," "disadvantaged" and underprivileged" crisis rhetoric within the black community to stir emotions.

What I have also noticed is that just about every other race in America reacts quite differently to the ending, or potential suspension, of welfare and other government aid. If whites are cut off from handouts, they merely acknowledge that their funds have run out or that there has been a cutback and try to do something else to survive. Maybe these poor whites reach out to relatives and friends to tide them over, or perhaps they actually go out and try to get a job to tide them over.

However, it is a much different reaction if blacks are cut off from the government trough, they scream and bitch about who's gonna take care of such and such, and why ain't dey ebt card working. Welfare is addictive and like a form of crack for most blacks, who are purposely given a taste of doing nothing all day, resulting in them enjoying being kept as opposed to standing on their own two feet.

Democrats have made the program almost synonymous with inner city blacks. So whenever there is any threat of cutbacks to the program, you will see mostly large and hungry-looking black women on television and videos, angrily lashing out at the social services in their cities and towns and being paraded about by the liberal media and Democrat Congressmen and Congresswomen as suffering "victims."

And upon seeing this reaction, white liberal Democrats immediately pounce upon this "crisis," to make it known that it's because of racism and wealthy white Republicans that blacks are in this dire situation. For the majority of inner-city blacks, welfare long ago ceased being just a temporary stop-gap measure intended for those in financial trouble and as a means of stabilizing their situation until they can get back onto their feet.

Many dependent blacks have made welfare a rite of passage, a lifelong right, and entitlement that they feel that they are owed. This mentality is bolstered by "helpful' white liberal Democrats who actively promote and target the benefits of these programs to the "disadvantaged" and "underprivileged" black and Hispanic community.

I recall seeing television commercials a few years back, where white and black liberals were imploring minorities to take advantage of all the free and "helpful" government programs that they were "entitled to." Democrat social justice warriors mailed out thousands of detailed pamphlets in English and Spanish, targeting specific areas in which to increase their welfare rolls, and by extension their voter rolls.

For decades, the Democrat Party have sent the clear, and unmistakable message that blacks have special needs and welfare should be there for them forever. It is this racial messaging which has allowed white liberals to develop the "entitlement" and "victimization" mindset needed to get blacks mentally imprisoned and dependent on all things government.

There is a third and little known component to this welfare scheme; convenience stores and big-box discount retailers, for many years, have been lobbying Democrats and Rinos and paying them millions to keep the welfare spigot wide open. Of the many places welfare recipients most likely shop and spend their monthly government stipend, Walmart is probably their number one destination and the biggest beneficiary of this setup. Even while many of their own employees are on food stamps and Medicaid, Walmart makes billions of dollars annually from their lobbying efforts to steer even more downtrodden welfare recipients to their stores.

For their reward, Democrats and Rinos are well compensated in this arrangement and in the process score points with the black community, poor Latinos, and whites by giving them the welfare scraps they so eagerly await the beginning of every month. In this symbiotic wealth redistribution scheme, discount and convenience stores make out with a massive flood of customers on the first of the month, and Democrats and Rinos get paid handsomely for their "services."

Oh, and the ones left footing the bill for all of this wonderful humanitarian "helping out" is the working middle-class taxpayers who are struggling to make ends meet themselves. But the gravy on the pork chop for the Democrat Party though, is that shiftless and lazy blacks will eagerly vote in droves for anti-American liberals to keep their handouts going and draining what's left of the middle-class.

Even more profoundly, the irony to all of this is that these exploited blacks, the vital cogs in this welfare kickback ploy, are not really sharing in the type of wealth that could drastically change their economic or financial situation. They are just conduits, like steel pipes, through which billions are being funneled. Welfare blacks cannot touch, nor can they ever access or have full use of this enormous amount of life-changing wealth in which they are an integral part of redistributing.

For their reward in this multibillion-dollar heist, these needy, manipulated, and used black pawns are relegated to a just a few hundred bucks a month, a food voucher, and substandard housing for their troubles. And at the end of the day when the dust settles, these go-nowhere blacks are still impoverished and waiting for the next first of the month to come.

In this sense, welfare redistribution is remarkably similar to a bank robbery in which white liberal Democrats steal billions and get paid millions for doing so, while complicit blacks involved in their elaborate welfare scheme are only being paid a few hundred bucks a month to drive the getaway car.

By the way, if you don't think that this is all just a racket and con job being played on hard-working Americans, just check out what SNAP stands for: *"Supplemental Nutritional Assistance Program."* This program is anything but, studies have been shown that the vast majority of welfare funds are not being used on healthy items as were initially intended, but are instead being spent at convenience stores and on things decidedly non-nutritional. *Hell, I've even seen auto parts stores advertising that they now accept ebt cards. What are welfare recipients doing there, are they gonna chomp on a muffler or radiator?*

This redirecting of funds intended for the purchasing of nutritional food for needy families is, again, due to liberal Democrats and the lobbying efforts of organizations such as the American Beverage Association (think Coke and other sodas), and the Snack Food Association (think potato chips and other greasy and sweet high-calorie goodies).

Lobbyists, working at the behest of these companies, are the ones responsible for taking the "nutritional" out of the SNAP program by arranging for greedy and corrupt politicians to bypass current laws and open up food stamp usage for much more than just the purchasing of healthy food items.

We all know that greasy junk food is like crack to lazy welfare recipients; this is why you will see a great many buffaloes and bison out shopping on "welfare day," usually occurring between the first and the fourth of each month.

To be honest, I don't think I've ever seen a thin welfare recipient in this country, even most of the pre-teen welfare children I've seen could be offensive linemen for the Los Angeles Rams. And with most of these welfare recipients, if you look closely, almost all of them have that same glazed-over look and blank stare indicative of a defeated and hollowed out soul, stripped of independence and resigned to their fate of not thriving but just existing.

Now, there's even more to this tragedy than meets the eye. The loosening of SNAP guidelines has also created a welfare-induced sedentary lifestyle among the poor, and thus, a perfect storm in which most of these recipients are overweight and unhealthy. This confluence of events has led to massive increases in juvenile diabetes, high blood pressure, and other diseases which disproportionately affects the black community. But there is always a silver lining to every dark cloud. This healthcare "crisis" dovetails quite nicely with the Medicaid program, another taxpayer-funded cash cow and "helping out" talking point for the Democrat Party.

So, in effect, white and black liberal Democrats have created an epidemic, an "obesity crisis" among blacks, by opening up the welfare program and making sure they are not only poor but eating unhealthy as well. Then these same "concerned" Democrats get on their media soapbox to tout that everyone needs "healthcare access" and to get enrolled in Obamacare, which is really just expanded Medicaid and another program rife with massive kickbacks, fraud, and corruption.

The rub here is that this convenient healthcare "crisis" allows a lot of pharmaceutical companies to also get into the wealth redistribbution fray, resulting in drug companies giving large donations to the campaigns of Democrats and Rinos to steer blacks and other minorties onto the new government healthcare system.

This flood of new medical "enrollees" ensures that these drug companies get a steady stream of chronically ill patients to inject with high priced drugs subsidized by, you guessed it, hard-working taxpayers. It's a win-win-win for all involved except for blacks who, because of their trifecta of sedentary lifestyles, bad eating habits and stress from poverty, have a lower life expectancy than just about every other race in America.

As to welfare's impact on young black women in inner cities, studies have shown that once a black and single woman has her first child, her being at risk of long-term poverty and long term dependency on government assistance is exponentially higher than those black women who avoided having a child while single. Nonetheless, Democrats promote welfare as a warm and caring blanket which blacks are to be swathed, a shelter of welcoming refuge in which an indoctrinated black suckling can snuggle up and tug at the teat of the party for all the sustenance needed for survival, but somehow never enough to thrive on.

You know, I really believed, naively, at one point that the numerous "helpful" government programs that Democrats advocated for and were ushering our people into were helping our communities. Having conservative values, I had always related this seemingly humanitarian gesture to the early struggles my family had gone through during my childhood. I believed then and still do now to a certain extent, that everyone in this country should have a safety net in times of financial need to help get them back onto their feet.

By all measures, our country is the most generous and compassionate on the face of God's green earth. Americans, mostly conservatives, give over $200 billion to charities each year. This is in addition to our country spending untold billions annually giving to other nations to help feed their people and rebuild their infrastructures. For 2018, right here at home, it is estimated that our government spent about 1.1 trillion on welfare; $668 billion on Medicaid and another $449 billion on other programs associated with welfare.

Even so, I didn't have the foresight in my youth to think about how blacks were being systematically stripped of self-worth, ambition, independence, and dignity by being on the government dole for such prolonged periods. Furthermore, welfare dependency has caused the majority of blacks never to demand anything, as other races have, of the party they support, such as the long-term underpinnings for prosperity like good schools, safe neighborhoods, and well-paying job opportunities.

In this sad state of affairs, a lot of blacks still view handouts as a viable way of existing within the greatest opportunistic and capitalist system on earth, never once stopping to think that their survival is solely dependent upon and subject to the whims of yearly legislative appropriations of money taken from others.

To further illustrate this, there was another video I came across of a rather large black woman who utterly destroyed a corner convenience store because either the merchant couldn't process her ebt card, or she just didn't have enough of a balance left for her purchase. Upon learning that her card wasn't being accepted, this crazed mastodon began to angrily and indiscriminately rake items off the shelves, creating havoc as a few hapless-looking men just stood idly by watching the carnage.

*Of note, our liberal Democrat-induced political correctness culture has made most males in our society powerless, providing no allowances, nor provisions, for men to physically restrain a woman, especially black women, because this "queenly" species is well protected by the Democrat Party's feminist "all men are evil" doctrine.

Probably a good thing for these men too, because I don't think they would've had enough force among them to bring this massive* *cornbread-eating, black-eyed-peas-snorting linebacker down any-ways.*

Anyway, it was just a disheartening and sorrowful sight to behold, a black woman so dependent on government assistance that she would resort to this sort of meltdown when the welfare spigot ran dry, albeit temporarily. Unfortunately, this woman's outburst was no anomaly, a lot of blacks are like welfare and section eight addicts continually looking for a hit from their pimp-daddy Democrat dealers: *"Man, can ya help a bro out with a little ebt or something? I need it, bro, got an Obama phone on ya?"*

These deeply dependent blacks need rehab badly, maybe they can try welfare anonymous or something: *"Hi everyone, my name is Tanishaweta, and I have had a welfare addition for ten years, and I am trying to get off my dependency...."*

You know, back in the day, a lot of blacks had a certain pride, and if they had to go on welfare or any other government assistance, they didn't want it to be known within the community and would look to get off of the program as soon as possible. But not too long after Dr. King's death in the late 1960s, there was a fundamental shift in the way blacks viewed welfare and all government assistance.

This change in attitudes among blacks can be directly attributed to the Democrat Party, which have liberalized away the stigma and shame of being on government assistance with their newly installed inclusiveness, tolerance, diversity, and equality social justice ideology. The result is that today, a lot of blacks not only want to go on welfare but will also unashamedly flaunt their stolen taxpayer funds, openly bragging about how they are working the system, not fully realizing that the system is actually working them and that their souls had been bought for the price of table scraps.

And to fund the welfare trough with even more taxpayer money, a lot of liberal Democrats spout the outrageous claim and narrative that poverty is the one problematic issue driving the violence we see among blacks today and that more welfare is sorely needed to address this issue.

This statement, as with most Democrat statements, would be inherently false of course, it just doesn't jive with how other races deal with being impoverished. Let's do a breakdown of welfare in America for context: There are roughly 41 million people on welfare in this nation, consisting of about 17.5 million whites, 8.9 million blacks, 11.25 million Hispanics and approximately 3.6 million people in other races who are on some form of government assistance, according to the Kaiser Poverty Foundation.

Now, I know, with these stats, blacks will scream and yell, *"See, told you more whites are on welfare!"* Fair enough, but just hold on there buckaroo!

Let's look at the "percentages" of welfare usage among the big players; whites are at 9%, blacks 22% and Hispanics at 20%. So, with the current population of whites in this country being at about 195 million, if they were at the same percentage, 22%, of welfare usage as blacks, there would be a humongous 42.5 million whites, alone, on welfare in this nation, eclipsing the entire amount of current welfare recipients among all other races combined.

While you are mulling over these numbers, and after the shock wears off, we'll just stroll on over to Owsley county in Kentucky to debunk the poverty-violence connection. The population in this county is about 98.5 % white, and the people there are dirt poor. I mean, some of these people probably still have outside toilets and possibly no indoor plumbing, and there's even a rumor going around that there's only one pair of socks for the entire population. This almost all-white town also suffers from stifling poverty, plenty of deadbeat welfare recipients and rampant drug use; crack, meth, weed, you name it, just like a lot of black communities, yet their violent crime rate is about half the national average.

How do we explain this? Why doesn't Billy shoot Jack just because he is penniless? Why aren't these whites indiscriminately shooting up their neighborhoods over drugs, cell phones, and sneakers and such?

So, with these myth-busting facts, this case study, in and of itself, demonstrably shows that poverty doesn't necessarily translate into genocidal-like numbers of homicides among whites, or any other race in this country, as it does among blacks.

It appears to me that many blacks are violent, perhaps, because they lack civility and God in their lives, coupled with the fact that most are easily swayed by short-term gains and immediate gratification, instead of slow, long-term economic stability and generational wealth building. This live-for-today mentality among blacks is borne out by the fact that we are probably the biggest consumers, but yet have the lowest household net worth in the nation.

Instead of buying houses and land, assets that build long-term wealth, the black community spends billions annually on things not rooted in appreciation and wealth building, like overly expensive autos and clothes, bling, numerous vacation trips, along with carrying high credit card debt. It is well known that a black man will buy a high-priced auto even if he has to stretch the monthly payments over twenty years. I will also note that there are a lot of blacks, who have been welfare dependent for decades, today, walking around with $800 iPhones while their children, some infants, are sporting $300 pairs of Jordans. I believe that this is commonly referred to as *"ghetto fabulous."*

To conclude this chapter I will say this, with welfare, blacks have been conditioned to always seek something for nothing and, thus, setting themselves up to always be exploited by white liberals. And because of their willingness to be kept like animals, the Democrat Party has created an addictive and never-ending welfare-induced poverty cycle among most blacks living on their inner city plantations, and have done so with a vice-like grip over the last fifty years and counting.

With that said, this control being exerted over an entire race could not have happened without the help of opportunistic and complicit Democrat blacks in leadership and influential positions. I know that, previously, we talked about black puppet leaders who were installed right after Dr. King's death in the latter part of the 1960s to guide blacks. However, today, many more "overseers" have been added to the Democrat Party's rolls, including black rappers, black anchors, and other black celebrities and sports stars.

Let's revisit this issue again because it just gnaws at me.

So, on to our next chapter....please.

Chapter Twelve

Black Millionaire Overseers

Ok, recap time: *After Democrats were able to pick up a few jungle fellas from the discount store "Slaves R Us" on the African continent, where blacks were eagerly bartered and sold by enterprising black chieftains, they put'em to work in the cotton fields of America's deep south in the 1600s.

*Democrats then beat their brand new slaves' asses until they, themselves, got their asses whipped in 1865 by Republicans and were forced, reluctantly, to free the black captives they had bred and sold in the deep south for centuries.

*President Abraham Lincoln then enacted the Reconstruction Act in 1865 to help these newly freed blacks recover from slavery. However, not be outdone, in return for his good deed, Democrats promptly killed him. *Oh well.*

*After killing Lincoln, Democrats would then create the KKK in 1866 and impose harsh Jim Crow Laws, Black codes, and segregation, along with many other restrictions on their former black slaves to let'em know they were still their property and "livestock."

*This animosity by Democrats against their black captives would go on for quite some time, until the 1930s, when the party figured out that even after lynching and whipping their former slaves' black asses for centuries, they could somehow get the black community's vote by simply offering welfare. *Who knew?* And like Rainbow Trout on a quite fruitful fishing trip, the black community eagerly snapped on the Democrat's dependency line and were hooked. *Welcome to the party!*

*But wait, there was hope arising with the 1950s and 1960s Civil Rights Movement when Dr. Martin Luther King Jr and Republicans, in 1964, finally got rid of the Jim Crow Laws and other restrictions hindering blacks in the south, giving them true independence.

*However, revengeful Democrats promptly, *you guessed it*, killed Dr. King just like they did Lincoln, and this time they installed their own black "Reverend leaders" *hello Jesse Jackson and Al Sharpton!* And shortly thereafter, distributed crack into black communities, *hello Marion Berry and Obama!*

*Democrats would then reach out to abortion-loving black women to cement their grip on the black community by offering more welfare and section eight, which they gladly accepted, of course. This sea change had the desired effect of destroying the black family and plunging the black community into chaos.

And so, here we are with more black overseers doing the bidding of white liberal Democrats, just to, uh, keep the new plantations going...wheeee?

◆◆◆

Now let's pause for a minute here and take note, there's a lot we can learn from great black intellectuals who actually lived during the era when Democrats were physically enslaving blacks; you know with whippings and leg irons and such. So, let's pay close attention to what Booker T Washington, who lived during this period, are saying about black "leaders" today:

"There is another class of colored people who make a business of keeping the troubles, the wrongs, and the hardships of the Negro race before the public. Having learned that they are able to make a living out of their troubles, they have grown into the settled habit of advertising their wrongs, partly because they want sympathy and partly because it pays. Some of these people do not want the Negro to lose his grievances, because they do not want to lose their jobs.

There is a certain class of race problem solvers who do not want the patient to get well, because as long as the disease holds out, they have not only an easy means of making a living, but also an easy medium through which to make themselves prominent before the public."

Booker T Washington, a black author, and educator, was born on a Democrat plantation and into slavery in 1856 and gained his freedom after Republicans won the Civil War in 1865. At nine years old, he took on whatever jobs he could find, such as coal mining and other menial labor to help out his impoverished family.

Although Booker dropped out of school early to seek work, he soon realized the importance of education and later enrolled in what is now called Hampton University. During his illustrious career, Booker would go on to teach other students and develop industrial training at his Tuskegee Industrial Institute in 1881 for other newly freed blacks. He would be instrumental in black progress during this period.

You see, in the 1800s, Booker T Washington believed in hard work and self-sufficiency, something many blacks lack today mainly because of their manipulation by black Democrat leaders. *So, again, If you seriously think the parties have somehow "switched," keep in mind, while reading this chapter, the era in which Booker T Washington, a former slave of Democrats, wrote the above statement about black puppets, and then compare to black "leaders" today shilling for Democrats in order to keep blacks underfoot and on inner city plantations.*

Working at the behest of white liberals, black puppets today are given power within the Democrat Party's political hierarchy and media structure as a reward for carrying out the party's bidding. Blacks at the top receive millions to spotlight any and all racial disturbances and grievances, perceived or not. Their job is to keep these issues going in the public eye and making sure blacks are emotionally upset, on the plantation, and their communities in chaos.

You will notice that there is a thread of duplicity and false brotherhood repeatedly occurring throughout this book because well-paid black Judases are selling out their own people at the drop of a hat to become the shackles and leg irons now being used by the Democrat Party to hold the black community captive. You will also notice that all of these black overseers today are always quick to sneer at and dismiss conservative blacks as Uncle Toms and coons while entirely ignoring black on black genocide and the real issues plaguing the black community.

Unfortunately, there is no shortage of these highly paid black social justice warriors who are being used extensively by the Democrat Party to sow racial discontent and discord among blacks. And because of their skin color, these liberal black overseers are somewhat imper-vious to any blowback from conservative whites and, thus, perform the heavy lifting of driving all racial narratives for their white masters.

The sole purpose and mission of Democrat black operatives are, by using race, to engage low-info blacks and steer them into liberal positions on policies and social issues, even if the policies and social agenda they are advocating for are detrimental to the black communi- ty and their well-being.

As I previously stated, white liberal Democrats have to use blacks to deceive other blacks to gain access into the heart of the black com-munity; much the way white slave owners used house Negroes against field negroes in the 1800s. Over the last five decades, blacks have been racially programmed by the civil rights "reverends" to harbor their own form of racism and bitterness against anything white or Republican, basing everything on skin color alone.

These duplicitous, conniving, and anti-American black overseers often tell rank and file blacks that there is oppressive and systemic racism at play in this country that's holding them down. Of course, this belies the fact that most of the members of the Black Caucus, other black leaders, and black celebrities saying this are millionaires living lavish lifestyles in white liberal neighborhoods, seemingly un-affected by the same oppressive, systemic racist institutions they warn other downtrodden blacks about.

In fact, members of the Black Caucus enjoy quite opulent life-styles while ignoring the daily, weekly, monthly, and yearly reports on poverty and black-on-black genocide in the districts they represent. Because of racial prejudices and unusually high sensitivity among the majority of the black community, these black puppets know that they can always blame white Republicans and the supposed lack of government funding as the cause for any and all issues within the inner cities that they, themselves, govern and blacks will fall for it every time.

To illustrate another type of black marionette that white liberal Democrats often use, there is a basketball player that comes to mind, and I won't say his name, who is a prime example of a low intellect

Democrat-controlled black. He is by no stretch of the imagination any Michael Jordan or anything, but there is no doubt that he will perhaps one day go down as one of the greats in NBA history when his career is finally over, which I hope is soon.

We will also note here that this player also will probably become a billionaire under the same oppressive "white supremacy system" he whines and bitches about so frequently. Recently, there was a big to-do over this baller "giving back" to his "community" when he do-nated a couple million dollars to help develop a school for black youths in the Cleveland area. On the surface this seems fantastic; however, we need to pump our brakes here because this NBA star is one of the best puppets liberal Democrats have in their arsenal at present.

Let me explain, first off, this school he is establishing is being heavily subsided by the taxpayers of Cleveland. So, as with most pub-lic schools these days, this initiative will probably turn out to be just another indoctrination cesspool of filth where transgenderism, homo-sexuality and other assorted ills will be foisted upon innocent and impressionable black children at some point by white liberals being handsomely paid to brainwash these newbies

Really, this "baller" could've saved his money and just send these kids on over to the Democrat National Convention for indoctrination, and be done with it.

Now, a couple of million spent by this fool seems like a grand ges-ture, however, it is not even a drop in the bucket compared to the over 22 trillion dollars spent over the last sixty years on the "war on pov-erty." A lot of that badly misspent and wasted moolah went towards ineffectual programs like welfare, section eight, WIC, and the Head Start debacle. Over the last five decades, a ton of taxpayer-funded aid has been given to benefit the black community to help them finan-cially until they could re-establish themselves. *Uh, yeah, that's it, uh, re-establish themselves. What a hoot!*

With the enormous amount of funds being spent on improving the situation of blacks, there hasn't been any real, meaningful change for most within the black community which, at this point, is just a vast, money-sucking black hole. *Oops, pun intended.*

With all of this money being drained from hardworking taxpayers, the lack of progress among blacks is not some unforeseen miscalculation on the Democrat Party's behalf. White liberals know that welfare handouts were never intended to lift anyone out of anything and were just enough sustenance for bare-bones survival. However, since the 1930s New Deal, black leaders have been encouraged by their Democrat masters to tout welfare as the silver bullet to prosperity for their communities.

Most blacks today remind me of that nest of baby birds, just chirping their damn heads off, waiting for the mother bird to come back with the worm. But unlike those young birds that eventually fly away on their own at some point, most blacks will sit in that welfare nest, grow old and die, still waiting on their Democrat momma bird to bring them that handout worm.

To reiterate, the greatest downfall of the majority of blacks in this country is that they, unlike every other race in this country, always need leaders, they need to be told what to do and how to do it, all the time, and this is where the Democrat Party excels, in exploiting this weakness. As for the "baller," I mean it is a nice soundbite and all, and great photo-op, for any athlete to say I did such and such or gave such and such to my community.

However, the systemic issues liberals have created within our communities will never be solved with just money alone because there are devastating internal and systemic issues internally, which require much more than just monetary relief to fix. The last fifty years have proven that the problems besieging black communities demand a concerted effort by blacks to change their thought process entirely; we must rebuild the family unit, have respect for each other, and establish a healthy and safe environment that promotes education, God, a strong work ethic, and moral character.

In that regard, blacks who have voted for Democrats the last fifty years, can go right ahead on and continue to do so for the next eight hundred years, but the things needed to repair the damage to our communities, which I just mentioned, will never be found by voting for Democrats, nor can these things be found on the plantations called inner cities.

Now back to this "baller," this fool could give half or even all of his earnings to the inner cities, and it wouldn't matter one iota. Because the "victimization" and "entitlement" ideology he espouses and teaches to the impressionable black youths he mentors will poison and mentally imprison these young charges and undo all of his so-called "charitable" work.

For instance, this muscular but whiny, and feminist, "baller" goes on television and proclaims that racism is holding "us" down as blacks and "we" blacks can't get ahead because of "systemic racism" and police brutality. He says this as if he lives within the same depressed Democrat inner cities as the blacks to whom he is speaking. And you would think by his angry tone that this fool had experienced something personally regarding law enforcement to make him go off this way.

But, strangely, this baller has never been accosted or arrested by police and is revered by whites and blacks alike in the same "white supremacist" country he detests and wants other blacks, who haven't made or got his kind of money, to hate. Unfortunately, starstruck black youths will listen to their hero's rhetoric and start being conditioned to feel "less than," and to feel that the liberal Democrat manufactured "institutional racism" is real.

And although their "hero" will go out and buy them backpacks and sneakers, and even give some money towards their "schooling," the structural damage to the psyche and mental foundation of these black youths will have been done, and in some irreversibly.

The material things the baller has purchased will not help develop the attitudes and self-confidence that young blacks desperately need to become self-sufficient and self-sustaining men and women of honor, integrity, and character. And by this measure, this baller's "give back" boils down to nothing more than just table scraps, and another handout with a side order of victimhood for black youths who will grow up holding onto the same racial attitudes and anti-American views he seems to have of this country.

Sadly, these youths, under his tutelage, will then use these excuses as the reasons that they cannot progress in this country. The relatively new use of sports stars by Democrats, in relating to black inner-city youths who idolize their sports heroes, their wealth and the trappings that come along with it, has proven to be one of the most effective ways for their party to bring young recruits aboard their platform.

Of note: In the 1940s and 1950s, Jackie Robinson, a Republican and sports hero, was fighting against Democrat imposed Jim Crow laws, segregation, discrimination and Black Codes in the south. And we must also remember that protests by Tommie Smith and Carlos Johns during the 1968 Olympics in Mexico were also against the oppression of Democrats,

Today, in an unusual twist, the same protests by these black sports stars are being used by white liberal Democrats against Republicans, the ones that actually helped the same black sports stars in the 1950s and 1960s fight the Democrat Party for their rights.

I ask myself, how can blacks today be so stupid? It is just so surreal in that back in those days, black stars weren't being used to promote anything for wealthy liberals. This thought was the furthest thing from Democrats' minds, who along with their KKK affiliates, were too busy beating and lynching Negroes in the deep south ever to consider using blacks in this manner.

So, to really think about it, in the 1950s and 1960s, I would suppose that it would have been quite odd, indeed, for liberal Democrats to have a commercial spot with a nigger hanging like an oversized pomegranate from an oak tree as a disembodied voice-over intoned about the tensile strength of rope from Home Depot.

A truthful commercial spot like this in the 1950s and 1960s probably wouldn't exactly spur massive black voting or endear the black community to Democrats, at all. No, the Democrat Party first had to clean up their atrocities, and image, of the 1600s, 1700s, 1800s, and 1900s to get black influential stars on board.

But, just how would they do that? How would they erase the enslavement, beatings, and lynchings they had committed against blacks for centuries? It would be a nearly impossible task to accomplish; there were history books and all, ya know. *Hey, wait a min-u-et! White Democrats figured it out and quickly. Most blacks don't read, so tell 'em that the parties "switched." Yeah, tell 'em that, even though*

Democrats were the only ones whipping slaves' asses and lynching over 4000 blacks from the 1800s to 1968, that they stopped, gave it up for lent, and it was the Republicans who were now their oppressors. Yeah, uh, that's it, it was Republicans! They did it!

Hold on, wait a minute though, this is stupid, blacks are way too smart and wouldn't fall for that hocus pocus jive right? Uh, er, oh yes they would, ever heard of the Bell Curve? Never, ever, underestimate the low intellect and lack of brainpower of the black mind, son!

The switch thingy was a gem and sleight of hand by white liberals who just spoketh it and it was made so. To make this thing butter, most oh so trusting low-info and welfare-dependent blacks didn't even bother reading anything, like they ever did, to validate this "switched" claim!

So, today with the Democrat Party's image being wiped clean like Hillary's servers, it's quite the different story on the usage of black stars by white liberals. If you will, picture this for a moment:

A multimillionaire liberal Democrat black sports star who has multiple mansions, a plethora of expensive and fancy cars and probably a few butlers and maids, suddenly picks a day to go slumming and descends from his ivory tower roost.

He then goes into the inner city and leads a black protest march against the supposedly "racist police" and "systemic, institutionalized racism" by having poor inner-city blacks dutifully follow him up and down the street shouting that they are all oppressed and that cops are hunting blacks to no end.

I mean, to them, the cops are just a shooting blacks all over the streets; on sidewalks, in cafes, diners, malls, churches, in the bathrooms, everywhere, even at the chicken joint for God's sake! These "persecuted" and "hunted" blacks get no rest from cops, in fact, most police agencies in black communities run out of bullets weekly while shooting at blacks. And, then there's the massive backlog on bullets in some police precincts within most black communities because cops there have also run out from all of their hunting of blacks. But no worries, these officers are being trained to throw rocks at blacks, sharp ones too!

Ok, that was fun, but let's get back on track here. After this march against law-enforcement, the indignant and self-righteous baller gets back into his Bentley and rides off. This SOB then goes back to Beverly Hills, where he is residing in a gated and secure mansion. There, he relaxes near his pool among his wealthy white liberal Democrat friends who pay him quite handsomely for his services, such as the one he just performed.

But back in the "hood," after this march for "equality" had concluded, the dirt poor, "protesting," no-pot-to-piss-in-and-no-window-to-throw-it-out-of inner city blacks went right back to their impoverished, drug-dealing, crime-infested neighborhoods, where the game of homicidal music chairs would then commence once more. The thought never crosses their little inactive minds that this baller fully and unconditionally supports the party whose policies is causing the unfavorable living conditions within the black communities that he is leading them in the march against.

Now, I'm not telling anyone to dislike this NBA star because maybe, just maybe, he doesn't know that he is a pawn of the party that enslaved his people, just like most of the other wealthy blacks who shill for the Democrat Party, but I wouldn't bet on it.

With that said, I'm now gonna double down on black puppets. Let's take a quick peek at two rappers; one is "Pimpin," and one is laid back and sipping on "gin and juice." They are both all-in, flaming liberal Democrats and really quite vociferous and fierce defenders of anything surrounding their party.

With these two quite successful rappers, when it comes to any racially divisive issues, they are everywhere white liberal Democrats want'em to be. These house Negroes are like the one-two punch of black manipulation. Just for ha ha's, let's break down their situations for a moment because they are both excellent examples of deceitful and traitorous "brothers" who would sell out their own for a ham hock and plate of collard greens.

They both came from rough, hardscrabble, inner-city neighborhoods, leaving behind the usual liberal Democrat grab bag of goodies of poverty, poor schools, violent gangs, drug dealing, and rampant homicides. *Ok, you say, what a lovely story, that's nice, and they have street cred too, fantastic, but's let's just pause for a minute there skippy.*

The surprising thing here is that the inner cities these two rappers both emerged from haven't changed one iota in the decades since they left. Democrats are still running these same cities, and yes there are still a lot of homicides, gang violence, and drug dealing with crippling poverty, subpar schools, and high dropout rates ravaging the community.

These two, uh, gentle and demure "rappers" somehow managed, by the grace of God, or by hook or crook, to get out of their respective dreadful and homicidal inner cities. And when they had accomplished this magnificent feat, what did they do? Well, they promptly turned around and aligned themselves with white liberals, which resulted in the both of them becoming multimillionaires and darlings of the Democrat Party.

Today, to "give back" to the black community, these two rappers are rabid supporters and advocates for the same Democrats whose policies are still causing the conditions in the inner cities that they were fortunate enough to escape and other poor blacks are still suffering from. *Do your head hurt yet? Mine do!*

I mean, old "Pimpin" and his "B" queen even campaigned during the 2016 presidential election alongside Hillary, the woman whose husband passed a bill in the 1990s that resulted in the imprisonment of many little inner-city Negroes, which she had then called "super-predators."

The Clintons put so many niggers in prisons during the 1990s that visitors to these correctional facilities back then thought they were at a BET awards show every time they arrived! So, how in the hell can any black in their right mind even try to reconcile the hypocrisy and duplicity by these two rappers, these "brothers," on display here? I certainly cannot, and I won't, but most other blacks can and will. These two incredible rap "stars," and gems of the black community have a massive following of uneducated blacks who are mostly piss poor and still living in dangerous inner cities but will hang onto every word these black overseers say.

The loyalty to white liberals by these rappers is no coincidence; just about every black who has gotten wealthy in Hollywood and the music industry is being controlled by Democrats and must do their bidding to retain their status. And talk about wealth? Old Pimpin and his Queen "B" even had a nursery built that cost anywhere from 500,000 to 1 million dollars! *You heard me, 1 million for a nursery, you know, where you put your little chil'ren in.*

But wait a minute, say it isn't so, these two black puppets of white liberals who absolutely adore their own precious children and will give them anything in the world, somehow supports the Democrat Party, the same party that exterminates over 200,000 other black children every year. *How can we reconcile this?*

I guess, for highly privileged black folks such as these, there just isn't any more room in that quite splendid nursery for a few of these, uh, commoners. These unworthy, murdered black children are the throwaways, just collateral damage in their war against America, but their kids are all snug and warm with not a care in the world. With these high-falutin liberal black Democrats, seems that their elitist infants are the in thing nowadays and are above every other commoners' children. These new house niggers, and overseers, have learned well from their white masters, indeed.

Whoaaa, went off on a tangent there, didn't I? What was I talking about now? Oh, that's right, now I remember!

Now, there are other well-known rappers on the cusp of becoming overseers for the Democrat Party, like the one who is as cold as an ice cube and currently melting like Frosty-the-Snowman from trying to please Democrats. And there's another rapper who was worth a solid fifty cents at one time but is being steadily devalued and is now currently at about forty-five cents from white liberal pressure.

The very effective ploy, by white liberal Democrats, of using wealthy blacks to herd the masses didn't just start with these black stars and certainly won't end with them either. For the origin of black overseers, I refer you back to the 1930s again, when the majority of blacks had migrated over to the Democrat Party because of welfare.

If you remember, it was during this period in which white liberals plied black figureheads, influential within their community, with political and financial incentives to bring the black vote over to their party. And in return for their traitorous deeds, these black "leaders" were handsomely paid, and Democrats even managed to throw a few crumbs at rank and file blacks, sorta like feeding the pigeons.

Today, droppings from the welfare table serve to keep blacks in the inner cities distracted, dependent, and suffering from the ravages of policies that have adversely affected their long-term stability and growth. It's like giving a terminally ill patient a morphine drip for cancer, it doesn't do anything to cure the disease, it only masks the pain of what's killing them and making their illness a little bit easier to bear in their final days.

Over the last five decades, the quite robust "racism" industry has spawned a lot of black millionaires in this country. Just look around at all the vaunted black "institutions" such as the once black NAACP, now a white liberal cesspool, and the wealthy civil rights "Reverends" such as Jesse Jackson, and Al Sharpton, who have been in the so-called "trenches" working for blacks for over forty years and are now multimillionaires themselves for their "labor." What have any of these do-nothings actually accomplished for the black community in their decades-long toiling in the "racism" fields?

But to further reward these dutiful black overseers for their work, white liberal Democrats, shockingly, recently gave old Reverend Al his own "show" on one of their networks. *To me, this man is as dumb as a flowerpot, and watching his show is like watching an angry cat trying to eat meow mix with chopsticks. I must say that was about ten minutes of my life I'll never get back.*

Meanwhile, the billions and billions pouring into black communities via various social programs to "help" downtrodden black victims, who supposedly cannot find their way out of poverty without this intervention, have done absolutely nothing for the stagnant, and now regressive black community. It is no coincidence that black puppets and black organizations were all put in place some time ago by the Democrat Party with the clear intentions of keeping rank and file blacks living on the hope and promise of good things to come tomorrow.

But the rub here is that the good things of tomorrow never comes for these blacks, and wasn't ever supposed to. Oh, but when every election rolls around, black leaders and white Democrat candidates tell ever hopeful blacks that there will be a chicken in every pot, a rooster crowing in every yard and that tomorrow the sun will come out and shine brightly upon everyone.

However, when all the campaign hoopla have subsided, and their black or white candidate elected and confetti swept aside, once again, duped blacks peek inside their pots early in the morning only to find that there's no chicken inside, it's still dark outside, and there's no damn rooster crowing in the yard. Nevertheless, most blacks are resilient and not too bright and, come next election, will repeat this cycle all over again.

To keep blacks believing in this alternate reality, and to smooth over their constant lies, the Black Pimp Caucus and other black organizations, along with the "Civil Rights Reverends, tell blacks to hold on because they are working diligently on their issues. Once all of the reassuring speeches are over with, and the black community placated, these black overseers just go right back to ignoring blacks and their issues as usual as they go about the business of endorsing and shilling for any and every other social cause on the left.

Even more disturbing, black puppets within the Democrat Party have cannibalized the Civil rights Movement, along with the lynchings and the bartering and selling of blacks during slavery. Atrocities committed against blacks for centuries are now being used as a foundation for other liberal Democrat social causes such as transgenderism, homosexuality, and illegal immigration.

This blatant perversion and prostitution of the black Civil Rights Movement is a slap-in-the-face to the black community and makes a mockery of the trials and tribulations endured by true black pioneers like Rosa Parks and Dr. King. In the 1960s, Malcolm X spoke of blacks such as these, who are used by white liberal Democrats in this manner to control emotional and ignorant blacks politically. *To this day, I firmly believe that this would be one of Malcolm's many statements on Democrats that would get him silenced.*

Today, looking at the make-up of the Congressional Black Caucus, there aren't any members who are conservatives or Republicans. Instead, there are only emotional, loud-mouthed, and unintelligent liberal Democrat lapdogs, especially the black women, who give short shrift to the minority communities they supposedly represent. Some of these black do-nothings have been in office for nearly forty years with nary a budge in the plight of blacks that are living in squalor and third world conditions in the districts that they supposedly represent.

If you look at wealthy Black Caucus members, they are all black Democrats who unabashedly and eagerly support and promote illegal immigrants over their own people, not giving a damn how blacks in their community fare with this Hispanic invasion.

These arrogant members of the Black Caucus, and other wealthy black overseers like them, are complicit in the never-ending and problematic issues plaguing unsafe and dangerous drug-dealing Democrat inner cities.

With that said, and to conclude this chapter, if you believe that these black puppets are something, well wait until you get a gander at the ultimate betrayal of blacks and their spirituality, which lies squarely at the feet of the devious liberal Democrat black pastors or, shall we say, "men of the cloth."

Let's talk about it. I want everyone to say Amen, and turn the page, please.

Chapter Thirteen

Democrat Churches, Dens of Iniquity

Ok, a quick and short recap: *Democrats took hold of blacks in the 1600s, lost them in the late 1800s, but regained them back in the 1930s with welfare.

* Democrats then almost lost their black property again in the 1960s, but held on; it was a close one! They had to kill Lincoln, Kennedy, Malcolm X, and Dr. King to accomplish this, but hey, sacrifices must be made.

*Today, defying all logic, the Democrat Party has enhanced its political weaponry using descendants of their former slaves and now have a plethora of black women, black congressmen, black sports stars, black rappers, black celebrities, black organizations, and of course, black Reverends on board the liberal Democrat train!

I don't know about you, but my head is spinning like the exorcist, but onward we go.

Malachi Chapter 3 Verse 18 KJV: "Then shall ye return, and discern between the righteous and the wicked, between him that serveth God and him that serveth him not."

Today, the two things most pervasive in just about any black community in this nation are churches and liquor stores, and you can find them on just about every street corner within most inner cities. In some strange way, these two just seems to go together in the black community. I mean, they both deal in spirts, really. Anyways, things have become so twisted in black churches, most blacks don't seem to know the difference between the two or which way is up anymore. What is the reason for this confusion?

You see, going all the way back to slavery, blacks were always so spiritual, right? Well, not so much nowadays, the community has certainly changed. Still, I know that God is always good, and it is my sincere belief that his word is written in stone and is immovable. I also believe that there are many decent pastors, black and white and whatever, doing his work and faithfully toiling in his service to bring salvation to the masses.

However, as to blacks in particular, there are those claiming they come in the name of God, yet pervert the Bible and revise scriptures for self-enrichment and political expediency. Surprisingly, just about all of the black "pastors" within inner cities across this nation are liberal Democrats and have a strong belief in an ideology wholly incompatible and inconsistent with the Bible and God's word.

Fortunately, there are real black Christians who are smart enough to never conflate true men of God with these sanctimonious, money-changing liberal Democrat serpents who have set up shop in the black community and posing as men of the cloth.

I will posit this truth right now; there is no way any pastor can ever serve the true and living God and still be a Democrat because the Bible clearly states : *"It is impossible to serve two masters."* The Good Book and the scriptures speaks specifically against homosexuality, abortions; the taking of life, and these are core tenets of the Democrat Party's platform.

Nonetheless, every Sunday morning from their pulpits, duplicitous black 'reverends' attempt to simultaneously serve God and their white liberal masters while steering their faithful and obedient flock onto the immoral based platform and ideology of the Democrat Party.

"Matthew Chapter 24 Verse 11 "And many false prophets shall rise, and shall deceive many."

Now, you would think that these "holy" men in crime-ridden and broken black communities across the nation would be more like Dr. King and help morally deficient blacks restore the lost spirituality that a lot of them once had in the 1950s and 1960s.

Well, let me tickle your trousers for a minute and share with you a true story about an experience I recently had with a pastor of a local church. About a year ago, I started attending this newly built Pentecostal Church, which was a quite spacious and impressive temple that had all the accouterments a black church would typically have such as drums, guitars, a piano, organs, and a soulful and harmonious choir.

The pastor seemed righteous and holy, and I could discern nothing untoward about his preaching or belief in God. So, I began going to their services on a somewhat regular basis and was really starting to feel the spirit along with some of the other blacks in the church, who shouted, screamed, and literally ran around the aisles like Usain Bolt on Red Bull, all the while praising the lord.

With this church, there was a very welcoming, warm, and happy atmosphere where this feeling of brotherhood and togetherness permeated the air, making me feel as if I was part of one big happy family. I was really enjoying myself; it was nice being around like-minded spiritual "brothers" and "sisters," in this holy refuge and sanctuary of sorts. And to top this all off, this church only passed the collection plate around once. *Did you hear what I said, once! ... have mercy! This was almost insane, it was like these people weren't black or something, or either they hadn't received the black churches' fleecing-the-sheep-memo yet. Their email server must've gone down. I mean, what was wrong with these people?*

Most black churches pass their plates around endlessly; before service, during service, and after service, even in the parking lot. The old, well-worn collection plate is usually passed around for the "building fund," for the "choir," for the deacon's wife who just had gallbladder surgery, and for mother Johnson who fell and broke her hip while cooking some black-eyed peas the other day, etc. Also, most black churches nowadays have gone high tech and have ATMs located inside, and will even take checks, credit, and ebt cards as payment for your salvation.

I recall some years ago when my younger brother told me about the time he investigated a new church that he and his wife had found at the time, excited at the prospect of finally having a spiritual home. However, upon his initial visit, this church directed both my brother and his new wife to the "financial" office where they were promptly given forms to fill out, which would disclose their assets and income in order for the church to determine their weekly "contributions." Needless to say, my brother declined their membership at the time and never went back, citing irreconcilable differences.

So now, it was refreshing for me to have found a church that wasn't just about money. Indeed; my place of worship seemed to fit the bill, in the respect that it stopped me from having to go through the hassle of getting change for my $5 bill on the way to church. Now I could just put the entire amount in the plate in one fell swoop. Life was good, praise the Lord, and this church was seemingly a blessing for me.

Just about everything seemed too good to be true, I should have knocked on wood because soon after I started attending, there would appear a crack in this "holiness" veneer that would end my spiritual contentment with this church. This dash of cold reality would jolt me out of my newfound religious-home stupor, diffusing my happiness and bursting my "brotherhood" bubble.

You see, with each service held during February, black history month, church leaders would pick out a notable such as Harriet Tubman, Frederick Douglas or one of the many other distinguished blacks in our nation's history in acknowledgment of their achievements. They would then display their biography and accomplishments upon a large screen for the congregants' enjoyment and edification.

I thought that this was a nice gesture by the members, to recognize the contributions of these black pioneers who had given so much for blacks to have the freedoms they enjoy today. Well, these feel-good moments and comradery that I had experienced and shared with my spiritual "brothers" and "sisters," would crash and burn just as the church was in the process of wrapping up its celebration of black history month.

It seems that while the pastor was away, the happy deacons had taken it upon themselves, or so I thought, to display a large image of a toothy and grinning Obama upon the church's screen in celebration of his "achievements," which really just boiled down to him being elected president while black.

I was stunned that the imagery of this man, who is diametrically opposed to Christianity and has extolled the virtues of the Islamic faith every chance he's gotten, would be shown in a building that was supposedly wholly dedicated to worshiping God and the Christian faith. Seeing this blasphemous and decidedly anti-Christian imagery displayed on the screen above me and being adored by most of the smiling and fawning black congregants, I just couldn't bring myself to stomach this treachery.

It was hard for me to reconcile this egregious misconduct by the deacons with the outstretched and forlorn-looking figure nailed to the cross in the near corner of the church. Feeling a bit numb and betrayed, I became furious and immediately removed myself from their premises.

About two weeks later, old pastor himself showed up at my home and relieved at his presence, I begin thinking to myself that maybe he had been unaware of what had transpired while away and was now coming over to let me know that there had been a gross error in judgment by his deacons, and to apologize. Well, to my surprise, it didn't exactly turn out that way in the hour that we spent together in conversation.

This particular pastor seemed to be all on board with what his deacons had done. This revelation would come as an eye-opener for me because, here was a supposedly God-fearing man sitting right next to me who would forsake the scriptures and Bible to align himself with that which was unholy and deviant, just because of skin color.

After my initial shock had worn off, I regained my composure and pressed on, fully explaining to him the reason for my displeasure and why I had left so abruptly that Sunday. In the heat of our conversation, I pointed out many historical facts to back up my stance and reasoning for my dislike of the Democrat Party and their anti-Christian ideology.

Unmoved, the pastor just stared blankly into space and mumbled something about Fox News and propaganda, along with regurgitating some other liberal talking points from CNN. It seems that "Fox News" is the go-to reflex response for blacks to defend Democrats.

However, the pastor was really taken aback, and visibly shaken, when I dropped the other shoe, blindsiding him with the fact that I had eagerly voted for and liked President Trump immensely. I went even further in telling him that I felt that Trump's presidency was the best thing to happen to blacks since the Lincoln administration.

I explained that Trump was the president mentioning God and Jesus regularly in his speeches and that he was the one protecting Christianity from the onslaught of the Democrat Party's anti-Christian ideology. This "man of the cloth" grimaced as if he had just sucked on a lemon as I continued admonishing him that it was president Trump who wanted prayers in schools, holding daily prayer meetings at the Whitehouse and inviting Pastors, black and white, over to lead these services.

I then went on to further contrast Trump and his predecessor, Obama, the only president in our nation's history ever to hold gay pride parties in the white house while pushing to have prayers taken out of schools. And finally, I exposed the fact that Obama never held daily prayers or any meetings with Christians in the Whitehouse and actually wanted their rights struck down. But after I had finished laying out the facts as they were, this blank staring, shell-shocked pastor just looked at me and repeated what most blacks believe nowadays, *that Obama has done a lot of great things.*

Of course, he couldn't name any of these "great things" Obama had done but the peaceful and loving holy man didn't stop there, he also hoped that Herr Commandant Mueller, the Democrats' special prosecutor, investigates Trump until he completes his mission of "finding" something, anything, to take him down. Again, this moment was surreal for me, almost like an out-of-body experience, because even though President Trump is hard at work protecting and fighting for Christianity and America, this "forgiving and loving" pastor didn't give a damn, he just wanted him removed from office to quench his immoral, liberal Democrat directed bloodlust.

In further conversation, my guest actually doubled down on his loyalty to Democrats, even going so far as to state that everything I previously told him was all propaganda and lies because what I had said wasn't what he had seen or heard on CNN or NBC. He just knew in his heart that Trump was racist, a Russian spy, and a misogynist working against blacks, women, Hispanics and Muslims, and everyone else in this country because this is what these networks had told him.

But under repeated questioning, this pastor couldn't come up with any evidence that would validate or support any of these wild assertions. I was stunned by his position, to say the least, and argued that he was on the wrong side of God and the Bible that he preached from every Sunday morning. I made it abundantly clear that his misguided support of Obama and the Democrat Party, and the bitterness he held in his heart for Trump, would lead to his spiritual ruination.

The now quite perturbed and flustered pastor, to establish his bona fides and authority in religious matters and to enlighten me on his extensive biblical "education," shared with me with how he was this great learned theologian who had studied in the Masonic Temples. At the time he had said this with an air of importance, with grandiose flare, as if this revelation meant a hill of beans to me. It didn't, but I politely acknowledged his religious "training" with a reflexive nod.

This "Holy-Ghost-filled" pastor had been like the Rock of Gibraltar, firmly and blindly entrenched in his loyalty, not to God and his word, but to Obama and the Democrat Party and there was to be no moving him from his position, at all.

After our conversation concluded, and the pastor had left, I pondered to myself, what if Jesus himself had come back today and run for the office of president in this country? *Can you just imagine the attacks upon him by the Democrat Party and this pastor?* As a presidential candidate, Jesus' advice on the campaign trail would, of course, include loving your fellow man as you would yourself, and abide by the Ten Commandments, all of them. Jesus' platform would also include the hot-button political messages of anti-abortion and anti-homosexuality, which would certainly strike at the heart of the Democrat Party's crowned jewels of social causes like Roe vs. Wade and newly cemented same-sex marriage.

Democrats, especially the black caucus, would all be out in

full force on CNN, NBC, MSNBC and other liberal networks in a frenzy. Can't you just hear'em now: *"This Jesus is a threat to our democracy; this is not who we are! "He is trying to destroy America and our ideals. This Jesus is a white supremacist and heartless!"* *" He is against women's rights and doesn't share this nation's values. "*

Then, of course, you would have the Asian weave-wearing, loud-mouthed black woman, or other dyke-looking liberal black women, along with their deranged liberal white woman counterparts scream-ing hysterically: *"It's a woman right to choose! This Jesus is gon-na set us back sixty years! He will destroy same-sex marriage and abortions, he's unfit and doesn't have the right temperament. He is colluding with the Russians! We cannot, in no way, let this sandal-foot mother...fker near the Whitehouse!"*

And just like when he had first made his appearance on earth, Jesus wouldn't fare so well today with either white or black liberals, nor their liberal media smear machinery. Democrats would all un-mercifully crucify him all over again, and this time with CNN and other salivating liberal media outlets gleefully covering it with neatly edited outtakes and soundbites. There would be breathless, and emo-tionally worked-up pundits detailing the many ways calamity would befall the nation if Jesus were ever to be elected to office instead of them stopping and nailing him to the cross.

Now just to be fair to the pastor to whom I had spoken, after our intriguing conversation had ended, I didn't come away with the impression of him being a dyed in the wool serpent like many of the other blacks in the inner cities masquerading as men-of-the-cloth. In-stead, after our conversation, I felt that he was just another misguided, brainwashed, and conditioned black who had been on the Democrat plantation far too long, trapped in the same liberal identity politics echo chamber which I had been subjected.

I had picked up, during our hour-long conversation, that he had been completely caught off-guard by a God-fearing and conservative black, a rarity today, and was emotionally and mentally unable to en-tertain any other reality than what the Democrat Party had created for him. I was a unicorn, something that wasn't supposed to be in existence, a figment of his imagination.

It seemed to me that, although this pastor was supposedly a righteous and holy man and loving what was just and Godly, his unflinchingly blind loyalty to the Democrat Party and its ideals and values had made it impossible for him to see past his skin color. With decades of conditioning, this pastor had been made to be highly susceptible to racial triggers that liberal Democrats have used to brainwash him, and most other blacks, into disobeying and forsaking God's written words. His "blackness" would not allow him even to entertain the thought that the party he follows, and the black former president he worships, represents that which is immoral, corrupt, and evil.

However, I can clearly see how some of these "holy men" can become so sidetracked though; religion, in a relatively short period, in this country has become a multibillion-dollar industry, and most prosperity preachers such as TD Jakes, Creflo Dollar, and Joel Osteen, now realize that the more churches adapt their scriptures and messaging to the secular world of liberal Democrats, the more prosperous they will become.

You know, I remember some time ago when it seemed like black preachers were humble and upstanding pillars of the black community, trying to live their lives as they preached and aligning themselves with that which was righteous and Godly. Preachers back then, except for a few, like Reverend Ike, were in the religion business solely to do the work of the Lord, spread his word and save souls. Nowadays most pastors, white and black, preach only for fame, power, and prosperity, and the adulation of their faithful congregants.

As a result, many churches, especially the megachurches you see today, are nothing more than money grabbing whorehouses run by former pimps and hustlers who prey on mostly emotional black women to fill their coffers. Pastors in these dens of iniquity, all teach that you should give, tithe, and sow your seed and the Lord will reward you abundantly but, oftentimes, the pastor is the only one who's being rewarded, and abundantly from your sown seed; he's the one reaping your harvest. I know that some of the poor and faithful churchgoing fellas have gotta be asking themselves: *"How come I gotta give pastor all my money? I am driving a 1983 Buick that still has chrome bumpers, while old pastor is leaning to the side and bumping a brand new Mercedes. Heck, he even went out and got two of 'em, one for his wife too."*

Today, the doctrine of most black churches have become deeply intertwined with the ideology of liberal Democrats, incorporating the deceptive and immoral-based platform of inclusiveness, tolerance, diversity, and equality in their services, thus, allowing homosexuals in their choirs and other places of leadership.

This liberalized indoctrination, foisted upon congregants in black churches, is being done by black preachers who are deliberately omitting passages from the Bible and misinterpreting scriptures to allow this perversion to flourish, unchecked and unchallenged, in their places of "worship," all in exchange for wealth and influence in certain political circles.

Furthermore, not only do a lot of black pastors in the inner cities steer their black "flock" to white liberal Democrat serpents but will also aid in setting up bus transportation services on "election day" to get their brainwashed black sheep to the polls to vote for'em. These inner city hustlers, falsely portraying themselves as men of the cloth, also will quickly turn against any real man of God opposing any of the Democrat Party's immoral platform or ideology.

President Trump recently had a few black preachers over to the Whitehouse for prayer meetings, and to have a discussion on how to adequately address the ills which have been adversely affecting the black community for decades. But with this news, suddenly a few of these black inner city "holy men" came out of the woodwork like enraged and demonic cockroaches to attack Trump and these men of God.

They lashed out publicly with name-calling and condemnation, not caring that it was very unseemly of so-called "men of God," and gentle "Christians," to exhibit this kind of improper behavior toward their fellow Christians. With their actions, the real masters that these black "pastors" served were now in plain sight for all to see. The black community is rife with these evil and wicked wolves in sheep clothing, who at the drop of a hat will entirely ignore all of Christ's teachings for political and financial gains.

Matthew Chapter 7 Verse 15 "Beware of false prophets, which come to you in sheep's clothing, but inwardly they are ravening wolves."

Matthew Chapter 24 Verse 24: "For there shall arise false Christs, and false prophets, and shall shew great signs and wonders; insomuch that, if it were possible, they shall deceive the very elect."

For many of these Democrat blacks masquerading as pastors today, Jesus Christ and the Bible mean absolutely nothing because they don't even believe in God themselves, and their churches are nothing more than fronts for money laundering and indoctrinating emotional, non-reading, low info blacks into the Democrat Party's ideology. These black vultures see their Bibles and scriptures as nothing more than props in their perverted Sunday sermons, just tools of the trade to hustle and fleece their very obliging and easily led black sheep.

I believe that long ago, most inner city black "reverends" made a pact with Satan to use their churches to brainwash and usher blacks, mostly black women, into the liberalized and alternate anything-goes "Christian faith" that their white liberalized masters have created. After the assassination of Dr. King in the late 1960s, many of these black "holy" men were given a mission, a directive by their white Democrat masters that the party needed black "churchgoers, especially," and to do whatever was necessary, to obfuscate and mislead about the truth of the living God and keep their "property" on the plantation.

Along with this duplicity by the black reverends, there has even been an ongoing effort by white and black liberals to disparage the Bible and diminish its teachings by promoting the idea that the scriptures were used during slavery to hold blacks down. Nothing could be further from the truth; many slaves, while in bondage to Democrats, used the Bible to learn how to read and, in the process, would come to know of the one true and living God.

And with their faith, these African slaves had the strength to endure their horrific treatment and time spent in captivity. The Bible and its scriptures would be the pillar and rock upon which a lot of black slaves would cling to while suffering at the hands of Democrats during slavery.

"Exodus 6:6 | Wherefore say unto the children of Israel, I am the LORD, and I will bring you out from under the burdens of the Egyptians, and I will rid you out of their bondage, and I will redeem you with a stretched out arm, and with great judgments:"

It must be said, the true church of God has always had a positive impact on the black community, with there being a direct correlation between the positive state of blacks with the majority worshipping God, as opposed to the negative state of blacks with the majority turning away from God. And, if we were to take a peek back to when Dr. King was alive and leading marches in the 1950s and 1960s, the black community was much more spiritual and less criminal versus today, where we see that the black community is much more criminal and less spiritual.

Truth be told, Democrats really prefers that there be no God or Bible in the black community, and if there were to be any religion in the black community, that they would be the ones controlling this "spirituality" of blacks.

In this sad state of affairs within the black community today, it is unfortunate that under the direction of Democrats, many black churches have veered away from their real spiritual roots, turning away from teaching the gospel and the truth of heaven and hell. These blasphemous dens of vipers have become bastions of liberalism and debauchery, chock full of black Democrats who treat God's house as nothing more than a bar or strip club.

The growing influence of liberal culture on most black pastors and the allure of riches have made them more secular, with most of their churches now having only a passing semblance of holiness. Underneath this righteous facade, the Democrat Party's immoral ideology of tolerance, equality, and diversity steadily plays a significant role in the black community's spiritual demise. It has gotten to the point today where, in most black churches, the preachers themselves are idolized and worshipped and can do no wrong in the eyes of their congregants.

"Jeremiah 14 Verse 14: Then the LORD said unto me, the prophets prophesy lies in my name: I sent them not, neither have I commanded them, neither spake unto them: they prophesy unto you a false vision and divination, and a thing of nought, and the deceit of their heart."

Case in point, black pastor Eddie Long, now deceased, was an "alleged " homosexual deviant who plied little boys with cash, trips and other goodies in return for sexual favors. He received the old "we forgive him" treatment from his congregation and kept right on "preaching" and "anointing" little boys. So, even when caught, these wolves in sheep clothing still do not want to ever give up their religious cash cow and will use every scripture in the bible, in any way they can, to prevent from doing so.

I truly believe in forgiveness for all, we are all human and fallible, but I also believe that if you purport to be a man of God and have fallen, and is now seeking redemption, that you should at least step down from the pulpit while excising your demons. Because of the always ready-to-forgive and forget mentality of their ardent and emotional believers and followers, there is no better racket for corrupt, lying former black hustlers and pimps to be in then the "holiness" industry.

Now, I am not gonna "tarry" too long on this church biz, because I think a lot of people get it by now. So, to take this chapter out, I am gonna ask quickly, why do the majority of blacks overlook criminal activities by Democrats and steadily vote for these criminals and convicts? The majority of the white community doesn't do this; however, many blacks have and will still today vote for Democrat candidates just because they are people of color, even if they are felons and crackheads.

Furthermore, the majority of blacks will also vote for Democrat candidates, black and white, even while they are incarcerated or have been just recently released from prison. One such example is Joe Ganim, a white Democrat from Connecticut, who served five years of a seven-year prison sentence for corruption. Yet, upon his release, this convicted felon was quickly elected mayor of Bridgeport, Connecticut, a predominately black and Hispanic city.

To contrast this with white conservative Republicans, and what they will accept from their elected officials, a few years back when John Rowland, then governor of Connecticut, was caught with his hand in the corruption cookie jar and went to prison for about three years, white voters wanted nothing to do with him once he got out of the pen.

With blacks, Marion Barry, a former black mayor, and cocaine abuser, caught with prostitutes on a few occasions, is now revered among them and actually has a statue in Washington, DC to commemorate his "achievements," pipe and all, lit too!

And let's not forget little Jesse Jackson Jr, another black Democrat felon, who once embezzled about $750,000 from his campaign funds, which was then used for trips and luxury items. He pleaded guilty in 2013, but even while under investigation in 2012, he was still in Congress casting votes and still beloved by adoring blacks. And with their support, amazingly, Jesse won re-election in 2012 with over 62 % of the vote in Chicago, home of black homicides, gangs, and drug dealing.

And to avoid substantial jail time, little Jesse came up with an, uh, sudden bipolar disorder, which was diagnosed by doctors, I suppose, probably sent in by the Democrat Party.

The results of this chicanery? "Ailing" Jesse Jr now collects about $138,000 a year in "disability and workmen's comp," payments from the hard-working taxpayers of this country. Oh, there was to be some "punishment," of course, for little Jesse Jr., who spent about twenty-two months in jail and halfway homes but was getting paid every step of the way in his ongoing "treatment," which was nice.

There are many more examples of wrongdoings and malfeasance by Democrat candidates and congressmen, black and white, who are still beloved and heavily supported by blacks today. Somehow, corruption and crime seem embedded within the black culture's DNA, this is why gangster rap is so prevalent in the community.

The majority of blacks seems to always gravitate, like fish to water, towards Democrat candidates and elected officials who exhibit thuggish and criminal behavior, even cheering it on. *With this said, it should be reasonable to conclude that the majority of whites in this country are much closer to Godliness and doing what's right, than the majority of blacks at this point.*

Unlike the white community, most blacks view criminal acts by their candidates as street cred, a badge of honor for their elected officials to have been locked up and to have served time. In just about any predominately black town or city, any black candidate who has been incarcerated or has been involved in criminal activities, and decides one day to run for office, would be a lock to win in that district. *"Yo, bro did a bid upstate, gotta get this bad mofo in office!"*

And once elected, it doesn't matter about the amount of crime, poverty, drugs, poor schools and homicides occurring in the newly elected Democrat's district, emotional blacks will still pour out into the streets like cockroaches at voting time to make sure he or she is elected again. This enthusiastic acceptance of criminality by most blacks shows a fundamental lack of morality and character among them and is a rebuking by the black community, as a whole, of God and his commandments.

I'm gonna go ahead and take this chapter out now, I think we've seen enough on this subject. So, in conclusion, most black "pastors" today have not only become a problem themselves within the black community but have also exacerbated the moral decline of faithful blacks attending their "churches."

Most of these black Democrat serpents know the Bible through and through and, yet, have perverted God's words to fill theirs and the Democrat Party's immoral wants and needs, and by extension their coffers. These "holy men" have sold their souls many times over for wealth and power, never caring about salvation or the commandments of God, much less the black sheep they are brainwashing and fleecing.

Wait a minute though, you think these unholy and corrupt Pastors and felonious Democrats are something? In 2008, Democrats fell upon some good fortune and got the ultimate black overseer for their party. They pulled off the unlikeliest of hoaxes and deception in getting their perfect black socialist marionette elected.

I mean, they had truly outdone themselves with this one. With the election of 2008, white liberals now had a black president, an all too willing puppet, to finish completely manipulating celebrating blacks who were so enamored with the prospect of a black man, a brother, in the white house that they didn't even care about his background, politics, or ideology.

How did this turn out, you say? Well, I already gave you a snippet of this black messiah earlier, now stick around and get yourself prepared for the full monte because this smooth move by Democrats will take us to the next chapter, and perhaps the greatest mistake the black community and this country has ever made.

Turn the page and behold, the black death, he that cometh to destroyeth.

Chapter Fourteen

Obama: Rise of the Black Messiah

Recap? *Ok, so Democrats enslaved and whipped blacks, starting with the 1600s. I mean they beat and lynched their slaves' asses all the way up to 1865 until Republicans stepped in and Democrats themselves caught a beatdown. *The white slave owners' defeat in the Civil War would also serve to free long-suffering African slaves and their offspring from captivity.*

*However, after killing Lincoln, the Democrat Party would create the KKK and turn loose their members on the newly freed slaves and impose some harsh restrictions, and lynchings, on'em in the deep south.

*But even with these restrictions still in place, welfare inducements in the 1930s would put blacks in the deep south right back on the Democrat Plantation; I guess they were so used to being sheltered and cared for, it all sorta worked out.

*However, in the early 1960s, and during the Civil rights Movement, Republicans and Dr. King happened, and persecuted blacks would finally get a breather from Jim Crow Laws, segregation and Blacks Codes with the passage of the 1964 Civil Rights Bill. *But, in retaliation, the peace-loving and tolerant Democrats would then kill Dr. King.*

*Then in 1968, after Democrats had offed the good doctor, they installed their own black "reverend" puppets onto their payroll to "lead" the black community, ushering in the "black power movement. And to finish blacks off in the 1980s, Democrats would exploit black women by offering them section eight and welfare, then sprinkled crack dust on the black community and removed the fathers out of their households.

*Moving along to the 1990s, Democrat homosexuals joined forces with the black community and with this solidarity, the number of black men on the down low rose precipitously, and so did aids among them.

*But, with the 2008 election, the crowned jewel of socialism, anti-Christianity, and perversion was still to come, and our nation would see the rise of the most powerful black overseer of all, Obama… king of the Democrat puppets.

You know, looking back on the 1990s, I remember Bill Clinton and how cool he was, an intelligent policy wonk who could rattle off economic stats on a whim. And I must admit, at the time, I was quite fond of this smooth-talking white southerner who had gone onto the Arsenio Hall show and played the sax like a pro. After old Bill's election, many smitten blacks had actually taken to affectionately referring to him as the first black president. And although I had cheered him on at the time, I still wasn't interested enough in politics to go out and actually vote.

It would take the prospect of the election of the actual first black president, or so we were led to believe, to get me motivated and off the sidelines and into the political fray, so to speak. As I previously stated, the 2008 election was the catalyst needed to finally get me to the polls and, surprisingly, also to research our great Democrat Party, once and for all.

Here was Obama, a supposedly authentic "brother" and first real black presidential candidate seemingly coming out of nowhere, giving soaring, emotional, and profound speeches that seemed to signal the much-needed hope and change that most Americans longed for at the time.

Obama was an enigmatic, and gifted teleprompter orator who proclaimed time and again while campaigning, that he stood for the values of our great nation and would work hard to unite us, regardless of race or color. Comparisons to Dr. King were immediately drawn by hopeful Americans all across the political spectrum, creating a sense of peace and harmony among many blacks and whites who had bought into Obama's seemingly candor, forthrightness, and intellectual demeanor. On the campaign trail, Obama implored us to be considerate towards one another, that we could have unity and be a better nation if we just strived together, regardless of our diverse backgrounds.

He vividly described his childhood; detailing being bought up within a multiracial family structure comprised of a white mother and Nigerian father. Obama intended to show us how if he could make it to the top, anyone could. We were mesmerized by his supposedly honest assessment of how far he had come as an individual and how we as a nation could also.

The election of 2008 was supposedly a political watershed, a moment of monumental achievement. This seemingly pivotal point in our nation's history was one in which the majority of the country had cast aside racial differences, eschewing deep-seated prejudices to finally live out Dr. Martin Luther King Jr's creed of judging a man by his character and the content of his heart and not by the color of his skin.

You know, for me, it wasn't so much about color as it was about uniqueness, I was caught up in the "first" black as president narrative that was being driven by the media and plantation blacks. At the start, I had been cautiously optimistic regarding this candidate, but most everyone and their momma seemed fully engaged and caught up in the enthusiasm and emotions of this unprecedented and historical event taking place right before their eyes. They were swept up in this feverish vortex of equality of the highest order. This Obama dude seemed to be something unique and different, a refreshing change and welcomed cultural shift towards a new and enlighten racial cohesiveness for blacks, whites, and every other race in America.

With Obama's ascension to the Whitehouse, it seemed that we were on the cusp of reclaiming our status as a real melting pot again, or were we? While the 2008 presidential campaign was surging ahead amid the mass hysteria over the prospect of the first "black president," I had excitedly started doing some research just before the election, and my antenna went up a little regarding some of Obama's past associations with shady, anti-American characters.

Chalking my findings up to fake news, I just brushed these revelations off, not wanting to believe any information at the time that the "brother" was anything other than what he purported to be. The main-stream media had conditioned me, at the time, to believe that any negative information about Obama was just right-wing smear tactics.

So, it was to be, in November of 2007, I relented and hesitantly voted for this raw and politically inexperienced community organizer. Despite my misgivings, I voted for this admitted former drug user because I believed, like most blacks and whites, that he was a "brother" who understood, by his speeches, what was needed for our community and our nation. I must say that after I had gone to the polls for that first time on that cold November morning, I came away with the feeling that I had been a participant in a significant milestone. I was proud of my vote and relished being a part of this historical moment.

It also would come as no surprise that Obama was elected the 44th president, in no small part, by blacks like me overwhelming the polls and voting 95% or more for our supposed messiah. Whites, on both sides of the political spectrum, would also turn out in massive numbers, I believe, in their misguided belief that with their votes, they were somehow absolving themselves of their guilt over slavery and all the atrocities that had occurred during centuries of black oppression, supposedly, by their ancestors.

However, it was the black community that went absolutely bananas and off the rails over Obama and his candidacy. For them, his election was like the Super Bowl of equality and his ascension to the Whitehouse was, somehow, to be a big part of their long overdue reparations. Old blacks, young blacks, middle-aged blacks, pregnant blacks, crackhead blacks, crippled blacks, drug-dealing blacks, deadbeat welfare blacks, toothless blacks, bedridden blacks, educated blacks, dumb blacks, blacks that were felons and blacks who had never voted, made sure they got to the polls to cast their votes in 2007.

Blacks came in staggering numbers, and by whatever mode of transportation they could find, arriving by bus, car, roller blades, stolen Segways, stolen scooters, borrowed helicopters, stolen trains, bicycles, motorcycles, skateboards, snowmobiles, parachutes, hang gliders, skis, and horseback. They came by boat, they teleported, they walked, and some even rolled in on stretchers, to make sure they got to vote for the self-described black redeemer. *Ok, I may have embellished a little on some of the modes of transportation, but I think you got the point.*

Note: Curious thing though, during this particular election no one was talking about black voter suppression or how blacks couldn't get ids to vote...hmmmmmm?

In fact, Obama pulled off the impossible during the 2008 election as some precincts, like in Philly, reported 115% voter participation on election day, all in his favor of course. Don't ask.

Now, the first inclination of the black community's, uh, high expectations of Obama would come soon after the election when jubilant young blacks begin dancing uncontrollably with excitement in the streets. They were screaming and carrying on about how their newly elected black messiah would suddenly make them wealthy, pay their bills, get rid of their mortgages and give them new cars, replete with 22-inch rims. To these blacks, with Obama now in office, there would be a chicken frying in every skillet and a rack of ribs on every grill. By this reaction from blacks, it was clear to see that this election, sadly, did not foster any independence or can-do attitude among the majority of the community.

Obama's rise had instead served to heighten their sense of entitlement and to further view our government as their ticket to prosperity. With his presidency, some blacks felt that they finally had a champion, a "brother," commanding the highest office in the land, who would be on their side and looking deeply into the issues which have plagued their communities for decades. He was one of theirs and were now in office with the power to go about effecting the change he spoke of so eloquently on the campaign trail.

To add to this lunacy, there was also a segment of militant blacks who believed that this newly minted "brother" would show whitey and the rest of the world what a black president could do now that he had obtained the most powerful-man-in-the-world status. They conveniently ignored the fact that there wasn't any significant or prosperous nations on earth currently being run by black leaders at the time, or any time prior.

Nonetheless, Obama's, the HNIC (Head Nigger In Charge) presidency was supposed to validate the hard-fought freedoms won with the 1950s and 1960s Civil Rights Movement. His election was supposedly an acknowledgment, and reward, for the sacrifices of black pioneers like Dr. King and Rosa Parks, who had shouldered the burden of searching for the seemingly elusive holy grail of true equality, now apparently found with this election.

This one profound act, and moment in time, of the election of a black man to the presidency, had seemingly shredded the notion that blacks couldn't ascend any higher than the white man would allow and bolstered the idea that despite our cultural differences we were all part of one race, the human race. Obama's election clearly showed times had changed for the better in this country and that anyone born in this country, regardless of race, color, ethnicity or nationality could aspire to ascend to the highest peak of the America dream.

It was a wild time and a lot of citizens; white, black, Latino, etc., had collectively concluded that racial harmony would now ensue and that our nation would be stronger than ever with this one colorblind act. We were, it seemed, in the throes of a new and optimistic beginning, and with our now reinvigorated and unified nation, most Americans believed that we would also be unstoppable on the world stage.

As with every hard fought election, there was to be some political divide and discontent after Obama's election and inauguration. But these grumblings would quickly subside and dissipate, and there would be no media outrage about how Obama was unfit for office, and no questioning of his temperament for the highest office in the land.

Before Obama took office, there had been no conservative anti-fascist organizations springing up with masks and baseball bats and assaulting Democrats, nor had there been violent and antagonistic conservative groups marching around publicly chanting that they wanted to kill cops. And, even after Obama's inauguration, there had been no rioting or looting, no conservative celebrities threatening to blow up the Whitehouse, no conservative late night talk show host shouting F..k Obama!, and no weekly protests of crazed conservative women marching in pussy hats and screaming obscenities at the president and Whitehouse.

Instead, when Obama had won, most Americans were ready and willing to embrace this change upon the political landscape and were pulling for our new, untested, and vastly inexperienced president to succeed. Even those initially against Obama and adamantly opposed to his election, resigned themselves to his victory and decided to give him a chance to see what would happen during his tenure. Their thinking was that maybe they had been wrong about him, and just maybe, given time, he was going to be good for the nation.

Oh, the liberal media absolutely loved and adored the new black president, and all throughout his presidency would never really challenge or pose any hard questions about his administration. During his eight years in office, Obama was never to be hit with any prolonged 24/7 negative wall to wall coverage.

In fact, most of the Democrat-run media fawned over just about anything our new commander-in-chief did and ran favorable piece after favorable piece about how America was entering a modern day of racial enlightenment. There were numerous softball interviews with reporters who gushed over even the most mundane of things regarding this president: *"What did he eat for breakfast?, How tall was he?, Where did his wife get her dress?.. etc..etc."*

Democrats, working alongside the Swedish government, even made sure that the new black president was given legitimacy and gravitas from the start by bestowing the, now tarnished forever, Nobel Peace Prize upon him just for being black and president. Surprisingly, there had been little to no vetting of this unaccomplished newcomer by the mainstream media, or anyone else for that matter. Most people just didn't seem to care about his background, even after he penned a book detailing his drug use.

This media blackout was deliberately designed as a buffer between the details of Obama's sordid past history and the fawning public. For white liberals, the undeniably racial aspect of Obama's presidency would indeed be used to strengthen the Democrat Party's control on the black community. All of their political power now coursed through their omnipotent, and deceitful, black puppet's veins.

In this respect, after Obama's inauguration, the Democrat Party saw to it that the red carpet would be rolled out, and would keep right on rolling throughout his presidency. Their new black marionette president was an instant celebrity and media sensation now, hobnobbing with Hollywood elites, wealthy rappers, and sports stars and drinking expensive champagne while eating fine caviar at nonstop parties.

Obama had come a long way from his days of being a crack smoking community organizer on the mean streets of Chicago. So, fascinated, as all of this inaugural carousing was taking place, I started looking back on the campaign of this president and recalled that, strangely enough, there had been only one network, Fox News, coming out with seemingly negative stories regarding his background. Conservative news anchors had urgently warned their viewers about so-called bombshell revelations on then-candidate Obama's communist ties, socialist views, and alignment with anti-American terrorists.

There were whispers Obama was in bed with radical Muslims, that he had actually been born in Kenya, and that he had applied for foreign aid as a student at Harvard. These stories were immediately swatted away as racist lies and fake news by the majority of emotional blacks and liberal mainstream news outlets such as CNN, NBC, ABC, CBS, and MSNBSC.

I mostly dismissed these stories as well, but not entirely, because deep down inside I wondered if there were any validity to any of these accusations. There was just too much smoke to say there wasn't a fire somewhere. Everyone had a past, especially someone who had admitted to using drugs so candidly, even before being elected to office.

I kept wondering, why would one network, Fox News, break with the rest of the outlets and say these things? And if they weren't true, why wasn't the other media outlets following up and running their own stories to clarify? Furthermore, why wasn't Obama, as arrogant and outspoken as he was, refuting these charges himself?

At the time, I was naïve, not thinking of the mainstream media as mostly Democrat operatives, so I just shrugged it off. After all, it was only on Fox News, and according to all the other mainstream networks and blacks, they were fake news, or so I thought.

However, something kept tugging at me; I had never before seen a time when most major news outlets were not even interested in vetting and fleshing out a presidential candidate's background. Here was a man coming from nowhere, with very little of his past being talked about, being instantly heralded as this great savior of our nation.

I asked myself, why wasn't there more scrutiny and digging into his background by all the media in our inquiring minds want to know society? Was it because he was black, or was there something more sinister afoot? There was no real trail of Obama's past, so to speak, everything just seemed so tightly choreographed like some well put together play or Broadway production.

Any negative issues popping up surrounding Obama was quickly attacked by a contingent of rabid liberal media anchors and pundits who promptly "debunked" any bad news with their very own liberal "fact checkers." There seemed to be a protective and almost impenetrable shield by liberal networks running interference and defending Obama, his candidacy, and his presidency at all costs.

For me personally, the cracks in the veneer of this black fairy tale would come about a year or so after the election, and after Obama's almost maniacal obsession with liberal social causes while ignoring the more pressing issues like the economy, black genocide, and the anemic jobs market. But for the majority of blacks, who were oh so enamored with the president's skin color, smooth talk, and charm, they forgot about their troubles and partied on with their new black king, and what a honeymoon it was.

Amid this delight and joy of electing Obama, the ultimate black overseer, overlooked was that most Americans were still suffering from the recession of the previous administration. And, as usual, blacks in mostly Democrat-run inner cities bore the brunt of this economic decline, disproportionately affected with increasing poverty, lack of jobs, poor schools, crime, drugs, and astronomical black on black homicides.

Obama's former hometown, Chicago, was a clear illustration of all these ills. Even with all of his years of organizing and speech giving, nothing had changed in this city for the black community. And after the election confetti had settled, it was plain to see that all of his time spent in these neighborhoods had only served as the black footstool upon which he would use to get elected president, resulting in a most dramatic, and fortuitous, change in his own personal fortunes.

Once in office, Obama not only ignored the issues which have plagued black communities for decades but would double down and exacerbate them by declaring that law enforcement was desperately in need of sensitivity retraining to deal with high crime areas in the inner cities and how they are policed.

So, to try to succinctly sum this mind-boggling proposition up; Democrats, for decades, installed policies in the inner cities that promoted the destruction of the black family, leaving black kids fatherless. Then these fatherless and directionless kids take to the streets to commit crimes. And to solve this problem they'd created themselves; Obama and other liberal Democrat Politicians were now declaring that police officers in these same crime-ridden communities are the ones needing to be retrained and not the black youths committing the crimes?

It defied reality that the first black president and commander-in-chief would actually be against law enforcement in any high crime black area in this country, especially his problematic hometown of Chicago. Why wouldn't Obama seek to side with officers who put their lives on the line every day in stressful and dangerous situations against black drug dealers and thugs to make these communities safer for the law-abiding blacks residing there? In this regard, Obama was a surprising hinderance to police officers trying to clean up drug-infested black communities. In fact, he would turn out to be just the opposite of what was sorely needed to stem the daily violence in high crime areas across the nation.

Obama epitomized the indifferent, callous and unconcerned, run-of-the-mill and mouthy black Democrat politicians, who for decades ignored black on black genocide in the inner cities while condescendingly patronizing the black community every election for political gain. But as it is with all Democrats, blacks still loved them some Obama, and there would never be any groundswell of awareness, nor protests, or riots over black on black violence and murders before, or during this president's time in office.

Personally, I couldn't quite understand this black "brother" president, it was amazing to me that he would not only allow blacks to kill one another like dogs in the streets but would actually go against anyone attempting to stop this carnage. Not that Obama was supposed to be a president for just blacks mind you, but when you have the black community breaking their necks to vote over 95% for a candidate, you would think that there might be some sort of addressing of the issues crippling a community housing such a crucial and rabid base of support for his party.

Since Obama had been on the ground and up close to the problems in Chicago during his "organizing" years, pressing issues troubling the black community should have been of utmost importance to him, so why didn't he seem to care? This lack of concern by Obama regarding the devastation of the black community didn't seem to matter to the majority of emotional blacks, they had already thrown their full support behind this historical trailblazer with wild abandon, blind faith, and uncompromising devotion.

This unconditional loyalty by the majority of the black community was roundly applauded by the scheming white liberals within the Democrat Party. Their black puppet king and other highly paid black overseers, by the sheer virtue of their skin tone, were keeping the majority of blacks happy and right where they were supposed to be, under the party's complete control and in conditions mostly resembling the plantations of the 1800s.

From his days in Chicago's black neighborhoods, Obama realized early on that the majority of blacks always demanded very little from Democrats, and was always given very little. Once elected, Obama had no need for these lowly black commoners, now that their job of voting him into office had been completed. Black civil rights leaders, the Black Congressional Caucus, black sports stars, black celebrities, black rappers, Black Lives Matter and any other black who was somebody, had also thrown their full support behind this fresh-on-the-scene black president, who was now at the helm of the greatest and most powerful nation on earth.

With Obama, there were other perks, any white who dared speak out against the new black emperor was promptly branded a racist by the complicit liberal Democrat wolf-pack mainstream media horde and forced to apologize, resign or retreat, and quite often quickly fired. Worse of all, any black conservative attempting to warn other blacks about Obama and the Democrat Party were summarily shut down and dismissed as delusional sellouts, coons, and Uncle Toms. In this regard, Obama was well protected by the Democrat Party's house Negroes, and was fully aware of his ride or die black bodyguards.

Obama was fortunate that he never had to answer any questions about his background or any of his salacious scandals, including Larry Sinclair, a gay man whom he is accused of having an alleged homosexual affair before his election of 2008. This quite emotional and teary-eyed gay dude gave a rather lengthy press conference, with graphic details, regarding a late-night crack-infused tryst that he and Obama enjoyed in the backseat of a limo. Now, I don't know if this reveal was true or not, but I sat and watched the riveting fifty minutes or so press conference in its entirety on YouTube.

Mr. Sinclair's demeanor was not one of a liar or hoaxer, but one of a scorned lover who had just been tossed aside like garbage after Obama had begun to become more prominent on the political stage and, to me, that was wrong. I actually felt terrible for this gay dude because it seemed that at one point he and Barack had a good thing going and that he had really loved him.

This love affair gone wrong was fascinating to me because we've had married Senators and Presidents, throughout this nation's history, who were known to have had extramarital affairs with other women, like Bill Clinton and John Kennedy. But we've never had a male president being accused of having a sexual relationship with another man and that man actually holding a press conference to proclaim it to the world. Of course, the Democrat mainstream media cartel would quickly bury the story, along with Mr. Sinclair. It was an intriguing affair, indeed.

However, I am still trying to wrap my mind around it, I mean, here was Larry Sinclair, this gay dude, openly and unashamedly detailing for the press how Pre-Senator Obama purchased about $250 worth of crack cocaine in one of Chicago's most dangerous drug-infested no-go zones. And while the black messiah was smoking his crack pipe in the backseat of a limo, old Larry was performing fellatio on our future 44th president. If true, this explosive affair would make old smooth and, uh, charming Barack historic in more ways than one.

However, because of the Democrat media's interference and suppression of every detail relating to this press conference, we may never know the whole truth. Really, this alleged homosexual affair was not like Trump's supposed payment to a female, which was plastered for months on end on liberal networks by the quite insatiable Democrat media hordes seeking to find out if he actually plugged a porn star.

I guess a white male billionaire having an affair with a female was much more newsworthy, and explosive than a black male Senator, in the dead of night, in the back of a limo, smoking crack, and having a romp with a gay dude.

*Being all things masculine myself, I find it quite shocking and repulsive that a man would let another man nibble on his noodle, but that's just me and to each his own.

Anyways, Obama also never had to answer any questions about his affiliations or any associations with anti-American operatives such as Bill Ayers, a prominent figure and advisor from his past. Nor did he ever have to answer questions about his pastor, old Reverend Wright, who displayed his venomous anti-American sentiment publicly during Obama's presidential campaign.

There's a lot more to tell. Take Joan Rivers, who declared in an impromptu interview that Obama was gay, and Michelle wasn't quite who and what she pretended to be, but you will have to look up Joan's video to get the full import, she wasn't kidding, at all, y'all. There was also the issue, unverified of course, of three gay black men, one in Reverend's Wright church, associated with Obama, all mysteriously killed in 2007 just as he was running for office. These are the things out there in the ether that Democrats are vehemently decrying as fake news, so I won't expound on them here, but do your own research and see if there is any validity to any of these assertions.

On that note, in the next chapter, I will detail how the gay community exploited a group of black lesbians in the 1990s to become a viable player on the political stage and an influence on our youth. This melding of blacks and gays dovetailed nicely with Obama and his presidency in that he had the ultimate platform to take the baton from these lesbians and further the homosexual cause in the 2000s, and would do so without hesitation and with great success.

So, despite it being so hard to get any straight, pun intended, info on our reticent black messiah regarding his background, the pieces of this puzzle, as laid out here, should start to form a clear picture at this point. In that vein, oddly enough, one of the first things Obama did when he got into office was to seal his records, and I mean all of them, from the eyes of the public so that the question of him applying for foreign aid as a student while in college could never be answered or addressed, nor his college grades accessed.

I thought it strange that this proud and supposedly intellectual president had sealed all of his records, including his time at Harvard Law School, from any and all prying eyes. This deliberate cloaking of his past nagged at me. Something wasn't quite right; he was too protective of all his pre-presidential doings and anything else surrounding his history as a young man. Although most people were aware of Obama's "organizing" in Chicago and his supposedly caring for blacks, we knew little else about the man except what the media would dress up and roll out for their viewers.

But as president, Obama's true stripes would soon manifest themselves as the black community was utterly ignored while he and his liberal Democrat cohorts actively advocated for increased illegal immigration from Mexico and Central America. This fetish for Hispanics by Democrats, along with job-killing globalist trade, made issues in most black communities, such as unemployment, poverty, and crime, more pronounced as these neighborhoods were the dumping grounds for newly arriving illegals and the drugs they bought with'em.

Now, you must ask yourself, why would a black president feverishly support illegal immigration, the very thing tearing down black communities, while neglecting his most loyal and ardent supporters? It would seem that Obama, like most Democrats in Congress, had all but brushed aside any sense of loyalty for the overwhelming support received from eternally hopeful and misguided blacks in 2008, and again in 2012.

In fact, right after Obama's re-election, a quite perturbed black councilwoman in Detroit lashed out at him in anger because she had been one of the many corrupt local black politicians who had vigorously championed and campaigned for the black messiah. She had also emphatically demanded, and prodded, blacks in her poverty-stricken city to get their asses out and vote for this supposed redeemer of the black community.

However, this "campaigning" by the councilwoman wasn't all about just getting a black man elected to office. Indeed, it seems that she and the rest of the enterprising blacks comprising the all-black Detroit city council had raped the city treasury, milking it dry of its pension funds and were now in severe financial trouble.

These black Detroit politicians thought that if they could just get Obama into the Whitehouse, that he would somehow help them out, and literally banked on it. But to their dismay, after Obama was elected, neither Detroit nor any other poverty-stricken inner city ever heard from him again. And in the blacks-are-stupid column, this quite vociferous and irate black Detroit councilwoman was not even aware at the time, that she had been caught on camera publicly airing a very illegal political quid pro quo, or kickback, for all to see. But no worries, this corrupt and politically explosive outburst was, of course, ignored by the fawning liberal Democrat media to protect our former El Presidente.

Speaking of Obama, he simply ignored this councilwoman and her whining, or in other words, he suggested to her, in no uncertain terms, *"Nigger, please!"* This black socialist trojan horse had much bigger fish to fry than the petty financial mess in Detroit. He was now in control of trillions and the largest economy in the world and viewed his election and presidency as a pathway, and mandate, by which to fundamentally and socially change America's demographics and moral fabric, permanently.

To begin the task of rearranging America's societal norms, Obama would, like Democrat President Andrew Johnson in the 1800s, appoint liberal activists, masquerading as circuit court judges, all across the country and select liberal Supreme Court Justices who viewed our Constitution as merely an annoyance, a living document to be rewritten and revised at will and at their whim. Obama would go even further as he advocated and backed assaults on Christianity, gun rights, and law enforcement. He would use a speech to the United Nations to endorse Islam and to conflate religions in the United States:

"The future must not belong to those who slander the prophet of Islam. But to be credible, those who condemn that slander must also condemn the hate we see in the images of Jesus Christ that are desecrated, or churches that are destroyed, or the Holocaust that is denied.

Let us condemn incitement against Sufi Muslims and Shiite pilgrims." "It's time to heed the words of Gandhi: 'intolerance is itself a form of violence and an obstacle to the growth of a true democratic spirit.' Together, we must work towards a world where we are strengthened by our differences, and not defined by them. That is what America embodies, that's the vision we will support."

This speech was just a pretext to Obama's future attempt at dismantling our Constitution and Bill of rights and destroying the Judeo-Christian foundation upon which it lay. And because of the dark pigmentation of this new president, Republicans was in quite the racial pickle; a political quandary that rendered their party impotent and unable to expose the truth or say anything negative about the new president without being branded racists.

This racial gag order on Republicans left the Democrat Party with almost unfettered power to carry out its socialist anti-American agenda. Obama now had free rein, especially during his first two years as president, with a Democrat-controlled House and Senate, to do whatever he wanted and would do so with impunity and without hesitation.

The overjoyed Democrat Party viewed their black puppet as the prized socialist nugget they had longed for forever and immediately went after control of our healthcare system and to assert gay rights over the will of the American people. Obama, while altogether ignoring rural America and the plight of the black community, quickly got on board to implement any and all of the Democrat Party's social causes.

Because of their racially-induced stupor, most blacks and low info whites hadn't even noticed when their new president started doggedly pursuing healthcare reform and homosexuality while black communities rotted, and welfare rolls increased. Healthcare reform and same-sex marriage would become the centerpieces of Obama's administration as Democrats cobbled together and quickly introduced legislation for both bills, which would irreversibility alter our society and nation forever.

This concentrated effort by white liberal social justice warriors in promoting these two core tenets of their party belied the promises given by Obama on the campaign trail, but liberal Democrats didn't give a damn, they now had their black trojan horse in place and felt embolden to remake our entire country into their image. As they attempted in the 1800s, Democrats were now determined to win by any means necessary even if they had to lie, cheat, use deception, and advocate violence to achieve victory.

The unbridled arrogance, political chicanery, and malfeasance of the Democrat Party would endure for two years and Republicans would not be able to effectively raise any opposition until after they were able to take back the House and Senate.

The thrashing of Democrat candidates would come about during the mid-term election of 2010 after voters, awakening from their Obama-high, suddenly realized that they had been deceived and duped into voting for socialism, immorality, and racial divisiveness. These newly enlightened voters finally saw their error in electing

Obama in 2008 and wanted to undo the mistake they had made. They came out to the polls in droves, voting en masse for Republicans to control Congress and was hoping that it wasn't too late to oppose the Democrat Party's immoral assault on our country. They desperately sought to deny the lawlessness and unconstitutional policies of the black would-be-king.

Democrats would have help in dismissing the damaging optics of these voters' wrath as their operatives in the mainstream media went into full spin mode, brushing off the devastating mid-term losses as something that historically happens in this country every election cycle. In this regard, the liberal media was still running interference and refusing to vet or cover any of the destruction being done to America by liberals and the Obama administration.

During his eight-year tenure as president, we now know that Obama weaponized our nation's governmental agencies, such as the FBI and Department Of Justice, against the American people. We know that he had his IRS target conservatives. We know that by using our government's agencies, Obama wire-tapped his political opponents, and allowed his Attorney General to illegally run guns to Mexico's cartels. And we also know that Obama sent, in the dead of night, billions in cash to Iran, a country that swears death to America every chance it gets and sponsors terrorism around the world

Today, there are many Obama holdovers and anti-American operatives still embedded and operating within most of our top government agencies, seeking to fulfill the Democrat Party's directive of completing the destruction of the Christian foundation of this nation. They are there, in our nation's capital, along with the activist judges appointed to various circuit courts around the country, challenging our Constitution, endlessly probing for any loopholes, anything to remove the Christian principles upon which our nation was founded.

The election of 2008 gave us a black president, black Attorney General, black National Security Advisor, and Black Muslim aides, all in the seat of power of the most powerful nation on earth. These wicked blacks were all Democrats, controlled by white liberals, running an administration that I believe was perhaps the most insidiously corrupt in the history of this country.

Never before in the history of this country have we had an out-going president send FBI operatives into a presidential candidate's political campaign to actually fabricate evidence paid for by that candidate's Democrat opponent, then try to use this fabricated evidence to gin up an investigation in an attempt to find a crime in which to overthrow this newly elected president.

Now, this wasn't much of a shock to me because this is what corrupt black leaders have done for ages in most African nations when in power. And we must also remember that it was during Obama's administration when we would suddenly hear unabashedly racist comments from black anchors, black groups, Congressmen and pundits on live television broadcasts proclaiming: *"Whites must become a minority in this nation."* or *"Straight White males are the problem in America."*

Which makes you wonder, what the hell happened to the "unity, and "hope and change " this "brother," Obama, had so eloquently and passionately spoken about on the campaign trail in 2007? Was it all just teleprompter Lies? What had occurred in our country from the short time he had been elected to office to now, to have caused this radical and extremely racist rhetoric permeating our nation? Hadn't Obama comprehended that he had won the presidency beca-cause of whites, and not because he had gotten most of the black vote?

There will never be enough blacks in this country to out-vote the white population, and for such an example we can note the failed candidacy of longtime black overseer Jesse Jackson. When old "Rainbow Coalition" Jesse had run for the presidency in 1984 and 1988, managing to get over 110% of the black vote, he still wasn't even a blip on the election screen.

To reiterate, not only did Obama incite racial division, hatred, and discord during his tenure as president, he also warred against Christians at every turn and wanted nothing to do with the Bible and God. With that said, even today, Obama's skin color is still protecting the remnants of his corrupt administration and still enabling the ongoing coup by his operatives left behind to overthrow our country. These communist "plants" are still there, misleading and hiding any and all of his wrongdoings; and as quickly as something surfaces on the nefarious dealings of Obama's presidency, it is just as quickly dismissed as nonsense and racism by the Democrat mainstream media.

One of the things that struck me most about Obama; here was a man born of a strong black Nigerian father and supposedly having "African Warrior" blood coursing through his veins, yet boldly proclaiming himself a feminist. So, it turns out that, all along, this proud and strong black man was nothing more than a wet, rainbow noodle, soft as a grape, and fruitier than an apple orchard.

This really hadn't shocked me that much, because a lot of black black men have been emasculated by the Democrat Party.

In fact, there is a whole damn epidemic of down-low men in the black community, masquerading as suave ladies men and spreading aids among unsuspecting black women.

This, of course, will lead us to the next chapter. Man-up or woman-up, and turn the page.

Chapter Fifteen

The Emasculation of Black Males

Ok, so Quick Recap. *Democrats enslaved, beat, and lynched blacks for centuries until angered Republicans soundly whipped their asses in 1865, thus, freeing blacks from slavery and toiling on deep south plantations.

*As a reward for their efforts though, these former black slaves turned on Republicans, their deliverers, and went straight back to Democrats, and their plantations.

*Democrats then put their newly reacquired blacks on welfare and crack, then Obama comes along and turn most of the men in the community gay…there.

◆◆◆

The majority of black men today are running around shouting that they are "African Americans" and proud descendants of fierce warriors from the "motherland. These blacks fiercely proclaim that they're from the continent where life supposedly began, the cradle of mankind, even going so far as to attempt to trace their roots back to some tribe in Africa and foolishly assuming African-sounding names.

I would say to these "Africans," *"whoaaaa, just pump your motherland brakes there, fellas!"* Black males born in America today are not real Africans, and could never be, their lineage has been diluted by centuries of involuntary and voluntary intermingling with white Europeans and just about every other race in this country.

Furthermore, to make matters worse, most black males have been emasculated by Democrats, and this is nothing new, the stripping away of manliness among black men in this country has been going on for quite some time. During slavery, many of the strong black male slaves, or bucks, that were bought over from Africa, was sometimes "broken" with sexual acts forced upon them by their nasty and fruity white homosexual Democrat masters who owned them. These invasive and submissive-inducing sexual acts were just one of the many ways in which Democrats asserted their dominance over their black captives, emphasizing their subservient roles in the new land.

I firmly believe that today, vestiges of this earlier introduction of homosexuality lives on and still can be seen in many black communities among many blacks. This now adopted lifestyle and attitude is currently on display in inner cities all across America as youths strut around with sagging pants and revealing their underwear, a behavior which some say originated with homosexuals in prisons wanting to advertise their "wares" to other male inmates.

A lot of black men in America today have been emasculated, or "frutinize," by following in the "inclusiveness, tolerant, diversity and equality" ideology footsteps of white liberal Democrats. This alarming shift in sexual attitudes has led to many black male youths accepting the entirety of the Democrat Party's platform, including gender fluidity, transgenderism, and the complete abandoning of their masculinity. As a result, white liberals now have the majority of black males living in the land of make-believe and pretendism, resulting in most now being softer than the women they lay with.

Homosexuality has always been a liberal white Democrat construct in this country, however, with the help of the well-paid black "reverends," liberal Democrat Progressives have been quite successful in aligning the gay community with the Civil Rights Movement of the 1960s and the black community as a whole. In the 2000s, during the homosexual community's quest for "equality," Obama and the Democrat Party combined their newfound homosexual "rights" and the ever-present black "victimization" into one Godless platform to endorse, promote, and eventually pass same-sex marriage into law.

I sincerely believe that this movement could have never gotten the traction, momentum, nor credibility that it did without the benefit of piggybacking off of black civil rights and the use of black reverend puppets. Crucial to the gay community, at the height of their movement, liberal homosexuals repeatedly called upon their black "reverends" to give heartfelt and indignant speeches: *"Gay rights are civil rights, and to deny them their rights is just like Jim Crow and the black lynchings of the 1950s. It's even worse than Emmett Till!"*

This messaging by these black overseers served to get the black community fully engaged on the issue of homosexuality and to feel a kinship with the gay community. However, if I may, I am gonna go out on a limb here and note that blacks in this country and homosexuality do not share the same history; never did and never will. Blacks are a race; immutable, and solidified, while homosexuality is a behavior and lifestyle; fluid, and can be modified, taken up, or dropped at any given time.

There is nowhere in our nation's history where you will find a bunch of gay men or lesbians, who were captured from the jungles of some homosexual, rainbow-infused country in the 1600s, being forced to pick cotton in the fields on southern plantations under a hot, sweltering sun while being whipped by gleeful Democrats. Nor were there ever separate water foundations and lunch counters for gays in the 1950s and 1960s. First off, unlike captured African men and women, male and female, during slavery, how would Democrats breed a bunch of gay men or a group of lesbians in order to restock their inventory of slaves?

Quite illogical, isn't it? Can you just imagine a bunch of gay men picking cotton under a sweltering hot sun?: *"Ow, ow, ow.. I just broke a nail on a stem, now I am gonna need another manicure! I just cannot do this. Mr. overseer! Mr. overseer!, these conditions are just deplorable, I quit! Oh, I'm not, like, picking another cotton ball for you or anyone else, and you can just go and tell the master, massa, or whomever, that!"*

Let that scenario tickle your fancy a bit! Somehow I don't think that the liberal Democrat manufactured gay "oppression and suffering" that the black reverends are paid to support and scream about, occurred in the 1600s, 1700s, or 1800s either because this was when white Democrat slave owners were actually the ones sexually "breaking" black men.

And I do not think gay oppression happened during the 1930s, 1950s, or 1960s when black men were being lynched by Democrats, especially since some of these white men were probably homosexuals themselves. Actually, there aren't any footnotes in our nation's history of any gay "oppression," so it would be nearly impossible to determine when exactly did this homosexual "history" occurred in this country.

Nonetheless, the ringing endorsements of homosexuality by the old black "reverends" is quite a serious matter, and the devastating fallout can be seen and felt today in black communities all across America. Studies show that over 40,000 HIV cases are diagnosed each year in this country, with about 50% of these new cases being located in the deep south and in predominately black southern cities like Atlanta, Georgia, and Jackson, Mississippi.

Like the astronomical black on black genocide in inner cities, the new aids epidemic remains largely obscured and mostly hidden from the public eye, simply because this scourge now disproportionately affects gay black men. Truth is, these black homosexuals are just collateral damage in the Democrat Party's ongoing crusade against this nation's moral values and Christian foundation.

To this effect, the black community, which used to be about the most spiritual in America, is now also experiencing a significant rise in aids among black women, stemming from closeted homosexual black men still on the down low because of the stigma associated with aids in their communities.

In our Democrat-created diversity, inclusiveness, and equality society today, black male youths in this country have become much more tolerant and accepting of homosexuality, quite unlike their so-called "brethren" still on the African continent who detest this behavior and lifestyle. In this regard, you would be hard pressed to find any African nation that readily accepts homosexuality within its society.

So, you must ask yourself again, just why are black men in America so welcoming of homosexuality these days? What exactly was the impetus for this sudden sea change and sexual revolution? We all know what happened during slavery, but today, where did this stripping of manhood begin for most black men in this country? And why is homosexuality so pronounced among black youths today?

Well, once again, we see black women playing a prominent role in pushing and ushering in the homosexual movement, and we all know by now that as the black women go, so goes the black community. One of the main catalysts, and turning points, in establishing homosexuality within the black community, and society at large, would come at the hands of black lesbians.

I was watching a quite interesting video of a black ex-lesbian who, after decades of this lifestyle, had turned her life around and were now professing to be a born again Christian. She revealed, in fascinating testimony, her days of organizing events in the early 1990s for large groups of black lesbians, and how they would gather at large functions to socialize. At the time, most of the gay community was basically in the shadows, underground, and was thought of as just a bunch of wealthy white gay men.

To counter this damaging narrative during this period, white homosexuals were attempting to have their behavior normalized, to be viewed by Americans as mainstream. But their timing was off just a tad because at the time many other issues were besetting their community which impeded their progress. Chiefly among them was the aids epidemic of the 1980s and 1990s, when it was found that homosexual men were averaging thirty to fifty partners a month in gay bathhouses in San Francisco, resulting in over fifty thousand aids contacts occurring every month. *I mean, there were so many loving gay families back then that it almost wiped out the whole damn homosexual community!*

Even with the attempted suppression of these stats by the liberal Democrat media at the time, aids became well-known as a gay white man disease because of the homogenous makeup of the homosexual community. Also, because of the stigma that came along with aids in those days, no sane politician was willing to get behind the homosexual movement to advance the community's cause. Which was no surprise, these politicians, always looking out for self, at the time saw no political benefit or upside in associating with this group's behavior and lifestyle.

So, stymied politically, these white homosexuals would soon hit upon an idea, deciding that they needed the emotional jolt of a Civil Rights Movement to "colorize" their community and give it "victimization" appeal. The homosexual community found that the aforementioned, already established and organized group of black lesbians was just the ticket for them to gain the political clout and attention needed to mainstream their behavior and lifestyle. These gay white men would reach out to the quite agreeable black lesbians and quickly bring them on board. This move would bring about the much needed "colorization" of homosexuality, which was then used to legitimize the nascent gay rights movement in the 1990s.

The "assistance" of these lesbians provided the emotional and "victimization" thrust needed for white homosexuals to gain access, and traction, in our schools, media, colleges and other areas of influence that possess the power to sway our youth. So, with the involvement and efforts of these black women, along with the Democrat Party's inclusiveness, tolerance, diversity and equality ideology, black civil rights and homosexuality were now inextricably linked together, and today the two are almost synonymous with each other.

This convenient marriage now serves to insulate the LGBT community from having to stand on its own nonexistent merits and, the truth of the matter is, by mainstreaming homosexuality, the Democrat Party is now advocating and promoting deviant behavior that was once thought of as a mental illness in the 1970s.

Don't get me wrong, I've never had any issues with gays, and I am not here to bash anyone because of their sexual preference. For many centuries, homosexuals have been among us, just like many other behaviors that have lurked in the shadows and have dwelled in the underbelly of our nation, and on the outskirts of our society. Starting in my teens, I had known of gays but had never really focused on or cared about what kind of sex they had or who they had it with, as long as it doesn't infringe upon me and my rights or hurt innocent children.

Matter of fact, I never really cared much about whom straight people were having sex with either. I never cared whether a man had sex with a mule, rooster, or squirrel, whatever their sexual preference was, as long as they kept it to themselves and didn't harm others.

To me, there are many things in society which I personally believe is just as immoral as homosexuality, such as prostitution, drug use, bestiality, and other deviant behaviors, but who am I to judge and censor all of these things, to each his own. It has always been my stance that is up to each individual and their God, if they believe in one, to sort each of these things out for themselves and determine if they are morally right or wrong.

With that being said, I do take exception to liberal Democrats force-feeding homosexuality and gender fluidity to our innocent and impressionable youth through their movies, our schools and colleges, and the mainstream media. The children of this nation are now being attacked relentlessly by white liberals who realize that these naive, and impressionable underage charges under their purview during school hours can be foolishly made to believe in eighty-two genders and transgenderism.

This demographics is in play because Democrats have all but given up on older and quite sane God-fearing people. This group is forever lost to the party's immoral social engineering and would never be convinced to believe that there are more than two genders, or of two men or two women comprising a "normal" family.

Honestly, until a few years back, I had never given too much thought about homosexuality, at all, and believed that people should just get along and not worry about what others do in their bedrooms. However, my thinking would change, drastically, after I had gotten into a heated debate with a gay activist dude on a social comment board of a popular website. He angrily called me a bigot after I stated that I believed marriage is reserved for a male and female, which it has always been from the beginning of time. I then advised him that I, being of sound mind and intellect, know for a biological and scientific fact that there were only two genders and not eighty two or so as he had emotionally asserted.

Fuming and highly upset, this quite emotional gentleman, in a somewhat vain attempt to validate his argument then, as most homosexuals do, used the analogy of male frogs changing their sex in the wild and copulating with other male frogs. I politely suggested to him that, if this was indeed the case, perhaps he should be dating frogs instead of humans.

I then went all in and informed him that, with homosexuality, liberal Democrats have made him believe in a race that never was, and that out of the seven billion plus people on this planet, including homosexuals themselves, not one was born of two men or two women to validate this newfound "race" argument. Furthermore, I stated that a black man could suddenly, one day, wake up and say that he would now be a homosexual, an alcoholic or a drug addict; however, that same black man couldn't, just one day, wake up and say that he was now Chinese or Mexican.

And finally, I politely pointed out to him the three things, which comes to mind, that is spread among all the populations on earth and readily found in just about every race; disease, addiction, and deviant behavior. I then asked of him; since every living human, including homosexuals, come from male and female, making it quite impossible for homosexuality to be on par with male and female as a new and separate gender, to pick from among the three categories, of which I mentioned, he would like to place the members of the extensively alphabetized LGBTQ community.

Oh, you should have heard the profanities he spewed at me, his emotional outburst and anger over my comments and scientific facts made me see that this so-called "loving," same-sex movement was not some peaceful endeavor by gays to gain their, uh, "rights" at all. Instead, this charade of pretendism was an all-out attempt at establishing and asserting special privileges for one group while attempting to subvert and deny the rights, beliefs, and free speech of another. After my brief but revelatory encounter with this radical homosexual, I haven't viewed most gays in the same light again. That said, I do not believe all of the gay community think this way, of course, just the rather large segment of radical gay Democrats who have infiltrated and morally plundered the black community to no end.

I have concluded at this point, that for homosexuality to flourish and gain the prominence in this nation that most in the gay community so desires, reality as we know it must end, Christianity must perish, and Bible scriptures "updated" to modify God's words for the acceptance of this behavior. As I previously noted, this is where the Democrat Party's usage of their black "Reverends" comes into play, to reinterpret God's word to advocate for, promote, and fit homosexuality neatly within the doctrine of their churches.

Through black leaders such as these, the gay community's repeated messaging of being kindred spirits with the black community has emasculated the majority of black youths, who are now being bombarded daily with sitcoms, commercials, and movies with prominent homosexual characters. Moreover, during the height of the same-sex crusade, liberal media outlets deployed their Asian weave-wearing, neck snapping, loud-mouthed, and unintelligent liberal Democrat black women on just about all of their programs. These highly paid black mercenaries screeched and screamed in emotional and incoherent torrents of racially-infused gibberish about how two men or two women going at it, or men wanting to change into women, was just like the generational atrocities of black slavery.

Democrats love their angry black "queens," who provide the racial ammo for all social causes debates on the left. Pay attention, and you will notice that at any time, and on any liberal broadcast during any hot-button issue, they will conveniently insert racially-charged "victimology" rhetoric into the conversation to stoke emotions and effectively end all meaningful dialogue. This advocacy of the LGBT community by black women has caused indoctrinated and confused black male youths being pushed into agreeing that same-sex marriage and Black Civil Rights are one and the same, and believing that gays not being able to marry was just like blacks being beaten and hung from trees during slavery.

Also, you ever notice that whenever a gay black athlete comes out of the closet, he is always Democrat and that white liberals, the Black Caucus, black reverends, and other black celebrities all rally behind him to eagerly bolster the gay community's diversity and equality narrative.

This "coming out" of the black male athlete is just another method which white liberal Democrats have used to "break the black "buck" all over again and destroy the masculine imagery of today's black men, just as they had done during slavery.

With that being said, there is no benefit or upside, whatsoever, for blacks to readily accept this faustian alliance with the gay community, to eagerly advocate for their deviant sexual behavior and lifestyle. The black community has enough problems of its own without having to align with homosexuals and the many negative issues that come with being attached to their agenda.

Now, for liberals, the purpose of having blacks on board the rainbow is twofold and rather conspicuous. First, by getting the black community to align themselves with homosexuality, the gay community and Democrats strip most blacks of their belief in God and that which is righteous, and this serves to keep most in chaos and constant state of flux.

And secondly, gays can now lay claim that they are just as oppressed and as much of a victim as blacks, thus, shielding themselves from any perceived attack on their community by using the cover of the black Civil Rights Movement.

Black male puppets in the mainstream media also play a significant role in black youths denying and shunning their masculinity. Just watch the soft-spoken and effeminate black "news" anchors and pundits on just about any liberal program; they are as soft as grapes and just facsimiles of real males. These black male feminists have beautiful manicures and eyebrows all done up and will get all emotional like females at the slightest hint of confrontation. And if you haven't noticed yet, a lot of skinny-jeans-wearing, latte-sipping black males in this nation have taken on the attitudes, soft vocal inflections, and cadences of white liberal Democrat males and have become increasingly feminine in their speech pattern and mannerisms.

The Democrat Party's inclusiveness, tolerance, diversity and equality ideology has ravaged the black community, spreading its culture of anti-masculinity and feminist values among black males like an uncontrollable contagion. And it only makes sense that the same

Democrat Party of the 1600s that forced homosexuality upon black males then would also, today, be the same party to continue to go about removing the masculine presence from young males within the black community.

Make no doubt about it, even now the LGBT community is actively and aggressively recruiting blacks. Just recently, Kevin Hart, a diminutive, wildly popular, and successful black comedian who was set to host the Oscars, came under fire by the gay community for old homosexual jokes he told over a decade ago. After a social media firestorm and dust-up, he apologized profusely to the gay community and backed out of hosting the award show altogether.

Nevertheless, liberal Democrat homosexuals saw an opening and at first deployed Ellen DeGeneres, a woman pretending to be a man pretending to be a woman, to gently persuade Kevin to strip himself of his maleness and bow down to the Liberace alter of perversion. Kevin balked at this, uh, offer, so Democrats bought in one of their high-powered black puppets in the hopes that his skin color would do the trick.

Don Lemon, a black male feminist, stripped of all visible masculinity, was then sent to engage and recruit Kevin as an ally of the gay community, with the intention that he would use his star power, as had other blacks in Hollywood, to entice and recruit young black men into the homosexual lifestyle. Sensing what was going down, Kevin wisely declined the offer to sell his soul to the Lgbt community, deciding right then and there on remaining a male and keeping his manhood intact.

Kevin may have been successful in escaping the homosexual dragnet, but the Democrat Party and their minions have been very adept in recruiting many other young black males, who are now mostly emotional replicas of their destructive and vindictive liberal black mothers. Because of the fatherless environment most of these youths are living in, they are easy pickings because they are much more likely to gravitate towards homosexual influences and tendencies, making their recruitment easy for the gay community.

In many black neighborhoods today, female emotions have supplanted essential and sorely needed manly rationale and critical thinking among the majority of male youths. And because of the stripping away of these innate and intrinsic traits endowed by our creator, the female qualities that these black males have taken on today creates dangerous and unpredictable situations in which the slightest insult or perceived insult can cause an overly heighten response to just about any offense.

Undoubtedly, it is this nitroglycerin-like volatility which serves to exacerbate the homicidal chaos within the inner cities we see today, where young black lives aren't worth a plugged nickel. With that being said, let's bring this section to an end because this will neatly segue into our next chapter of course.

Turn the page and peruse, if you will...

Chapter Sixteen

Black Lives Really Matter? Negro, Please!

O k Recap?…oh, I don't think that I need to at this point, so let's just continue…shall we?

◆◆◆

I have never ever, in my life, come across a more oxymoronic and immensely deceptive misnomer than Black Lives Matter. What kind of brainwashing, gobbledygook gibberish have blacks fallen for this time? What's wrong with my people, if stupid were money they'd all be living as millionaires in the inner cities and not waiting on the first of the month for dey government funds. I don't even know where to begin, I just can't.

Why do I even have to write this for blacks to get it? Oh well, I guess someone's gotta do it, I reckon, because there are some very low-info and intellectually-challenged blacks out there who actually believe in and are following this white liberal Democrat-sponsored terrorist organization.

This innocuous sounding organization, Black Lives Matter, founded by black lesbians, enriches itself by playing up racial incidents for the Democrat Party, thereby keeping blacks confused, angry and mentally unbalanced. And make no doubt about it, this violent group is a vital cog and considerable part of the Democrat Party's anti-American weaponry, just like Antifa.

In fact, going back to the KKK of the 1800s and the Black Panthers of the 1970s, just about every violent group throughout our nation's history has been an offshoot of the Democrat Party. *At this point, I will throw down a challenge, I defy anyone to name any hostile group ever created by the Republican Party. Go ahead, I dare ya.*

Today's gang members, Hispanic and black alike, that are shoot-ing at each other within inner cities are all Democrats and criminally flourishing in their Democrat-created hellholes and drug dens. To that end, both Antifa and Black Lives Matter have just one goal which they have been tasked with, foment racial divisiveness and chaos, especially among black youths. Strangely though, given their name-sake, it's curious to me how a group like Black Lives Matter seem to somehow mysteriously avoid tackling high homicide rates among blacks in inner cities like Chicago. Because in this city alone, there have been over 4000 *blacks* murdered by other blacks, and that is just during Obama's two terms in office.

One must then ask, what is this organization's real intent? And why is it then that Obama, Antifa, and Black Lives Matter, who are supposedly so compassionate about the loss of black lives, cannot be bothered with the mind-numbing daily, weekly, and monthly loss of black lives in inner cities all across this country? I suppose, to these "caring" Democrats, blacks being killed by other blacks could never be used for political gain; therefore, these deaths would fall under business-as-usual and viewed as just collateral damage in the Demo-crat Party's war against America and law enforcement.

With that being said, you didn't think, I mean really think, that black lives really mattered to wealthy black stars, the Black Caucus, and other rich black celebs who live among their affluent, white liber-al Democrat pals, did you? Did ya really? No, you couldn't have. You did? Ok, I think the best way to illustrate how much black stars, black congressmen and congresswomen care about black lives is to bring this all together with actual incidents and their selective "outrages" over each one.

We'll start here, it's just as good a place as any to begin, I suppose: On July 20, 2012, a white guy shoots up a theater in Aurora Colorado, killing 12 white people and wounding another 70. In response, there was this sudden fiery and outraged reaction by the liberal media and white Democrats, along with the Black Caucus, Black Lives Matter, the black reverends, and many other well-heeled black puppets: *"It's time for gun control, the NRA needs to be abolished. It's time for our kids to stop dying. Those dreaded AR-15's must be banned once and for all. White Christian males need to be put down!"*

This selective outage continued for months on end and would be memorialized by liberal Democrat candidates and gun control activists for political gain during every election campaign after that. However, in August of 2012, and nearing Labor Day weekend in Chicago, 37 blacks were shot and 9 killed. Strangely, with these black on black killings, the reaction was quite tame, ho-hum, and even matter of fact from the liberal media, white Democrats, Black Caucus, Black Lives Matter and many other black puppet pundits:

"This just illustrates that there are still some shootings in Chicago, but the numbers are trending downward over the last 25 years, or so. Historically, we are seeing a decline in shootings within the inner cities. Besides, those guns are coming in from somewhere else, from other states."

On all of the liberal networks, this shooting in Chicago was less than a two-minute soundbite between commercials, dying off quickly and never to be heard of again. Over on social media, some of the black stars, feeling forced to weigh in, had merely said: *"That's a damn shame man."*

Ok, now let's go to December 14, 2012, when 26 white children were killed in Newtown, Connecticut by a deranged white Democrat youth. Again, there was fiery outrage from the liberal media and white Democrats, the Black Caucus, Black Lives Matter and many black celebrity puppets:

"It's time for gun control, the NRA needs to be abolished. It's time for our kids to stop dying and those dreaded AR-15's banned. These are all of our children! We need to get more laws on the books to protect the innocent. Why is this still happening in America in this day and age?!" "Why are Republicans endorsing this!"

Now with this shooting, there would be massive protests by demonstrators, along with "crisis" loving Democrat Senators who gathered around microphones, speaking empathically about saving the children while gun control advocates screamed at them: *"We must do more to protect our kids! do something about guns, create more laws."*

Hollywood Celebs also got involved, from the safety of their gated communities, of course, making commercials and pleading for more gun control as Democrat lawmakers in Connecticut rushed to reduce the capacity of gun magazines to about two bullets or something. With this particular tragedy, every year, there is the remembrance and push for another gun law to add to the existing five thousand or so on the books already.

Even Obama, the black messiah himself, who did absolutely nothing when over 4000 black youths were being killed in Chicago during his tenure, got into the action because the political capital to be gained from the Sandy Hook tragedy was just too much to resist. He quickly flew to Connecticut on a red-eye and, not waiting for the plane to land, parachuted down onto his podium without even getting his $10,000 suit wrinkled, mic at the ready. Once there, Obama cried like a baby for the cameras as hordes of liberal media jackals captured his crocodile tears for political posterity.

Now, once again, let's juxtapose this with the daily black on black killings in this country: During the weekend of August 3rd, 2018, 72 blacks were shot and 12 killed in Chicago, with the tally for the entire month, 319 blacks shot, 273 wounded and 46 killed. Again, these blacks deaths were met with the same tame and ho-hum reaction by the liberal Democrat media, the supposedly caring white liberals, the Black Caucus, Black Lives Matter and other wealthy black puppets:

"It appears that there are still some shootings in Chicago, but the numbers are trending downward over the last 25 years, or so. Historically, we are seeing a decline in shootings in the inner cities. Besides, those guns are coming in from somewhere else."

The Democrat Party and the liberal mainstream media, along with their black figureheads, have fully mastered the game in regarding which deaths to feign outrage over.

More astonishing to me is how the majority of the black community is so easily distracted, and diverted, from the quite routine deaths of their own people to become so emotionally invested in the murders of others outside their race.

In 2018, during the month of August, while daily black on black killings were occurring in Chicago and inner cities all across America, as a diversion, the mainstream media, and white liberals, along with black Democrat leaders, had most blacks focusing on the anniversary of the Charlottesville, Virginia riot where one white woman was run over and killed by a supposedly white nationalist. Black media pundits went all-in on this single death, huffing and puffing and just beside themselves with the news of this white woman dying after being hit by a car driven by, of all things, a "white supremacist!"

During a Whitehouse press conference, white and black liberal Democrat reporters badgered beleaguered press secretary Sarah Huckabee relentlessly about this woman's death. These "journalists" pressed her on the president's reactions and why he wasn't "denouncing" the white nationalist who flatten and killed this "unarmed and minding-her-own-business" white woman in Virginia.

But, while questions were being raised about this one white woman being killed, nothing was being said about dozens of black youths dying in the inner cities, yet the oh so "concerned" reporters still feigned anger over this one supposedly "white nationalist" incident. *So, to sum up, with these black leaders and pundits, all of their ginned-up anger was focused on a lone white woman in Virginia, and not on the hundreds of dead "brothers" and "sisters" lying on the gang-torn streets of Chicago and other Democrat inner cities.*

Now, it's not like these black on black shootings are one-offs and reporters simply miss'em because they are so elusive. No, these are daily and weekly occurrences, and in plain sight. These "journalists" didn't have to wait for an "incident" and protest every six months to get a scoop on homicides in this nation.

But just watch any of the liberal Democrat mainstream media outlet shows, and you will most likely see a black conservative on the panel with about three, foaming at the mouth, and deranged liberal "news" pundits. And pay close attention to the loud-mouthed, unintelligent, Asian weave-wearing black liberal female or liberal Hispanic woman, and it will go something like this:

Black liberal Democrat host... *"I wanna talk about the tragedy in Charlottesville and the woman who was killed. Trump's reaction spoke volumes to his bigotry in not condemning and denouncing the KKK and white nationalists he seems to be aligned with"*

Black conservative... *"Well, there was a clash between the violent Democrat sponsored Antifa group and the so-called white nationalists that occurred last year. However, I wanna talk about the 400 blacks killed in Chicago so far this year, along with the thousands of blacks killed every year in the inner cities. Why isn't there any coverage on your network."*

Cue the black liberal female... *"Yeah, you wanna ignore what's going on and cover for Trump. He didn't apologize for the death of that white woman in Virginia and condemn the white nationalists enough for us, so why don't you just say he's a racist and part of the KKK."*

Black conservative... *"But, Trump isn't racist, he has done a lot for blacks in just under two years, much more than Obama during his eight years and..."*

Here comes the loud-mouthed liberal Hispanic woman interjecting and cutting him off... *"That's Obama's economy, which was on the precipice of taking off, and did take off soon as Trump took office!"*

Then the black liberal Host gleefully, and falsely, declaring...*"Yeah, it does seem that historically, the numbers would show that there was some lowering of unemployment for blacks during Obama's administration."*

Black Conservative now frustrated that the subject has changed... *"But, but how can this economy be Obama's when it was Trump who rolled back Obama's regulations that were actually hindering and hurting the growth of businesses.*

It was Trump who established and accelerated the growth in our economy we have now with tax cuts, which give incentives to small businesses to expand and hire more employees. He's created over 700,000 jobs for blacks at this point. It's a fact that under Trump, black businesses has increased by 400%. Now, can we please get back to the killings in Chicago?"

Enter the fuming black liberal female once again...*"Ok coon, if that's what you wanna believe, Trump hasn't done anything for blacks.*

He's racist against blacks, Muslims, and Hispanics, he abuses women, he's unfit for office, and he has conspired with Russians." Smiling black host... *"unfortunately, we're outta time."*

This is the way it typically goes on liberal networks; paid black millionaire pundits deliberately ignoring and burying any issue that would illuminate the real distress within black communities, while sarcastically dismissing anything good that Republicans are trying to to do for the black community. These black overseers obfuscate the facts, cloud the details, and misdirect with made for television emotionalism that their white Democrat masters love.

Well-paid black puppets you often see on liberal networks have one mission only, to shift the focus of the narrative and conversation back onto the Democrat Party's ideology of inclusiveness, equality, diversity, and tolerance.

Ok, so let's move on and take a look at one more Democrat exploitation-ready "incident." On August 26th, 2018, 9 people were shot and 2 killed by an alleged "white man" in Jacksonville, Florida. *Ah, some white folks being killed, now we'll get some action from Democrats again!* And just like that, and as if on cue, the fiery outrage of the liberal media, white Democrats, Black Caucus, Black Lives Matter and other black puppets:

"It's time for gun control, the NRA needs to be abolished, it's time for our kids to stop dying, and those dreaded AR-15's banned. We're gonna get more laws on the books."

I could go on and on because there are so many incidents and circumstances which drive home the point that black lives do not matter to well-paid black puppets, nor to the liberal white masters that control them. Strangely enough, the loss of a black life never seem to really matter to most rank and file blacks in the inner cities either, that is until their white, and black liberal leaders give the order that they do.

When Trayvon Martin was shot and killed while in the act of beating the hell out of old George Zimmerman, our black president had then intoned: *"Why, that could have been my son."* Really Mr. black messiah? None of the other 4000 or so black kids that were shot and killed in Chicago during your barf-inducing eight-year tenure as president could've been your son? Not one was qualified? I mean, we're talking on average about 500 children, some as young as six years old, being shot every year in Chicago while Obama was president and none, I say none, could have been his child because they had the misfortune of being killed by other blacks. Only a few errant, and criminal, black youths killed by white cops was worthy of being his son?

I wanna say here, there was another really tragic story out of Chicago that really touched me, and one the liberal Democrat media quickly buried. A little nine-year-old black boy was on his way to school, playing innocently with his basketball, when a group of young black gang members, thugs, approached him and inquired as to the whereabouts his father. Of course, the little fella didn't know of his father's location, hardly any of the black youths in Democrat-run cities know where their fathers are today. Anyways, not happy with the answer they received, this group of black thugs then took the little child into an alley, stood him up against a wall and summarily executed him.

Now, I can only imagine what went through this little innocent child's mind in those final moments of his short stay on earth as bullets tore into the tender flesh of his little body, smashing bones and piercing organs until his life was no more. He probably wondered, in his last seconds, what he could have done so wrong to not have any real chance at life.

With his death, there were to be no t-shirts made, no marching, no nothing for this little black kid, because he didn't fit the political narrative of white liberal Democrats. There would be no protests or racially-incensed mobilization of black celebs, no angry, puffed-mouthed black sports stars and black rappers or any other high profile blacks threatening anyone on liberal media outlets, nor any blacks wearing t-shirts and hoodies for this kid.

There was also to be no sensitive, sniffling, and almost crying black anchors detailing for weeks how this innocent little boy was executed. And there was barely a whimper on social media or on any of the liberal networks. This child's death was blacked out and omitted like the thousands of other black on black killings occurring each and every year in inner cities across our nation.

At the time, I was speaking to a big-mouthed liberal black male, who was whining about cops hunting blacks, and when I told him about this story, he just goes: *"Oh, I didn't know that happened."* I told him other stories about little black kids being killed in the inner cities by other blacks, and each time I had finished, he always had the same response: *"Oh, I didn't know that happened."* Sadly, this is representative of a lot of blacks; most don't know a damn thing outside of the Democrat Party and liberal media, which doesn't show or tell them the truth about their own people.

I have noticed recently, with black Democrat leaders, prized remembrances and tributes are reserved only for the few blacks that are killed by whites. These rare white on black killings are the only deaths that seem to matter because militant blacks can then get the chance to parade around screeching police brutality," while looking for an opportunity to perhaps get on television and if lucky, get the black reverends involved and sue somebody.

Uh, "grieving" black mothers, who knew their sons were out slinging drugs, shooting people and committing robberies, will always sue the city for their "unarmed" sons' "undeserved" death if a cop was involved in the shooting. Strangely enough though, according to most all of the mothers of these "victims," their black sons being killed by officers while engaging in criminal activities, were somehow good boys and every last one of them was supposedly on the path to getting their lives together at the very moment they were shot.

A lot of inner-city blacks are hip to the game of musical lawsuits and quite aware that a liberal media-driven racial "incident" can prompt a city to settle for millions with the victims' families, and quickly. So, in Chicago, and just about any other Democrat inner-city hellhole, a criminal black young'un being killed by a white cop is like hitting the lottery for most of these mothers.

I think whenever one of'em gets shot and killed, the mother holds her breath like waiting on the results of a Powerball or scratch-off ticket to see if she had won. In the case of an inner city mother's child being killed by another black youth: *"Damn nothing, poor little Jaeqckeni, told his ass to stay away from that gang, I need a go-fund-me or something."*

However, if it is a white cop shooting and killing her son, it's a whole nother matter for this black mom: *"Yessssssss, they killed my totally unarmed and minding-his-own-business good son, and the media is here, got my hair did, where's the NAACP? "Where are the black Reverends and lawyers?" "Where's my millions!"*

So, it would appear that, for a taken black life to matter to most inner city blacks, the killing would have to be able to fit within the very narrow confines of that rare white-on-black racial incident within the black community. It's almost as if a black youth killed in the inner city would have to first meet specific criteria, as given by liberal Democrats, to actually qualify for the exalted status of mattering to black celebrities, black rappers, rich blacks, the Black Caucus, and white liberal Democrats.

On those rare occasions that this stringent test has been met, and the death determined by white liberals to matter, the old black "Reverends" and black organizations are called in to give speeches about blacks being hunted by racist cops. Then, and only then, would the protesting, looting, and rioting commence. I mean, for most blacks to get agitated and upset about the incident themselves, they really have to confirm with Democrats and the liberal media that the dead black youth lying in the street, riddled with bullet holes, was indeed shot by a white person, preferably a white officer.

Now, if it happens to be a black cop who had shot and killed a black thug, white liberals and black leaders will then neatly fit this death in under the "all law enforcement is racist" theory to qualify the incident as racist. For instance, in Charlotte, Virginia, an incident occurred in which a black officer, who reported to a black chief of police, shot and killed a black guy holding a gun. It wasn't until after the liberal media got ahold of the story and twisted the hell out of it that, amazingly, blacks started screaming "racism."

This animal-like mentality and low intellect among the majority of blacks are enjoyed immensely by the mainstream media and wealthy black pundits, sitting in cozy "news" studios sipping lattes with white liberals while whipping their inner city zombies into a racial frenzy. Ok, by now I think you understand, with black and white Democrats, that not all black lives are equal, and that some are more special and politically important than others. So, let's try to gain some insight into which black deaths can qualify for a riot, get noticed by the black reverends, and bring 24/7 media attention.

We'll start by visiting, and contrasting, two mothers of slain black inner city youths to make our point. Our first scenario will showcase a Democrat reporter from the mainstream media, unknowingly interviewing the mother of a black on black shooting victim:

"Ma'am, can you tell us what happened, we are just trying to ascertain the facts of this incident so we can fully cover it on the six o'clock news."

"Well, (sniffle), my little Taquandrella was shot by Jhermal, he lives down the street aways, I believe the police have him now."

"Ok, is Jhermal black as well?"

"Yes, he is sir."

"Uh, er, do you know if this Jhermal happens to be an officer?"

'No, he's...I don't think so; he actually was in a gang and sold drugs."

"Uh, er, Robby cut; I think we have just about all we need."

"So, do I get to be on the news?"

"We'll get back to you ma'am, sorry for your loss."

"How about appearing at the Democrat convention with Hillary or somebody?"

"Ha, ha, ha... We'll get back to you."

So, as this scene demonstrates, blacks killed by other blacks go virtually unnoticed by the Democrat media and are brushed aside; just forgotten inner city collateral. Oh, other blacks in the neighborhood will do their usual and quite frequent ritual of lighting candles and placing teddy bears and flowers at the site of the black on black shooting, all while giving their almost rehearsed feelings and grievances that so and so didn't deserve this and people need to wake up and stop the violence.

But this "tribute" by neighborhood blacks doesn't even begin to compare with the privilege and sainthood status bestowed upon a black youth shot by law enforcement, especially a white cop. Blacks killed by law enforcement never, ever truly die, they just seem to live on forever, memorialized and deified through t-shirts and militant black celebs and rappers.

These exalted "victims," even in death, enjoy a barrage of 24/7 media coverage for months on end and are given look-back tributes every year to commemorate the "racist incident." Most fallen, inner city black "heroes" are given plaques and medals of Honor for their bravery and courage while being shot by a cop in the course of dealing drugs or committing other criminal activities in their community.

Furthermore, the circumstances of these "unarmed" and "minding-their-own-business" deaths are then taught in universities by white liberal Democrat "professors" in the hopes of inciting even more blacks. And to top all this memorializing off, tear-jerking Hollywood movies are made for posterity; of these innocent black scholars who were all hunted in the inner cities like deer, all victims of "racist police brutality" and the supposedly unequal justice system.

With that said, let's now go ahead to our second scene and listen in on the questioning by a liberal Democrat reporter. He is interviewing the mother of a black youth who was slain by a white cop, which is without a doubt the holy grail of "racial incidents" in the inner cities, and a political candy store for Democrats:

"Ok, Ma'am, can you tell us what happened, we are just trying to ascertain the facts of this incident so we can get it covered on the six o'clock news."

"Well, my son, who is usually out all times of night on the corner was, just hanging out with his great friends. You know, just reciting Shakespeare and going over questions on his upcoming PSAT exam. And all of a sudden, this white cops pulls up out of nowheres and gets to shooting, killing my son just cause he black."

"A white cop?! Did you say a WHITE cop shot your unarmed, minding his own business son?! This is unbelievable? How are you holding up ma'am?"

"Ok, (sobbing), I guess ok, this is the third son that's been taken from me?"

"Sorry for your loss ma'am, but wait a minute; were your other two scholarly sons shot by cops as well?"

"No, street gang members shot my other two, they were just hanging out at a party, enjoying themselves."

"Uh, er, ok, yeah, well right now we'll deal with what matters. Cops should be held to a higher standard; this racism has got to stop. This is a despicable and heinous act by law enforcement."

"Yeah, they need to stop hunting our people; I've had enough of this police brutality. My son didn't du nuffin and didn't deserve this."

"Don't worry ma'am, we'll get this on the air right away, we'll expose the blatant disregard of your son's rights, and other unarmed black men caught up in the systemic racism that runs rampant throughout law enforcement and the justice system. Have you called the Reverends and filed a lawsuit already?"

"Yeah, (smiling), I did that earlier today."

" Ok Robby, cut, get this back to the station as soon as possible, gotta get it edited, gotta get my hair and makeup done for this horrific and tragic story!"

And this is how it goes with the black community, ignoring the annual genocide of over 6000 black on black killings, to mainly focus on the yearly 300 or so media-directed racial incidents involving a cop protecting the decent people within the black community from the criminal elements in their neighborhoods.

This "systemic racism" ploy by the Democrat media and black Reverends seem to work all too well because long after the St Louis incident involving the Mike Brown shooting, there's still those manipulated, and really dumbed down blacks exclaiming: *"Remember Mike Brown bro!" "Yeah, damn cops shot'em, and he was unarmed and innocent!"*

Meanwhile, from the time old Mike was shot in 2014 to now, there was probably another 25,000 blacks killed by other blacks in the inner cities; however, these collateral blacks will be ignored like so much road kill by Democrats and their black marionettes. You can't make this stuff up, it is unconscionable, the disregard by blacks for other black lives snuffed out by blacks within their own communities, but on and on it goes and where it stops no one knows.

It seems that daily and weekly black on black shootings in the inner cities is now like watching a long-running, made-for-television drama where a black being shot by a white cop is just a commercial break. *Can't you hear the voice-over now narrating the stoppage of this regular programming when a white cop shoots another criminal black:*

"We will now take a commercial break from our regular shooting of each other to riot, loot, and destroy property, but don't go away, we'll be right back to shooting each other!"

Ok, ok, I think you get the picture....no, you don't? So, you think it's hyperbole? You really think cops are hunting blacks?

Well then, let's go to some numbers and, in this instance, we are gonna use black on black homicides in just Chicago alone, Obama's old stomping grounds when he was broke and smoking crack. You see, even with all of his supposed organizing, it seems that Obama could not make a dent in the massive homicide rate in his hometown.

So, just for ha...ha's...we are gonna take a trip to the windy city and take a snapshot of the homicidal madness among blacks. Let's now go ahead and compare and contrast shootings by law enforcement and inner-city blacks during the nine years of Obama's tenure, and right on up to 2018, shall we?

Year	Cops killing blacks	Blacks killing blacks
2009,	19	459
2010,	13	436
2011,	23	433
2012,	8	514
2013,	13	455
2014,	17	464
2015,	9	511
2016,	11	808
2017,	11	682
2018	18	381 as of August 2018

Total: 128 blacks killed by the police. 5143 blacks killed by other blacks.

Now, even with the undeniably stark reality these numbers portray of wanton violence and homicides among blacks, after every cop shooting of a black criminal, black sports stars, celebs, black rappers, the Black Caucus, and the black Reverend leaders will all still get on television and social media to vilify law enforcement and foam at the mouth: *"F'ng pigs hunting blacks, white racist mofos, no justice no peace!"*

Now, I don't know about you, but from the numbers on the above chart, it appears that inner city blacks are much more capable and efficient at "hunting" other inner city blacks than law enforcement could ever be. And to think that cops, according to most blacks, are the ones who are supposed to be trained to "hunt'em" down and "get'em."

Well, just maybe these officers patrolling the high crime areas of our country's dangerous inner cities need to bring in a few of these side-shooting, saggy pants fellas to enlighten them on their wildly successful technique of hunting and killing blacks. I mean, according to those stats above, the cops in Chicago could only peel off about 128 of these little fellas from 2009 to 2018, while blacks were able to kill over 5000 inner-city dwelling blacks during the same exact period!

To me, this just shows that law enforcement's hunting and black-kills ratio in Democrat inner cities like Chicago is very, very dismal compared to sharp shooting inner-city blacks. *Don't these officers ever go to the range? Practice, practice, practice man, we're talking about practice!* What game is afoot here you ask? Why are these supposedly well-trained professional lawmen hitting and killing so few blacks while sagging-pants, stoned-on-weed blacks enjoy a much higher ratio of black kills in Democrat-run inner cities?

I may be wrong, but I think I might've figured out the primary cause of this massive disparity in the number of black kills between inner city blacks and law enforcement. It seems that blacks who are shooting and killing each other in Chicago, and in every other inner city, don't really give a damn as to who they hit or why. These inner city side-winding blacks will shoot at boys, men, girls, women, school children, kindergartners, roosters, cats, dogs, mice, crickets, etc. And they couldn't care less about the ages of their victims either, they'll shoot ya from one year old to one hundred years old and beyond.

*Inner city blacks will even shoot a baby in the womb, which would not even count as a murder to the old black "Civil Rights" Reverends and white liberal Democrats, I would suppose, because these black Democrat deviants would undoubtedly just classify the baby's death as a late-term abortion under their Planned Parenthood guidelines or something.

For added bonus points, a lot of blacks will shoot other blacks over a "look" or a diss and will kill for designer sunglasses and a pair of new Jordans. Many blacks will kill another black wearing the wrong colors in the wrong neighborhood, and they will kill for a cell phone, and it doesn't even have to be an iPhone either! Most inner city blacks kill because they are bored, and murder because they are excited.

Blacks will shoot each other at award shows, rap concerts, at barbecues and at funerals. Some blacks will shoot anyone, anywhere, and at any time, doesn't matter the weather or the season. I think that with these blacks, their trigger fingers move even while they are sleeping, probably stemming from some disorder like SBWSA, Shooting Blacks While Sleeping Apnea, or something. Ever heard of DWB, (Driving While Black)? Well how's about SWB, (Shooting While Black!)

With the many ways blacks kill other blacks these days, there's just no way in hell for law enforcement in Democrat inner cities ever to match their kill ratio, unless they also devalue lives like inner city blacks do and target, indiscriminately, whomever and whatever to shoot. I don't think this will happen, of course, because most lawmen are decent and honest folks and are upstanding citizens endowed with a conscience, something the majority of blacks lack.

The reluctance by law enforcement to follow in the path of trigger happy inner city blacks, makes inner city blacks, hands down, the best hunters and killers of other blacks by an overwhelming margin. It is also worth noting that with almost any community, city or region in this country that is predominately black, you will also find a lot of violence and very high homicide rates. It's also worth noting a weird coincidence, that Democrats, the same social justice warriors supposedly looking out for the welfare of blacks, run all of these inner cities. But just don't just take my word for it, look up the homicide rates in any of the predominately black cities, such as Baltimore, Detroit, Washington, D.C, Chicago or Milwaukee.

It seems that wherever a lot of blacks are concentrated, you will also find much higher incidents of violence and killings then you would see in any mixed communities that have a much lower percentage of blacks. Looking back over the last forty years or so, over 250,000 thousand blacks, and counting, have been killed by other blacks on inner city plantations across this country without even so much as a whimper from liberal Democrats.

This epidemic has gone mostly unnoticed by the public due to the civil rights "reverends" and mainstream media continually running interference and downplaying the staggering number of black deaths at the hands of Democrats. The black reverends are especially adept at distracting and diverting the attention of blacks away from the genocide of their own people and, in return, are well rewarded with wealth, fame, and the opportunity to live in exclusive gated communities alongside their liberal white masters.

These black overseers, along with the Black Caucus and effeminate and corrupt black news anchors, black sports stars, black rappers, and other house Negroes, run the black community like a gang, directing their anger in the direction as their white liberal masters have commanded. I have witnessed this misdirected anger time and time again among many low intellect blacks as they wait and watch for cues from their black "leaders" on what actions to take after a supposed "racial incident" occurs.

Most blacks, like trained animals, lurk on inner city plantations, biding their time until well-paid black leaders within the Democrat Party get on social media to let them know who or what their next prey will be. And boy, these hierarchy blacks and house Negro celebrities on television and social media sound and look so angry as they rachet up the racial tension, exhorting poor and uneducated inner city blacks not to take it anymore, to rise up and fight!

They use all the right words; "institutional racism," "white supremacy," and many other racial dog whistles in demanding blacks take a stand and protest and riot. This tactic works quite well on most uneducated and emotional black inner city dwellers who do not care about facts, due process or civility. They just care about what the black basketball star, Hollywood celeb, Black Lives Matter, the black "reverends" and the Black Caucus tell them. They were all "brothers" and "sisters," and what they said must be true, because we blacks were all together, right?

The difference between the wealthy black instigators and the poor black rioters is when the well-off black Democrat has finished appealing to poor inner-city blacks to riot and protest, he goes to Starbucks and have a latte with his well-heeled white liberal Democrat friends.

And while there, with his $1,000 iPhone, he yucks it up with'em while discussing his upcoming trip to Paris, or dishing about his stock holdings and real estate investments. Meanwhile, inner city blacks, among whom he has stoked emotions, are rioting and tearing up their own neighborhoods and yelling "institutionalized racism" and no "justice, no peace."

After destroying their own neighborhoods, these poor, riled-up blacks go back to their substandard and dilapidated housing in the same drug-infested communities, where a lot of them will be subsequently shot like roaches by other drug-dealing blacks. However, the survivors will wait patiently amid the poverty, drug dealing, and killings for the next racial "incident" to occur; and for their instructions from white liberals and their black overseers on how to react.

The sad thing is, when you speak to a lot of these dumbed down blacks about black on black crime, most of them don't say we have to do something about our children being killed. No, these liberal fools ignorantly and foolishly shout: *"Whites are doing it too, why ain't you talking about that son!"* Well, let's go to the numbers again to see how this plays out; the white population is about 195 million,

Hispanics about 60 million, (give or take a few million illegals or so), and the black community comes in at approximately 39 million.

So, to dispense with this racial equivalency theory often touted and tossed about by highly sensitive, low-info blacks to justify black on black killings; if whites all of a sudden decided to kill about 40 million of their own people one day, could blacks somehow match them one for one and continue as a race in this nation?

I would think not unless you could somehow use the Democrat Party's common-core math or something. *My people, my people...* FBI stats show that whites and Hispanics in this nation, combined, average about 5700 killings a year among themselves, while blacks in Democrat inner cities average over 6000 deaths a year among themselves.

These numbers should give the black community some pause. We are the only race making ourselves extinct, not any other group of people and certainly not our now vilified law enforcement. Undeterred, black overseers still will go into hyper overdrive concealing these facts to protect their benefactors, white liberals, even going through great lengths to try, at every turn to "debunk" any stats that will expose the actual condition of homicidal blacks in Democrat-run inner cities.

You know, a thought keeps nagging at me, why is it that black lives can only matter when blacks are given the go-ahead by white and black liberal Democrats? Why are inner city blacks being told which killings to get angry over and pay public tribute to, and which ones to ignore? If we can just go back for a moment and touch on the foundation of this apathy among blacks regarding the lives of their brethren.

Since the 1600s, devaluation of black lives by other blacks was designed by Democrats to keep plantation blacks in perpetual emotional flux and to destroy any unity that would pose a threat to the slave industry in the deep south. You see, by having blacks view each other as worthless during slavery, there would never be enough togetherness of the over four million slaves for a rebellion against their white masters.

Today, this mental conditioning has produced a self-defeatist attitude where the dependency by blacks on the financial largess of their white liberal Democrat masters far outweighs any compassion they may have for any black lives lost to other blacks in their communities. As I pointed out before, there has always been other blacks, such as house Negroes taking advantage of black violence.

Today, the Black Lives Matter organization benefits significantly from chaos in black communities. They have deftly exploited the weakness of most blacks, who always seem to need a leader, and is merely a replacement for the old radical, do-nothing, black "civil rights" reverends.

These long-in-the-tooth, corrupt black guards have lost their mojo on the black youths of today and are on their way out. They are no longer relevant among this new cadre of emotional and extremely violent young black social justice warriors of the Democrat Party. But don't feel sad for these old, race-baiting reverends, they have already made their millions from decades of blackmailing and race hustling off the backs of poor blacks and is now merely handing the 'racial incitement" torch off to those that are now more capable.

Black Lives Matter pays homage to the old, corrupt "reverends" by purveying all things racial with an enthusiasm that matches, and sometimes exceeds, the energy of their captive inner-city black sheep and have now taken over the shepherding of these racially sensitive, susceptible, and emotionally vulnerable black youths.

If you look closely, there are tens of millions of dollars flowing from white liberal Democrat billionaires and corporations into the coffers of this group. *Why is that you ask?* These are just advance payments to these new, young black overseers for steering indoctrinated and illiterate blacks onto the Democrat Party's platform and ideology.

Because the founders of Black Lives Matters are lesbians, this dovetails quite nicely with the gay community's diversity and equality pitch. Truth is, just like the black reverends, nothing has changed in this set-up, the militant youngsters heading up Black Lives Matter will be the only ones really profiting from the poverty, homicides, drug dealing, and gangs ravaging the inner cities. This organization's "directors" and "employees" will make millions and will live not in the inner cities among the poor blacks they "lead," but among their well-heeled, white liberal friends in beautiful, safe communities.

One of the most disturbing, and little known facts about all the killings in Democrat cities like Chicago, is that there is about a 70% unsolved murder rate, which means that a lot of black murderers are walking the streets with impunity, and in plain sight, within the same neighborhoods where their victims once lived. However, in many of these cases, there is never any demands for justice in these neighborhoods. There is no rioting and no destruction of property, no chanting of "no justice, no peace" from residents until these criminals are caught, nothing.

I suppose that the people living in these communities know who the killers are and have just resigned themselves to living with it, maybe out of fear or just plain apathy. And with all things considered, I would guess that it would be the former. Most inner city blacks, especially the children, are desensitized anyway from the frequency of homicides in their neighborhoods and have grown accustomed to the almost daily occurrence of violence from their own people.

The only ones speaking out about this issue is black conservatives who are deeply concerned about the future and direction of the black community and our black youth. However, conservative blacks are continuously ridiculed, attacked, and summarily dismissed as coons and sellouts by wealthy black puppets and other plantation blacks.

Most blacks living in violent inner cities today are taught to absolutely hate black conservatives, just like house Negroes in the 1800s were taught to hate field Negroes and runaways. And because of their mental brainwashing and conditioning, plantation blacks nowadays do not share much in common with independent and free-thinking black conservatives, nor do they share their clarity of thought. Black conservatives today are much like their defiant ancestors who, during slavery, had escaped the stranglehold of Democrats while other blacks remained ensconced in their poverty and misery, dependent on their white masters and content in their status on the plantation.

So, in concluding this chapter, I will say that, until blacks learn to value other lives like their own and take a tough stance against the Democrat Party's dominance of their lives, they will always be failures and losers.

*Until plantation blacks recognize and call out the ills of the hellhole inner cities that white and black liberal Democrats have created for them, they will never become financially stable and economically viable in this nation of wealth.

*Until blacks truly unite and demand action to cure the problematic and systemic issues plaguing the inner cities that they face daily, and until they require that they are treated like humans beings instead of property and political pawns, they'll never gain respect from white liberals or anyone else.

*Until blacks treat every single black death in their cities with the same venomous anger, rioting, and looting, there'll never be any legitimacy to the Black Lives Matter movement or its organization. Finally, until blacks can look into the mirror and say I am somebody and matters, and that every other damn person's life matters, regardless of race, they will be a lost cause and will endure needless and endless suffering under their white Democrat masters for many more generations to come.

*But hold on, wait just a cotton-picking minute here, what is this I hear? For decades, white and black liberal Democrats have been telling the black community that all they need is just a little more black leadership at the helm of these violence-prone inner cities to right the ship.

Ooooooookk, alrighty then, let's just take a quick stroll into this leadership fantasy that black Democrats leaders have forever conjured up for the majority of poor blacks that have foolishly bought into this nonsense. This should be good, so stop staring and turn the page.

Chapter Seventeen

Handicaps and Special Needs Victims

O k, I am not recapping anything at this point, gonna let it ride and marinate for a few chapters. Hopefully, everything is sinking in so far as to who the enemies of this country and its citizens are, we'll summarize later...

I was watching a forum recently, a town hall meeting on the topic of violence in Chicago, and it occurred to me that this particular discussion was most insightful on the way most liberal blacks think. The broadcast peeled back the liberal media's concealment of back genocide and exposed the frustration of the city's residents regarding the massive amount of black youths being killed annually on their streets. This truth just so happened to be revealed on none other than Fox News, the station hated by liberal Democrats but the only one bold enough to air what was actually happening within the black community.

As I began watching the show, I just knew that it was gonna be good, so I got my popcorn ready, and just as I assumed, it was predictable and didn't disappoint. The segment started off with a panel of concerned-looking black "leaders," who were called together to have a meaningful dialogue and discuss solutions for their community's problems.

This brain thrust and think-tank consisted of three black men; a Chicago Democrat Congressman, another running for mayor and a stern-looking West Indies professor who rounded out the table. The panel's robust and timely discussion centered on how to address the quite sobering daily homicides, gang violence, drug dealing, and stifling poverty devastating the black community.

Sure enough, following upon the predictable path of liberal Democrats, the black Congressman pro-offered that the only way for black Chicagoans to rise from their decades-long quagmire, created by Democrats, was to remove the current white Democrat mayor and elect a black Democrat to the position, which would be himself of course.

The inference here, by this opportunistic black "brother," was, that only by increasing leadership positions for black Democrats in city government, could the unique needs of the stressed black community be genuinely addressed. This statement, in and of itself, is quite absurd and condescending and insightful as to the devious race baiting nature of black leaders who see political power as just a pathway to self-enrichment.

For decades, black candidates and congressional leaders have been directed by their white liberal masters to perpetuate the myth that they are highly upset at the problems that have been troubling their communities for decades. These deceptive and duplicitous black serpents slyly tell low info blacks repeatedly, that if elected they will search diligently for ways to deal with the violence and poverty plaguing the inner cities that people like themselves have created.

But underneath this "caring" facade, liberal black leaders view inner-city blacks as being helpless without their aid and guidance, treating most like mentally retarded and handicapped special-needs victims who just needed to be handled with care so as not to damage their feeble and fragile minds. You know, I've always wondered, just what are these extraordinary needs I keep hearing about that the black community has which are so different from every other race in America?

I would venture to guess that one of these manufactured "needs," is the never-ending and cyclical, supposedly, lack of voter Id among blacks, an election-time ruse created entirely by the Democrat Party and their liberal media cohorts. Only during this time, to stir voter turnout, does this unicorn rears its racial head as Democrats angrily declare that the black community is just so disenfranchised and unable, for decades, to figure out how to get a proper id because of voter suppression by Republicans.

This every-election, racially-charged proclamation by black "leaders" regarding the seemingly endless failure of downtrodden blacks to procure an id, really implies that most just aren't smart enough to know where the DMV office or any other government building is located. However, for decades, the majority of these same blacks have had no problem finding the welfare office and obtaining the proper id needed to get "dey" benefits.

Still, yet, some of these easily led blacks will watch liberal networks like CNN, continually beating the voter Id "victimization" drum, and get highly upset, believing that most blacks in their community cannot get an Id because of some right wing suppression.

If you think that any black in the inner cities is without Id's, go ahead ask any of them if they have an Id and there's your answer.

So no, black voter suppression doesn't exist today and haven't since Democrats placed the KKK at the polls to intimidate blacks, starting with Reconstruction in 1865 and ending in 1964 with the signing of the Civil Rights Bill. Nevertheless, during every election, black pundits on liberal networks flap their gums and foam at the mouth, screaming that poor blacks are being disenfranchised and that their votes are being suppressed.

This is just one of the Democrat Party's tried-and-true methods of perpetually entrapping blacks in a mental state of victimhood, telling them that they are not capable or smart enough to do anything on their own. For instance, look at blacks who think that they cannot get into most prestigious colleges by their own merit and hard work because of some fictional institutionalized "systemic racism."

They are being told that, because of centuries of enslavement, blacks today need affirmative action and shouldn't have to get the same grades as their white and Asian counterparts to attend the same colleges. *So really, are liberal Democrats saying that the majority of blacks are so stupid that they have to have college tests dumbed down for them to compete with whites and Asians? The irony to all of this?*

It's weird that these same proud "African Americans" asserting this claim today are the same ones who believe that during slavery this country was built by the creative hands of black slaves. *So how can it be that blacks, coming from this lineage of smart, dutiful, hard-working black builders, now need a dumbed-down sliding scale to get into most colleges?* I am completely mystified by this paradox; it seems to me that any type of affirmative action or dumbing down of anything for blacks would be seen as patronizing and condescending; an insult and the ultimate "less than" slap in the face of proud "African" blacks.

I personally believe that Affirmative action for blacks is like giving a wheelchair to a man who is quite capable of walking himself if he tried. *It is one thing to need a hand up, and entirely another just to want a hand up because you feel entitled.*

Take Head Start, another wealth redistribution ploy crafted and promoted by white liberals and launched in 1965. This waste of a program was designed, supposedly, for so-called "disadvantaged and less fortunate" black children and was a part of Democrat president Lyndon B Johnson's 1965 "war on poverty." However, we all know how he really felt about blacks: *"With the signing of this civil rights bill, niggers will be voting Democrat for the next 200 years."*

Anyway, Head Start, supposedly an educational equalization tool for underprivileged three and four-year-old black kids, was to be implemented at an early age to, uh, level the learning field with young white kids of the same age group. But as with most programs put in place by Democrats, what was supposed to be an eight-week program soon turned into a massive year-round expenditure of taxpayers' money with minimal results to show for it.

In 2002, a study by Human & Health Services sampled over 4000 children in the Head Start program and, over several years, compared them to other black children who were not in the program. At first, there appeared to be some modest gains by those participating in the program, however, by the time these Head Start enrollees got to elementary school, there was no noticeable difference in these kids versus the black kids not entered into the program.

Furthermore, prior research by the Westinghouse Learning Foundation in 1969 concluded that any gains made by black kids in the Headstart program had all but disappeared by the early grades. As a result, this "helping out" program was nothing more than another re-distribution of wealth albatross draining more taxes from the middle class to fund and "staff" this slush fund.

To date, over 30 million kids have gone through Headstart at the cost of over 100 billion dollars with little results. Even now, taxpay-ers are quietly being ripped off to the tune of about $8 billion each year with still no discernable difference in educational improvement among kids in the black community. And to further bolster these re-sults, other federal studies in 1985 and 2005 also concluded that there was no difference between the kids that had gone through the pro-gram and those who did not. So, what gives?

Well, here's a thought, Head Start which was initially founded to "help" disadvantaged black children, was created just so liberal Democrats could have another pool of money available to spend on whatever social causes they wanted. To note, most of the funds in this program have now been redirected to fund early schooling for foreigners and illegals.

Today, the participants in Head Start are comprised of about 37% Hispanics, 31% blacks, 7% mixed Indians, and about 5% percent Asians. This follows the modus operandi of white liberal Democrats; first utilize their inclusiveness, diversity, tolerance, and equality ide-ology to create a massive pot of taxpayer money for one cause and once established, redirect the hell out of it for whatever purpose they want, all while skimming funds off the top for their "staffing" expens-es, like vacations and casino trips.

Also, to note, when it comes to the Headstart program, whites are barely on the scale as to participating in this wasteful program that funnels money to the Democrat Party's minions while creating more unnecessary, and redundant, government positions.

To continue in this vein, take social security as another exam-ple of taxpayer funds abuse. This seemingly well-intended "help" for retirees, who had worked and paid into the program, currently have billions being taken out and redirected, again by Democrats, to able-bodied people in their 20s, 30s, and 40s, all claiming disability. In fact, due to the startling uptick in new disability cases since the

1960s, the dirty little secret is that there are more people on disability in this country today than on welfare. This change in the SSI program came about with the loosening of once stringent rules that now allow depression, stress, simple aches, and other pains as qualifiers.

This massive Social Security fraud being perpetrated by Democrats is a relatively new "welfare scheme, and another means by which the party can garner more votes by "protecting" these new "rights," while draining what's left of social security. In public though, these same Democrats put on quite the show, often screeching and howling about how they must protect social security while, supposedly, admonishing Republicans not to touch this sacred program because retirees paid into this program and have earned it. This dishonesty just shows the duplicity and deviousness of two-faced Democrats.

An entire book could be written on Social Security, the new welfare, but I won't go any deeper into this subject at this point. However, everyone needs to research this for themselves and become aware of everything liberals are doing against the hard-working taxpayers of this country.

Getting back on track, I would like to state that there are more poor whites in this nation, probably more than the entire population of blacks and Hispanics, combined, yet, the black community, in their "victimized" stupor, still fall back on their liberal taught default position when they fail to achieve their goals: *"It's the white racist system holding me down, and I need help."*

The Democrat Party has pushed this "institutionalized, systemic racism" and "helpless victim" narrative onto the backs of dumbed down blacks for decades. So much so that the majority of blacks living in inner cities genuinely believe they are mentally handicapped and special-needs victims, utterly incapable of standing up as men and women on their own two feet as with other races.

So, to conclude this chapter, I wanna say that blacks are not special-needs victims, nor are they handicapped, most are just plain lazy and always looking for something for nothing. Furthermore, blacks are not unique in any way, shape or fashion and, nowadays, the only thing so unique to black culture is the high degree of sensitivity most in the community exhibit towards any and all perceived racial slights.

The majority of blacks have the most delicate and thinnest of skins in this regard, which is so strange for supposedly strong African Queens and fierce black Mandingo warriors from the harsh and unforgiving jungles of the motherland. Nonetheless, these same proud "African Americans" have specific words they say all the time among themselves and within their own neighborhoods, but the majority of them will act a complete fool and wild-out when other people outside their race say these same exact words.

Somehow this duplicitous behavior is viewed as normal and part of black culture, which I think is quite silly and dangerous. Today, I sincerely believe that most of the black community done gone and tasted too much of the rainbow and have been fully immersed into the Democrat Party's inclusiveness, diversity, tolerance, and equality Kool-Aid. I mean, these fools have become absolutely staggeringly stone drunk off this suicidal elixir.

You know, at this point, I wanna talk about it.

Turn the page.

Chapter Eighteen

The "N" Word and Other Racial "Triggers"

N o recap, we are just gonna dive right in on this one. But I'll be back, I promise.

◆◆◆

You know, it is my sincere belief that some flustered Democrat overseer, on some plantation in the deep south, probably first used the "n" word on a troublesome slave who wasn't picking cotton fast enough for his taste.

Somehow, over time, this awful word became embedded in our vocabulary and entrenched in our culture, and has been with us ever since. Today, this word and other racial insults and slights have been taken from the cotton fields of the Democrat plantations of the 1600s,1700s, and 1800s, and have been refurbished and refitted for usage by select members of our modern society.

Yes, the "n" word is now being used extensively by white and black liberal Democrats as a highly political and destructive weapon to denigrate and character assassinate Republicans and conservatives alike. It is also the default go-to defense and racial incitement tool for others seeking to elicit an emotional response, and violence, from the black community.

Take Omarosa Manigault for instance, a black woman who had worked alongside Trump during his historic campaign for president in 2016. She had known him for over twenty years and when he became president, had been generously rewarded for her loyalty by being given a cushy do-nothing $170,000 a year job in the Whitehouse. I mean, she was like the head of the African-American-sit-down-be-quite-Ur-ban-Renewal-and-Renaissance-committee or something. But because of her uncontrollable anger and "black woman" attitude and many other undisclosed issues, the job wouldn't last for long for Omarosa and Trump would have to let her go.

However, after being summarily dismissed, this black woman, whom Trump had considered a friend for many years, decided to write a tell-all book in which she suddenly recalled hearing him say the "n" word, even though she had absolutely no proof whatsoever to substantiate this inflammatory claim.

Now, if I may say so, it is my firm belief that after Omarosa was fired, she sought the most hurtful and destructive thing she could think of to hit back at Trump and in the process, attempt to gin up sympathy and anger from the black community. So, with her "insider" book, the question arose for those with sanity, why did Trump, inexplicably, wait until this point in his life and after his sixty-ninth birthday to finally utter the "n" word?

Oh, I would suppose that after over twenty years of being in her presence, according to Omarosa, Trump just couldn't hold it in any longer and just had to whisper the dreaded "n" word to her. During her obligatory round of Trump-hating liberal media interviews with salivating liberal "journalists," Omarosa publicly intimated that she had indeed recorded this racially explosive conversation, but, er, had a glitch on her cellphone at that very moment, thus preventing the playback of this quite offensive utterance by Trump.

But surprisingly, her efforts at pumping up her book sales by using race baiting would fail spectacularly, and not because most blacks were enamored of Trump. It seems that brash and outspoken Omarosa had run afoul of liberal Democrats during Trump's 2016 presidential campaign, drawing their ire and disdain. As a result, most liberal networks and Democrat pundits she had crossed earlier now turned on her like a pack of hungry wolves, including black marionette "reporter" April Ryan.

With Democrats and Conservatives now dismissing her as just another fired and disgruntled ex-employee, the publicity for the "tell-all" book that Omarosa thought she would generate by turning on Trump never materialized. And the other devastating shoe would drop on her book sales when, oddly, the black community at large was as silent as a closed funeral home.

Omarosa learned a lesson right then and there that liberal Democrats were in control of the black community, and that rank and file plantation blacks wasn't gonna be given any commands anytime soon by the black reverends to attack Trump on her behalf. So, just like that, the majority of blacks had "heeled," like obedient pit bulls obeying the commands of their Democrat masters as they ignored Omarosa's racist claims entirely. Conservatives weren't fooled by this nonsense either, they realized that Trump had been around over sixty years in the public eye, among many blacks, Democrats, and Republicans, without a hint of this "racism" nonsense.

Of course, Omarosa's racial incitement failure was a rare one-off because liberal white Democrats absolutely love it when blacks use the "n" word to assail Republicans and Conservatives and often use this word themselves to incite the black community. But on this occasion, Omarosa wasn't to be rewarded for her betrayal because liberals hated her as much as Trump, perhaps even more so.

Meanwhile, there was the quite public and explosive, coded, use of the "n" word by Bette Midler, a seventy-year-old liberal Democrat, whom I believe is quite an ugly white woman. She recently tweeted:

"Women are the n-word of the world Raped, beaten, enslaved, married off, worked like animals; denied education and inheritance; enduring pain and danger of childbirth and life in SILENCE for THOUSANDS of years. They are the most disrespected creatures on earth."

This tweet was sent out in a fit of anger and frustration over President Trump's recent nomination and confirmation of Brett Kavanagh to the Supreme Court, a straight white male, and very conservative anti-abortion nominee. Democrats had tried just about everything to stop him, wanting so desperately to keep this judge off the Supreme Court and had failed, miserably.

So, old triggered Bette Midler, in an act of sheer desperation, was forced into a Hail Mary and used the racially combustible "n" word in her tweet, piggybacking and playing off of black civil rights and black enslavement in an attempt to stoke fear and anger among blacks. She was supposedly sending a secret message, like the bat signal, to the Democrat Party's base of mercurial liberal plantation underlings that Brett Kavanaugh, the new Supreme Court Justice, was racist and that they needed to get out and vote and pronto.

But to me, Old Bette's messaging was strange in that there had been no accusations emerging during the confirmation hearings of any racial incidents regarding this clean-cut, vanilla Judge. So, it would seem, her emotional outburst would turn out to be just another white liberal Democrat milking black emotions for all they were worth for political gain and attention.

I thought about this tweet long and hard, almost shrugging it off and dismissing as the ranting of an old, senile, and washed-out liberal hag. Then I got to wondering, what was it that had made this old nag shortened the racially offensive and taboo word she was so eager to tweet? Why had she just used the "n" word and not use the word in its entirety? Really, if this "n" word she had tossed about in anger on social media was so offensive to her where she could only use the first letter, why would she even attempt to use it at all? So, I tested out the import of this word in real time on other Democrats.

The following day I spoke with a white liberal Democrat friend, telling him about this tweet while using the word in its entirety. He winced like he had just caught a massive cramp and stated, emphatically, that he didn't like the word at all, and admonished me not to ever use it around him again. Fair enough, I expected this reaction, yet I am betting that this same fella had no problem with Bette Midler saying the "n" word in her tweet, which deliberately implied the very same word which I had just spoken.

Here was the hypocrisy and craziness of the left up front and on display. This friend is a proud supporter of the Democrat Party, the party which created the "n" word during slavery and still uses it today, albeit, in its shortened form whenever they deem it necessary. So, to me, it is quite strange that he finds that saying the "n" word is per-

fectly ok, yet the entire word was quite offensive to him, even though the two are the same and mean the same. Whew, are you following me on this yet?

With that said I ask you, the readers, should I abide by my friend's hypocrisy and duplicity and tread cautiously with the usage of the dreaded and highly inflammatory "n" word here in my text? Or should I just let loose and use this word in its entirety as old Bette really intended to do?

Oh, before you answer that, let me first ask you, do you know what the "n" word in its entirety is anyway? I think everyone has a right to know, don't you? Ok, so you've convinced me, I'm throwing caution aside and letting loose just so we can get everything out in the open. So, for the uninitiated and faint of heart, the "n" word means *"nigger,"* plain and simple.

Wow, there is no turning back now, I feel better already getting that off my chest! With that being exposed, let's now go back to old Bette Midler and her racial incitement tweet. Let's now reveal what she had actually said, and meant, during her social media outburst on Twitter, un-redacted of course:

"Women are the niggers of the world Raped, beaten, enslaved, married off, worked like animals; denied education and inheritance; enduring pain and danger of childbirth and life in SILENCE for THOUSANDS of years. They are the most disrespected creatures on earth."

Ain't that a hoot, an old, liberal white Democrat detailing centuries of atrocities committed against blacks, yet supports the same party, as history tells us, that is responsible for all these atrocities. This just shows that these liberals are delusional, at best. You just cannot make this stuff up with these anti-American racists.

Now, with the entire word on display, Bette's message seems to be a tad more incendiary, and this is what she really wanted plantation blacks to see and feel. Nevertheless, this old hag of Democrat Royalty bears the distinction of being one of the privileged white plantation owners, so all she had to do after her racial "faux pas" was merely issue an apology, of sorts, and all was forgiven in the black community.

And although she had supposedly repented for her public outburst, in her mind her mission had been accomplished, having been able to successfully get her intended racial message out to the dumbed down portion of the black community.

Of course, the silence by black celebs was deafening; there was to be no stoned-looking Snoop Dog, no JayZ, Black Caucus, black Reverends, or any of the other black overseers shouting "racism!" *To me, this wasn't shocking but was highly predictable, so I'll just move on.*

Now, let's take Roseanne Barr, a comedienne who tweeted that Valerie Jarret, a former Obama cabinet member, looked like a cross between the Muslim Brotherhood and the Planet of The Apes. *To note, although Valerie Jarret looks black, she is actually more Iranian than anything else, but we all know that most blacks will still get their knickers in a bunch just because of her skin tone.*

Personally, I thought that the comment was old-school hilarious and laugh out loud funny because the target of her tweet did indeed resemble the comical mashup she had so humorously described; it was comedic observation at its finest. In this regard, black comedians have always made jokes and poked fun at the appearances of other blacks in their standup routines, calling some porch monkeys and fried-faced baboons and such, which I have always found to be some funny stuff.

But in Roseanne's case though, by the reaction of Democrats, you would think that she had just nuked the gay bathhouses in San Francisco or something. The fake outrage and righteous indignation from black and white liberal Democrats alike were almost instantaneously palpable and would quickly develop into a national firestorm, which would not be abated until her head had been called for.

I mean, Roseanne's comment became a spectacle of epic proportions as the liberal media all pounced upon her like hungry lions on raw meat and ABC, part of the Democrat cartel, citing racial insensitivity and some other liberal goobley gook standard fare like, *"that's not who we are,"* promptly canceled her very successful sitcom.

Even though she had never uttered the dreaded "n" word, which old liberal Democrat Bette Midler had done with impunity, Rosanne wasn't given a pass but was instead treated much harsher only because she leaned conservative and supported Trump. She had found out the hard way that anything said with any racial connotations is copyrighted and patented for exclusive use by white liberals, in certain circumstances of course, and plantation blacks. Only these two groups have the license to wield this formidable weaponry of racism that had been tempered in the hot forge of black enslavement.

So, coming full circle, even though it was white southern Democrats who constructed this word centuries ago to degrade and humiliate their black slaves, here it was today, the same word, now a robust part of the Democrat Party's platform and arsenal. *Wow, how did that happen?* Well, if you've read this book up to this point, you should have a clue by now.

*It is my personal belief that the word nigger, which is derived from Negro and meaning black, was first used by dumb and illiterate white Democrats in the 1600s because they probably couldn't get the hard pronunciation of Negro correct. I suppose that it was during this time when the word would become a sort of slang for their black African captives. *As an aside, I also sincerely believe that a lot of blacks today get their "lazy language" from their white slave masters as well, butchering words and saying such mispronunciations as doe instead of door, flo instead of floor, ax instead of ask, etc. Being black, at times I find myself doing this as well, I guess, because of the environment in which I had been immersed.*

So, in this regard, the lazy language phenomenon within the black community today is just a holdover from southern, illiterate, white slave-owning Democrats.

With that being said, let's go all in on this toxic and mysterious "n" word and thoroughly dissect it, shall we? As I stated earlier in this text, at the start of the Civil War in 1861, the Democrat Party had about four million slaves under its thumb. So, I'm gonna go out on a limb here and guess that the word 'nigger" had to of been used at least four million times plus by southern slave-owning Democrats at some point during this time:

"Nigger, pick that cotton! "Nigger, fetch me some water!," "Come here, Nigger!" "Hang that Nigger!" "Don't run, Nigger!"

I imagine that these words were sweet sounds to these whites back then and, to a large extent, secretly, to a lot of white Democrats today. Of course, they wouldn't dare say it out loud today because most of'em are in government positions or heads of major companies, running large and successful organizations and living in the cozy suburbs watching reruns of Ellen. Also, most of'em would probably get their heads bashed in by blacks if they were to ever utter the word in public without advance notice and permission by the black reverend leaders and Black Congressional Caucus.

Oh, I can also imagine that the word nigger was probably used even more vehemently by white Democrats after Republicans whipped the snot out of their asses in 1865 and freed the slaves. And Democrats must have been really pissed off to no end to have to accept the fact that their former slaves were now free just like them and their liberal white families: *"Damn uppity niggers done went and got themselves freed because of them damn radical publicans." "Sumabitch!" "They gon always be niggers to us though. We'll git their black asses back on the plantation, you'll see."*

White liberal Democrats today usually feign outrage over the word nigger but will readily use it, shortened of course, and packaged neatly within the politically correct "n" word to incite the black community. And if you haven't noticed yet, on all of the liberal mainstream networks like NBC, CBS, MSNBC, CNN, ABC, etc., racial comparisons and innuendos are frequently tossed about by black and white liberals to validate and legitimize every social issue that the Democrat Party promotes and advocates for, whether it's abortion, socialism, homosexuality or illegal aliens.

Just listen carefully to any broadcast showcasing liberal pundits and watch when the topic runs hot and heavy, and they become stymied by facts, you will suddenly see strands of slavery and Jim Crow begin coursing throughout the discussion panel, and whichever pundit can connect the social cause of the day to slavery the best, wins. You just know that deep down inside, white liberals today are just chuckling with delight over how the word nigger gets most racially sensitive blacks stirred up. Just the utterance of this word by some will throw a lot of blacks into a rage and hissy fit and have them screeching "racist" for months.

But hold on, amazingly enough, there appears to be a silver lining regarding the usage of the word nigger. *Say what? How can that be? Man, you jiving!*

No, I'm not, it seems that this highly offensive and racially-charged word is not so bad after all when used correctly. The much-maligned nigger appears to have now somehow gotten its blessing by the majority of the black community for other blacks to use for commercial and entertainment purposes.

This shouldn't really come as much of a surprise to anyone nowadays, blacks have been casually saying nigger within their own communities for decades and even the black young'uns, barely able to talk, can say it upon command. Yes, toddlers in the black community may not be able to say "da..da," but they can certainly say "nigger!"

Also, you can go back and find comedians like Richard Pryor and others who have used "nigger" quite frequently in their stand-up comedy routines. And you can also go back to the black comedies of the 1970s, like the Jeffersons and Sanford and Son, which used this now taboo word many times on their television sitcoms as well, always to hearty and side-splitting laughter. Being old school myself, I actually understand the usage of this incendiary verbiage and its comedic value. Like a lot of blacks, I have used the word much like the stars in these sitcoms, not with racial malice but to elicit laughter from other blacks. I have laughed many times when black comedians in the aforementioned sitcoms of the past have used this word, and today still see their racially raucous comedy as funny as all get out.

So, as it were, it would appear that for some blacks, the word nigger seems to have this duality to it, a good and evil so to speak, sometimes offensive and other times a humorous term of endearment and acknowledgment of brotherhood. However, with some blacks, even the sound of the word comes across as very offensive and if left up to them, would never be spoken by neither whites nor blacks in their presence in any setting.

271

Even though old nigger is banned in sitcoms nowadays, it is still commercially in demand and used quite often by other blacks, especially rappers trying to turn a buck within the music industry. *So, although I'm a black, cornbread-eating southerner, I am still working my way through all the usages of this word, and I think I just about got it now.*

Liberal black rappers have, for many years, eagerly exploited and turned this offensive word on their own community for fame and profit, keeping nigger relevant in today's black society and the nation as a whole with their recordings. This turn of events has, for decades, made the exploitation of blacks much easier, because most all of these black rappers are hardcore Democrats and will promote their party's platform whenever they are called upon to do so.

Just listen to a lot of rap songs today, and you will hear liberal black rappers slinging the word nigger around with impunity and swagger while other black and white liberals bop along to the infectious beats, blithely ignoring the racist and crass lyrics.

Oh, hold up…wait a minute here, I have just been handed a memo! It has come to my attention that I am in error and that the proper spelling and pronunciation of the "n" word is now "nigga" and not nigger. Looks like I have been out of the loop on this one and was late in getting the updated racist word reconfiguration memo that my other "brothers" received. Astonishingly enough, black Democrat rappers, from what I've just learned, have sorta cleaned up the most racially inflammatory word in our nation, ever, just by replacing the "er" with an "a" on the end of nigger.

Well now, why didn't I know about this sooner? I mean if this had indeed been the case, that it had only taken a simple exchange of letters and a slight change of pronunciation to sanitize old nigger, the neutering of this word could have been done decades ago. Wow, I had no idea that just by removing the "er" that it would completely cleanse nigger of all racism and centuries of Democrat atrocities, and remake the word into sort of a cordial black greeting, a black salute even.

With the "a" now adorning the end and replacing the racially-charged "er," nigger has been remade into the nice, relatively inoffensive and palatable "nigga," which is now easily digestible for all. For me, this development certainly changes the whole complexion and scope of the entire discussion on the so-called "n" word. *It's a horse of a whole nother color, no pun intended. Ok, pun intended, there.*

This radical change of the once highly toxic "nigger," seemingly, bought about a whole new era of racial enlightenment for the black community, and now it appears as if it's ok for blacks, and some whites, to say a word sounding similar to nigger, without actually saying nigger. *Very convenient, I like it.*

And to think, all it had taken was some brilliant black Democrat rappers to figure this out! Strangely enough, the revising of this word was eerily reminiscence of the switch that the Republican and Democrat parties had supposedly undergone in the 1960s. You know, the "switch," where all of the atrocities committed against blacks by Democrats during the 1600s, 1700s, 1800s, and 1900s, being somehow conveniently switched over to the Republican party in the 1960s. Isn't it just amazing what doctoring a word or "switching" around a political party can do in the fight against racism?

It's sorta like Democrats using industrial hoax detergent and myth bleach to get that really tough slavery stain out. Cue the commercial, please:

"Are you a Democrat and having trouble getting blacks to believe that you didn't whip and lynched their asses for over 200 years? Do you want blacks to forget you opposed every civil right for their asses?

Do you want blacks to never find out that you were the ones denying them education and land ownership for over 300 years?

Well, there's good news! Get "Switch-Out "and make your party new again!

Wash that 400-year-old slavery stench right off ya! Put it on someone else! Yeah, that's right, on someone else!

For the low price of an ebt limit, and a 40oz, starting at $400 a month. you can now make your problems with the black community disappear, guaranteed for at least 200 years.

So, call now and make the switch, and get "switch out, your plantation niggers will love you for it!" Keep'em happy, keep'em ignorant, keep'em poor, get switch out!"

Anyways, it was strikingly similar that, just as the parties had supposedly switched in the 1960s, merely by the decree of white liberals, the word "nigger," had also been conveniently switched to "nigga" by the decree and consent of liberal black rappers sometime in the 1980s as well.

But back in the real world, we all know that the parties never changed, and that old "nigger" is still around and on standby to be used publicly, but only by black rappers, and liberal white Democrats in political emergencies, provided they shorten nigger to the "n" word and speaketh not its entire breadth.

Ok, so at this point and getting up to speed, we now know that among blacks the word "nigga," which is a derivative of the Democrat created word "nigger," means brotherhood and unity and is not racist at all in this context. We also know that the word nigger is highly toxic and racist in most other settings but can still be used by white liberals in the form of the "n" word in case of a political emergency. Got it?

Wow, this is brilliant the way old nigger has been cleaned up, it's sorta like a nasty killer drug dealer who gets caught doing his criminal deeds, and his attorney cleans him up, puts'em in a suit and tie and presents him to the judge as a choirboy. And just like that, walla! An overnight, magical transformation, turning this dangerous drug dealer into a clean-cut "law-abiding citizen," and, thus, absolving him of any wrongdoings just by his appearance. *I see, ok then.*

Everything was going swimmingly until a chorus would arise among some blacks who wanted old nigger entirely dead and gone from their community; they were just plain tired of this racist and antagonistic fool. This desire was quite commendable on their part; however, I do believe, as history shows, that this is highly unlikely and entirely unachievable because there have been others, like Richard Pryor in the 1970s, who have tried to kill old nigger by publicly denouncing the word, and yet it survived.

In fact, I believe that the quite resilient "nigger" was even buried at some point by our very own self-righteous and indignant-sounding black civil rights "reverends" who, at one point, was on a sainted mission to stop the usage of this painful word, like forever. For these black, duplicitous overseers, in public, it was very, very heartbreaking for them to hear this racially denigrating word but in private circles, they still canoodled with black rappers, comedians, and others who said these words all the time and often used it themselves within their own communities.

With that in mind, these good "reverends" would endeavor in utmost, uh, sincerity, well the most Democrats can come up with anyways, to do away with this offensive word once and for all. So, giving it a try in 2007, the NAACP chapter in Detroit, now a liberal-run "black organization," along with the "reverends," supposedly held this much anticipated going home funeral service for old "nigger" with the liberal media in tow. The "reverends" proceeded with a solemn march, including horse-drawn carriages and all, and gave emotional speeches, rattling off all the hurt and pain that this nigger had caused the black community over the years, but wouldn't be able to do so again because it was supposedly finally being laid to rest.

However, when this touching ceremony had concluded, the demise and interment of nigger were still in doubt by many blacks, who believed that its death may have been greatly exaggerated. Their suspicions would soon prove to be warranted, because while everyone was focusing on the burial of nigger, his sneaky accomplice, nigga, got clean away and made its way back into the black community's vernacular.

Now nigga, which was actually a clone of nigger, had not only survived this so-called "elimination" of its racist counterpart but was still circulating and actually thriving in black communities, mostly on rap records and in Democrat inner cities. For a while, everything seemed fine because for a lot of blacks, nigga, which was like nigger-lite and less filling, was ok and was eagerly welcomed as a replacement for the old racist troublemaker.

But, as rumors and urban myths go, this new nigga got lonely one night and had gone to the racism cemetery and dug up nigger, his almost identical twin, which was still alive and well and none the worse for wear.

Unsure of how they would be viewed, "nigga" and "nigger" slipped quietly back into town together, not knowing how they would be received after that splashy televised funeral and big to-do over nigger's burial. However, to their surprise, the next day, they were both heartily greeted and welcomed back into the black community with open arms.

I believe that one of the primary reasons that nigger is still in play within most inner cities today is because it has become ingrained in our culture. It is sorta like the seasoning and flavoring of black neighborhoods, and I would suppose, at this point, would be quite tricky for blacks even to try to fathom substituting nigger for the "n" word on the rough streets of Democrat inner cities.

Oh, er, but wait, let's see if we can fathom it! I can sorta imagine a cleaned up conversation in the "hood" going something like: *"Yo, what's up my "n" word!" "My "n" words on the corner, making that paper yo." "Man, let's roll and wet them "n" words."*

Oh well, that didn't work, not as smooth, and doesn't quite roll off the tongue as well as it should. Maybe then, it is ok for inner city blacks to use "nigga" because although "nigger" and "nigga" may sound just alike, we know, wink, wink, that they are not.

Here, we must ask ourselves this question; why in the world would any black person want to use the same offensive words that racist Democrats created for blacks during slavery to remind them of their second-class status citizenship in this country? And why would any black use any word that sounds anything remotely like nigger?

No other race would take a degrading word used against them by their former slave masters and turn it against their own people for profit. *And it is no surprise that a lot of blacks today will politely say "n" word in public and in mixed company, but will yell "nigger" at home at the drop of a hat in private.*

However, everyone, blacks, whites, and whoever else, can still hear the entire word on records being promoted and sold to everyone and their momma right now, even as we speak, because "nigga" or

"nigger" lends street cred and is a big selling point for most gangster rappers. *Just as a side note, strangely, there hasn't been any outcry by touchy white liberal Democrats to ban this word or anything sounding like it in our now highly sensitive culture. Why the pass?*
Just for tickles, imagine if gangster rappers ever decided that they were never using either nigga or nigger in their lyrics again and that they were gonna replace both with the politically correct "n" word in their, uh, songs. Personally, I think it would be quite ridiculous and hilarious to try to substitute these words in hardcore rap, it just wouldn't go over so well with the demographics black rappers target, but let's give it a shot, shall we?:

"Ladies and gentlemen, throw yo hands up for MC Mad Gangster Killer Dog, straight outta Rikers from an eight-year bid!" Boom, boom, boom, shik, shik, shik.... "Uhn, uhn..... yo, me and my "n" words gonna cruise, got nuthin to lose, "n" words on my block but I got my Glock. "N" words messing with me, dumb mofos just wait and see, those n-words are crazy......"

Ok, ok, I think I see the issue; however, I cannot ever imagine that, say, the Chinese would happily rehab and exploit the racially offensive "chink" word for profit and their community's rabid consumption. If they ever were to do so, I suppose, this would entail changing the racist "chink" to something like "chunk" for a similar sounding but less offensive word.

Can you just imagine Chinese youths walking around saying: "Yo, my chunk, whaddup yo!" I don't think that's ever gonna happen, nor are Chinese celebs and politicians going to be carefully recrafting the word chink into the "C" word in the hopes of using it as a political tool against their adversaries.

Neither will you find any Hispanics rehabbing the word spic or wetback saying: "Yo my spac brother, what's happening?" Or what's up wetbic! Come to think of it, I haven't seen or heard of any other race trying to rehab and remix racially offensive words in an attempt to diminish its psychological and emotional impact for commercial use.

No, there are no "offensive" words among other races being supposedly switched, cleaned up, and recycled for use within their communities and society at large. But to pull this off with blacks, Democrats have taught most how to deceive themselves by utilizing the "switched" concept as they did with the parties switched hoax. This provides the needed deflection away from any and all of their misdeeds and misconduct, thus, absolving blacks of all accountability for their words and actions.

I firmly believe that white liberal Democrats today thoroughly enjoy blacks using the word nigga, mainly because it is another tool to help them maintain control of their inner city plantations. I would suppose the word reminds today's Democrats of a time long ago when their ancestors could openly say "nigger" themselves while sipping lemonade on their plantation porches as black African slaves toiled in the hot sun picking cotton in their fields.

Today, liberal Democrats in Congress, descendants of slave-owning white southerners in the 1600s, 1700s, and 1800s, probably reminisce about the time their ancestors could freely utter the word, especially when they had black slaves stretched out in the sun and gleefully creating welts on their backs with a whip: *"Whooo whee, look at the bubbles on that nigger, Jimmy!"*

Ahhhhh, those were the glory days for the Democrat Party. So, I imagine that a lot of white liberals today really appreciate the hard work and effort that many black rappers and comedians, who enthusiastically support their party, put in to keep the word in play. And even though the "er" has been removed and replaced with an "a" in many circumstances, white liberals still love the sound of the word because Democrat and "nigger" go together like peanut butter and jelly.

Only thing is, I wonder, why do black rappers who use this word so often themselves, are so hypersensitive to any and all perceived "racist" comments by others? I mean, you can have a hardcore killer rapper shouting nigger all day long on his recordings and making millions from it, but let a white guy offer him some crispy fried chicken and this black fool would translate this gesture into being called a nigger and a fight would soon ensue, so what gives?

Also, seems racism is getting kind of convoluted these days, it's getting harder to figure out because you have a lot of young white kids now walking around with sagging pants and listening to black gangster rap music. I remember one day pulling up to get some gas at a station, and a rap song was blaring something like this from a radio: *"Gonna get you niggas when I'm done wit my hos...we gonna ride those mother..fkers. Niggas can't see me, but wanna be me..."* I glanced over and was quite stunned to see two white guys in an expensive-looking car, sporting 22s, and smoke billowing out the windows, moving their heads to these "racist" lyrics.

There was also another incident which occurred some time ago, when I was playing basketball with a group of "brothers" and a few white guys, and in the heat of battle, one white guy shouted at the other white guy: *"Nigger, pass the ball!"* I looked around, waiting on a bloody confrontation but there wasn't even a ripple among the black "ballers" and the game continued without missing a beat. It would seem that these white "ballers" had achieved the ultimate and quite lofty goal dreamed of by white liberals, the distinction of being off-color "honorary blacks" who were allowed the usage of this racially-charged language in the presence of other blacks without any repercussions.

I believe this privilege is similar to wild game conservationists getting overly friendly with the lions and tigers they were in constant contact with, laboring under the illusion and false premise that they both fully understood each other's language because of their familiarity and proximity to one another.

I realized much later on that the connecting thread and commonality of both whites and blacks on the basketball court that day was that they were all liberal Democrats and of the same ilk, loving gangster rap, and the word nigger, regardless of their skin tone.

But just how did gangster rap really get its start and prominence within our culture, you ask? I can remember when rap used to be about silly themes, false bravado, and wordplay, and about which rapper could spit the dopiest rhymes to defeat their opponent in lyrical combat. Rappers like Kurtis Blow, and LL Cool J, and groups like the Sugar Hill Gang and the Fat Boys personified this type of fun loving and harmless rapping.

Along with the break-dancing craze, this music was a shared, non-violent passion and interest among many blacks at the time. I can still recall people walking around with their boom boxes, some as big as refrigerators, blasting this innocuous rap music all over the neighborhood. Those were some good times, even amidst the troublesome crack epidemic and gang violence. It has even been rumored that break-dancing and rap duels back then served to keep some of the violence down and a lot of brothers out of trouble; gang members would have dance-offs instead of shoot-outs.

However, there would be a sea change in the music industry, introduced, again, by liberal Democrats, when a white Jew signed and promoted NWA (Niggaz Wit Attitudes), one of the first gangster rap groups to burst onto the scene. This group epitomized black exploitation, and in the 1980s sold millions of records that denigrated women and promoted violence while making themselves and their white liberal masters wealthy.

The eager acceptance of this rap genre by the black community helped create a whole new and dark subculture in which future generations of children would be subjected to wanton violence and indioctrinated into the mindset of easy money, gangs, excessive bling, and drugs. As previously mentioned, gangster rap was being introduced to the nation at about the same time Democrats were busy pouring crack into black communities.

And it is this confluence of events which would result in a whole new lingo contemporary to the times and popping up in black neighborhoods all across the country: *"Nigga, pass that pipe!"*

Now, the "n" word isn't the only racially inflammatory word that seems to set most blacks off, oh no, there are many other racial triggers in the ever-expanding "offending blacks dictionary." The black "reverend" leaders and white liberal Democrats have managed to create an entire list of continually updated racial "triggers," words that they often use when they want blacks to riot or get stirred up for political purposes.

We know that most blacks really get excited over being called names such as "monkey," "gorilla," or "ape." It's almost like Africa doesn't have any other animals that blacks think reminds them of themselves. What about giraffes, crocodiles, or hippos? Aren't they all part of Africa too? Somehow, these fellas have been cruelly left off of the list of the who's who's of animals blacks are to be offended by.

But why do blacks take such umbrage at being called names such as monkey and ape? I mean really, who started this comparison of blacks to animals anyway, and why do blacks accept and validate any inference of them being similar to apes or gorillas by getting highly upset when called these names? Recently, the Democrat Party went even further and got a lot of blacks worked up over inanimate and historical objects as well. *Lord help my people.*

Most blacks, especially southerners like myself, have been around the Confederate Flag and statues for decades, and have totally ignored them. Hell, a lot of southern blacks watched Dukes of Hazzard religiously back in the day and enjoyed the hell out of it too, confederate flag car and all!

Blacks never cared one way or another about anything concerning these historical monuments, that is until white liberal Democrats demanded they get downright angry over all things Confederate. Before this dictate though, most blacks couldn't even spell Confederate and wouldn't know the real story behind the rebel flag and statues if it hit 'em in the head, much less what any of them represent.

Nonetheless, at the urging of white liberal Democrats and their black puppet leaders, many in the black community became sudden-aggrieved and highly incensed. I mean, some blacks became so outraged and emotionally distraught over these "racist" objects, which they had been around for decades, that if a Confederate flag or statue was anywhere in their vicinity, they couldn't breathe, sleep, eat or function properly knowing that these "white supremacy" artifacts and remnants of America's past racism existed anywhere on earth or the universe.

Really, some blacks were literally foaming at the mouth, and would become even more irate after liberal networks rolled out, you guessed it, their Asian weave-wearing, loud-mouthed, liberal black women, who began screeching about the horrific and racist civil war era statues and monuments that must come down now in order to protect their black youth from racist Republicans.

In pointing out the glaring duplicity and hypocrisy on display by these deceptive and liberal-controlled black women; they were feigning anger and outrage over these supposedly racist, inanimate objects, yet eagerly embraced and supported the same Democrat Party that actually created the Confederacy in the 1800s. Furthermore, these same deranged liberal Democrat black women will never speak about the suppression and manipulation of blacks, who are today barely existing on inner-city plantations and suffering from the real issues of drugs, poverty, and gang violence caused by their white masters.

Now, there is one new and intriguing "racist" entry just recently added to the black triggers list by Democrats: *"Build the wall."* Sounds innocent enough, right? After all, we're only talking about a wall, but to some blacks, after being given their command by liberal Democrats, these became fighting words!

With that being said, I remember a few years back when the white mayor of West Virginia got fed up with the Obamas and their hateful and racist rhetoric and called our, er, first "lady" Michelle Obama, an ape in high heels. There had been a massive backlash and outrage by blacks, who lashed out with threats of violence until, eventually, the official was forced to step down from her position.

Ok, so let's go ahead and contrast this animalistic outrage by blacks over "shook to the core" Michelle Obama with that of a recent attack on Candace Owens, a black woman who happens to be conservative and a runaway slave from the Democrat plantation, of which I believe Michelle is an overseer.

Tom Arnold, a liberal white male who was featured on Roseanne Barr's earlier sitcom, and a few of his liberal white comrades took it upon themselves to publicly attack Candace Owens with gutter language on social media, just for her speaking out against Democrats and their centuries' long exploitation and abuse of blacks.

Candace appropriately responded to these white men by making a statement for herself and Kanye West, a rapper who also at the time supported Trump, our newly elected Republican president. She tweeted:

"When @PerezHilton @TomArnold and @ShaunKing, 3 white men, rush to viciously attack the freedom of two black people who refuse to be pawns to a leftist ideology-it should ring as a wake-up call to the world about who the real racists are. None of you white men own my blackness."

Now, after this tweet, no other black men, uh, African warrior, spoke up to defend this conservative black woman, their Queen. So old Tom Arnold, now emboldened with this black silence, went much further in his reply to Candace by saying:

"That's a lot of extra words @RealCandaceO so you can suck racist d- by trying to insult an actual hero @ShaunKing hahahaha. #MAGA"

So, everything was laid out into the open and made manifest; here we had white male Democrats, in the public square, telling a black woman to suck their penis because she had the gumption to break the oppressive shackles of Democrat enslavement and escape the plantation. Oddly enough, there were no "African Warriors" and no other black celebs "weighing in."

This cone of silence was quite perplexing to me because, in our racially combustible society where even an inkling of a racist slight, like with Roseanne Barr, could draw the full wrath of the black community, there was no black backlash whatsoever. Indeed, this denigration of a "black queen," of all things, by racist, liberal Democrat white men, that was blasted all across social media to millions of people, including blacks, was met with stone cold silence by black celebs.

There was to be no drugged-out looking Snoop dog yelling, *"racism!, I'ma get those mofos!"* Nor was there any scowling Samuel Jackson gazing menacingly into cameras and berating these white men, nothing. And there would be no NAACP, no black reverends, and no other black males getting upset and condemning, denouncing, or going after these white Democrat males who had publicly degraded a black woman on social media. Also, there were no loud-mouthed black liberal women, snapping their necks about and getting emotional on their "networks" in defense of their black "sister."

And most obvious, no Black Caucus members were grandstanding at microphones yelling: *"It's just like slavery and Emmitt Till!"*

This reaction spoke volumes and when taken upon its face, would definitively show that all of these blacks are house niggers who are well paid by liberal Democrats to shut the hell up while white males are busy sexually abusing and publicly putting down conservative black women who are no longer on the plantation.

Furthermore, if rank and file blacks ever wanted to dig a little deeper into the ills plaguing the black community, just go down this more expansive list of house niggers; black anchors, liberal Democrat black women, black civil rights reverends, black rappers, the NAACP, Black Lives Matter, the Congressional Black Caucus and just about any other black star in Hollywood. It is within this group that you will find plantation blacks such as these not only allowing the abuse of conservative blacks but fully endorsing this treatment towards their "brothers and sisters" as well.

So, the duality and hypocrisy among these black overseers and the black community as a whole; for their precious and extremely protected Godless and liberal Democrat black women, there is always an enormous backlash by black plantation males over anything hinting at their denigration. However, for conservative black women, who are shamed and denigrated publicly by racist whites, liberal black males mostly side with and even promote this behavior, and the putting down of their strong and independent black sisters.

With Candace, the silence from all of the proud black "African" warriors and black "queens" was deafening and shameful, to say the least. The treatment of this conservative black woman was beyond reprehensible and similar to proud African women, during slavery in the 1600s, 1700s, and 1800s, being raped by white Democrat males on southern plantations as their shackled black males stood by helplessly watching.

Today, the shackles holding these black males back are not made of iron or fear. Instead, it's the millions these, uh, fierce "African warriors" are being paid by their white Democrat masters which forces them into being bystanders while a particular segment of their black women, their "queens," are being violated. Just imagine, what if a white Republican male had told Michelle Obama to suck his penis? There would have been death threats on his life, and he would have needed to go into a witness protection program...like forever.

Today, black males run around yelling that the black woman is their mother earth and queen. But as I just illustrated, when it comes right down to it, these same liberalized, effeminate, and neutered black males are very selective in which black women are their "queens." Seems like only the loud-mouthed, mentally-imprisoned, liberal black women still on the Democrat plantation, are the only ones to qualify for this sacred black queenship designation in most black communities.

Meanwhile, the growing segment of God-fearing, intelligent, and independent-thinking conservative black women are shunned like pariahs by the majority of blacks for leaving the plantation and liberal groupthink.

Since slavery, this is how white Democrats has programmed most blacks, conditioning and brainwashing them to deny and resist any and all thoughts and actions that would go against the party's platform and ideology, even if they have to go against members of their own race to do so.

So, with that, we've seen just who can use the word nigger and who cannot, and we've also noticed that immoral, baby killing liberal Democrat women are fiercely protected while Conservative and Godly black women are not. Unfortunately, this is now the state of affairs for the majority of blacks living in inner cities all across these United States.

So here, I will note that if you are black in America today and have gotten this far in reading this book, and still supporting the Democrat party, then you are what I would call a devoted Niggercrat. Yeah, that's it, I said it.....a Niggercrat.

Ok, I think that I have spoken enough on this subject, for now, and would like, er, all blacks to stop using the words "nigger" and "nigga." Much easier to do, I suppose, is to have conservative whites stop using the names of any animals from Africa around blacks because they just might slip up and use the wrong one.

The Democrat Party has almost irreparably damaged most blacks with trigger words. If you will indulge me a bit, let's just imagine this scene in, say, the year 2030 when a white guy, sitting in a lunchroom, gets into an argument with a liberal black guy and name calling ensues.

After a brief exchange, the white guy quickly thumbs through his manual:

"Words That Do Not Set Off Blacks" and stammers...." You, you hare!

The black guy, sensing a probable racial slur, bristles, and thumbs his way through a copy of: "Word Blacks Are Offended By."

After a few seconds, his buddy peers over his shoulder and mutters: "Yo, hare's not in there, it was black rabbit that was added last year, not exactly the same, he's ok." The black liberal shrugs the insult off and laughs at the white guy.

The white guy wipes the sweat from his brow and makes a mental note to himself to purchase the 2031 updated copy of "Words That Do Not Set Off Blacks."

This seems funny, but it could happen. However, trigger words aren't the crème de la crème of black exploitation by the Democrat Party. No, the one thing which indeed shows that a lot of blacks are intellectually-challenged, easily manipulated, and misled is that the majority of blacks are unwittingly helping Democrats erase their own relevance in America, and at quite an alarming pace. For decades, white liberals have been amassing an army of Hispanics, mostly illegal, to so-call "brown' this nation and make whites the minority while in the process replacing blacks.

Today, when a lot of misinformed and dumbed-down blacks hear the word "brown" from white liberals, they mistakenly think that they are also to be included in the future spoils and riches of this nation if whites were ever to be relegated to minority status. This is stupidity beyond the pale; blacks are rapidly being replaced and still yet have foolishly bought into the Democrat Party's web of deceit and lies as they have done for decades.

Enthralled by the "inclusiveness" umbrella of their white masters' tolerance, diversity, and equality ideology, blacks are happily complicit in their own demise and dwindling political power base. In this regard, Democrats have once again proven to be highly successful in carrying out another nefarious plot to make the black community care about an issue, and threat, that they should be up in arms over.

Most blacks are honestly not getting it; white liberals are using the black community's own history of enslavement and the hundreds of years of oppression our ancestors endured, to implement their grand design of turning this nation brown with illegals.

Blacks have bought into the belief, propagated extensively by Democrats on liberal media outlets, that just because blacks and Hispanics share the same brownish tint to their skin, that both somehow also share the same culture and behaviors, and that the two distinct races are all one people and must look out for one another. This couldn't be further from the truth as to what is really happening to the black community with the influx of illegal Hispanics.

The hard work and sacrifice endured by black pioneers like King and Rosa Parks during the Civil Rights Movement to make blacks relevant in this nation are slowly being undone by this new liberal "pigmentation brotherhood" ideology. This exploitation of borderless-thinking blacks will take us to the one thing, illegal immigration, that white liberal Democrats have been advocating for and getting, and in the process boosting their political hold on our nation.

However, this is also the one thing that is guaranteed to effectively relegate blacks to nothing more than third class citizens in America. So, hold on to your ponchos and burritos amigos, it's gonna be a wild ride.

Turn the page....Si.

Chapter Nineteen

Democrats & Illegal Aliens

"*2nd Chronicles 14:7 Therefore he said unto Judah, Let us build these cities, and make about them walls, and towers, gates, and bars, while the land is yet before us; because we have sought the LORD our God, we have sought him, and he hath given us rest on every side. So they built and prospered.*"
   Proverbs 25:28, "*He that hath no rule over his own spirit is like a city that is broken down, and without walls.*"

◆◆◆

Before we get started, I want to provide some context for this chapter. Right now, as I am writing this book, President Trump is in a heated and protracted battle with anti-American liberal Democrats over funding for a wall and border security, which our nation so desperately needs to stop the massive influx of illegal aliens into our country.

The Democrat Party and Rinos have stood steadfast, for decades, against protecting the American people, while simultaneously encouraging illegal immigration and providing for every need for illegal aliens at the expense of hard-working taxpayers.

When the subject comes up, of building a wall to stop the massive influx of illicit drugs and illegals, along with the financial and crime burden on the taxpayers of this nation, liberal Democrats always have the same refrain: "*There's no money for the wall, it's $25 billion wasted.*" Or " "*Maybe, we could have some small fencing and some drones.*"

You would think, by this response, that Democrats are fiscally responsible hawks and just looking out for the hard-working taxpayers' purse strings. And you would be dead wrong, of course, because

Democrats have always had politically forked tongues. Earlier, when they knew there was no chance of passing any immigration bill whatsoever, their top leaders rabidly supported border security and a wall and gave impassioned speeches declaring the issue was so pervasive and threatening to the American public that something must be done and quickly:

Obama 2006: *"The bill before us will certainly do some good, it will authorize some badly needed funding for fences and better security along our borders, and that should help stem some of the tide of illegal immigration In this country."*

Hillary: *"Well, look I voted numerous times when I was a Senator to spend money to build a barrier to try to prevent illegal immigrants from coming in, and I do think you have to control your borders..."?*

Chuck Schumer was much more expansive and effusive on illegals in 2009:

"When we use phrases like "undocumented" workers, we convey a message to the American people that their government is not serious about combatting illegal immigration."

"Above all else the American people want their government to be serious about protecting the public, enforcing the rule of law and creating a rational system of legal immigration that will proactively fit our needs rather than reactively responding to future waves of illegal immigration."

"People who enter the United States without our permission are illegal aliens, and illegal aliens should not treated the same as people who entered the U.S legally."

With these revelations, funding for a wall and securing our borders was never the issue because our country spends billions, annually, on illegals and to help other countries. Over the last two decades, we have spent over $6 trillion in the middle east on unwinnable wars in Iraq and Afghanistan. And that is just the tip of the iceberg of how many countries we are helping, annually.

Let's quickly go over some more numbers taken from the website "Howmuch" on government spending in foreign aid. The United

States spend over $36 billion a year helping other countries, outspending the next largest donor, Germany, by about $10 billion.

Here are the top ten countries that were given our taxpayers' hardearned funds in 2016, broken down to the exact dollar amount:

1. Iraq: $5,281,179,380 (for conflicts, peace and security)
2. Afghanistan: $5,060,306,051 (for conflicts and security)
3. Israel: $3,113,310,210 (for conflicts, peace and security)
4. Egypt: $1,239,291,240 (for conflicts, peace and security)
5. Jordan: $1,214,093,785 (for conflicts, peace and security)
6. Kenya: $1,143,552,649 (for policies and security)
7. Ethiopia: $1,111,152,703 (for emergencies)
8. Syria: $916,426,147 (for emergencies)
9. Pakistan: $777,504,870 (for conflicts, peace and security)
10. Uganda: $741,326,448 (for policies and security)

To top off all this spending, illegal aliens in America cost taxpayers over $135 billion a year and, according to Forbes, this includes almost $19 billion annually just in healthcare cost alone for these non-citizens leeching off our medical system. *But wait a minute, hold onto your nachos, there's more!*

Illegals also fraudulently claim over $4.5 billion annually in child tax credits by using ITNS (Taxpayer Identification Number), provided to them by white liberal Democrats. Remember, in our abortion chapter, in socialist California about 25% of the state's healthcare costs go towards Medicaid to cover the costs of illegals having newborns, resulting in over 200,000 illegals being born in this country every year, all paid for by taxpayers. *As of this writing, there's a total of about five million of these illegals, and counting, who were born here that are walking around on our soil. Hispanics are being bred by Democrats.*

It is incredible that the Democrat Party eagerly endorses spending on other countries and illegals to the tune of almost $200 Billion annually, but are staunchly opposed to a one-time charge of $25 billion for a wall to secure our borders and the safety of Americans. Democrats are also against e-verify and getting rid of chain migration, along with opposing ending the visa lottery. All of these changes would drastically reduce the annual $136 billion-plus expenditure by taxpayers on the 22 million plus illegals already in this country.

Keep in mind that these numbers are just guesstimates, and really conservative numbers because Democrats have blocked all info on the real cost of illegal aliens, which could be costing the taxpayers of this country well over $300 billion annually.

However, the stats above, alone, should shine a spotlight on our real enemy and let every hard-working American know just who is working against our nation's best interests and its citizenry. Ok, so now that we've got the numbers out of the way, let's go into what we stand for as Americans when it comes to immigration, and I believe that the Statue of Liberty sort of epitomizes this: *"Give us your tired, your poor, your huddled masses and illegal aliens...."*

Well, just hold on there sonny, wait a minute, something about this Statue of Liberty inscription is amiss and fishy, and I bet you know what it is. Can you spot the out of place words in this quote boys and girls? I bet you can if you're an American patriot. What you just read was CNN's and the Democrat Party's revisionist lady liberty quote, updated to accommodate criminal Hispanics hopping our borders unlawfully. The real inscription for lawful and legal immigrants reads:

"Give me your tired, your poor,
Your huddled masses yearning to breathe free,
The wretched refuse of your teeming shore.
Send these, the homeless, tempest tost, to me:
I lift my lamp beside the golden door."

The Statue of Liberty was completed in 1886 and was given to our nation by France to celebrate the end of the Civil War and slavery. The broken chains at her feet symbolizes and acknowledge freedom for blacks; thus, Lady Liberty should have been called: *"The Negroes are free from the Democrat Party statue."*

Now that we've gotten that out of the way, just how did this massive influx of illegal aliens we see today get started in this country, and just what are their real purpose? Also, why are Democrats so protective of these illegals over Americans nowadays? To get these answers, we'll have to go back to the start of the illegal alien invasion.

According to History.com, before the 1965 Immigration act, most immigrants were of European descent, and each of these immigrants coming over to America stood on their own merits, assimilated into our culture, learned our language, and were self-sufficient. In the decades leading up to the 1960s, a lot of Mexicans and Central Americans were coming over, as well, to work on the farms and after the harvest season was over, would always go back across the border to their families.

This was an excellent setup for the farmers of America; they got the help they desperately needed, and Mexican workers got the money they needed. And best of all, our nation didn't have to provide massive welfare handouts for these seasonal migrants. It was a win-win for all. Well, this would all drastically change in the 1960s when the Democrat Party seized upon a cunning political ploy, and like most things with white liberals it was a corrupt, self-serving, and politically motivated idea.

You see, Democrats thought, because of the signing of the Civil Rights Bill in 1964 and removal of the KKK's voter suppression, the striking down of restrictive Jim Crow Laws and segregation in the deep south, that most blacks would perhaps learn the truth about their party, wake up one day, and leave the plantation in disgust.

Anticipating this swing by blacks over to the Republican Party, Democrats surmised that their party would then need a new subservient group of voters to replace their former slaves and moved on to another downtrodden and impoverished group to exchange welfare benefits for votes. *Viva La hombres!*

*of note: The Democrats' concerns were unfounded, blacks moving over to Republicans would never occur because of the "switch" hoax.

But even with this stroke of good luck, the Democrat Party would continue on with their plans to create a new voting bloc and would call for our immigration system to be reformed into one that was more inviting. So, it would come about that in 1965 the Cellar-Hart Immigration act would be conveniently introduced by two Democrat Senators, Emanuel Cellar, and Philip Hart, and heartily supported and backed by liberal Democrat Senator Ted Kennedy, God rest his Chappaquiddick soul.

Leaning on the emotions of the still-warm Civil Rights Movement and just passed Civil Rights Act, the immigration trojan horse bill was quickly adopted by Democrats in Congress. The passage of this bill would serve to remove established merit-based immigration principles which had worked exceedingly well for decades in building this nation into an industrial and economic powerhouse.

Previously, our immigration policy focused on hard-working Europeans who were coming over to work, learn our language, and develop businesses while gladly assimilating into our culture. The Democrat-enacted Cellar-Hart legislation would revise this immigration policy and stance into one of inclusiveness, tolerance, equality, and diversity and taking care of the world's poor. This drastic, and detrimental, change in policy saw a massive influx of destitute immigrants from Latin and African countries coming over without any work requirements, without ambition and depending on taxpayers to support'em with welfare, food stamps, and other government assistance.

Of course, this change in policy created a massive rush of not only legal immigrants but also of illegal aliens stampeding across our borders like ashy-mouthed welfare recipients on the first of the month at Walmart. The word had been put out by the Democrat Party to illegal Hispanics: *"Just get to America shores, and we'll hide you, and help get you integrated into the system. We'll procure ids, ebt cards, social security cards, driver's licenses, housing, medical care, and schooling, just vote Democrat when you get here."*

Mexicans were so happy and grateful to Democrats that they told people in El Salvador, Honduras, Guatemala, and other impoverished craphole countries to come on over and to top it all off, they would even be given free passage through their country. Democrats found that this new group of Hispanic immigrants were just like many American blacks, emotional and extremely grateful for any table scraps given to them and most of all, would eagerly vote Democrat as repayment for their government aid.

In recent years, white liberals and their black puppets, not shy about what they are doing to America, can barely conceal their glee at the tremendous increase of new illegal voters. You can often see these liberals preening and snickering on liberal "news" programs declaring that America will be "browned" in a few short years from all the illegal aliens coming over in their welfare-induced invasion. And you can always catch Democrat pundits on liberal networks, excitedly boasting that white Republicans had better watch out because they are gonna be the minority, and soon.

This is not far from the truth; at the time the 1965 immigration bill was passed, the white population was about 154 million, blacks approximately 14 million, and all other foreign-born population, including Latinos, were about 9.5 million. Today, because of the 1965 Cellar-Hart Immigration Act, and Democrat protection for illegals, the Hispanic population has risen dramatically from 9.5 million to about 60 million today, including the 23 million or so here illegally.

Now, let's bring our low-intellect, exploited blacks into this equation and get a complete grasp on the big picture and full impact on the black community and the endgame for Democrats. From the 1965 Immigration Act to present, the black population only grew from 14 million to about 39 million; however, to reiterate, during this same period the Latino explosion, with the aid of Democrats, was leapfrogging the black population and would grow from 9.5 million in 1965 to about 60 million today.

The manipulation of both demographics by the Democrat Party was derived from a straightforward formula that white liberals concocted for increasing and maintaining the population of illegal aliens in this country. By perverting our laws and Constitution and melding it with their newly created inclusiveness, tolerance, diversity and equality ideology, liberals have struck upon the perfect formula for political power.

In today's Congress, the Democrat Party has reinterpreted the 14th amendment of our Constitution, *which was intended for newborns of newly freed black slaves in the 1800s,* so that now, under this amendment, an illegal alien woman who is pregnant, can hop our border today and have a child on our shores tomorrow, and that newborn would be an automatic "citizen' who could then bestow citizenship upon his or her parents. Then these illegal parents, and now new "citizens," could go on to sponsor other relatives in a never-ending chain of amigos coming over to this country.

To top this off, the newborn baby of an illegal alien automatically qualifies for welfare benefits, which also transfers unto the parent, and Walla!, immediate government assistance for the entire brood. *This is called "birthright citizenship" and "chain migration."* In this regard, pickings are ripe for illegal border hoppers, and in fact, today, over 63% of Hispanics in this country are currently on welfare or some other form of government assistance.

It is also a fact that Hispanics, as a whole, consistently vote 70% or more for Democrats, every election. This is why there is always aggressive pushback and lawsuits being filed by Democrats and Rinos against anyone even suggesting getting rid of Chain Migration, the visa lottery, or preventing illegals from exploiting the 14th amendment birthright citizenship loophole. The removal of these unconstitutional immigration policies would thwart the Democrat Party's ultimate goal of obtaining dictatorship power within our governmental agencies and having political dominance by overwhelming the voting booths with illegal voters.

You think the corruption we have seen from Hillary, Obama, and other Democrats is something? Well, just wait until the Democrat Party fully accomplishes its goal of entirely open borders and the saturation of this nation with illegals. To flesh this out in detail, we're gonna go into the numbers on immigration for a bit but first let me, in case you didn't know, explain to you the difference between illegal aliens and legal immigrants.

Legal immigrants apply for citizenship at various points of entry, like Ellis Island, to gain access to America, and later go through a naturalization process where they take a test, pledge allegiance to the flag and America, and become productive and contributing members of our society. These new citizens have the utmost respect for our laws and are eager to learn our language and assimilate into our culture because they have proudly earned the right to be here by going through the steps required by our immigration laws.

Legal migrants recognize the opportunities afforded them to establish businesses, raise their families, and enjoy all the things that this country have to offer. And to accomplish this, these lawful migrants are often willing to sacrifice a lot, even paying the high cost of admission, which usually includes a long wait in line and, sometimes, spending thousands to enter into this one of a kind nation.

In contrast, illegal aliens hop our borders like cockroaches at any access or non-access point they can, and do not pledge allegiance to America, nor do they abide by our rules, customs, or laws. Illegals do not have any respect for this country or the law-abiding citizens in it. These criminals also do not take any naturalization or citizenship test and prefer their native language over English.

Furthermore, I have found that most illegals do not ever want to assimilate into American culture and have a desire to change our customs and laws to be more like the countries they recently fled. *Why is this? I don't know, it's a mystery to me. Maybe it's because a pig loves slop?* There has always been an assimilation problem with migrants coming from countries other than of European origin.

As an example, even the refugees among the 1.5 million we take in annually through legal immigration, from countries like Syria and Somalia, don't assimilate well into American culture. Studies have shown that even after five years of living in America, about 60% of these refugees cannot speak any English and are considered functional illiterates. *But I am betting that somehow they can pronounce "welfare" and "Democrat" quite well.*

These refugees, as with illegal Hispanics, don't see the vast opportunities like Europeans and Asians, they only see the welfare benefits and other government assistance that our nation provides. In that vein, these illegals and refugees have the same belief system and entitlement attitude held by many American-born blacks.

Moreover, today, illegal alien Hispanics are being bought into this country at an accelerated and unprecedented rate to bolster and, in some cases, even replace the black vote. It is no secret, for those in the know, that illegals and blacks are crucial voting blocs for the Democrat Party and are the tie-breakers, during close elections, needed to push their candidates over the finish line. This is the main reason you now see the hard stance and circumvention of our immigration laws for illegal aliens by white liberal Democrats.

Today, right before our eyes, another powerful minority filler voting bloc is being created in real time. Illegals are now the new voting spackle, ballot filler, used by liberals to plug votes in wherever needed during an election. Because of newly created motor voter laws, illegal aliens are obtaining drivers licenses and registering to vote at an alarming rate in states like California, Connecticut, New York, New Jersey, Massachusetts, and other liberal hellholes. These illegal alien-friendly "laws" provides plenty of illicit voter spackle for Democrats in blue states.

And if conservatives within Democrat run states, in any election, ever happen to turn out in large numbers to the polls, white liberals can now reach into that ever-expanding bucket of illegal alien spackle and just paste right over their votes. Nice, isn't it?

The endgame here is that Democrats, right now, is working diligently to get enough illegals voting in this country to negate and counter any and all foreseeable party defections that white, blue-dog Democrats could make in future elections.

The use of illegal voters allows the Democrat Party to literally nullify the legal votes of American citizens and control local and state elections and, at some point, our federal elections, no matter how American citizens vote. In most liberal states, this takeover of the polls has already occurred. And for those residents residing in most blue states today, Democrats make it appear that the election process is fair and above board, but behind the scenes, the outcome in many of these races have already been predetermined even before the contest had begun.

It's a nasty political game, but one which white liberals have been working on for decades. However, the one problematic issue they are facing at present is that most illegals are bunched up in a few sanctuary stronghold states like California, Connecticut, New York, and New Jersey. Never fear though, Democrats are now feverishly at work trying to figure out how to get enough illegals into every state in our country, via catch-and-release or whatever other methods, and onto the voting rolls to take over the presidential election as well.

So, as it stands, conniving white liberal Democrats, with the help of their media comrades, have all but blurred the lines between illegal and legal migrants. And as with many anti-American socialist causes, most blacks are eagerly on board, even though most illegals and refugees are being dumped into their already impoverished and financially strapped neighborhoods. To soothe over these easily placated welfare-dependent blacks, their black leaders tell them that illegal and legal migrants are victims of oppression just like they are, regardless of whether they had hopped the border unlawfully or entered legally through a port of entry.

Gullible blacks are then told repeatedly that it's racist Republicans who want to keep these poor, persecuted Hispanic men and women and, oh God, the little children from coming into our country. If you ever notice, when Democrats give speeches about the illegal immigration issue, they always use the term "migrants," thus, making no distinction between legal and illegal.

To me, this would the same as not drawing a distinction between a burglar and a houseguest. Just imagine if you will, how this theory of Democrats would play out in your own home: *There's a welcome mat at your front door, and this is universally known as an invitation for people to knock on your front door if seeking entry.*

You have invited friends over for a gathering and are awaiting their arrival. After some time, the doorbell rings and while you are answering the door to let your invited and waiting guests file in, eight other uninvited people whom you do not know, and cannot speak your language, climb through your windows, while another four breaks into your home via the back door.

Eventually, you and your guests stumble upon these uninvited trespassers that are not only in your home chillaxing but also helping themselves to your food and services that you had laid out for your invited guests. And when you tell them they have to go, they defiantly respond that you should shut the hell up and that they have a right to your living space, your food, and everything else in your home.

Once you have relented, because they have friends down at town hall telling them that they are just undocumented guests, these criminal trespassers now know that they cannot be easily removed from your home and will invite more of their friends and family over to partake of your home and services.

Under the Democrat Party's inclusiveness, tolerance, equality and diversity ideology, you would just kindly advise your waiting guests, who had entered via the front door and the right way, that the disrespectful criminal trespassers have just as much a right to your home and everything in it as they did and everyone should be ok with the uninvited "guests."

You would then tell your invited guests that, since your trespassing "guests" are all broke and not working, you'll need more money from each of them to buy more food and drinks to accommodate them.

Ok, that was nice, now back to the real world. Truth is, the guests you invited are the people to whom you have extended an invitation, and who have politely waited to enter with your permission. And you know by their civil and lawful actions that they will most likely respect your home and abide by your rules. However, the uninvited "undocumenteds" breaking into your home are trespassers and brazen criminals who do not care about you, your rules, your home or anything else in it.

So, it is with our nation, and the glaring existential issue we face, not only of the massive influx of illegal aliens but also of an entire party standing behind these invaders and enforcing their illegal entry as well. Under Democrats, illegal aliens are not only coming across our borders like a swarm of locusts and utilizing taxpayers' funds for their every need but are also being encouraged to participate in our political system and vote.

Often, you will hear the liberal Democrat talking heads on television: *"There's absolutely no proof of illegals voting in our elections. There have been scattered instances of irregularities, but those are outliers."*

Fortunately, smart Americans don't even need stats to figure this one out, just enough common sense to know that there are millions of illegals voting in our elections every year, and even more so in the eight years when the black messiah was in office. To prove this with pure logic, let's lay it out in black and white, shall we?

*So, a bunch of illegals cross dangerous territories with their little rugged-assed children, slip past dangerous gang members and break our laws by sneaking across our border.

*Then these Hispanic trespassers and criminals brazenly steal social security numbers, make fake ids, apply for welfare, go on Obamacare, obtain housing, put their kids in our schools and then march in our streets carrying Mexican flags while screaming America is racist.

*And, then the Democrat Party, which promotes, advocates for, and protects these same law-breaking illegals over Americans at all costs, would have us believe that all 22 million of these criminal trespassers would be too timid and afraid to go to the voting booths during elections.

* Democrats, to defy logic, would then have us believe that no way, no how, bold, border hopping illegal aliens would ever fill out a ballot or pull a lever for their party's candidates; their benefactors and staunch advocates, and sole reason for them being unable to be deported. Really? Ok then.

Also, illegal aliens are not the peaceful migrants the liberal media portrays, most are nothing more than emboldened criminals, backed by powerful and influential Latino organizations and liberal lawyers and judges who are now well entrenched within our judicial system. These well-funded entities and individuals are all working overtime for the Democrat Party cartel to keep the illegal immigration spigot open. In this regard, we frequently hear misleading and racially conditioning phrases from leftists and liberal Democrat Hispanics: *"This nation was built by immigrants!" "Republicans are just afraid that whites will become a minority."*

Well, let's take a look at the validity of these anti-American statements. First off, as I stated before, this country was founded by white European settlers, and they were not immigrants eagerly welcomed when they landed upon these shores. They were invaders and took this land by force from Indians who were in the process of seizing land from other Indians by force.

Now, liberals will scream: *"Yeah, white men colonized the Indians, and this is their land!"* And I say to them, "Oh yeah; Indians fought whites back in the 1600s and 1700s…and lost, so clearly, whites have controlled the country since. And, if Indians haven't risen from the 1600s, 1700s, 1800s, 1900s, and now the 2000s, with enough power and force to "take back" their land, it ain't gonna happen. *So, move on."*

And yes, this still is a predominately white country, with about 195 million whites out of the roughly 325 million citizens in the United States today. With that, I guess Democrats would be correct in saying that America is a "white supremacy nation," sorta like Mexico is a Hispanic supremacy nation or African nations are black supremacy countries or Asian countries are Asian supremacy countries and so forth, so what? *Why can't America be a white supremacy nation, it's mostly white, isn't it? I don't see an issue here, do you?*

This is the way it should be; whatever race founded or conquered the land are the dominant ones; they are the ones who get to determine their borders and choose which system of governance, laws, and rules they want established and their people to be under.

As for illegal Mexicans and their claim that part of America is their land? Well, in the run-up to the American-Mexican War of 1845, the United States, under President James Polk, advised Mexico that we were taking Texas and some other land they had and that we wanted badly. Mexico said no way Jose, which was a bad move for them because we promptly went to war with these hombres and whipped them within an inch of a burrito.

A badly beaten and defeated Mexico then, of course, gladly signed the treaty of Guadalupe Hidalgo in 1848, making Texas ours with the Rio Grande as the new border between our two countries. With the signing of this treaty, a relieved Mexico also threw in California and other land to boot so we wouldn't take their whole damn country from'em.

Although we were some bad muthers, our nation was terribly nice about everything though and even let the Mexicans in California and Texas become automatic citizens, which is the absolute best thing that could have happened to them, by far...really.

Today, illegal aliens, embolden by anti-American Democrat activists, are marching in our streets with Mexican flags, chanting that they are gonna break whatever treaty was signed in the 1800s and take their land back from the United States. Very foolish indeed, it's like a social justice hyena approaching a lion in the forest and saying: *"Hey lion, that spot you lying in, remember long ago when your ancestors took that piece of land from us, it was wrong and... I am here to take it back!"*

I would venture that this would not go over so well for the hyena because the lion was still a lion and still the baddest in the jungle, and what he took was his until when, or if, he decided to relinquish it. The hyena, like the illegals in this country, fails to realize that from the time the lion acquired the spot he was lying in, to present day, his position of strength never changed, nor had his ferociousness waned.

I would suppose that the foolish hyena thought, with the passage of time and all of the inclusiveness, equality, diversity and tolerance changes in the forest, that the lion would feel some kind of feline guilt and regret his ancestors' actions and willingly give up his spot to this now "victimized" and "entitled" descendant of his forefathers' victims.

The politically correct hyena would be badly mistaken, of course, so would the arrogant illegal aliens parading in our streets. As with the lion, so it is with the United States, we are still the baddest and most powerful nation on the planet with tens of millions of patriots ready and willing to back it up at a moment's notice. We have not lost our moorings as a nation in this respect, the mainstream media just make it seem so with their 24/7 spin cycle of tolerance, equality, and diversity sob stories.

The Democrat Party would have blacks in this country believe that all brown people are the same and that they should feel, in some kind of way, a comradery with Hispanic invaders that want to overwhelm the white population and "brown" the country. Not surprising, the majority of blacks have bought into this "brotherhood" with Mexicans, even though most Mexicans cannot stand their black asses.

As to "browning" the country? Well, I am black and sane, and must say that I do not want to ever live in a country that is overwhelmingly brown or black, nor do I ever want to be in a country that is run solely by "brown" or black people. Because currently, there really isn't any country on earth being run successfully by black or brown leaders, none whatsoever.

Brown and black run countries all over the world are mostly shitholes, real poverty stricken, crime infested, and corrupt cesspools where the people primarily depend on the largess and kindness of Americans to just exist. To these African and Latino countries, our nation is like one big limitless ebt card they continually swipe, all while sending their criminals and deadbeats to us to finish siphoning off our taxpayers' hard-earned money. Still yet, the Democrat Party's conditioned and foolish plantation blacks, privileged enough to be born in this country, will ignorantly spout: *"America is racist and full of white supremacists; black and brown people don't have a chance here!"*

Really? I suggest to those blacks or Hispanics and anyone else who think that America is "racist," or is suddenly a bigoted and intolerable "white supremacy" capitalist nation, to seek out a country of their "color" or "nationality" and go to it, there's lots of 'em to choose from.

The reality of the situation is that a lot of people; brown, black, yellow, green, and everyone else all over the world are dying to come here, longing for the freedoms and ideals of this nation and the many opportunities that it offers. Even Japanese schools teach their students English out of respect for our country, and to get a leg up on assimilation when, or if, they ever decide to migrate to the United States.

Hell, in fact, people from countries with all brown and black government leaders are literally dying to get the hell out of wherever they are and into America, the supposedly racist, white supremacy country they detest. Strangely, once these brown and black people have fled from these brown and black, uh, supposedly non-racist, tolerant, and utopian countries run by all brown and black leaders and get into this country of racist white supremacists, you can't seem to get'em out.

I mean, once here, these illegals leave claw marks on the ground when you try to deport'em. Why is that? Why do we have such a devil of a time getting illegal brown and black people to go back home to brown and black run countries that they say are great places and not shitholes?

Why would these unlawful invaders, brown and black, scream, howl, and kick against being removed from this racist 'white supremacy" country of evil white men? When illegals are caught and are in the process of being deported, they don't scream: "*Viva La Mexico!*" Or "*Hellllo Honduras!*" And they don't say: "*Thank God I'm caught amigo, now I can go home to my beautiful country that is not racist.*"

No, instead, it is quite the opposite reaction, when caught by ICE, illegals hire immigration lawyers, funded by Democrats, and get liberal judges to block, obstruct, and delay their departure from our racist country as long as possible. Illegal aliens also employ white Democrat Senators, to parade them about on liberal networks, showing their families in tears and emotionally emphasizing how the poor family is being torn apart and how they wouldn't survive for two minutes back in the country they lived in for forty years and just recently came from.

I've always asked, why do have to separate illegal families anyway? Why not just send the whole damn bundle back to their country as a package? I mean, cable and insurance companies and other industries in this nation insist on bundling, why not the same for illegals? With that being said, today there is no better country for blacks, or any other race, to be in than America, period.

However, most blacks born here are just too stupid, and emotionally caught up to realize that when they are born in America, they are born into privilege and that at birth they already have it better than the majority of people around the world. This is the freest land under the sun, a nation ripe with golden opportunities for those who apply themselves, regardless of race, color, or nationality.

It is so sad, and sickening that, while entitled-minded indoctrinated blacks, born in America, are running around screaming that "da man and da white supremacy institutionalized racism" system has kept them down, people from all over the world, when they gain access to this country, fall and kiss the ground and thank God that they are finally here.

To counter this truth, though, dumb American born blacks say: *"They don't understand this country. They didn't go through what we have gone through here."* I would say to these blacks, nigger please, you're dumb enough to vote in droves for the party that actually enslaved and whipped your asses, impede your progress for centuries, and today are still too emotional and ignorant to figure it out. Sit down and shut up.

Truth is, a lot of these people coming over here today are just recently removed from many of the very same things that blacks went through hundreds of years ago under Democrats, so American blacks need to move on. Now, I do understand that this whiny, entitlement mentality of most in the black community is symptomatic of the decades of brainwashing by white liberal Democrats. So, let me help these seriously misled blacks understand a few things.

America is supposedly a melting pot consisting of people of all races, creed, nationalities, and colors. We are the most generous nation on earth when it comes to immigration, taking in over a million people each year. We are also the most compassionate nation, one of the main reasons people flock to our shores, seeking a better way of life. Even though we allow over a million people a year to come here legally, there are those who still are skirting this process by crossing our borders illegally and cutting in front of those standing in line.

At first blush, and amid the media sob stories hysteria, you would think that liberal Democrats have all this caring, compassion, and love for people supposedly seeking to escape the alleged persecution in their countries so badly that they would risk breaking our laws to do so. To drive this narrative home, with every imminent deportation of a caught illegal border hopper, the liberal media quickly flood their networks with imagery of sad looking and supposedly impoverished illegals who are wanting a better life.

Then there's always the heart-wrenching sob stories being propped up on liberal networks like this:

"Poor Juan Gonzalez Lopez Fuentes Hernandez was bought over to this country, through no fault of his own, and now the racist Republicans wanna just rip him away from his family of eight children and wife. This is not who we are."

This may sound sad and all, but look closely at the two-year-old illegal who's weighing in at about 200lbs, and the rest of the "children" who look like members of the Baltimore Ravens offensive line. Most of these illegal alien leeches are on welfare and are taking taxpayers for a ride. The liberal media uses these illegal families in this emotional capacity to extract sympathy from American citizens, while at the same time getting these non-citizens on the voting rolls to nullify their votes.

Democrats always whine about how we have to help end world hunger, which is just a smokescreen for their fraudulent election activities. Most of them know that it would be an impossible task to help all the world's poor but rely on the ignorance and emotions of Americans to sympathize with law-breaking illegals. Educated people know that our country and all of the industrialized nations combined, utilizing all of their resources, could never end world hunger; wouldn't even put a dent in it.

Roy Beck, a prominent public policy analyst and president of NumbersUSA, illustrates, in vivid detail, the insurmountable task of solving world poverty. Using gumballs as a visual aid, he demonstrates the absurd notion of trying to erase world hunger and poverty by flooding America with poor immigrants. You must look up his video to get the full import.

There are over 7 billion people in the world today, and that includes about 4.5 billion who make less than $2 a day. In Africa, approximately 650 million people earn less than $2 a day. India has another 890 Million people making less than $2 a day.

China has about 480 million people making under $2 day. And

the rest of Asia has a staggering 810 Million people making less than $2 a day.

Central America, with a combined population of about 180 million destitute Latinos, is comprised of seven countries; Belize, Costa Rica, El Salvador, Guatemala, Honduras, Nicaragua, and Panama. And there's also Mexico's population of approximately 130 Million, all claiming persecution.

Statistics show there's about 5.6 billion people living in countries poorer than Mexico, and although there are many more non-Hispanics in poverty around the world, Latinos are the most heavily sought after prize by Democrats because of their proximity to the United States, not because they are the poorest.

Today, given the green light by Democrats, tens of thousands of Central Americans are being told to claim violence and persecution in their countries and are now rushing our borders and looking to enter our country forcibly. So, it begs the question, if all of these Latino countries are under siege, wouldn't all 180 million Central Americans be in danger and need asylum? And wouldn't we, under Democrat immigration rules, have to take in all of them? But, just how would we be able to do this without bankrupting our nation?

To reiterate, as a nation, we take in over 1.5 million legal migrants annually, which I think is a bit much already. But going by the numbers which I just pointed out, even if the United States were to take in 50 million poor migrants a year, it wouldn't even begin to make a dent in world poverty because net new births are well over 80 million annually within poverty-stricken African, Asian, and Latin countries.

So, to stem world hunger as Democrats suggest, the United States, with a current population of 325 million, would have to absorb another 5 billion poor people and possess the capacity to feed and care for all of them. By continuing listening to and buying into the inclusiveness, tolerance, diversity and equality ideology of Democrats, all we would ever hope to accomplish with open borders and unlimited immigration is the eventual collapse of our nation and turning our home into a third world country, and shithole, like the ones these migrants fled.

As of this writing more blacks, whose communities are being hit the hardest by illegal immigration, are waking up from their de-cades-long slumber and educating themselves and are actually walking away from the plantation. But there isn't, I believe, at this point, nearly enough of them leaving the Democrat Party to save their community's future.

You see, blacks have been hit with a devastating two-prong attack by Democrats and don't even realize it yet. Let me try to explain by weaving it all together for my brothers and sisters. Remember Margaret Sanger, the Democrat hero and Founder of Planned Parenthood, who once stated that blacks needed to be exterminated like weeds? Now, remember when Democrats passed Roe vs. Wade in 1973, the law legalizing abortion under the guise of a woman's right to privacy?

So, piecing it all together, again, while Hispanic births were off the charts, and unimpeded after Democrats introduced the Cellar-Hart immigration act of 1965, during this same period, over 20 million babies were being aborted by black women who took advantage of the 1973 Roe Vs. Wade abortion law which was also put in place by Democrats.

On top of that, Hispanics have gained enormous power and have set up influential Latino organizations that really advocates for their people while also increasing their political power. These organizations are well funded by white liberal Democrat billionaires who see illegal aliens as the new blacks, but much more temperamentally malleable, in their highly anticipated future fiefdom.

So even though blacks are slowly being relegated to nothing more than noisy Democrat doormats in favor of these border hoppers, they still stupidly and irrationally defend illegal aliens' "right' to be in this country, once again disregarding their own self-preservation and interests.

To belabor the point and sum this all up again, and for us to get a better understanding of the absolute dagger that has inserted into the heart of the black community with illegal immigration: *Democrats have been systematically putting policies and laws in place to grow, for decades, the Hispanic population, while simultaneously putting policies in place, for decades, to slow the growth of the black population.*

What would it take to wake blacks up? Was all lost for our communities, and was blacks cursed with being predisposed to an ignorant gene or something? Were blacks destined to walk this earth "disadvantaged and "underprivileged" forever and depending on government assistance without end?

God sent the black community Abraham Lincoln, John Kennedy, and Dr. Martin Luther King Jr, all to no avail, the Democrats took all of these great leaders out to prevent blacks from ever gaining independence. But there would be one more chance, and I believe the last one, for the black community to help themselves.

An outsider and unlikely hero and savior would arise, one who would expose the layers of deception and the depth of corruption of white liberal Democrats. This Deliverer would shine a glaring spotlight on the plight of the black community, which has suffered mightily from decades of Democrat exploitation and stewardship of the civil rights "reverends" and the corrupt, self-serving Congressional Black Caucus. This outspoken, take-no-prisoners, white billionaire businessman would ask of blacks the single question that would send tremors throughout the established political system and across America: *"What have you got to lose?"*

This golden-maned lion of law and order would descend from the safety of his lavish and opulent towers to champion hard-working Americans and everyday struggling citizens. He would sacrifice his own comfort and well-being to bring hope to our nation again, to instill confidence in Americans once more.

During his 2016 presidential campaign, he would fire a thunderous shot across the bow of politics-as-usual with his proclamation that he would weed out the corrupt, the immoral, and evil inhabitants lurking in our nation's capital and ensconced in its corridors of power. Having always been up to the task, this eagle-like savior would have no fear of the daunting swamp of evil serpents slithering about in Washington DC.

This champion of the people would, at this critical juncture in our history and with our nation faltering, take upon his mighty shoulders the challenge to restore America, this once great and promising land we call home.

Indeed, here was this alpha wolf, heeding the call that our nation desperately needed a leader, someone who would fight to arrest the alien swarm and secure our borders, expose liberal Democrat corruption, save our children from Democrat pedophiles, get rid of political correctness and bring back our jobs.

This warrior would hurl himself into the political fray with reckless abandon and with dedication and purpose like no other. He would task himself, against all odds, with the seemingly overwhelming responsibility to make our neighborhoods safe again, make our schools safe again, make our vets whole again, make our country respected again and make our military strong again.

But most of all, this hero took on the mantle of righting the sinking ship we call home, and in no uncertain terms, he would make it clear that he was here, with us all in this disastrous moment in our nation's history, and on a mission to...

Make America Great Again.

Need I say more?

Chapter Twenty

Make America Great Again

Recap; as previously detailed, from the 1600s and slavery, to the 1800s and the Civil War, to Lincoln and Reconstruction, to the 1930s New Deal, to Dr. King and the 1950s and 1960s Civil Rights Movement, to the 1980s crack epidemic, and to the 1990s and 2000s homosexuality movement; blacks have been exploited and denied their rights every step of the way by Democrats.

But Democrats are not done, not just yet, they have another mission for blacks. There's a new target, whom they so deeply despise, and one that these plantation owners want to bring down, just as it was with Lincoln in the 1800s...

Nehemiah 4:18 For the builders, every one had his sword girded by his side, and so builded. And he that sounded the trumpet was by me.

Psalms 94:16 Who will rise up for me against the evildoers? or who will stand up for me against the workers of iniquity?

Just for a moment, regarding blacks, I wanna go over some key points in Trump's life before he became president, and the constant target of white liberal Democrats. There was a much gentler time when he hung with, and helped, many blacks such as Jesse Jackson, Oprah, Al Sharpton and Spike Lee, and black rappers like Snoop Dog, Fifty Cents, along with boxers like Mike Tyson, Floyd Mayweather, and George Foreman.

But with what we've learned so far, it comes as no surprise that since Trump ran as a Republican for the presidency, most plantation blacks are set against him. This is because the good things about

Trump is difficult to find on the internet. Google, facebook, and most liberal websites, leftists in the services of Democrats, are hard at work scrubbing, omitting, and distorting any and all information regarding his presidency.

So, if you are trying research anything Trump or Republican by "googling," be careful of misdirection by so-called liberal "fact checkers." As an alternative, try Duckduckgo, you may have better results.

Now, a few tidbits about the Trumpster, prior to him being branded a racist by white liberal Democrats, and we can go from there:

In 1986, Trump won the Ellis award, along with Rosa Parks and Muhammad Ali, and many other notables. This award is given out by the National Ethnic Coalition Of organizations, and to be eligible, recipients must meet their criteria, which includes integrity, having compassion and being a humanitarian.

Courtesy of truthrevolt.org, in 1998 and 1999 Trump worked with Jesse Jackson and his rainbow Coalition to help get more blacks into corporate America and help with building projects in Harlem. Old Jesse fell all over himself praising Trump at the time.

In the 1990s, Trump defied the tradition of the other clubs in Palm Beach by allowing blacks and Jews into his Mar a Lago club. He was met with fierce resistance by liberal Democrats but ultimately won out.

There's also the story of the homeless black woman living free in Trump Towers for over eight years, which you can go on Youtube and view.

* *George Foreman also recounted how in the 1990s, when he was nearing bankruptcy, Trump came to his rescue, promoting a fight with Evander Holyfield to get him back on track when no one else would.*

There are many other stories of Trump helping blacks and many other people of all races in the 1980s, 1990s, and 2000s. For the sake of brevity, I won't go into all of them here. I just wanted to give some context in this chapter that will illuminate the viciousness of the Democrat Party's political and media machinery when at full thrust against an individual they immensely dislike or feel threatened by.

Stories about Trump, like the ones above, are currently being taken down by leftists or distorted on a ton of other websites run by white liberals who falsely claim that they are "debunking" these claims. But this is ok because the information is out there in the ether and cannot be removed entirely, you just have to really look and ignore the liberal "fact checkers" and their so-called debunking websites.

As I alluded to in the previous chapter, for Democrats to be elected, it really comes down to "minority filler votes," comprised mainly of plantation lacks and illegal Hispanics.

Contrary to belief, in this nation, there are slightly more conservative whites than there are liberal whites. So, it is essential to note that if Democrats had to rely solely on whites to get elected, there wouldn't be any Democrats in Congress, at all, and you could just forget about a Democrat ever being president again.

This is the primary reason Trump caused quite the stir with his history-making candidacy in 2016 when white, blue-dog Democrats awakened to the truth about their party and where it was leading them and defected by the millions to vote Republican and, thus, throwing the Democrats' election calculations of illegals and black voters askew and in chaos.

With this development, during the election, the Democrat Party's lovely candidate, Hillary, fell behind and the numbers could not be made up with less-than-enthusiastic-blacks, dead voters, and the vast amount of illegals white liberals managed to sneak into polling stations all across the country. Aggrieved Republicans and white blue-dog Democrats had overwhelmed the polls, giving Trump a resounding victory over the shell-shocked ice queen.

Democrats were stunned, to say the least. You see, they had bet bigly on their media cohorts damaging Trump's campaign beyond repair and making it easy for another one of their corrupt comrades to take the presidency. But on election night, they realized the error of their ways in underestimating the will of the American people and it was a little too late in the game to stem the tide. Upon their defeat, Democrats had then concluded, while licking their wounds, that white blue-dog Democrats were not as gullible as most blacks and could always shift at any time, making this group an unreliable voting bloc for their party going forward. The writing was on the wall for the party of slavery and racism as more Americans were catching on to what was happening and waking the hell up.

This devastating blow of the potential loss of defecting and suddenly unreliable white voters was alarming and cause for concern for Democrats as they realized that if this trend held for future elections, it would undoubtedly become an untenable situation for the future of their party.

But the much bigger issue looming for Democrats was how to character-assassinate and tear down Trump, this loud-mouthed behemoth running roughshod all over their party. Wildly popular, this authentic and historical outsider, who declared at the onset of his 2015 campaign that he was "America-first" and anti-establishment, was doing a number on the entire political system as they knew it.

Trump, the wily billionaire, and novice politician managed to out-game the decades-long status quo politicians entrenched in our nation's capital and thoroughly thrashed any and all establishment candidates; Republicans and Democrats alike. And as he drew nearer to victory during his campaign, Democrats, now realizing their worst fears was about to come to fruition, concocted a plan using operatives from the previous administration.

During Trump's campaign, anti-American Democrat plants were placed inside our government agencies as an "insurance policy" to obstruct, resist, investigate, and to block Trump's administration and crush his America-First agenda for the hard-working taxpayers of this country at all costs.

As I am writing this, it just seems so surreal that we have an entire party working against Americans at this juncture in our history and that these socialist, Nazi-like liberals still have supporters, especially blacks, who will gladly assist them in destroying this nation, and their home. The tactics that Democrats are engaging in against our Constitution and our country today is indeed frightening for those who actually get it, and would also help explain the animosity against any patriot attempting to help Americans.

As an example, Trump, a very successful celebrity billionaire who often hobnobbed with liberals, conservatives, blacks, and whites, for decades, went from being a carefree philanthropist, respected author, reality show star and successful businessman of forty years... to now all of a sudden, and in the blink of an eye, a racist, misogynist, homophobe, Islamophobia, Nazi sympathizer, white nationalist, white supremacist, a Russian spy and unfit and temperamental.

Those with some intellect will wonder, how could a very public person such as Trump, possibly be all of these things and keep it under wraps for almost seventy years? How could all of the people he hung with, as previously mentioned, during those many decades not have an inkling of such dastardly deeds by Trump until he ran as a Republican for president? Strange, isn't it?

It seems that with the win-at-all-costs Democrats, smears, ruthlessness, and violence has always been par for the course and is nothing new. As I detailed earlier, this behavior dates back to the 1700s and the Democrat Party's initial, and successful, attempt to hold onto their black property and the slave institution. So, to put today's white liberal Democrats and their constant attacks on Trump into context, we will have to, once again, journey back in time.

As I noted earlier, not too long after the Constitutional Convention of 1787 when Northerners had declared that all black slaves were free in their states, rebellious pro-slavery Democrats in the Deep South had adamantly maintained that their black slaves weren't free, well, not in their states anyway. This is the point at which we would need to begin, I believe, to explain the main reason Democrats are so dead set against Trump. Bear with me as I connect the threads of centuries of Democrat malice:

*Remember when our first Congress was being formed in 1789? And remember when the Democrat Party was attempting to count their enslaved blacks in the deep south to gain additional seats for political power and dominance? In this set-up, black slaves were to have no rights whatsoever but would still help fuel the Democrat Party politically.

*Remember when, in order to hold onto their black slaves, Democrats shot Lincoln in the late 1800s during Reconstruction? Remember when Democrats in Congress would then oppose every constitutional amendment for freed slaves, such as the 13th, 14,[th] and 15th to stop black progress. So, to sum up, Democrats murdered a president to hold onto their black property. They would also double down and impose Jim Crow Laws, segregation, and Black Codes on southern blacks at this time as well.

*Remember when Democrats created the KKK in 1866 to intimidate and control their former slaves while burning Black Wall Street down and murdering hundreds of blacks? *Here, equality and civil rights were stopped dead in their tracks and southern blacks suppressed and controlled by white, pro-slavery Democrats once again.*

*Remember when Democrats smeared, jailed, and killed Dr. King in the 1960s to prevent black independence and continue their stranglehold on the black community? *Here, again, Democrats would turn to murder and kill a black leader who was guiding blacks off the plantation.*

As unlikely as it seems, through all of these events and centuries of abuse, the majority of blacks today are still the property of Democrats, lock, stock, and barrel. With that said, let's piece this thing together.

Today, if you look closely, as with King and Lincoln, Trump is just the latest iteration in the string of threats to the Democrat Party's centuries-long hold on their black property and their quest for permanent political power. As I've clearly stated, with Democrats, their political fortunes have always revolved around their control of the black community, which has been the voting filler they've desperately needed to win elections. This is one of the main reasons why the 2016 election of our 45th President, Donald J Trump, is such a severe threat to the Democrat Party's plan of continued political relevance.

Furthermore, to compound the Trump issue for white liberal Democrats, the spotlight is now being shined on the decades-long illegal immigration into this country, hindering the coveted and unfettered massive influx of new Hispanic voters, the new blacks, so desired by white liberals. Also, unlike other meek and mild Republicans in the past, Trump publicly and unabashedly reached out to the off-limits black community, the Democrat Party's most reliable voting stooges for decades, and questioned them on their stupidity of being political pawns for so long.

When stumping on the campaign trail, he asked of the black community a straightforward question: *"You have had broken communities, poor schools, high crime rates, and poverty under Democrats for fifty years, what have you got to lose?"*

It wasn't the eloquent or traditional political speak of erstwhile Republican candidates, nor was Trump's inquiry of plantation blacks wrapped in the usual ambiguous election jargon of life-long politicians. His question to them was just a plain-spoken, yet forceful urging and pleading to a race that really didn't have anything else to lose when you think about it. But by Trump uttering this one statement, it served notice that he knew of the inner workings of the Democrat Party, and was fully aware of the black-vote cinder block which has been supporting them for decades.

Trump was, in no uncertain terms, wooing the black community and telling them that he was ready to roll up his sleeves and have a serious conversation about their issues. He made it known that, if given a chance, he would be their pathway to independence and economic viability, something that horrified Democrats. Now, any other race in America would have wholeheartedly welcomed and embraced any president who addressed them as sincerely and directly as Trump had, without the lies, without the condescending attitude, and without being patronizing.

Blacks should have absolutely flipped with joy over the prospect of a president in power, telling them that he was behind them all the way in achieving freedom from welfare dependency. Trump was indeed publicly spotlighting the black community's ills so that they could get the help they so desperately needed.

Not welfare help mind you, but instead, jobs creation, proper education and other things of substance that would promote long-term growth and economic viability. However, many within the black community were unfazed, and Trump's sincere outreach would be met mostly with deaf ears by low-info and directionless blacks who had grown accustomed to living in Democrat-run, broken inner cities. There was no rhyme or reason among the majority of blacks anymore, they just know they vote Democrat, and that's it. *The majority of the black community nowadays are more like primal cavemen and cavewomen: "Me black, you Democrat, give me welfare, food, me vote you!"*

During his campaign, Trump learned that most subservient plantation blacks are almost immovable in their support of the Democrat Party, and that many are like barnacles clinging fiercely to the hull of a welfare-dependent ship to nowhere, and proving just as hard to remove. Trump, at this point in his presidency, is slowly beginning to realize that he will have to work really hard to scrape blacks away from their liberal host. I mean, it's almost like he would have to get a set of grip pliers and a blowtorch to remove these fools from their plantation hellholes.

As previously noted, to create this type of passion and fierce loyalty among blacks, Democrats today utilizes skin color and identity politics to influence rank and file blacks. To pull this off, the party often relies on their willing house Negroes and staunch black overseers like Maxine Waters, Sheila Jackson, and Kamala Harris of the low-intellect Congressional Black Caucus, along with many other overseers, such as puppet black celebrities, black rappers, black organizations, black civil rights leaders, black news anchors, and black sports stars. These black traitors were the ones, during Trump's presidential campaign, who delighted in spearheading the Democrat Party's manufactured "racism" accusations and smears against everyone associated with his campaign.

However, undeterred, Trump continued right on campaigning, and there was nothing ambiguous about his actions as he boldly visited black churches and consulted with black preachers to get the lay of the land. He applauded the few blacks that voiced support and ignored those black detractors and others who attacked and vilified him. This was absolutely terrifying to the Democrat Party, that any black would be interested in listening to, or supporting, Trump.

So, Democrats would ramp up the hyperbolic racist rhetoric by piggybacking off of Trump's *"Mexicans are bringing over rapists and killers"* comments made on the campaign trail. And would soon begin splashing their own revised edition: *"Trump is racist against Mexicans and therefore racist against blacks,"* all over the mainstream media.

To reinforce this narrative, white liberals quickly pushed their eager black overseers onto liberal network "panels," and the smear-Trump crusade was enjoined in earnest and taken to new heights by white and black liberal "anchors" and "reporters" whose sole mission was to stop him from becoming president at all costs.

Trump had committed the cardinal sin, daring to touch the forbidden third rail of politics in attempting to appeal to blacks directly. And much to the chagrin of Democrats, even amid all of their media-driven contrivances, Trump displayed the tenacity and courage to withstand whatever shock was produced from their never-ending attacks of fabricated racism. He held on, defying all odds, not succumbing to the liberal media's hit pieces.

Surprisingly, not only did Trump take on and absorb all of the blows liberal Democrats dished out, but he also seemed to relish the battle, defiantly returning the favor and attacking the Democrat Party and their media henchmen with a ferociousness Republicans hadn't seen since the beginning of the 1861 Civil War.

The most salient observations that I see today, and ones that Democrats fear most, is that Trump's policies are targeting the two things, stopping illegal immigration and bringing back manufacturing jobs for blacks, that if successful will eventually move a lot of blacks and Hispanics over to the Republican Party. For Trump, a man not taking any salary, his candidacy and presidency were never about a political game or stunt, he was always sincere in his belief that he could Make America Great Again, as his interviews from decades ago will attest. *Who would've thunk it, huh? I mean, a billionaire and reality star becoming the president and helping hard-working Americans?*

Stepping back for a moment, somehow, I just knew in 2015 when Trump announced his candidacy that he would become president, and had excitedly told all those around me. At the time, I was laughed at by many of my friends and ridiculed for my insight, but I persisted and said to them that Trump was authentic and gutsy and reminded me a lot of my grandmother and mother. To me, Trump was a throwback to the tough John Wayne and General Patton types, having old world grit, and bluntness in his assessment of any situation and would tell you the truth whether you liked it or not. And this is something beta males, and plantation blacks will never, ever identify with.

Cutting through the liberal media's hocus pocus and false, inflammatory rhetoric, when Trump began his run for the presidency you could see from the start that he was real and a genuine patriot who loves this nation. And when he spoke on the campaign trail, he was merely stating what a lot of people in this nation were thinking but couldn't say out loud for fear of losing their livelihood, homes, and businesses in the racially charged and sensitive political correctness society of inclusiveness tolerance, equality, and diversity created by Democrats.

I believed that, right from the start, Trump was the only candidate strong enough to break the corrupt political machinery of the Democrat Party and beat the white liberals at their own game. He was what was badly needed at this time in our nation's history because, going back decades, many Republican candidates had morphed into button-down Democrat-lites, and forming a uniparty with corrupt liberals, all prospering from special interests, bribes, and lobbyists' kickbacks to the tune of millions

I imagine that a lot of people today don't do this at all, but just sit back and think for a moment about how our government is actually being run right now. Going back to perhaps the 1930s, we Americans, the people, are no longer in control of this nation and haven't been for quite some time now.

Outside organizations and entities, some foreign, are the ones influencing our elected congressmen and women and deciding how they will vote on policies and discharge their duties in government. In this political racket, known as our government, there are billions at stake in this massive game of political quid pro quo that is being played out daily in our nation's capital by officials who are supposed to be representing the American people's best interests.

Even though members of Congress get paid a whopping $175,000 annually with full benefits, and receive top of the line paid-for insurance coverage for about 162 days of work a year, most are still on the take and bilking taxpayers out of their hard-earned cash every chance they get. As a result of their malfeasance, there are millions flowing into the hands of greedy and corrupt Democrats and RINOS. These illegal payments are made to ensure that contracts and policies are steered into the direction of whomever, or whatever the lobbyists and special interest groups desire. In this regard, the American citizens' voting power has been made null and void, resulting in the ballots they've cast during elections being made meaningless.

The power of "We The People" is now being usurped and redirected by those in political power, the elected officials we have blindly sent to Washington to represent us. Furthermore, covert Democrat-created groups like the rogue deep state, or whatever you wanna call'em, in powerful government positions within our now weaponized FBI and Department Of Justice has all but deemed themselves as the sole and final arbiters of our fate. White liberal Democrats, to continually cover-up and maintain their corruption and crimes, have installed many of their evil anti-American operatives within our government agencies, along with activist judges, who are hard at work circumventing laws and reinterpreting our constitution.

When Trump spoke about the swamp in Washington during the 2016 presidential campaign debates, you could almost feel his passion and disgust emanate from your television screen as he detailed the corruption and the criminal elements that have taken over and are now operating our government. As he stood on the debate stage, publicly shaking the skeletons out of the Washington elites' and corrupt powerbrokers' closets, the fear, and angst among Democrats and RINOs in the audience were almost palpable.

The scene was startling in that here was Trump, a candidate who wasn't accepting any money from any of the aforementioned corrupt lobbyists or special interest groups, standing among politicians, claiming they were working for American citizens, seemingly alone in his quest to stem the tide of corruption in our nation's capital.

Trump was the rarest of political candidates in that he could not be bribed or bought; a very dangerous man in a cut-throat and corrupt town such as Washington D.C.

From the very beginning of Trump's campaign, the political uni-party and establishment, the powers that be, all held out hope that his political "sideshow" would somehow fizzle out and they were banking on it. Once Trump was removed from the primaries, Democrats thought, then they would dine on their usual fare of demure and feckless conservatives and would trash each and every one of them in the media without a strong rebuttal or fight, just like Mitt Romney in 2012. *To this day, with that election, I still believe Mitt threw the presidential election to Obama. I could be wrong, but just go back and watch those debates again for yourself.*

Going back to the 1700s, immoral and violent Democrats has always held a political advantage over Republicans; they were ruthless and used no holds barred win-at-any-costs tactics and physical confrontations to accomplish their goals.

In contrast, God-fearing conservatives were always the ones seeking the ethical, honest, and compromising routes in their political endeavors and staying above the mudslinging fray. Harkening back to the beginning of their party in 1854, Republicans just didn't see it as "gentlemanly" to get into the weeds with their adversaries, they had a limit as to how far, or low, they would go in their fight against their opponents. *The lone exception would be the Civil War, of course.*

Conservative Republicans, by nature, are conscientious and polite, and it is this genteel and diplomatic approach to politics which has cost them equal footing in a lot of debates and election cycles against the do-whatever-it-takes liberal Democrats. Unfortunately, these virtuous traits of Conservatives play right into the hands of the Democrat Party and their newfound, weaponized inclusiveness, tolerance, diversity and equality ideology they use nowadays as a cudgel to bludgeon their opponents into submission.

Over the last five decades, liberal Democrats have managed to establish and hone the political correctness culture in which we now live. And in every recent election, this oft-utilized tool of the left has turned out to be quite advantageous for their party. Today, most Republican candidates are deathly afraid of being seen as noncompliant with this political correctness ideology and have been tiptoeing and dancing around hot button social issues generated by liberals for quite some time.

This media-driven climate of virtue-signaling 'gotcha" has resulted in most conservatives having a deep fear of the mainstream media splashing anything negative across all of their networks in a manufactured smear job. And if caught in the crosshairs of some social issue, most of these weak Republicans will backtrack and apologize profusely even when they are right in their stance or position. These brazen tactics by liberal Democrats have cowered many a Republican elected official and candidate running for office.

Enter Trump, the only unapologetic, anti-establishment Republican candidate in history who could out trash talk, out loud, out bold and out brash liberal Democrats. For true Americans, he was the much-needed bull in the political correctness china shop, an unafraid outsider who took on the demonic Democrat Party with unmitigated zeal, trashing their establishment leaders and the famed black messiah of the previous administration without hesitation. *To me, this was perfect and quite refreshing, like lying on the beach on a warm and sunny day watching blue waves crash onto white sandy shores while sipping on a cool, iced drink.*

Like millions of Americans, the frustrations and anger that was pent up inside me for the previous eight years were now being unleashed by Trump, our golden-maned conservative warrior, and unconventional hero. I remember viewing the 2011 Washington Correspondent's dinner where Trump was being lambasted and ridiculed by Obama and his liberal media cohorts, daring him to get into the political arena. By Trump's reaction, you could see that he was thinking very deeply about the reckless abandon and rising incivility of the Democrat Party and had probably decided right then and there, that at some point he would be needed to step in to save this nation.

Before Trump's political ascension, there had been too many weak and indecisive Republican candidates who had stood idly by while Democrats dictated their terms of surrender to them, but not our guy. Trump broke with this staid, button-down Conservative Republican protocol and Washington "decorum" by simultaneously declaring his candidacy for president and immediately attacking the political establishment and lying liberal media all at once. *I was so happy at Trump's boldness and aggressiveness, I hit my head on the ceiling, twice, while jumping for joy!*

Now, that they were getting a dose of their own caustic and bitter medicine, suddenly liberal Democrats, after hanging with Trump for forty years, were howling and hooting, declaring that now he was somehow unfit for office. Corrupt establishment Republicans, who were on the take themselves, also screamed and yelled that Trump was destroying their party's good name, as if they had one over the last three administrations.

Along with millions of hard-working Americans, I knew that Trump was remaking the party for the good and was giving Republicans what they sorely lacked, real leadership and the backbone they once had in the 1800s. I firmly believe that God sent Trump not only as a messenger to the suffering people of this nation but also as a warning, and sign for us conservative Americans to not ever give up in our fight against Democrats and their evil ideology.

I also believe that God, in Trump, delivered to us an unconventional and uncouth wrecking ball to smash the levers of corrupted power entrenched, for many years, in our government and to give this country just one more crack at redemption before he completely destroys it.

To the unwashed and truly uninformed masses, the liberal media and Democrats will have you believe that Trump is a brand new 40ish upstart; a broke, drug abusing community organizer from Chicago, fresh on the scene or something...*oops, that was Obama, sorry.*

No, as I stated before, Trump is a white seventy-year-old billionaire, a battle-tested and successful businessman who has been in the public eye for over forty years. This man is not a newly minted and crisp $100 bill America just happened to find, no, Trump is an old, earned-the-hard-way, crinkled $100 bill that this country always had sitting in a drawer somewhere. He was like that money saved for a rainy day that we knew was there all the time and had taken it out on occasion, inspected, and always placed back in its hiding place.

Beginning in 2008, there was a downpour of epic proportions, it was raining immorality and corruption in America, and the resulting liberal Democrat torrents was absolutely destroying this nation. And there would be no relief from this political correctness monsoon until 2016 when fed-up Americans would reach into that rainy day fund drawer and retrieve that $100 bill called Trump.

During Trump's seventy years on earth, there had never been any mystery to the man, so to speak, and there wasn't ever any hint of corruption. So, today, it still amazes me what the onslaught by the liberal media of manufactured "racism" and revised history of someone's past can do to that person's reputation and character. We see lies unfold every day with liberal "news" outlets such as CNN, NBC, ABC, MSNBC, CBS, and other Democrat operations as they run fake story after fake story on Trump for their low-info viewers.

All of the things about Trump's life that the mainstream media, white liberal Democrats, and black racist overseers are feigning outrage about today is old, recycled news that has been rehashed and repackaged for dumb sheeple who cannot tear themselves away from the hordes of anti-American media termites that has infested our nation's information sources.

Trump has circled the globe many times, hung with world leaders and potentates, hobnobbed with Republicans and Democrats, dabbled in the promotion of boxers and schmoozed with Miss America Pageant contestants. He has also employed and helped many blacks, whites, Hispanics, and just about every other race in his business and personal dealings over his many years in business.

During his illustrious career, Trump's businesses, best-selling books, reality shows, pageants, bankruptcies, divorces, wives and ex-wives, endless tax audits, and just about everything else Trump has been looked over, dissected, and processed by the media ad nauseam and there really isn't much more to learn or to be told about the man's life.

As I alluded to earlier, not once during his fifty years or so of hanging with Democrats, Republicans, movie stars, sports stars, rappers, hosting parties and making cameo appearances, etc., was Trump ever called a Russian spy or racist. Yet, after running as a Republican, he was quickly branded a racist, and everything else, by those who had known him for decades. *Similar to blacks being called coons after leaving the Democrat Plantation.*

These venomous and fabricated attacks came about because of Trump's almost unbelievable presidential run, which was historic and masterfully done. With his ascension as a Republican, he had pissed off anti-American Democrats to no end. And the pivotal turning point in Trump's presidential campaign would occur when Hillary, the Democrat would-be queen, reeking of elitism, called his every day, hard-working supporters deplorables. She stepped in it bigly when she publicly proclaimed that Trump's blue-collar voters were uneducated and uncouth, unworthy of being acknowledged by high and mighty wealthy Democrats such as herself.

As to Hillary's statement on the intellect of Trump supporters, well hold on, let's just go ahead and pump the brakes here. With Hillary's "educated" supporters, and not to put my peoples down, it's not like there's a ton of black and Hispanic scholars running around in shithole, crime infested, Democrat inner cities and illegal alien sanctuary strongholds with book bags teeming with intellectual literature, noshing on tofu, and engaging each other on the works of Shakespeare.

Au contraire, most Democrat-voting, inner-city denizens are high school dropouts, illiterates, and welfare-dependent livestock awaiting the first of each month for government aid and table scraps. I mean, for me personally, any black dumb enough to believe the myth that the political parties somehow "switched" in the 1960s, from the same party that whipped and hanged their asses for centuries, are right at the bottom of the intelligence totem pole. *Even a beaten-down dog would know who kicked him in the ass for years and would bite his nuts off the next time he sees 'em coming.*

Anyways, as I write this book, the Democrat Party is right now tearing the kitchen sink off their political playbook wall to throw at our President, Donald J Trump. And one of the best lines of attacks, and schemes, they have conjured up each, and every election and effectively employed against Republicans continuously is "victimized" women.

Trump was to be no exception, during his presidential campaign, I still can remember Democrats screeching and screaming like constipated hyenas: *"Trump slept with women ten, twelve, fifteen years ago and God knows how far back, and now he doesn't wanna admit to it, but we'll make him! We'll get 'em!*

The Democrat Party loves this line of attack, because, *"by God, we're talking about women here, the women! Our fairer sex is being abused, I say, abused!" Yada yada.*

This brings us to the Democrat Party's corruption and shenanigans during Alabama's special election for a just opened Senate seat in 2017. When they saw that Roy Moore, a conservative firebrand, was going to win the election, liberal Democrats immediately pulled out the old victimized woman card and suddenly there were sexual assault "victims" galore, replete with fabricated sordid details from forty and fifty years ago.

And it was no surprise for me to see unintelligent and ignorant blacks, especially black females, suddenly popping up on television and yelling about how Roy must be stopped. This manufactured dust-up by conniving Democrats costed Roy Moore, a good man, a seat in the Senate.

And after their mission was accomplished, all of these distraught "victims" just quietly disappeared, like most of them do, never to be heard from again, until the next election of course. After the election was over, there was the same low-intellect, plantation black women on television again, laughing and celebrating, *"Yeah, we stopped Roy Moore."*

These idiotic black women, as commanded by white liberals, also went out and voted for Doug Jones in droves, a man who told them to their faces that he would flood their communities with illegals, kick'em in the ass and endorse anti-black Democrat policies once he got into office. *It's like Democrats could tell black women that there were unlimited ebt cards and hair weaves at the bottom of the Grand Canyon and that they needed to go over the edge to retrieve'em. In about two weeks, the canyon would be filled up with'em, all dead, Asian weaves and all.*

Now, where was I? Oh yeah, talking about Trump, wasn't I? Damn ignorant Negroes got me sidetracked.

Ok, ok...so Trump, a young, good looking, promiscuous billionaire and international playboy back in the day, who actually ran the Miss America Pageant and was surrounded by tons of beautiful women, won't indulge the Democrat Party on his sexual prowess. *And this is a national emergency and political issue?*

Trump coyly refused to even entertain the thought of telling liberals whom he had slept with and how many, and if he had ever paid any of'em to keep their flap shut about any trysts they may have had. But according to pissed-off Democrats in Congress, under smear rules 101, this arises to treason, unless it's a Democrat like Senator Menendez from New Jersey and his pedophile ring.

Nevertheless, the old sexual victim playbook didn't work too well with the Trumpster, this man was fortified Teflon. I remember when that private tape was strategically released in the media, you know when Trump said: *"Grab 'em by the pussy."* Yeah, that's the one, didn't even put a scratch on the MAGA Train.

Remember when suddenly, highly sensitive and aggrieved "go low and go high" Michelle Obama, the black first lady (questionably) responded at the time, saying she was "shook to the core," and nasty black rappers saying they were deeply offended?

First off, our former first lady's husband abused drugs, as mentioned in his own book, and was accused by a gay dude, Mr. Larry Sinclair, of having an illicit extramarital affair with him, as I previously detailed. The Obamas have hung with, listened to, and entertained gangster rappers at the Whitehouse, many times, who have spewed profanity and filth about women on their recordings for over twenty years.

Oddly, neither Michelle nor her "sweet-and-low" hubby and young daughters, was ever "shook to the core" by any lewd lyrics by these black gangster rappers. Hell, black rappers were even riding dirty with their queen Hillary, showing up at one of her small rallies, standing alongside her onstage and shouting, "my niggas" during the 2016 presidential campaign.

Furthermore, not only do a lot of blacks listen to this woman-bashing, misogynistic "music" by black rappers, they will actually go out and spend their money on this "music," and will allow their small children listen to it as well. *So, in other words, disingenuous Democrats such as the Obamas, will pay rappers to sing offensively to them and their children in public, but feign outrage when Trump says offensive words in private? Ooook.*

Anyways, when the "victimized women" ploy failed to register with Americans and did little to derail Trump's campaign, the big guns were bought out. Nearing the end of the 2016 election, Democrats would drop their nuclear smear bomb, rolling out about twenty women, uh, oops, twenty *"victims"* for the media.

In the final days of the 2016 presidential election campaign, these conjured up "sexually victimized" women made their customary rounds on leftist networks such as NBC, ABC, CBS, CNN, MSNBC, and other Democrat-controlled outlets. And they were all claiming Trump looked at'em thirty years ago, might've had sex with'em twenty years ago, that he slept with'em fifteen years ago and didn't leave a tip and somebody needs to know that he had been frisky when he was younger...yada, yada, yada. They were all victims, why? *Because they said so, that's why, and "we must believe the women," and "they must be heard!"*

These, uh, "saintly," abortion loving, pussy-hat wearing, and well-paid liberal Democrat activist "metoo women" was all too eager to give us salacious details, a blow-by-blow (pun intended) account of the supposedly most humiliating and embarrassing "victimization" of their lives which had, uh, happened twenty, thirty or forty years ago at the hands of a lustful billionaire.

Now, of course, they all needed an attorney. *Hey, I know one How about attorney Gloria Allred? Yeah, she's sort of an unknown, a raw talent, but just might do the trick.*

So, now that they were lawyered up, these manufactured "victims" would go the usual route of getting maximum exposure for their suddenly "painful experience" with Trump by having a flurry of softball interviews on all of the Democrat-controlled media outlets. *How about, er, uh, they start with CNN perhaps? Yeah, let's interview 'em there, CNN is an upstanding "news only" outlet...really...uh...no?*

Once these "victims" were in front of the cameras and in the spotlight, it was like watching overwrought, badly produced soap operas. They all wore sad and anguished faces on cue just by calling on their distant memories of all the "sexual abuse" that supposedly occurred forty years ago, never mind the fact that one of these "victims' had now been happily married for over thirty five years, has eight kids, four grandkids, a dog, rooster, and a happy cat. Yet, after all those years, these "victims, uh, er, still were able to manage uncontrollable tears for the cameras, real tears. *Uh, zoom in now, close, get a tight shot!*

I remember there being "concerned-looking" liberal Democrat interviewers on various "news" outlets just being so attentive and really listening to these now petrified women, and becoming visibly upset and aghast at the alleged sordid details being finally fully "exposed," for the world to see, and on their broadcasts! I hooted and howled with laughter as these, uh, "victims" expounded on how they just couldn't seem to get over how Trump, a good looking billionaire playboy, looked at'em twenty and thirty years ago. *Some of these dogs should be so thankful.*

Real American patriots paid little attention to this made-for-sheeple spectacle and after Trump was elected, in spite of this charade, pissed off Democrats tried just one more "super-victim" and rolled out their old retread, Stormy Daniels, to "get Trump" *as old black and dumb-as-rocks Auntie Max would say.* Democrats were just so sure that if a lawyer could make Trump say that he indeed, at least once, had sex with a former porn star, who had slept with scads of other men while being filmed and getting paid for it, that this would be the "gotcha moment" which would undoubtedly lead to his downfall and impeachment.

Really, who could stomach a rich and handsome billionaire sleeping with a female porn star ten years ago? *Arrrrrgh! I mean, was this supposed to be more lurid than some beta male black Senator from Chicago allegedly having sex with a gay man in the back of a limo while smoking crack or something?*

With gender-conflicted Democrats, Trump, an alpha male, having sex with a female just wouldn't do, they were petrified. Oh, feminist, liberal male "anchors" was simply aghast that an alpha male was actually sleeping with "females," they were absolutely hysterical, going on ad nauseum about who knew what, when, and who paid who.

Well, this ploy didn't seem to pan out either. Trump just shrugged off this round two of "sexual victims" foolishness and fought back with his own threats of lawsuits. In other words, he advised these "victims" to do the one thing that they couldn't do, prove these allegations or put a sock in it. And it worked, they all seemed to just disappear overnight, except old Stormy, whom at present has been ordered to pay the Donald over three hundred thousand dollars for his troubles. *Whew, that was certainly fun just to relive these moments of Trump snookering Democrats. I could reminisce all day on these fond memories, however, let's move on to: "He's a Russian spy, and we'll get the goods on 'em yet."*

So, what game is afoot, you ask? Well, just like during the Civil War of 1861, the election of 2016 was a high stakes contest between Americans and Democrats, winner keeps all, with the United States and our Republic at stake. With the 2016 presidential election, Democrats thought they were holding onto the winning hand because they had Obama, their ace of spades, spying on Trump and campaigning for their ice queen, Hillary, who was one of the best and, for decades, a remarkably cunning player in the business of politics and corruption.

Liberal Democrats, sure and cocky of the hand they held, smirked, just as they had done during the roasting of Trump at the correspondence dinner in 2011, as they declared: *"Take your defeat like a man, I hope you don't stir up any dust after you are defeated, loser!" "You just don't know when to fold'em, cowboy!"*

Democrats were all smiles, giddy with excitement, as they placed their stacked and fraudulent election cards on the table that cold November day, displaying a full house of illegals, deranged whites, dead voters, and black welfare-dependent plantation fools.

At the sight of this sure winning hand, the Democrat-controlled media went berserk, proclaiming right then and there that Hillary was indeed the winner as they had forecasted. With this hugely anticipated announcement, there was overwhelming joy in liberalsville. However, their victory wouldn't last long, for it was at this pivotal moment in our nation's history when something wonderfully strange happened.

Just as the celebratory liberals were reaching for the nation-altering pot on the table, Trump tipped his ten-gallon MAGA hat back just a tad and slowly showed his hand, revealing a Royal Flush of hard-working Americans, defecting Blue-dog Democrats, Christians, and freedom-loving Conservatives.

There was a collective gasp as the entire room grew silent, with those in attendance unable to process the enormity of what had just occurred. Yeah, Trump had won, he'd whipped their asses, and was flushing the establishment and elites right down the toilet. Oh, the Democrats were in complete disbelief and frozen stiff; they had huffed and bluffed all campaign long that they, in no uncertain terms, held the best hand in the house.

They sincerely believed that all of the odds had been stacked in their favor, their media comrades had all but assured them not only of victory but total annihilation of Trump. And Hillary, smiling and giddy with excitement after she had been guaranteed victory by the same liberal media which gleefully broadcasted her imminent crowning for months on end, was now dejected and deflated and understandably flummoxed.

From the start of the 2016 presidential campaign, it was a foregone conclusion by many Democrat elites across the country that Hillary would indeed ascend the throne and take her rightful place, her long overdue inheritance of the Whitehouse, and assume ultimate political power after this foolish "election" formality nonsense was over. She would trounce this reckless reality billionaire, send him packing and finish Obama's, the ace of spades, destruction of America.

But the tables were now turned, and the 2016 election would become like a funeral for demented white liberal Democrats and subservient, welfare-dependent plantation blacks, who wailed and thrashed about while gnashing their teeth demonically at their loss, refusing to come to terms with the total destruction of their vaunted can't-lose candidate.

After Trump laid his cards on the table, showing that he was indeed holding the winning hand, a chorus born of defeat ensued from distraught Democrats: *"Cheater, you must have hidden cards up your sleeve, the hand is a fraud!" "You're not legit, you're an imposter!"* So, to dismiss these claims of fraud, Trump, without further ado rolls up his sleeves for Democrats and all the American people to see.

When his sleeves went up, there was another collective gasp by all, because his bare arms did not show the soft and pampered limbs of a multi-billionaire. Instead, Trump revealed the rough-hewn, muscular, and sinewy arms of the forgotten hard-working men and women of this nation who had been looked upon by the coastal elites as uneducated, inconsequential, and of little use to Democrats or their Party.

It was then, at that moment, on election night of 2016, when Trump's purpose was made manifest for all to see. It was evident then that our nation had witnessed and experienced a victory by a true champion of the people, for the people, and by the people. Trump had stood in the gap, steadfastly and unselfishly, and on the founding fathers' values, principles, and beliefs, leaning not on his own merits but on the dreams of the working poor, the ones who thought their futures had long since passed, to nevermore be.

Trump, the non-political and anti-establishment outsider, had connected like a flash drive of hope inserted into the USB port of the rust belt and former robust manufacturing towns, where well-paying jobs that once sustained thriving communities were no longer. Where residents of these ravaged areas had seen, over the years, their way of life packed up and moved offshore by Democrat policies and their hopelessness had long since set in.

Trump went about transferring the beaten down aspirations of these rural Americans upon himself, uploading their angst, frustration, and desperation onto his MAGA laptop during his campaign. And with his election in 2016, Trump is now currently in the process of reprogramming this nation's powers that be to accept the blue-collar apps of these hard-working Americans, so they're once again included in this nation's main server of prosperity.

Out of work, men and women in rural America and urban cities finally had a champion to call their own, one who honestly had their backs. With their champion's improbable election, there had been a collective sigh of relief and growing anticipation of wonderful things to come. As with anything patriotic and American, it should come as no surprise that blue-collar workers in this country are an anathema to the Democrat Party, despised by snooty liberal elites and Hollywood types, and is a group no longer relevant in their political plans.

In contrast, liberal Democrats and RINOS love foreign blue-collar imports, as demonstrated by the 500,000 or so HB-1 visas they advocate for each and every year to bring Indians and other foreign nationals over onto our soil to take well-paying jobs away from struggling Americans in the heartland of this nation. Upon Trump's victory in 2016, heralding the end of the foreigners-over-Americans status quo, enraged and out of touch Democrats pondered to themselves: *"How were their hand beaten so badly by this guy, this reality star who were representing know-nothings and working stiffs? He wasn't even supposed to be intelligent enough to understand the political landscape and game they had mastered for centuries.*

Hadn't they, themselves, shuffled the cards, cut the deck and even had a quick peek at some of the cards which he had been holding? Democrats wondered *"Who fed him the winning cards, who? He was a newcomer to this game and should have been out of his league."*

Although the Democrat Party was in turmoil with their resounding defeat, this game still wasn't over for them, not by a long shot. The beatdown they suffered in 2016 at the hands of Trump had been a critical setback, but one which they felt they had to overcome, and quickly. The election had been one that their party sorely wanted, and in fact had been a must-win for them to continue the game of re-writing our constitution which Obama, the ace of spades, had started. They also desperately needed, at all costs, to cover for the corruption of Hillary, their queen.

Democrats had come oh so close to winning, and yet so far, how did it happen? Prognosticators in the media, and, uh, really wise pundits and polling seers had all but written Trump's candidacy off, foolishly drinking their own liberal echo chamber Kool-Aid, which didn't include the people who actually worked for a living and were hurting from decades of anti-American Democrat Policies. To me, the election of Trump also reminded everyone how blacks are stupid enough to let emotions and manipulation by Democrats continually hurt them and their communities, for decades, without so much as a whimper.

The majority of blacks are forever in total lockstep to vote whichever way liberals demand, without hesitation, and there's absolutely nothing Democrats can do to make most blacks turn against them, nothing. *White liberals can kill their mommas, slap their babies and kick'em in the ass, continuously, and most blacks will just brush it off and wait for the first of the month and dey ebt cards.*

However, the majority of whites don't play that nonsense, damn an ebt card, and will shift a vote on liberal Democrats' asses in a heartbeat. The 2016 election served to illustrate that most whites are not just gonna sit around in a welfare stupor while the Democrat Party go about destroying what's left of their communities and our nation without a fight. *Oh, hell-to-the-no.* So, in the 2016 election, over nine million newly enlighten whites, realizing what was happening, shifted from Democrats to Republicans, abandoning the liberal Titanic upon which they had been riding. But to no one's surprise, for the majority of blacks, the band of entitlement kept right on playing on the deck of the sinking ship "Handout," and they were just a hanging on for dear life.

*Sadly, if left up to just deadbeat and low-info blacks to save this nation, anti-American Democrats would never lose another election. With that being said, I feel that I must give another heartfelt shout out at this point, and say thank God for moral and intelligent whites!

After the election and their defeat had sunken in, an evil and wicked thought occurred to Democrats as a rictus of a smile ran across their satanic faces. The Grinch-like and wily liberals came up with a clever little plan; they would stop Trump from accomplishing anything for the American people, especially the hard-working middle class. They would have their unfettered illegals and open borders after all. With their liberals in courthouses across the nation, they would have their activist judges stop any plans that would help this country.

They would obstruct and resist any and all appointments of American patriots to Trump's cabinet and would gin up investigation after investigation to distract from their corruption and to anger people against him. There would be no wall to protect this nation or its citizens. There would be no helping the insects in the Midwest, no helping the black community, no economic revival, no manufacturing jobs, and no making anything great again. Why they would simply find a way to impeach and remove him from office before he even got started.

Democrats, with their cold and ashen Grinch-like hearts, delighted in the knowledge of the political sabotage they had in store for Trump. All was not lost; they would stop his presidency from coming. As with Dr. King, Democrats would pull out their old "smear" and "fabricate" media-driven playbook of deception and lies often used to target Republicans.

After the 2016 election was over, Democrats were panicking from the promise made by Trump during the presidential debates, to thoroughly investigate the corruption and crimes of old Hillary and her minions. However, liberal Democrats already had their "insurance policy" in place, with well-entrenched and corrupt deep-state operatives in all of the executive and judicial branches of government, ready to carry out their nefarious plot. They now just needed something, anything to generate an investigation into Trump and cause chaos within his administration. My theory:

*First, the Democrat Party contacted Fusion GPS, one of their deep state operations, and then they got shady British operative, Christopher Steel, to fabricate a dossier on Trump. This would also *be the same dossier which just so happened to be bought and paid for by Hillary and the Democrat National Convention.*

*Once this file was produced, one of Obama's holdovers, FBI agent Peter Strzok, was then sent to present the fabricated dossier, or "evidence" of Russia Collusion, to a secret FISA court(Foreign Intelligence Surveillance.), which I believe is totally corrupt as well.

*At the FISA court, old Peter got his judge "friend" to sign off on a warrant to wiretap Trump without any hearings to determine the validity of the underlying fabricated "evidence." **Just think about it, this federal Judge, who was supposed to uphold the constitution and laws of our nation, had given the ok on a meritless and baseless warrant to spy on Trump and anyone associated with his campaign without even blinking an eye.

*Using this newly obtained warrant, based on their completely fabricated "evidence," other holdovers from Obama's administration, and deep-state members of the FBI, CIA, and DOJ, infiltrated Trump's campaign and his transition team to try to plant this "evidence" among the members.

*Then the falsely obtained and baseless warrant was repeatedly signed off by Rod Rosenstein, an Attorney General appointed after the convenient recusal of Jeff Sessions, a milquetoast and, I believe, a covert Democrat operative who inserted himself almost at the very start into Trump's campaign. This slick southerner, at the behest of Democrats, managed to ingratiate himself as a loyal friend of then-candidate Trump, and gaining his confidence. However, Trump soon got a whiff of the FBI's corruption, and attempted coup, and fired FBI Director James Comey, another plant and Obama holdover.

*Now fired, Comey, who is also a friend of Rod Rosenstein, the acting Attorney General, still had a deep state connection to Robert Mueller, who was involved, in the 1980s and 1990s scandal involving Whitey Bulger, a gangster on the payroll of the FBI at the time.

*So, Comey would send Robert Mueller as his replacement to lead the FBI, but he was subsequently turned down for the position by Trump. Nonetheless, Democrats were undeterred, they would get

Mueller, in some capacity, around the Trump administration and close enough to do damage.

*To slip Mueller in the back door, James Comey, the recently fired and, I believe, corrupt former FBI director, suddenly writes notes to himself and then leaks these same notes to his reporter friend as a supposedly powerful memo showing Trump was colluding with Russians, all based on the fake dossier he helped create, and one he knew to be false.

*This "reporter" buddy would then get this "explosive memo" over to Rod Rosenstein, the cunning deep state Democrat Attorney General, who then acted surprised and quickly pounced on this info as if he wasn't in on the fabrication of this "evidence" all along.

*Rosenstein then uses this same "leaked" memo to declare that an investigation is warranted into "election meddling" and then appoints his old buddy Robert Mueller as Special Counsel, the same deep state operative Trump turned down just days ago for FBI Director. Now, with this turn of events, old Mueller is in a position to investigate Trump based on the fabricated evidence that he, Comey, and his buddy Rosenstein are all in on.

*Of note, seems that old Mueller, being the FBI director in 1993, when twenty percent of our nation's uranium was sold to Russians, has a vested interest in preventing Trump from ever uncovering all of the Democrats' corruption.

*Anyway, old hangdog-faced Mueller then starts an investigation using the false "evidence" which was paid for by Hillary, the Democrat queen, who was also involved in the uranium deal along with Mueller.

*With their Russian "insurance plan" and coup d'état in full motion, Mueller, the uh, supposed honorable Republican, and nonpartisan prosecutor, according to the complicit liberal media, proceeded to gather sixteen other deep state liberal Democrats and Trump-hating lawyers to fill out his "team" of "investigators."

*Then this cadre of conflicted, liberal Democrat socialist lawyers, all use the same unsubstantiated and "fabricated evidence," provided by their Attorney General buddy Rod Rosenstein, as a basis to attack

everything and everyone around Trump to distract from Obama's, the ace of spades, corrupt administration and Hillary's crimes and misdeeds against our nation.

Whew, I hope you kept up with that one.... it's a tangled web of deep state deceit and anti-American intrigue that is still being unwoven even as I write. At this date, Mueller has finished his report, with nothing found, but now new Attorney General William Barr is looking at the corruption of Mueller, Obama, the Clintons, and many other Democrats...stay tuned.

Although a lot of people have some knowledge as to what is actually happening in this country, it is very difficult to sort through because liberal media outlets like CNN, MSNBC, CBS, NBC, ABC, NY Times, WaPo, Facebook, Google, and other Democrat tabloids and talk shows have been running interference by distorting, distracting, omitting and outright lying to the American people, all while propping up this fabricated "Russian" investigation.

After installing their diabolical "insurance plan" and having their false propaganda disseminated among the public, delighted liberal Democrats and their media wingmen waited and waited. They leaned to the side, ears cuffed, anticipating the wails of Trump supporters, listening for the sweet sounds of deplorables crying over his impending impeachment and removal from office. It would indeed be a thing of pure joy, hearing deplorables thrashing about in their misery and seeing these "uneducated supporters" lose faith and turn on Trump, how delicious!

Liberal Democrats were absolutely delighting in the prospect of their media soldiers crucifying Trump daily on their broadcasts and driving a public stake through the heart of his presidency. They had paid an enormous sum for the fake Russian dossier and were now awaiting the return on their investment.

But as they strained to hear the expected weeping and gnashing of teeth of his supporters, a faint and curious noise arose and grew louder. What sound was this? It wasn't the sounds of sorrow and gnashing of teeth, why no, it was the sounds of happiness. They hadn't stopped his presidency from coming, it came, and not only was Trump unscathed but he was also still running around, jubilant as ever and holding massive rallies all over the country to cheerful and appreciative Americans.

The economy was booming, Isis was being decimated, North Korea was tamed, manufacturing jobs were roaring back, illegals were on the run, stock markets were through the roof, the corrupt kickback Iran deal was pulled, and black and Hispanic unemployment was at the lowest ever. Why, Trump even had time to fund historically black colleges, set up venture capital for minorities and push through tax cuts for the working man! Democrats fumed, where, just where did they go wrong? They thought long and hard; their crazed, anti-American minds repeatedly going over all of their tried and true methods from their character assassination and smear playbook. Their wicked little heads almost exploded from frustration, they had just about exhausted everything on their list of vicious smear tactics and had pulled out all the stops with their "investigations" and 24/7 media misinformation onslaught. Heck, they had even managed to get a lot of Trump's staff fired with false innuendos and accusations.

However, Trump, their primary target, and impediment to keeping their corruption hidden, was left unfazed and standing. What would it take to bring his presidency down and stop him from helping the American people? For white liberal Democrats, this was now an emergency, and they wondered how they would get the American people to turn on Trump. They went over their political character assassination checklist once more:

* They had tried to get him with a false "evidence" investigation, they paid fake sexual victims to lie, paid a porn star to embellish her sexual encounter with Trump, talked about his divorces, claimed his realty university was a sham, hinted that he was a tax evader and denounced his bankruptcies.

*They had thrown claims of homophobic, Islamophobia, misogynist, transphobic, racism, and bigotry at'em. They had doubled and tripled down with accusations that he was a newly discovered KKK member, a Nazi colluder, a white supremacist and a secret agent for Russia.

* They had attacked his wife, children, in-laws, dog, cat and the air he breathed, and they harassed his staff and called him Cheetos and bone spurs.

* Black gangster rappers and MS-13 members had threatened him, liberal Democrat celebrities, sports stars, and talk show hosts all mocked and hurled profanities at'em him nightly on their various programs and talk shows.

*Hollywood degenerates and pedophiles had put out numerous infomercials denouncing him and marched in pussy hats, screaming about how they were gonna blow up the Whitehouse.

* There were Antifa and Black Lives Matter members rioting, destroying property and blaming Trump for any and all shootings, while other liberals held weekly witchcraft seances to cast spells on'em. Some liberal fools even went on hunger strikes, screaming and howling at the moon while wrapped in cuddly blankets and playing with crayons.

*The Democrat media; NBC, CNN, ABC, MSNBC, and CBS, BBC, PBS, and others had all gotten in on the act as well, parading out Obama's corrupt ex-CIA heads and other anti-American ex-government officials to exclaim in all the grave hyperbole they could muster: *"We, as a country are facing imminent danger every single second that Trump is in office!" "It's the end of the world, we won't survive another day; this president is a clear and present danger!"*

However, nothing seemed to work against Trump because real Americans and patriots saw through the deception and stood steadfast behind their champion. Besides, I sincerely believe that a higher power had his back as well:

Isaiah 54:17 "No weapon that is formed against thee shall prosper; and every tongue that shall rise against thee in judgment thou shalt condemn. This is the heritage of the servants of the LORD, and their righteousness is of me, saith the LORD."

*You know, lately, sometimes I drift off, imagining that Democrats had suddenly become sane and rational people and that just for a moment, *through their own, love, peace, tolerance, diversity and equality ideology their party espouses*, that maybe, just maybe they would see that Trump was right. And perhaps they would buy into all the beautiful things he was doing in trying to fix our country and help everyday hardworking Americans just like he promised. Just maybe, they would think, he will go down as the best president ever. Just maybe... *Whooooa...I'm back, let's pump our brakes together on this one.*

Democrats doing some serious analysis of themselves and their behavior isn't happening, ever. This party has always been the same ruthless and immoral party as it was in the 1600s, 1700s, 1800s, 1900s, and now the 2000s. If you look closely and without political correctness blinders on, you will see that Democrats have been relatively consistent ever since their inception in 1829 and nothing has ever changed for these violent and deranged anti-Americans. So, this movie doesn't end the way I imagine it should. Oh, I wish it did, but it doesn't.

Right now, liberal Democrats are in shock, and even more volatile, over the notion that President Trump is actually trying to do what he said he would do, that he meant the promises he made on the campaign trail. Democrats and RINOS are wondering, what politician does that? Trump was breaking with political norms, shunning the glad-handing and underhanded establishment traditions and precedents which had gone back decades, and perhaps even to the founding of this nation.

To Democrats and RINOs, it was almost a rite of passage for politicians to embellish and lie to get into office, but once elected they were supposed to quickly "pivot" to establishment guidelines, protocol, and procedures while smiling and wearing their "for the people" raiment in public. However, these anti-Americans severely underestimated Trump's will and determination in this regard. There would be no "pivoting" to the left or right, Trump proved that he was first and foremost a traditional constitutionalist and patriot who honestly loves our country and has demonstrated, by his actions, that he is a man of conviction and cannot be swayed one iota from his MAGA mission.

And to the Democrat Party's dismay, Trump fiercely fights any ideas or actions that would revise or remove even one word from our

Constitution and Bill of Rights. His victory in 2016 left the Confederate Democrat Party's quest for political dominance in disarray, crushing the eight-year socialist momentum they enjoyed under Obama.

To white liberals, Trump, the SOB, was going to appoint like-minded conservative Constitutionalists to the Supreme Court; justices who were not activists and ones that would interpret the constitution as written, restoring the voice and will of the American people as our forefathers intended. To make matters worse for Democrats, their daily, full-throated, and constant screeching about "Russia" and other alarmist attacks against Trump is still proving ineffectual, and just bouncing right off of'em like rain sluicing down the sides of a newly waxed car.

The Democrat Party's dilemma, it would seem, is how do you stop someone who is his own man and doesn't need your money, lobbyists or special interests?

* *How do you stop a man who isn't taking any salary to do the hardest job in the world, and under 24/7 unprecedented scrutiny and negativity?*

How do you stop a man who doesn't give a damn about what Democrats or anyone else say about him and can give as good as he gets?

And how do you stop a man who is well-equipped to obliterate your most prized weapon; political correctness?

Answer.... you can't, unlike the always on-the take, quid pro quo establishment politicians who are raping the taxpayers of this country, Trump is not even taking a salary and has nothing to lose, and with the reluctant aid of Twitter, has now awakened people to the true intentions of the Democrat Party, the real enemies of this nation. And that isn't hyperbole in any sense, just think, the overhyped, vaunted, and much ballyhooed Russian collusion investigation, after over $25 million spent, thirty Russians indicted, and a couple of jay-walking tickets handed out to nobodies, devolved into a who-paid-who-for-sex scandal that allegedly occurred twelve years before Trump became president.

Old hang-dog-faced Mueller, the very special counsel, was turned into nothing more than a glorified ambulance chaser, hunting down thinly-connected people for tax evasion from decades ago and other petty process crimes that have nothing at all to do with Trump or his campaign. However, Mueller's "investigation" has served the two purposes for which it was intended:

*One, by investigating Trump non-stop, his law-and-order administration was too tied up and distracted, for years, to investigate Obama, Hillary, other Democrats, and even Mueller himself for all of the crimes and corruption they have committed against this country.

*Number two, Democrats have no one to run, effectively, against Trump in 2020 and seek, with the help of 24/7 negative coverage by their liberal media operatives, to throw enough unsubstantiated Russian foolishness, or whatever nonsense, at the wall that they would make Trump unelectable.

As for the black community, Democrats still have most of them on plantation lockdown, telling them that this Russia hoax really matters and to hate Trump, even though every sane person and their momma know at this point that it was corrupt Democrats who actually took money from Russians under the Obama administration while Mueller was the FBI director.

Doesn't matter though, most of the black community are bereft of common sense and logic and have been attacking the Democrat Party's new prey, Trump, like obedient and rabid Pit Bulls obeying their liberal white masters' commands. The majority of blacks blithely ignore the fact that it isn't Russia destroying their communities, creating fatherless homes and allowing poverty, gangs, drug dealing, and high homicide rates to fester in their neighborhoods; it has always been Democrats and their policies.

But despite the baseless and unwarranted hatred from these dumbed-down plantation blacks, right now Trump is in the middle of accomplishing great things for their community. He is creating blue collar jobs, funding black colleges, getting illegals out of the country, and bringing school vouchers and choice back. Trump is not only helping blacks but all Americans, from the rust belt to the east and west coast.

However, liberal Democrats know that they can never, ever acknowledge the positive impact that Trump's policies are having on the black community and this nation as a whole, and must either hide or distort the truth or mislead and misinform the public. In this regard, if you haven't yet noticed, since day one of the Trump administration, there has been nothing but "investigation" after "investigation," all of the Democrat Party's attacks have been solely personal in nature, simply because liberals are all about power and have no suggestions themselves on fixing anything for Americans, never did.

Liberal Democrats are no longer disguising their hatred for this nation and our culture, and have pulled out all the stops to see America fail in their quest for dominance. It is incredible to me how many people in this nation are still supporting and aligning themselves with their platform and ideology at this point. Unfortunately, due to the constant misinformation by the liberal mainstream media, the bulk of our nation's population is now mostly dumbed-down zombies, content in their ignorance as our society deteriorates.

And this is even more pronounced in the black community. With that said, let's conclude this chapter. I wanna do a little contrasting of both Obama's and the Trump Administration. Just for ha ha's.

If you will, turn the page, please.

Chapter Twenty-One

Trump & Obama In Contrast

O k, so let's recap and take a gander at how far we've come, shall we? *Democrats enslaved blacks in the 1600s, but after centuries of whippings, beatings, lynchings, and restrictions, Republicans would defeat the Democrats in 1865, forcing them to release their captives.

*Then Abraham Lincoln tried to help blacks with Reconstruction, and in retaliation Democrats promptly assassinated him and created the KKK, who then turned around and burned Black Wall Street to the ground and lynched thousands of blacks with impunity.

*With all of that, in the 1930s, blacks still went over to the Democrat party for welfare table scraps, but Dr. King would come along in the 1960s and break the Jim Crow laws and segregation in the south, freeing blacks once again.

*Angry Democrats then promptly killed King, and this time installed their own liberal Democrat-friendly black civil rights "reverends" to lead the black community.

*So, after five decades under the leadership of these "reverends" and the Democrat Party's welfare "assistance," most blacks today are directionless, uneducated, on crack, in poverty, and gay. Still yet, "resistance" plantation blacks have yet another opportunity in Trump, to become men and women again, if Democrats don't try to kill'em first…

Let's just suppose, for a moment, that America is one big neighborhood and all the houses in this neighborhood are in various states of disrepair and in dire need of landscaping and upkeep. Obama, a charming and smooth, self-described landscaper, happens by in his chauffeur-driven Bentley and pulls up to a tree badly in need of pruning, gets out in his $5000 suit, looks the situation over and says to the homeowner:

Well, ah, my beautiful madam, we have ta get measurements on this tree, and ah, get the proper saw and ladder, uh make sure we're not disturbing any birds that may be up there. And ah, we need to determine the trajectory of any fallout of the branches.

Furthermore, ah, we hope to change this tree in the future for the betterment of everyone in this community, blacks, whites, gays, straight, transgenders, Hispanics and, ah, everyone else. It is ah, incumbent, ah, upon me ta not be derelict in the discharge of my sworn duties to the American people that, ah, have entrusted me with the security and economic, ah, er, safekeeping of this country.

I will assign the appropriate committees and resources for funding and ta look into the causation of maladies such as these that affect the way of life for so many of you in your community.

After speaking, Obama gets into his Bentley, leaving the bewildered and confused homeowner behind. Eight days later he shows up again, the tree still in need of pruning, grins and says to the homeowner: *Dear lady, this ah, er, this tree cannot be pruned, it's ah, impossible, no one can do it, so, ah, the environment may be harmed. It's just the way, ah, things are now, and you'll just have ta live with it.*

The homeowner asks, *"How much do I owe you for your effort?"*

Obama says: O*h, you'll pay, I'll send everyone in this neighborhood a bill. You owe me everything, your devotion, loyalty, your votes for my candidates, your everything.*

Done, he gets back into his Bentley, puts on his $2000 pair of shades and instructs his driver to leave, never to return.

Ok, so now, along comes Trump, a rough around the edges and relatively new landscaper who is just beginning to learn the trade. With his hard hat on, he pulls up in his beat-up 1999 Ford Ranger; his jet is parked at home. He gets out, surveys the tree, and after checking it over, grabs his saw, throws on his climbing boots and says to the homeowner: *"Let's make this tree great again!"*

Trump rolls up his sleeves and goes up the tree, saws the limb off, comes back down all sweaty and says to the homeowner: *"I cut the son of a bitch off for ya, the branch was dead alright and was hanging really badly. That last rat bastard you hired to do the job a long time ago didn't know what the hell he was doing."*

The homeowner says, *"Thank you very much, it's been that way for eight years now, and we really needed it done. How much do I owe you?"*

Trump says: *"Nothing Ma'am, not one damn dime, it was my pleasure to do it, someone should've done it a long time ago, a long time ago and if I would've been here it would've been done, a long time ago, believe me."*

Trump then tips his hat, gets back into his Ranger, and rambles up the street towards another house. After some time, and at the next community meeting, the flabbergasted homeowner tells her neighbors at the gathering about this abrasive but wonderful new landscaper and his salty language. Appalled at his tone and off-color language, some homeowners are offended and put off by the new guy and longed for the old smooth-talking landscaper because, even though he didn't do much, he was funny, sweet and charming. However, some of the other homeowners remembered how well-kept their homes and streets used to be prior to the "charming" guy becoming their landscaper and were eager, despite the new guy's tone and language, to finally get their homes and neighborhood back into the shape they were before.

So, the community becomes divided between those homeowners who wanted to see things get done, regardless of the language and brusque tone of the new landscaper, and those homeowners who wanted to be talked to sweetly, where no one was being offended while their homes went to pot. I think this pretty much encapsulates the essence of the two vastly different administrations.

Obama was the effeminate, anti-American, socialist driven puppet who saw this country as a wealthy nation that owed other oppressed nations and fancied himself the conduit by which he, and his new world order handlers, would have America give up its sovereignty and become governed by an international body like the United Nations and its council.

In stark contrast to the elitist and condescending anti-American attitude of Obama and his ineffectual governing, Trump is a take no prisoners, meat and potatoes, no holds barred leader and astute businessman who fully understands what is at stake. America has always been the country where he, along with other white, black, Hispanic and Asian and other eager entrepreneurs have tapped into the many opportunities this nation has afforded them to become millionaires and billionaires by the fruits of their own hard work, ingenuity, and intellect.

Contrary to Obama, Trump sees America as the most celebrated Christian-based nation on earth, a powerful country that must always have unchallenged sovereignty and the strength to control her own destiny, thus, his emphasis on producing our own products and rebuilding our military. Our 45th President doesn't believe in handouts or reparations to other nations; he believes, rightly, that they are their own country, let them develop themselves as we have.

Trump knows that these struggling countries have intelligent grown men and women, and if they needed western intellect or loans to help them become a more industrialized nation, perhaps we can lend them a hand, nothing else. To go a bit further in our contrast, I wanna take Obama's actual words and deeds vs. the words and actions of Trump to drive my point home.

On June 1, 2016, Obama held a Town hall meeting while campaigning for then-candidate Hillary Clinton. A black Carrier employee in Indiana, fearful that he was losing his factory job and hearing that Trump could possibly bring back manufacturing jobs, stood up and asked Obama what could be done.

Here is Obama's response: *"What we have to do is to make sure that folks are trained for the jobs that are coming in now because some of those jobs of the past are just not going to come back."*

And says this about Trump: *"When somebody says, like the person you just mentioned who I'm not going to advertise for, that he's going to bring all those jobs back, well how exactly are you going to do that? What are you going to do?"*

"There's no answer to it" "He just says, well, I'm going to negotiate that? What magic wand do you have? And usually, the answer is he doesn't have an answer."

Let that sink in, a black Democrat president, while in office making millions from globalist policies that have decimated manufacturing and factory jobs that working blacks in this country have depended on for decades, telling another black man, who is fearful of losing his job and means to support his family, just to suck it up and learn something new.

This disappointed Carrier employee, this "brother," should have discovered in 2008 that there was no hope with Obama, heck, there wasn't even any change, just a snake oil salesman peddling his wares of fake economic tonics which held no therapeutic or curative value for working Americans whatsoever.

Now, the optimism for American workers in Trump's own words in 2016: *"Right now, 92 million Americans are on the sidelines, outside the workforce, and not part of our economy. It's a silent nation of jobless Americans..."*

"My economic plan rejects the cynicism that says our labor force will keep declining, that our jobs will keep leaving, and that our economy can never grow as it did once before."

*These two outlooks from vastly different administrations serves to illuminate the distinctiveness between a smart, intelligent, and selfless leader for Americans, like Trump, and a money-grubbing shrill for the Democrat Party's platform and ideology, like Obama.

Now, after Obama gave his callous summary and take on the manufacturing job losses that are disproportionately affecting black communities, he goes back to the Whitehouse where he would continue to throw lavish gay pride parties and entertain movie stars, Black Lives Matter, black singers, and other celebs while continuing to spending taxpayers money to no end.

With Trump, there have been no parties at the Whitehouse, no revolving door of celebs, and no concerts. He has been a working president ever since his inauguration, steadfast in his Make America Great Again agenda as promised As you know by now, the man doesn't sleep, he knows there's too much to do, and undo, to get this ship we call America righted again.

Trump is a throwback to the founding fathers, who desired and created a Republic, a government representative of the people, by the people, and for the people. He knows exactly how our nation has gotten so far off course, how we have strayed from a path of economic and military strength; he's been saying it for decades. Don't believe me, for evidence, just go back and look at his old interviews of twenty and thirty years ago.

A billionaire who has never used drugs, smoke or drink, and is a very successful businessman, during his 2016 presidential campaign, Trump looked the everyday hard-working American in the eye and said: *"I've got your back,"* and meant it.

True to his word, Trump gets to the white house and immediately invites black college presidents over and holds meetings with prominent businessmen and job creators. He invited hard-working construction workers over to the Whitehouse, honored ICE, and congratulated border patrol and everyday law enforcement officers for a job well done. Trump also rolled back crippling Obama regulations and cut taxes so that small businesses could flourish and to give some relief to middle-class taxpayers. *Yet, none of this is seen on the liberal media.*

To contrast again, Obama, during his presidential campaign in 2007, and like every Democrat before him, used the tried and true political ruse of pretending to be for the little man only to enrich himself and gain political power. I mean, this man was a pivoting fool once elected. Just go back to when he was a Senator and compare his campaign promises with what he actually did when he got into the Whitehouse, which he used as his own personal piggy bank.

Trump, a man without pretense, was never seeking fortune, fame or power, he already had that, and for many years. His only mission was to restore the sovereignty of our nation and the manufacturing base that the on-the-take politicians had previously given away. In 2008, we had blindly and emotionally elected a smooth talking, community organizer and former lawyer who once abused cocaine. Somehow, we were led to foolishly believe that he could do the work of a drug-free, brilliant, and highly successful businessman.

During his eight-year tenure, Obama spent about eight trillion dollars to stimulate the economy, but it was money poorly spent. For starters, about 13 million more people, especially blacks and Hispanics, was placed on welfare to bring the total of deadbeats on government assistance to approximately 47 million, the highest ever recorded in this nation. And with these welfare numbers, it would stand to reason that we would also see the highest rate of poverty in fifty years during Obama's tenure as well.

Millions, and perhaps billions of taxpayers' funds went to Obama's "pet projects" such as Solyndra, a company guaranteed over $500 million in government "aid," and other startups, that failed bigly and quickly. *I'm not even gonna talk about that $800 million healthcare website that Obama had his friends, uh, create.* Still, there were billions more of Obama's "stimulus package" going to some of his other friends and secret slush funds for radical organizations such as Black Lives Matter and anti-American Muslim outfits.

Now, there were legitimate bailouts of companies like AIG, of course, but imagine if Trump had gotten elected in 2008 and was at the helm of this nation with this type of money, $8 Trillion to spend, at his fingertips. Oh, my, America would have been off the charts economically back then. I mean, right now today, even amid all of the Democrat witch hunt investigations and resistance, Trump is already saving our nation tens of billions by reworking lopsided trade deals and getting other countries to pony up funds for their own protection.

These results illustrate the quantifiable differences between an astute businessman and a know-nothing chatterbox who just throws money at a problem while dipping into the till himself, as most Democrats are wont to do with vast sums of money at their disposal.

The takeaway here for Americans: *" Never let an alleged former crackhead near your money."* As for the black community, I will venture this, it is my firm belief that Trump is the best thing that has happened to blacks since Lincoln, in spite of the large segment of Democrat-controlled, hate-filled blacks who are far too deluded and conditioned to see the forest for the trees.

Most black Democrats, when asked if Trump is good for their community or being told about his documented and amazing accomplishments in getting manufacturing jobs back and helping fund black colleges and black entrepreneurs, they say: *"Man, I don't believe that nonsense, that's fake bro, Trump's a racist, stop watching Fox News and Hannity."* But ask these simpletons about Obama's achievements, and you get: *"Man, he done a lot yo, he put a lot of things in place."*

It seems that the majority of blacks in this country do not possess enough rationale, critical thinking, or intellect to discern those things which imperil their own survival. Even the wild animals in the forest can instinctually sense when a forest fire or catastrophe is looming and will take actions to ensure their survival. *I guess the most noticeable difference here would be that the animals in the wild do not have other radicalized and socialist animals in their neck of the woods spouting inclusiveness, tolerance, equality, and diversity while pushing them towards the forest fire.*

You know, I've also noticed that most blacks get puffy in the mouth whenever someone says "Make America Great Again." Why is this? *Are these fools not proud of being in this country? MAGA, which is meaningful and straightforward words about patriotism and being proud of your country, triggers blacks? Really?... Seriously?*

With all that Trump has accomplished so far, and what is he is continuing to do for blacks and all Americans, white liberals have blacks still running around screaming like banshees: *"Yeah, make America white again!" "White nationalist mofos!"* These dumb plantation blacks would also revive the old decades-long and tantalizingly smooth never-ending classic: *"Trump wants to send blacks back to Africa!"*

As a sane, conservative black man let me tell you what Make America Great Again means to me. I can remember back in the day, in my pre-teen years in the 1970s, when we could and would leave our doors unlocked night and day and other neighborhood kids could and would just walk right in like family. We had a community that in the summertime, neighborhood children would hang out all times of night playing tag, catching fireflies or just talking and singing under the streetlights.

Even though I did have some great white friends that would come over to our house at times, our neighborhood was mostly black and peaceful, like a village where ever-watchful parents would sit in rocking chairs on their porches, sipping iced tea or lemonade on hot and sultry summer nights while laughing at our carefree and foolish play in the streets. And if a kid got in trouble at another kid's home, that parent would give him a beating and then send him home for another.

It was this sorta discipline which kept most of us on the straight and narrow path, and as I remember, we never had any serious crimes among us. There was no shootings, no stabbings, and no drug dealing on the corners by sagging pants thugs. The most violence we experienced around our neighborhood back then was when two of the fellas would get into a beef every once in a while and scuffle with each other to settle the matter. We would all gather around and watch them duke it out of course, and when it appeared that one had gotten the better of the other, we would then pull the victor off the defeated and in a day or so you would see these same two guys hanging out, laughing together as if nothing had happened.

I also remember the times when there was plenty of blue-collar work for blacks, and how my brothers and father would grab their lunch pails and head out to work every day to the mills and factories to work in good, honest, well-paying hard hat jobs. And when the weekend would come, they'd shower, get dressed, and hit the town looking good and feeling good. From around the neighborhood, you could often hear the strands of the Commodores, Doobie Brothers, Isley Brothers, Al Green, Parliament, etc., you know, the good stuff, not this crap that's being passed off as music these days.

There was an overall feeling of good vibes in the air in those days, and there is a YouTube video you should see which captures this mood precisely. If you ever have the chance sometime, check out the Rufus Thomas and the funky chicken video, which I think epitomizes the era and atmosphere which I am referring to, where tens of thousands of blacks are having a simple, carefree, and clean unified blast of a time at his concert.

So, when I hear Make America Great Again, this is what it means to me; a restoration of respect for law and order and each other, and an atmosphere of civility, prosperity, and peace, and well-being. And yes, I guess you can say that I am a black nationalist, because I was born in America, speak only English, and have a deep and abiding love for the only country I've ever lived in. All Americans should think about what this nation can be again, because this is our house, our only home, and if we lose this home to invaders from other lands that do not speak our language, and who insist on remaking our culture, what will we have left of ourselves?

Although Trump has put many policies in place that directly, and indirectly, affects blacks positively, white liberal Democrats want him stopped. Blacks working and becoming educated and independent would be devastating to the party's political plans.

As of this writing, under Trump's administration, our country has a booming economy and red-hot jobs market where over 400,000 manufacturing jobs have been created, and over 700,000 more blacks have gained employment. Coal mines that were once shuttered by the Obama administration's relentless attacks on their industry are now being reopened, along with other factories and companies in the manufacturing sector.

A relentless Trump has created over three million jobs in just two short years in office and has achieved unprecedented economic growth and success in bringing back blue-collar jobs, significantly enhancing opportunities and financial viability for the black community. With all of this happening, why is there still such an overwhelming black "resistance" to Trump? And why it is so crucial for white liberal Democrats to have most blacks resist Trump at all costs, even amid this tremendous black job growth, business opportunities, and development for their communities?

To understand this, we must backtrack a little and rehash a few of the things we've gone over in previous chapters, but bear with me, if you will. Again, this black "resistance" ties in with the Democrat Party's early exploitation of blacks, and the need to keep them dependent and underfoot. To flesh this out, we must first quickly rewind to the early 1900s.

Before the industrial revolution, most jobs were in farming. But by 1880, and for the first time in our nation, a majority of our workforce was in non-farming Jobs. So, it would come about, in the 1900s, that cities like Cleveland, which was a leader in oil refining, and Pittsburgh, a mecca for iron and steel production in the United States, would become shining examples of our country being an industrial behemoth that were producing many well-paying jobs for Americans. Then, our government protected these blue-collar jobs by placing high tariffs on steel and giving large grants to railroads, which was central to our ever-increasing industrial productivity.

The well-paying jobs that came along with this economic boom in the early 1900s provided a meaningful living wage for those without degrees, and would also be instrumental in helping many families support themselves, live comfortably, and send their children to college. *Note: During the early 1900s, most blacks in the south still worked farm jobs and were still being suppressed by Democrats, so in order to obtain factory work, many would have to migrate to northern cities.*

In the north, early on, blacks would initially encounter discrimination and stiff competition with European immigrants. But soon thereafter, World War I would create many more manufacturing jobs as the demand for steel rose, and blacks would make tremendous employment gains in places like New York, Baltimore, and Detroit.

Fast forward to 1950s, 1960s, and 1970s, blacks were working in factory jobs and, with Dr. King's stewardship, most families remained intact and exhibited a strong work ethic, belief in God and a focus on education. Back then, all of these positive attributes were central to our community's success and was the engine that drove prosperity among blacks. However, as previously noted, with blacks rising economically in the deep south and becoming much more independent in the 1960s, Democrats saw their black political support slipping away and quickly eliminated Dr. King.

And although rioting and chaos ensued after his death, black families mostly remained intact and self-sufficient, working and providing for their themselves right on up through the 1970s and into the 1980s. But then, white liberal Democrats would install their black "civil rights" overseers, who would work feverishly to not only get blacks firmly back into the slave mentality of dependency and develop new plantations but also to destroy the family unit which had grown stronger during the Civil Rights Movement.

Of note, the Bill Cosby show of the 1980s would be one of the last television shows to depict an intact two-parent black family, headed by a male and female who were successful and intelligent, with no shucking and jiving, and with no homosexuals or transgenders prominent in any role.

As I detailed earlier, in the 1980s, crack would be introduced to the black community, along with welfare and section eight which was being emphasized by Democrats as the silver bullet for black prosperity. However, the crippling of the black community and rural whites would be significantly accelerated in the 1990s when Democrat President Bill Clinton signed Nafta, the North American Free Trade Agreement, into law. This partnership with Canada and Mexico, according to white liberal Democrats, was supposed to expand our exports and be the panacea needed to boost our economy and create many new jobs for Americans.

The NAFTA agreement, a globalist contrivance of Democrats, was to produce this symbiotic trade relationship between our three partner nations which would, in turn, help each country's economy and mutually benefit American and foreign workers. The way the agreement was intended to work was that one country would sell something to us that they were good at producing, and in exchange, we would then sell them something that we were good at producing.

The fly in the NAFTA agreement ointment would soon arise when both Mexico and the United States started producing the same goods. Canada and the United States, historically, have had similar levels of low and high skilled workers, but there had always been a massive imbalance in the skill level of workers between these two countries and Mexico.

And because of our south of the border neighbor's mostly low skilled workforce, compared with the relatively small amount of low skilled workers in Canada and the United States, Mexico could produce the same goods we were making but at a much lower cost because of their much cheaper labor.

Before the NAFTA agreement, our country placed a tax, or tariff, on all of Mexico's products coming into our country to level the pricing playing field for our manufacturers. These levies allowed for products made in the United States to be sold to our consumers here at home for less than Mexican products coming across the border. With this protectionism in place, products coming from Mexico never posed a serious trade threat to our manufacturers here at home.

However, after the signing of Nafta, and in just a short period, our tariffs on imports coming across the southern border fell to zero and unleashed Mexico's low wage workforce to fully compete with American workers. The removal of these tariffs placed our manufacturers at an economic disadvantage and started a massive hemorrhaging of blue-collar American jobs in the 1990s.

To further exacerbate the impact of the Nafta agreement, there was a devastating domino effect with the significant loss of peripheral jobs such as local diners, coffee shops, and department stores, etc, where waiters, store clerks, and other workers, dependent on the patronage of manufacturing and factory workers, saw a steep decline in jobs. Hardest hit though, was the deep south and the Midwest where blacks and rural whites, who depended on these well-paying manufacturing and factory jobs to provide for their families and send their children to college, saw shutdowns and massive layoffs.

Never ones to let a crisis go to waste, these job losses played right into the Democrat Party's hand and were the silver lining they were looking for as they quickly rode in on their handout horses and offered more "help" to the black community in the form of welfare.

Today, under Trump, there is a reversal of sorts as his administration is in the process of providing millions in grants to cities like Detroit to attract manufacturing jobs back to depressed black communities and devastated rural white areas. This blue-collar revival is also happening in Georgia, Michigan, and South Carolina, along with many other states that, historically, have had economies dependent upon manufacturing and factories.

Our rejuvenated economy has seen car companies such as Honda, BMW, and Toyota expanding plants in the south, along with openings of once-dormant coal mines in Pennsylvania and West Virginia. The Trump administration is also allocating $100 Billion for the restoration of urban areas with his newly created Urban Revitalization Council. *Now, you won't find this stuff on NBC, CNN, MSNBC, CBS, ABC, PBS or any of the other liberal Democrat-controlled networks, it has been totally blacked out. You will have to go to YouTube, or places like the Daily Caller, Breitbart, Washington Examiner, and other sites with true objective journalism to get real news about this administration.*

You know, I feel so good about spreading the truth that I just want to rehash here for a moment, if you don't mind: Under President Trump, over 700,000 blacks have gotten jobs and are back working again. In just over a year and a half as president, Trump has created over three million jobs by cutting taxes and allowing our businesses to flourish and compete fairly with other countries. He has reduced the Obama-era regulations that had stifled innovation and growth, unleashing the entrepreneurial spirit in this country once again.

With President Trump, black business startups have risen over 400%, and with his steady "America First" guidance, there has been a resurgence in the optimism of blue-collar workers. Under this administration, a lot is happening in this country, and all of these developments are crucial for this nation's workers and job opportunities, especially for the black community.

Trump, unlike many presidents that came before him, aptly embodies the notion that platitudes and rhetoric will never change attitudes and economic situations; it takes strong, meaningful actions and hard work to achieve positive consequences and results. His administration is bringing back income opportunities for workers of all stripes across this nation like never before, with the end goal being to make sure that all Americans, including blacks, have great job opportunities and safe neighborhoods and communities to live.

Some blacks are seeing first hand just what can happen when a president really talk the talk and walk the walk. They are taking notice of what a real agent of change, and someone who truly cares about the welfare of all Americans, can actually achieve when he is indeed working in this nation's best interest. It's quite amazing to me that we have an elected president who had gotten only about 8% of the black vote, yet still listens to and works tirelessly for the black community as if he had received 98% of their vote.

And even though a lot of blacks, at the Democrat Party's urging, are staunchly against him at every turn, this man is still creating an economic environment for blacks, and all Americans, that hasn't been seen in decades, or ever, in this country. His policies have been a welcome blessing for a lot of struggling blacks and rural whites who had silently suffered in poverty under the last administration and Democrat policies.

Trump's unwavering and steadfast demand that our immigration system be reformed, along with his newly created blue-collar jobs and accelerated removal of job-killing illegal aliens, will be a tremendous employment boon for blacks and all Americans in this country. And again, with only 8% support, Trump didn't owe the black community a damn thing and didn't even have to acknowledge our plight. He could have pissed on us just like Obama did for eight years as he pursued white liberal Democrat social causes, but he didn't.

Like Obama, Trump could've given slick, lacking in substance, teleprompter speech after speech just to hear himself talk, but he didn't. He could have gone into office, eat caviar, throw lavish parties, and ignore the black community and would have been justified in doing so, but he didn't. Unlike his predecessor, who gouged the hard-working taxpayers at every turn and placed millions more Americans, especially blacks, on the welfare rolls, Trump, who is not even taking a salary, wants to break the Democrat Party's hold on the black community and release them from bondage, just like Lincoln did in the 1800s. His actions are speaking volumes to those who truly understand what is occurring under this president.

Trump's administration has certainly been a refreshing and welcome change from the last hellhole of a corrupt administration which ignored poor blacks and destitute whites while raping the middle-class in this country.

Under the previous Administration, we were bilked out of billions to fund programs like the Obamacare albatross which has been nothing more than another redistribution of taxpayers' money for illegals and welfare deadbeats. In speaking with many blacks, I often tell them that this economic window of opportunity Trump is creating right now is the best thing that could've happened for them in the history of this nation and to take advantage of this time in their lives; it may never come again, especially if Democrats get back in the Whitehouse.

Still yet, the black "resistance" remains strong among the majority of ignorant and emotional plantation blacks who are still screaming that they hope Mueller and the Democrat Party topple Trump; just find some way to take him out. Now, I don't blame these blacks entirely for their illogical and irrational behavior because they have been told repeatedly that they are not supposed to take care of themselves or their families. The majority have been led to believe that their survival would always fall under the purview of our government, with rich white liberal Democrats rationing out their table droppings upon their community as a farmer would his cattle.

These blacks don't quite understand what their decades of Democrat alignment have done to them and fail to see that their "resistance" to all things American is only resistance against themselves and their children's prosperity and future.

White liberal Democrats know that for the sake of their party's future, they cannot let Trump succeed in fully restoring the manufacturing base back into this country, nor can they ever allow him to bring good-paying, blue-collar jobs back to the black community. If this should ever happen, the Democrats' black "property," the engine that makes their party tick, would then become taxpayers and these employed blacks would then gain independence like they were starting to in the 1960s before Dr. King was killed.

If it were ever to come to pass where the majority of blacks were working in this country, and fully understood taxation, it would be much harder for white liberals and black overseers to keep them on the plantation. But for this to happen, blacks must first be educated enough to develop the necessary skills to get the well-paying jobs being created by Trump. This is a big no-no for Democrats, whose party, since the 1600s, has prevented most in the black community from attaining real education and self-sufficiency.

As I detailed in previous segments, welfare dependency has been the independence-draining scourge causing many blacks to lose ambition and purpose. Along with the lack of knowledge, very little job skills, and no self-sufficiency, government dependency has been at the root of most of the black community's ills.

With that said, let's go to our next chapter to see what Trump is doing about all of this, shall we?

Chapter Twenty-Two

Blacks, Education, and Back to Work, No?

O k, so no recap at this time, let's just dive right in. If you are still with me at this point, you should fully grasp everything that has been happening so far.

As a businessman, Trump is no stranger at understanding the needs of his employees and realizes that to get most blacks back into the workforce that they must first acquire the necessary skills to be able to compete in this red-hot and booming economy he has created. And that for most of them, this means schooling and training to fill the surging blue-collar jobs that are now readily available.

Because of decades of welfare dependency, many blacks are lacking in educational and vocational skills, so the task is a little difficult, but Trump is determined. Strangely, for years, white liberal Democrats have screamed in just about every election campaign about the absolute necessity of a college education and a white-collar job, knowing fully well that this is not the path for a lot of rural whites and blacks who like working with their hands. Today, liberals still howl like coyotes caught in leg traps: *"Everybody deserves free education, it's a human right!"*

These conniving Democrat serpents recycle this rhetoric ad nauseum every election, all the while advocating for illegal immigration and killing our manufacturing base by outsourcing and offshoring blue-collar jobs as fast as they can to other countries. Their self-serving, "free education" rhetoric is used to brainwash a lot of blacks and rural whites into thinking that only a college degree can provide them with the necessary education to get a good paying job. The result of this "education is a right" myth is that we now have many broke college graduates with worthless gender studies or liberal arts degrees walking around with tremendous debt load, still not finding that gem of a "white collar" job that the Democrat Party promised would be there upon graduation.

This whole shell game of "get a college education" is a complex and elaborate scam, but let's simplify.

First off, with the black community, the Democrat Party starts by denying school vouchers to blacks in the inner cities, as Obama did in Washington DC, hoping that they drop out of school and become dependent on the government. And after dropping out, liberal Democrats bet on the constant chaos, violence, and poverty in their inner cities to cause a lot of these blacks to get stuck being either being dependent on the government or engaging in criminal activities to survive.

For those blacks making it through high school and graduating despite these obstacles and barriers, once they get into liberal colleges, white Democrats just scoop'em up and train'em to become overseers and social justice warriors for their party.

*So, just to sum up, blacks drop out of school and become dependent on the government, liberals win. And if blacks happen to make it through the inner city gauntlet of poverty, drugs, and gangs, and get into college, they are then thoroughly brainwashed by their liberal professors into helping steer other blacks with less education unto the Democrat Party's platform, and liberals win again.

Not surprising, most black "leaders" of militant liberal Democrat groups, like Black Lives Matter, have all gone to liberal schools and through this brainwashing process. Many colleges and universities in this country today are nothing more than tax-payer funded indoctrination centers that promote the deceptive and weaponized inclusiveness, tolerance, equality, and diversity ideology of the Democrat Party. The truth of the matter is, these higher learning institutions are mostly just another form of wealth redistribution where students are encouraged to take out huge loans, backed by our government, to pay for their tuition.

And the kicker here is, because of our government's "generosity," we taxpayers are on the hook guaranteeing these loans, so if the student ever defaults, we get the bill and the shaft. And since the taxpayers are footing the bill, these satanic cesspools called liberal colleges can keep raising their tuitions. *Nice, isn't it?*

To summarize again, Democrats continually stress that everyone in this country must have a college education, and will advocate for the use of taxpayers' money to guarantee loans to get students into their liberal learning institutions. Once in college, these students are then brainwashed into becoming full-throated social justice warriors and graduating with mostly worthless gender studies degrees.

Also, while white liberal Democrats have a lot of blacks rioting, looting and protesting over Confederate flags and statues, well-paying factory jobs are being created, some with six-figure salaries, and are going unfilled as there are not enough skilled workers in America to fill them. You see, most in the dumbed-down black community are made to look at shiny racial objects, while in Washington the Democrat Party is actively advocating for and recruiting foreign workers to fill skilled and high paying technical and blue-collar jobs that Americans should be trained for.

With that, you must ask yourself, why are American students being taught liberal arts and gender studies while people from India and other countries are being trained in vocational skills that are in high demand in this country?

Why then, you say, would Democrats and Rinos need millions of foreign workers to flood the country if they are beating the "college" necessity drum for Americans? It would seem to me that we would have tons of trained and ready workers in this country to fill these high paying jobs if students were being taught about careers for the real world and not have a curriculum focusing on the rainbow universe of the LGBT community.

Even amid recent employment downturns for American workers, with factories being shut down in the Midwest and families losing their jobs and homes, white liberal Democrat were still clamoring for even more HB 1 Visas for foreigners. This demand is nothing new, Democrats and Rinos have been steadily calling for more HB-1 Visas and increased foreign workers for decades, always citing a pressing need by tech companies and other blue-collar industries.

But think about this for a moment, white liberal Democrats in California, running multibillion-dollar tech companies in Silicon Valley, and among the richest in the nation, are now funneling money to the lesbian-created Black Lives Matter organization for their "inclusiveness, tolerance, diversity and equality" agenda.

Yet, these same companies have very few blacks actually working for them and are mostly comprised of white liberal Democrat males and imported Indians. It's almost as if these Democrat billionaires are paying a few blacks large sums of money to keep the rest of the black community away from their doorsteps, sorta like a protection racket. Why don't these rich white liberal "inclusiveness" billionaires, who supposedly love and care about diversity so much, actually hire and train blacks and other Americans for these well-paying jobs instead of importing foreigners from thousands of miles away and paying big salaries?

As my book title asserts, there is an agenda at play, *Americans Vs. Democrats*, and it is no coincidence that these are the same liberal billionaires who hate Trump and are fighting him at every turn to increase the amount of HB-1 Visas to keep decades of unfair trade and employment practices in place. Their job is to keep most manufacturing out of this country, thereby preventing a lot of blacks, rural whites, and many other Americans from obtaining financial independence via good-paying blue-collar jobs.

As of this writing, the Democrat Party is highly incensed over Trump and his policies because he has hit upon the root cause of what is really ailing the black community and is doing something about it. He realizes that most of the disillusioned college graduates in this country end up with meaningless degrees, tremendous debt, no job, and bleak future.

And let's be real, most Americans weren't meant to go to college anyways. For many high school students, it's only after being pressured by their parents or friends, do they just assume that college is the next logical step in their higher learning process and a rite of passage.

To counter this unproductive narrative, Trump, along with his daughter Ivanka, recently called an unprecedented meeting with companies like Boeing, Apple, and FedEx, whose executives pledged to create 4.5 million jobs over the next five years or so, and train American workers to fill them. *You won't find this anywhere in the liberal media either.*

This bold initiative is just part of the newly created National Council for the American Worker, an apprenticeship program where minorities and other youths will be trained in the skills necessary for them to be competitive in the marketplace.

With Trump's administration, students of all races will have the opportunity to enter into blue-collar programs that will train them to become engineers, electricians, plumbers, construction workers, etc.

In the end, these youths will have great paying careers that will come without the smothering debt, and indoctrination, of liberal universities and colleges. This ambitious endeavor by the Trump administration will help rebuild our workforce here, in our country, with American-born workers, instead of outsourcing to other countries or importing foreign immigrants.

Today, the opportunity for the black community is tremendous and unparalleled; it makes no sense to have able-bodied adults here in this country stuck on welfare scraps and living in drug infested, violence-prone cities while we import foreigners to take these well-paying jobs so that they can live comfortably in beautiful neighborhoods among their wealthy liberal benefactors.

In this regard, Trump's election has severely hampered the Democrat Party's end goal, of having the manufacturing sector remain decimated in this country and blacks forever relegated to underclass status, on welfare, subservient and beholden to their party. Trump has been instrumental in combatting and reversing the New World Order "service industry" ideology that Democrats so greatly desires. And his administration's actions and belief in American workers and of

American ingenuity, going forward, will be of utmost importance for the rebuilding of our morale, strengthening our infrastructure, and restoring our industries.

Trump is also making huge inroads with a lot of struggling rural whites, who are incredibly grateful for his outreach and understanding of the issues they face. And perhaps he is converting a small segment of minorities; however, many in the black community is still in "resist" mode and will need to be bought along slowly, like infants.

Truth be told though, how can blacks ever become educated and assimilate into America's culture when white liberal Democrats and their black puppet "leaders" are having the majority of them rebuke their own country every chance they get. Most plantation blacks are still distracted by their "Africanism" and " Black Power" nonsense, even sneering at our American flag and calling our national anthem racist.

You often hear them say things like: *"Man, they cut that part of the anthem out that had slavery in it, this country is racist."*

Really?, with that being said, let's conclude this chapter because I believe that this is the perfect time for me to broach the subject of the quite wealthy, but somehow still downtrodden black slaves now residing on the opulent Democrat plantation known as the NFL... or Negroes are Fools League, if you rather.

We're in the fourth quarter of this book and on our socialist opponents' five-yard line, ready to score some more points to wake Americans up and put this game away.

The ball has been snapped, so turn the page you football Neanderthals.

Chapter Twenty-Three

NFL Ballers, Anthem, & Trump

We are gonna once again skip the recap and just go right ahead and onto the field.

◆◆◆

A few of the hot button issues President Trump is quite adamant about, and have obsessed over, is respect for our country and flag, and rightfully so. It would seem to me that patriotism would just be a given for people privileged enough to be born in this country.

In this regard, we should all be proud nationalists fiercely protecting the freedoms and opportunities that this unique country affords all of us, regardless of race. However, true patriotism, our flag, and the National Anthem are all currently under assault by anti-American Democrats, the enemies of this country and its citizens. So, it comes as no surprise that some of their plantation blacks, the weapon of choice for the Democrat Party, even while making gobs of cash from playing in the NFL, are now disrespecting our flag and National Anthem and calling themselves slaves. *Ain't that a hoot?*

As a result of this quite perplexing anti-American stance, these rich blacks have made themselves a target of Trump's wrath: *"If these players wanna kneel and won't respect the flag, the owners should get those sons of bitches off the field!"*

With these words, Trump caused a backlash among these emasculated malcontents but echoed my sentiments exactly. It struck a chord with me, and I know that I am not alone in my feelings on this matter, the way President Trump responded to the disrespect shown our country by these wealthy blacks. There are millions of other disgusted and hard-working Americans that agree, wholeheartedly, with his honest assessment and brutal admonishment of these pampered black NFL "slaves."

Everyone in this country who works for a living should find it insane and repulsive for blacks or anyone with this kind of opportunity to provide for themselves and their families, to display that kind of animus towards the very system giving them the chance to have wealth beyond most Americans' wildest dreams.

Don't get me wrong, the bulk of NFL players and a lot of other black sports stars are good people who cherish the opportunity to get paid millions to participate in a game they would gladly play for free on inner city asphalt basketball courts and grassy playgrounds. The thing I find most frustrating, and confusing; seems that you can never ever assemble Democrat blacks in any sport in overwhelmingly high percentages and expect lasting peace and harmony.

If you look at Football and Basketball where blacks make up about 80% and 90% of each league respectively, there is always pouting, disruption and grumblings of discontent by a few who have a grievance with something or somebody, over some perceived inequality issue. These wealthy, overly sensitive Democrat blacks are never satisfied, and never happy, always mouthing off on social media and in front of the cameras.

But if you take hockey, for instance, which is a mostly white sport with a few blacks sprinkled in for flavor and seasoning, there are no such issues. I never got into watching this particular sport, but these players make millions skating around on ice and hitting a puck, and seem incredibly grateful that they do.

In the baseball league, you have an eclectic potpourri of whites, Dominicans, and other foreigners, and there are barely any issues because these players are much more appreciative of having the privilege of coming to this country and making millions for playing a game they've loved forever and played for nothing even before setting foot on our shores.

And you can take a look at the multinational soccer leagues, with all races competing, there are no racial issues, no whining, and no malcontents. However, when you get enough homegrown, Democrat

Party indoctrinated blacks as the dominant race in any sports league, watch out.

I know that not all of the black NFL players are racist simpletons, just a few dozen or so, but it's sad that any of'em are feeling the way they do while making the kind of money they do. These oh so sensitive and soft "social justice warriors," masquerading as tough gridiron warriors, supposedly have a gripe based on their false premise of "police brutality," the foundation for their kneeling on our anthem, continually declaring that it is too pervasive in black communities and blacks are just being hunted by cops to no end.

Uh..huh, sure, right. I will refer these ignorant blacks back to my Blacks Lives Matter chapter for stats on this one.

Anyways, you will hear these idiots say things like: "My kids gotta know to watch out for racist cops, cause they be hunting blacks." Well, if their kids, these little future Black Lives Matter rioters and didn-du-nuffins are being hunted by law enforcement, what neighborhoods are they in and what the hell are they doing to be hunted? These little unarmed and minding their own business Democrat scholars wouldn't happen to be dealing drugs, car-jacking or robbing and shooting folks, would they?

Nonetheless, a lot of zombied liberal media blacks actually believe that white cops are out hunting blacks like southern whites hunt squirrels, but reality and the numbers contradict this of course. According to FBI stats, blacks on average kill each other at over a six thousand or so clip each year, while law enforcement, on average, may kill a few hundred black criminals yearly, but, never more than they kill white criminals though.

Truth is, black kids in black neighborhoods are hundreds of times more likely to be killed by other blacks than by a cop. And since they commit over 51% of all violent crimes and homicides in this nation, blacks are the biggest threat to other blacks and every other race, period. Yet, white cops hunting blacks is the narrative being taught by black and white liberal Democrats.

If you had to make an analogy of this foolishness it would go sorta like this: *"Here, little negro, hold this lit stick of black dynamite in your hand. It's ok, it's safe, but just watch out for those evil white cops giving you sparklers to hold, they are dangerous!"*

I often wonder why these same, oh-so-fearful-of-cops, NFL players don't just tell their kids to respect everyone whether they are law enforcement or not, believe in the Lord, pull their pants up, get educated, get a good career and be somebody. This would seem to solve a lot of the "fear" of law enforcement within black communities.

Also, I wanna point out that if people want to live in safe neighborhoods, then a lot of Democrat blacks should absolutely be looked at and with more scrutiny than any other race in America. For the hard of reading, let me repeat this just one mo gin, blacks are 13% of the population, yet commit over 51% of all violent crimes and homicides, which actually means that blacks are much more violent than every other race in America, combined. With this enlightening info, what other race are the cops gonna profile in predominately black, drug dealing, and gang infested Democrat run cities…the Irish?

To repeat a stat, in the last five decades, over 250,000 blacks have been killed by other blacks in Democrat run inner cities. In contrast, only 58,000 Americans were killed in the Vietnam War.

I'll tell you this, there are many decent black folks in high crime neighborhoods that are just begging for more policing and for troublesome black youths to get their asses whipped, and I agree. Yeah, that's it, I do believe that black kids should have their asses whipped more often than any other children of any other race because I've concluded that they're naturally more hard-headed. Black children need far more parent brutality, just like I had when I was growing up.

Out of the eleven children that my mother had, none of us have ever been in prison, none of us have ever fought a cop, and none of us have ever been shot at by police. What kind of secret sauce had my deeply religious mother stumbled onto that would accomplish this remarkable feat? Did our family have some sort of immunity that today's black NFL players don't?

No, it was a quite simple formula really; an old fashion remedy that is a little outdated in the current black community nowadays. We were taught discipline and was bought up to be men and women who respected authority and our elders. I always remember hearing my mother say: *"You can learn your manners at home, or the streets will teach you."*

Uh, we learned at home, mom sorta forced it upon us whether we liked it or not. She was religious alright but would pop a shoe, iron or whatever else she was holding at'cha if you got out of line. My mother never spared the rod or any other weapon of ass destruction. This crazy woman, for our punishment, would on occasion, grab an extension cord or the dreaded "switch," which she sometimes, if in a good mood, gave you the honor and privilege to go pick out yourself, and she would beat us just short of manslaughter.

Although I may have gone a little overboard in describing our punishment back then, today, I now realize that there was a method to my mother's madness for which I am grateful today. Many black youths nowadays lack respect for others because of the absence of this sort of no-nonsense discipline in their households.

This brings me to that particular segment of NFL and NBA players who whine and moan about every little racial issue that they are encouraged by their liberal Democrats masters to champion. These hoopsters and footballers work out and often develop strong muscles, athletic ability, and talent, but inside they are not masculine men. A lot of NFL and NBA "superheroes" are sensitive milquetoasts and just as soft as grapes. Many are whiny and emotional like females; having mannerisms unbecoming descendants of proud African warriors who were able to shoulder any adversity with quiet dignity and courage.

I mean, true African warriors back in the day hunted lions and tigers, killed anacondas and ran four hundred miles, barefoot, over thorny brush-covered plains in two-hundred-degree weather, all without complaining to the chief about dey equality and rights and how little Timbuktua down the street talked about their momma.

Even when some of these Democrat ballers amass a fortune from the so-called "white supremacy" system they supposedly detest, they still complain and are bitchy and catty like a bunch of runway models with broken high heels. Some of these black "stars" pout and foam at the mouth over the slightest hint of a perceived racial offense and run around sashaying and vogueing on the football field or basketball court like transgenders having an emotional meltdown over a "reassignment" surgery gone wrong.

Oh, these must-see black "stars" can go out onto the football field and make crazy runs and acrobatic catches, or have monster rim-rattling dunk-a-thons, but some of these petulant "ballers" still haven't overcome their liberal white masters "victimization" conditioning: *"We're being treated just like slaves, they just don't understand our issues. Oh why, oh why is Trump saying such mean things to me. I've never heard such a tone. He shouldn't have said sons of bitches, he really hurted my feelings."*

Yet, these damn fools hear rougher language every single day listening to filthy and nasty gangster rappers on their headsets while preparing for dey "games." And when these black "heroes" visit the inner cities, they often hear kids, some as young as two years old, saying things far worse than Trump ever said, and in public.

I remember this black girl on a video teaching her young toddler to curse. The sad thing about it? There were other black adults were sitting around laughing and applauding this child's improper behavior. Really, this little kid was barely walking but could spit out "bitch!" upon command.

Now, just to be fair, I know that a lot of today's black youth are at a severe disadvantage because most are in fatherless homes and unfortunately, most of their heroes and "Role Models" are these wealthy and effeminate black sport stars crybabies who are not real males. Parents today need to turn the emasculated NFL and NBA off, and turn on hockey or something. Most of the black stars of today, are not the strong men of mettle that used to do battle on the gridiron or basketball court from back in the day.

Guys back then played like men in rough and tumble contests where fights often broke out. They were gladiators, not like these "players" today. Watching the NFL and NBA nowadays is like watching the Black Gay Pride Bowl, or Black Lives Matter Diversity and Tolerance Playoffs and Transgender Equality championships. Today, these tender players pout and scream about how they are racially discriminated against and how they are always disadvantaged.

At this point, you may be wondering, just how did these soft ballers of today come to be? If you remember, in my "homosexual" chapter, I detailed how the gay community's agenda started taking off in the 1990s when gay white men were able to enlist a group of black lesbians to colorize their movement. Prior to this change, football, and even basketball were brutal contests where men would scrap on the football field, gouging eyes out, knocking out teeth and stomping on their opponents, all without repercussions or whiny beta males crying in their warm buttermilk.

In fact, players back then wore injuries from their battles on the gridiron like badges: *"Man, see this gap? Yeah, mean Joe Greene knocked my teeth out! And I'm not having it fixed either, just leaving it like it is so I can show my grandkids someday!"*

Over in basketball, during this same period, it was no different, medical staff would be on standby for players who loved "going to the rim." Before the gay community's makeover of sports, players would bite, scratch, claw, mutilate and punch each other, and loved it. They were warriors, real masculine men who took no mess, or prisoners.

But after the homosexual movement of the 1990s gained prominence on the political stage, along with the Democrat Party's feminist and emasculating ideology of inclusiveness, tolerance, diversity, and equality, with today's black beta football and basketball players, a broken fingernail will get'em sidelined for at least two weeks.

If you look closely, now it is the white players in the NFL that seems the manliest, so, therefore, if the NFL wants to get back to the glory days of real sports, why not have more white players signed. Yeah, why not have affirmative action for whites? By the numbers, the NFL is about 80% black, so why isn't there an outcry from white players saying they want true equality in the league?

Why isn't there a rule, like the "Vanilla Mayonnaise Mandate" or something, that states that no sports league can be more than 40% of any one race at any time during the season? Why isn't Congress, especially the, uh, White Caucus, "looking" into to this and why must there be a demographic lock in the NFL that favors wealthy black dissidents and anti-American malcontents?

Old, "give all" Kaepernick, who started the anthem "protest," was raised by white parents and made 14 million dollars a year playing football. That's $14 MILLION a year playing just 16 games a year, which breaks down to about $875,000 a week!

This Muslim male declared that his kneeling was to protest police brutality and a racist America, but we must also remember that old Kap was in the same NFL, the league run solely by white billionaires, for about four years before he felt so "aggrieved." Then we find out that, lo and behold, that he had recently gotten a Muslim girlfriend, so the pieces started falling into place. His "protest" was never about police brutality, this was an assault on America's Christian based ideals under the guise of black victimhood and backed and pushed by white socialist liberals within the Democrat Party.

Kap was sent to kneel on our flag and anthem to show that our way of life did not comport with his beliefs and that we must redo our Constitution to reflect the Democrat Party's values. It would seem that Kap was just trying to finish what Obama started; weave Muslim ideals into our society, especially among our youth, and destroy our very foundation of Christianity. He was playing the white liberals' identity politics, the race card, as planned and never really wanted to be on any NFL team again. He was and still is, an activist and operative for his Democrat masters and football just provided him the platform to carry out their plan.

To drive this point home, when the Baltimore Ravens was on the verge of signing Kap, his Muslim girlfriend then tweeted that the owner of the team was like a slave master. This was an orchestrated move. I believe that they both devised to ruin his chances of ever getting a contract and playing football again.

Now, this slavery thing by NFL players actually tickles me because what self-respecting white plantation owner is gonna pay any slave millions a year just to catch or throw a football? If the fool is a slave, his owner can make him do all these things and whatever else for free and beat his ass if he doesn't. Seems old Kaepernick and his minions didn't get the memo about plantations run by Democrats in the 1600s, where black slaves barely got fed water and gruel and were worked all day in the steaming hot sun without pay, never mind that "$15 an hour minimum wage."

By these measurements, NFL team owners today are really lousy at this enslavement thing and is really giving away the farm to blacks. They are also really giving the slave institution a bad name by paying such exorbitant salaries to their black captives. *What's wrong with 'em, is dey fool?*

My guess is that these owners may have been just adjusting for inflation or something and got carried away, because their black slaves on the NFL plantation are making far more than just about everyone else these days, including run of the mill whites, Asians, Hispanics and, especially, all of the other blacks still on the inner city plantations. Hell, it would take us free folks about twelve years or more to make what old downtrodden slave Kap made in just one week. Furthermore, if old Kap is somehow still a slave while making over $800,00 a week, what do you call his maid or butler working a lowly 9-to-5 in his services and making $70,000 to $80,00 a year?

Anyways, do white NFL slave masters know that their black slaves could be beaten and made to work for free? I suppose that if they ever found out they've been had, they would undoubtedly make these black NFL slaves, outside of playing football on Sunday, pick some cotton, maybe plow a few fields in the hot sun on their days off or something as repayment? I was also wondering, every once in a while, just to reassert themselves as their masters and superiors, shouldn't NFL slave owners have to whip some of these black players' asses anyway as a reminder that they were still slaves, or lynch a few of'em just for fun?

I just think that it is despicable and inhumane for NFL and NBA plantation owners to force these black slaves to accept millions of dollars a year for playing a game. So cruel for these once poverty-stricken black people to be subjected to this involuntary servitude and degradation while making such massive wealth.

Oh, wait a minute, I just thought of something important, do black youths, still playing high school sports and college ball right now, know of this lucrative "slave" system awaiting them? Shouldn't someone try to warn these innocent black youths that, on draft day, they are walking right into a trap of enormous wealth?

These unaware black youths need to be stopped before they make the mistake of getting drafted by a slave owner who will savage them with a contract and untold riches. They need to at all costs, avoid this dangerous, racist and oppressive "white supremacy" system that will force millions upon them like the plague and just opt to get a regular old nine to five like I have.

Now, it is well-known that the black mind is something else entirely and to prove this; when some of these unsuspecting black youths are signed to lucrative NFL contracts and can buy a Bentley and dey mommas' new houses, they are at first incredibly grateful for the opportunity to make an enormous amount of money from their efforts and talent.

However, give these newbies a few years of living in luxury and being manipulated by white liberals and these same black youths, coming from the mean streets of poverty-stricken Democrat-run inner cities, will become so sensitive that they will kneel on our flag and Anthem and whine at any perceived hint of a racial slight.

Seems that just about any Democrat today who has a measure of political power or social media platform can lead most blacks, regardless of their status in life, anywhere they want, all they have to do is just tell them that whites, especially white conservatives, are racist and cops are hunting and killing blacks. For example, all Kap had to do was kneel and tell other highly paid black-ballers to do the same and a lot of these easily-led players quickly and foolishly gave him a platform to kill their own livelihoods while simultaneously carrying out his mission against America, their home.

Somehow, intriguingly enough, this brings to mind, again, that most blacks always need "leaders" to follow and cannot seem to form one coherent, independent thought for themselves. They just repeat what they heard from others, chanting the same racist mantra taught by their white liberal Democrat masters like overly sun-tanned Buddhist monks.

These so-called descendants of "African warriors" are desultory migrants, wandering aimlessly and directionless until they are told by their liberal masters of the path upon which they must tread. If we look deeper, some blacks in the NFL are really emotionally unhinged, because it is quite illogical and irrational that any "African American" would be doing so well and making so much money in a "white supremacy" system that supposedly hates blacks.

In reality, both poor whites and blacks are living in the same "white supremacy" system as these well-paid NFL players, yet there is a massive disparity in income between black sports stars and ordinary blacks and whites in this nation. With this reality applied, it appears that race has nothing to do with the divide in this country and that the chasm in this nation is more along the lines of wealth, the haves and have-nots.

I mean, under this supposedly white racist supremacy system, how can we say that old Samuel "Django" Jackson, Oprah, Tyler Perry, Beyoncé, Spike Lee, Snoop Dog, Kevin Hart and many other celebrities, black doctors, lawyers, CEOs, and other blacks are being oppressed and can't get ahead? These uh, black "slaves" are living among wealthy whites and have learned to work our capitalist system to its fullest.

With that said, it appears to me that black sports stars are much more like the wealthy white liberal Democrats they live among in gated communities than the poor blacks in the inner cities they came from, yet they continually claim "every" black in America is still oppressed. To debunk the asinine narrative of white supremacy, if you look at our population, with whites being about 195 million and blacks approximately 39 million, there are more poor whites in this country than the entire population of blacks.

Where do these poor whites fit in, are they oppressed too? Has their own "white supremacy" system failed them? And just who do they call to lead them against their own "white nationalist" system? How do we reconcile and right this injustice against poor and impoverished whites? Also, why don't white players who were once impoverished like blacks and now making tons of money playing in the NFL, also get to kneel, bitch, and moan or at least throw tofu or mayonnaise at somebody?

Really, whites have much more of a stake in America's professional sports than blacks could ever have and should be much more upset at the inequality suffered by their race in the NFL and NBA than blacks. If you think about it, white men created football, baseball, and basketball as well as hockey, along with just about every other sport being played in this nation today. Blacks didn't invent a damn one, but this is not even the biggest issue I have with these liberal boot-licking fools.

Today, the issue I have is that these wealthy and successful blacks actually search for ways to be aggrieved and will "manufacture" racist incidents to fit their white liberal Democrat masters' narrative of "victimized" blacks. Jackie Robinson, a Republican and strong black male of honor and integrity, played baseball in the 1950s when there was real, and dangerous, discrimination by the Democrat Party. During this time, white southern Democrats were lynching blacks like no tomorrow, but Jackie Robinson would persevere and become one of the black pioneers, with courage, quiet dignity and real manliness, who would help erase this sort of thing from our society. He opened the doors for every black sports star you see today, without continually bitching and moaning about how the Democrat KKK was after'em.

In black America today, where manliness has mostly gone out the window, the world has devolved since Jackie's playing days. So, the question looms, if indeed there was this blatant systemic racism that whites wanted to hold onto, why in the world would supposedly racist white owners let blacks, at any time, dominate any of their sports, whether it was basketball, football or twiddly winks?

Was this a coordinated effort by these white owners to have blacks perform like highly paid, black organ-grinder monkeys in minstrel shows for adoring whites to see and jeer at? Or, was it a smart business move to form an enterprise where black athleticism creates entertainment and a must-see spectacle for children and adults of all ages, who will readily pay to view and root for their hometown team, regardless of race?

I'll opt for the latter because if you look at soccer, a game not dominated by blacks and comprised of many nationalities, it is probably one of the most prominent sports in the world and having the most ardent and rabid fans. Also, if NFL owners were oppressing black sports stars, why would they let them form a union and negotiate astronomical salaries for just a few months of their time out of the year?

Really, if black players are so "distressed" about police brutality, why aren't they, in the offseason, marching and protesting in the streets? You won't ever find'em doing this, why?

These "ballers" are usually too busy at this time of year spending their millions on trips and lavish vacations, making it rain in strip clubs, splurging on bling, buying new cars, partying, and other idiotic things like paying bail money after beating their girlfriends, or boyfriends, the hell up, among other things.

But once the season starts, some of these partied-out offseason "ballers" get their eyebrows done and manicures looking just right, then they all get choked up, scowl and foam at the mouth and dig in their high heels on protesting the greatest nation on earth.

Our National Anthem is only a few minutes long and you mean to tell me that these black NFL players, making on average about $300,000 a week, cannot suck up their sensitivity and feminist ways for three minutes, once a week, for a total of sixteen times in the season? That's a total of just 48 minutes during the entire NFL season in which these emasculated black players cannot seem to get past the, uh, "police brutality" and "racist America" thingy stuck in their craw by their liberal Democrat masters.

Out of all the active NFL players active every season, I haven't heard about anyone of'em ever being shot by cops during any season or offseason over the last twenty years or so, or ever. Although I have heard a lot about players committing criminal activities like NFL player Ray Carruth, who killed his pregnant fiancé because he didn't want to pay child support.

And I have also heard of other NFL players being charged with drug possession and distribution, like Sam Hurd, who used to play for the Chicago Bears, but no player was ever assaulted or shot by cops while engaging in their criminal activities. However, there have been NFL players who have been assaulted by other blacks or shot like Sean Taylor, who played for the Washington Redskins.

Seems like he made the huge mistake of inviting inner city Democrat blacks into his new home for a party. It appears that after surveying his possessions, a few of these black "friends and invitees," thinking he was away at training camp, snuck back to pick up some of his valuables and belongings that he wasn't using. Unfortunately for Sean, he was home at the time and was shot and killed by the same black "friends" whom he had just entertained a few nights before.

There was to be no protests or riots over this senseless killing of a young black man trying to make it because, as the black community sees it, his death came about because of "friendly fire" between blacks, which doesn't count in the liberal Democrat world.

Today, as I detailed earlier, it means absolutely nothing when a black kills another black but, again, whenever you point out the insanely high black on black killings in black communities, most blacks get defensive and wanna broaden the scope outside of Democrat inner cities to include whites, and you will often hear'em say: *"Whites are killing each other too!"*

I find it quite perplexing that blacks always wanna drag whites into the conversation for false equivalency on these matters. But will never point out that whites have much lower homicides, percentage-wise, lower out of wedlock birth rates, cleaner neighborhoods, and more two-parent households.

Most blacks are taught by their white plantation masters to utilize diversion, false equivalency, and distraction as a means to lessen the impact of the carnage happening in their communities.

With conditioned blacks, their entire focus must always be on the small puddle of police "brutality," and not on the massive wave of black on black crime that has raged for decades on the streets of Democrat-run cities all across this nation.

But back to sports, just imagine; what if these "aggrieved" NFL and NBA blacks were somehow successful in their protesting-the-anthem endeavor and had managed to run away their paying audience, effectively shutting their respective leagues down? They won't be the ones getting hurt the most because they have already gotten paid and are enjoying the good life. No, it will be the thousands of black youths still playing ball in high schools and colleges, coming from poor, crime-infested inner cities that will be harmed. These youths will lose out on the chance at an opportunity to obtain life-altering money that the current black miscreants are making, just because of a manufactured "social justice" campaign by a Muslim Democrat who hates America.

The message that these black sports stars are sending our black youth is that they are always a victim, that it doesn't matter that a white man pays them enough money to have multiple Rolls Royces, numerous mansions, a maid, butler, and chauffeur. And it doesn't matter that they can now afford to do just about anything they want and able to help their family out, they are still just a nobody and "less than," just for being black.

A lot of black NFL and NBA players today are downright ignorant and plain dumb, but I've noticed lately that most of'em are quick to throw on a pair of glasses and strut around like they have some brain cells in their head. However, just by opening their mouths, these fools prove that they are no brain surgeons, yet are still looked up to by most blacks as scholars just because they can throw or catch a ball.

This unwarranted admiration is quite unlike the disdain the majority of blacks have towards conservatives like Dr. Ben Carson, a brain surgeon, pre-eminent in his field, who fled the Democrat plantation years ago and who is now hated by most in the black community for doing so.

The black community's hatred and bitterness towards intelligent and hardworking blacks like Dr. Carlson illustrates just how much most blacks have gotten their "heroes" all wrong. The brainwashed majority have steadfastly rejected accomplished blacks like Dr. Carson, but readily idolizes any dumb and nasty rapper, black celeb, or ignorant woman-beating sports "star."

With that being said, President Trump realizes that this behavior of whiny blacks, rich and poor, is merely an outgrowth, a symptom of being conditioned and brainwashed, for decades, and that the vast majority are not in control of themselves or their destiny. Trump also understands that this "victimization" and "entitlement" mentality, so pervasive among blacks, must be stopped and reversed in order to reset the community and is giving a lot of these blacks, especially males, what they have been sorely lacking for quite some time. I wanna talk about it, turn the page.

Chapter Twenty-Four

Blacks, Trump Is Your Daddy!

No recap just yet, I wanna plow right into this one!

♦ ♦ ♦

Unlike Obama, his beta male predecessor, President Trump is the ultimate alpha male, and I firmly believe that he is providing something for a lot of black men that they never had before; an influential and masculine father figure. There is a saying that I believe, lends some credence to this statement: *"You are known by the fruit you bear, and the fruit doesn't fall too far from the tree."* Say what you want about Trump and his divorces, infidelities and such, but just look at his children; they are all well-educated, disciplined, respectful, drug and drink free, and are all well-mannered and well-spoken.

Some people will be quick to say: *"He's rich, he can afford the best care for his children."* I tell these idiots that money has nothing to do with being a real father or what values get instilled into your children. Just look at all the "upper class," snobby celebrities in Hollywood who have drugged-out, foul-mouthed, gender-confused and criminal-minded little bastards they have birthed and call their children. And look at all those rich liberal Democrat sports stars who would kill a woman, and their kids, just to avoid paying child support.

Trump has been and still is, the quintessential, fatherly male figure his children needs and dote on, regardless of whatever else he's done in his life, and it shows. Just by the way his children often look at him, as if he's their ultimate hero, is a testament to the splendid job he has done in bringing them up to be respectful men and women.

To me, Trump's disciplined rearing of his children is the ironclad and indisputable proof that he has always placed his kids' welfare first and foremost. He sets the standard of how black men should be, real men who take care of their families and responsibilities.

The last president in office was an effeminate male, and for the eight years of his tenure, a lot of black men patterned themselves after his emasculating ways, feminist mannerisms, and immoral values. The last president was telling black men that it was ok to be feminine, to accept homosexuality into their lives and that it was ok to try to change genders and to always squat while peeing.

Trump comes along, and it's a shock to watered-down black males, but the greatest irony of all was to hear supposedly hard and street-tough black gangster rappers pouting on social media: *"f' Trump," "we need to off that mofo, he ain't no Obama, bring Obama back!"* These downy-soft "African Warriors" can't take it that Trump is a strong and unabashed alpha male, an unapologetically singular bastion of machismo and not afraid of offending the sensibilities of both men and women.

In going directly against the Democrat Party's ingrained feminist driven ideology which has been systematically stripping the masculinity from our society, especially among black males, Trump has been a one-man revolution. His relentless assault on the entrenched liberal political correctness plague, which has been allowed to fester like a canker sore, is one of the aspects often missed when he says, "Make America Great Again."

One of Trump's primary purposes has been to redirect and reset the societal norms in this country back to that which have served us well since the founding of this country and the beginning of mankind. This means that, for our society to continue, there must be a restoration of men-as-men and women-as-women in this nation. With this being said, I firmly believe that manliness among black males can never be achieved while they are supporting anything Democrat. So, it would stand to reason that it is only when a black male takes the red pill and flees the Democrat plantation, does he then become a man; an intelligent, rational thinking real male.

This is where Trump attacks the black community, with a brazen openness, daring black males to reclaim their masculinity, their dignity, and self-worth, to restore their communities and families by having faith in God, hard work and education. Don't misunderstand me; I am not painting all black men with the same feminist brush here, because there is a sliver of decent black men in this country who are influential father figures and raising disciplined, properly educated and respectful children.

Unfortunately, there is also an epidemic of overly sensitive, child-like black males within the black community who do not fall into this category. They have shirked their duties and responsibilities and, with the help of morally deficient black women, shun the children they have fathered, and it's killing the black community.

These black men are in desperate need of someone like President Trump, an unflinching, authoritative father figure to mete out discipline and to warn the black community against the political correct, and feminist ways their males have taken on and have grown accustomed to. Trump is, in no uncertain terms, telling overly sensitive Democrat black males to pull up their pants, get back in school, get an education, and become men again. He's telling them to take responsibility for the lives that they have created, build a family and legacy to be proud of and to have their children look up to them as their heroes, instead of whiny sports stars and Godless celebs.

Our 45th President is saying to these black males, "I'll help you any way I can to achieve any goal you want, but you have to first have the ambition and drive to do so for yourselves, because I am not here to hold your hand, and I'm not here to be your babysitter." With that said, I think the point has been made, so I'll just go ahead and conclude this short chapter. I believe it has served its purpose.

Let's get on to the next segment, shall we?

Chapter Twenty-Five

Value Of Blackness

Recap: Ok, so Democrats enslaved blacks starting in the 1600s and treated them like livestock for centuries. Republicans freed blacks in 1865, but most blacks would drift right back to Democrats for welfare, which would cause crime and poverty to devastate their communities. Not satisfied with their handiwork just yet, Democrats would then get a lot of blacks hooked on crack and also get them to align themselves with the gay community and their homosexual, transgender, agenda.

Today, outside of the voting booth, Democrats considers the majority of the black community worthless and devalue blacks because blacks devalue themselves by being, for a pittance, in the services of the ones who enslaved their ancestors...

As I noted earlier, the majority of blacks in this country today are being made to obey the Democrat Party and their anti-American ideology, not by whip and chains but by well-paid black overseers and welfare table scraps.

Hell, in a strange turnabout, blacks today, like the KKK of the 1800s through the 1960s, are now the Democrat Party's violent enforcers, and like trained chimps, most of'em will riot, attack, and destroy property upon command from their white masters. But what makes'em this way? And how do we quantify their value to Democrats? Is the party getting a good deal from their plantation blacks? In further analysis and comparison, what did it really cost to feed, house, clothe, and provide medical care for slaves in the 1600s, 1700, and 1800s?

Back then, slave masters on each plantation had to pay all costs out of pocket for African slaves, or maybe took out loans with their black property as collateral. Then, plantation owners had to also determine the cost of transportation of each slave from Africa, the value of each at the market and calculate the amount needed to care for their property. Mostly, they had to determine breeding costs and plan a budget, just like a cattle rancher would do for his livestock.

However, unlike white slave owners maintaining their black slaves in the 1800s, white liberals now have use of taxpayers' funds to keep their black livestock contently grazing in "entitlement" pastures in their inner city corrals. This set-up is ingenious and cost-effective for Democrats, who now have little to no out of pocket expense to bear for the upkeep of their black cattle.

Today's Democrat Party doesn't have the headaches of trying to figure out any of the out of pocket costs as their ancestors during slavery, they just utilize government funds. In this relatively new redistribution scheme, hard-working taxpayers' monies are today being used to care for inner city blacks, which serves to achieve the same obedience from this group as whips and chains once did in the 1800s.

As a result, for the majority of blacks today, the only thing that has changed from the Democrat plantations of the 1800s to the Democrat inner cities of today is the form of labor; instead of picking cotton for Democrats in their fields at harvest time, now blacks are picking votes for Democrats in the ballot boxes every election.

It's a neat trick indeed, and devious sleight of hand for the Democrat Party to pull off in plain sight, to have the descendants of their former slaves still in their services, and strong supporters, after centuries of abuse and suppression. Under the guise of their inclusiveness, tolerance, diversity, and equality ideology, liberal Democrats, after using money from hardworking taxpayers to herd inner city blacks onto their plantations, can now sit back and tell the black community *"See what we've done for you, you owe us, so vote Democrat!"*

After decades of being dependent on government aid for their sustenance, most blacks today have lost their blackness and worth and is in dire need of a real black president to reappraise and revalue them. I believe Trump is that real first black president. *Did I just say that? That Trump is the real first black president?* You damn skippy I did! No, not in color, don't be silly, but I do genuinely believe that our current president, Donald J Trump, number Forty-Five, is the real deal and the first president to actually really get it with the black community.

And not only does Trump get it, but he is also taking bold steps and actions to address the community's ills in doing something most black males seem incapable of today, he is manning up. So, I ask here, what is blackness, is it just the tone of one's skin? Is this the only qualification? I dare say that is far from the truth. What would then qualify one to attain the status of being truly black?

To illustrate, I will tell you what I believe being black is not, and why I think Trump, if not entirely black, demonstrates the essence of what blacks used to be before the Democrat Party took over their communities:

I know that being black is not the undignified wearing of your pants down to your knees and slinging drugs to your own brethren in your neighborhoods.

Being black is not the proliferation of mostly futureless, bastard children in our communities who have no male guidance or hope.

Being black is not being forever dependent on government handouts for your daily survival and sustenance, and being black is not trashing the place where you live.

Being black is not standing or sitting on a stoop all day long smoking and drinking with your buddies, waiting for something to happen.

Being black is not killing the people in your community who looks like you, nor killing, assaulting and robbing others who don't.

* *I believe that being black imbues us with a particular bearing and hardiness, sustaining us through the harshest of times and the lowest of points.*

It is with certainty that I believe, the most essential element in our DNA and the hallmark of being truly black is to have a complete acknowledgment of our spirituality and connection to God, whom most blacks have now shunned to follow the immoral path of Democrats.

*I believe that being black is having the courage and fortitude, like the blacks of the 1960s Civil Rights Movement, to overcome impossible odds and struggles, and taking satisfaction in the dignity and rewards of education, honest labor, and achievement.

*I believe that real blackness encompasses love, caring and support for our children and the elderly as a village and respecting the lives of our fellow man, regardless of race, from the womb to the tomb.

*I believe being genuinely black denotes colorblindness and steadfastness of character that fosters integrity, honesty, and happiness within.

These things which I have just mentioned are elements mostly lacking in much of today's black communities, but are the cornerstones which inform and promotes the furtherance of our race and any other group in a civilized society that adheres to these tenets. President Trump, I believe, embodies these principles, this blackness, and all of the aforementioned traits our community once had which has long since been stripped from the majority of blacks by Democrats. He has exemplified and tapped into the things that blacks need for building long-term prosperity and a promising future for themselves and their children.

Even with most in the community eschewing Trump the president in favor of the Democrat Party, Trump the God-fearing businessman still works nonstop and diligently for blacks just as he does for all Americans and not seeing rejection by most in the black community as a slight at all. Trump is crass, bold, and unapologetic but is also honorable and trustworthy and tries to keep his word at all costs, rewarding those loyal to him. He holds no grudges against the black community for turning on him as a candidate and as a president, for he realizes that they know not what they do.

As with an African warrior facing down a lion in the jungle, Trump displays the raw courage and conviction to face and stare down dangerous anti-American foes such as white liberal Democrats, Antifa, Black Lives Matter, the NAACP, the Congressional Black Caucus, the LGBT community, black "civil rights" leaders, the mainstream media and others who would keep blacks stagnant, suppressed, and under their thumbs forever.

Like the tough and gritty men of yesteryear who battled America's enemies to become victors, so must Trump become as fierce as his adversaries to save our country. We are at war; everyone must know this by now. As most can surely sense a brewing storm by the gathering of dark clouds in an angry sky, so must we then discern the storm we now face as a nation, before it's too late.

Turn the page patriots.

Chapter Twenty-Six

The New Civil War

As the title of my book suggests, right now there is a new civil war taking place in our country, and I want to flesh this out, but first let's set the combatants of the two opposing and solidly entrenched sides:

Americans: Republican Vs
President: Abraham Lincoln
Slogan: We The People.
Life, Liberty & The
Pursuit of Happiness
Weapons:
Trump
God
Family
Constitution
Country
Bible
2nd Amendment
Truth
Conservatives
Bill of rights

Democrats: Confederacy
President: Jefferson Davies
Slogan: Diversity, Tolerance,
& Equality and inclusiveness
Weapons:
LGBT Community
Radical Muslims
Antifa & Black Lives Matter, RINOS
Illegal Aliens,
Globalists
Congressional Black Caucus
Liberal colleges and Universities, FBI,
DOJ
Deep State Operatives
CNN, NBC, MSNBC, CBS, NY Times,
Google, Facebook, Twitter, ABC, PBS,
BBC, Washington Post, NPR Radio,
Espn

Although certainly not complete, I believe that we now have the two sides defined at this point. To draw the connection as to how our nation got here, we must again go almost to the start of our nation's political system. So, I'm gonna rehash just a little for context, if you don't mind. During the run-up to the Civil War of 1861, the Democrat

Party mistakenly believed that they could achieve their goal of political dominance by using violence and force to conquer this nation.

Defiant, pro-slavery Democrats were then looking to tear up our newly written Constitution and bend our country's will to their own. At the time, they believed wholeheartedly that muskets, bayonets, and cannons were a means to this end. Well, history shows that their plans for using violence to overthrow our government would fail miserably as their party was soundly defeated in 1865.

Today's Democrat Party is cautiously aware that most Conservative Americans are well-armed and still cannot be taken by force. So, even though liberals do use some violence when they deem it necessary, nowadays they are focused primarily on cultural upheaval and social chaos by using political sabotage, identity politics, their liberal media henchmen, and other resources as mentioned earlier. With the sides firmly set, let's dig into the actual methods by which white liberals have been stealthily accomplishing their goal of destroying the Christian foundation of our nation in their quest for political dominance, shall we?

1. Attack and indoctrinate the youth: Starting with preschool and right on through college, children are the most sought after demographic by Democrats. Disney which was once thought of as wholesome family fare, is now introducing homosexuality to children via their movies and cartoons. Some grade schools are now teaching gender fluidity, the tenets of Islam, and promoting transgenderism to impressionable small children.

Our youth is the foundation of the next generation, and if Democrats are successful in brainwashing them, that's the ballgame. The Democrat Party's' endgame here is to finish breaking the family unit apart and attacking anything dealing with Christianity by confusing our youth.

2. Flood the country with Democrat-voting illegal aliens: To reiterate, there are about 22 million or so illegals in this country, mostly Hispanic, in states like California, New York, New Jersey, and Connecticut, that have been issued driver's licenses and registered to vote. *Which begs the question, if these aliens are "undocumented,"* *how do they get "documented" to get licenses?*

Anyway, in these blue states, white liberals make it abundantly clear, all that is required for any of their "residents," illegal or not, to vote in their elections is to show their newly issued driver's licenses at the polls, making voter fraud pretty much cut and dry. Over the last ten years or so, because of the large numbers of non-citizens voting in these areas, the coastal states have been locked-in as Democrat strongholds.

And if you look at the 2016 presidential election, Hillary won the popular vote by almost four million over Trump in California, which just illuminates the strategy by Democrats to flood every state in our country with illegals and to slowly turn red states, like Texas, blue.

Let's go into detail for a moment and talk about the 2016 election. Hillary ended with a total of 65,844,610 votes, while Trump had a total of 62,979,636 votes. So, it would appear that Hillary won the popular vote by a few million; however, the election results would also show that Trump won the bulk of the electoral votes by a margin of 306 to 232, which is what counts in our presidential elections.

Now, on the surface, this seems patently unfair, but let's dig a little deeper to show just how vital our electoral college is and why the founders were so wise to have this in our Constitution. Hillary bested Trump by almost 3 million votes overall, but let's take a look at where this margin came from with a simple chart:

California(estimated 11 million illegals): Hillary 7.5 Million votes and Trump 4 Million votes. *..Hillary wins by 3.5 Million.*

Washington D.C(illegal alien stronghold): Hillary, 266,000 votes and Trump, 11,500 votes. *Hillary wins by 254,500 votes.*

Massachusetts (illegal alien stronghold and sanctuary state): Hillary 2 million votes and Trump 1 million votes.....*Hillary wins by 1 million votes.*

New York(illegal alien stronghold and sanctuary state): Hillary 4.2 Million and Trump 2.6 Million votes.... ...*Hillary wins by 1.6 million votes.*

So, with the numbers, in California alone, where illegals are voting in rather large numbers, Hillary beat Trump by about 3.5 million votes, more than enough to comprise all of her "popular vote" margin of 2.86 million votes in the 2016 election.

Today, liberal Democrats, using these illegal alien buttressed numbers as proof that the popular vote should matter, are now calling for the elimination of the electoral college altogether. Shrewd and cunning indeed. Now, as previously mentioned, according to CDC stats, estimates today show that there are about 4.5 million anchor babies in this country that were born to illegal aliens and another 200,000 being born each year and increasing. All of these illegal aliens' births are being paid for by Medicaid and taxpayers money. *So, in effect, Americans are unwittingly being made to fund their own demise.*

With that being said, I don't think that I need to go any further for you to understand that if the electoral college is ever removed from this country, all of our future elections will then forever be determined by illegal voters, leading to Democrat dominance, forever. This constitutional change may yet come to pass because it has been shown that in the last mid-term election of 2018, that over 90% of districts Democrats won had out-sized numbers of foreign-born voters.

3. Liberals invade and infect red states: A quick anecdote, I have a liberal friend who recently moved from a blue state because of high taxes and headed to North Carolina, a red state with low taxes. His relocation came about after he had lived in this blue state for decades; voting for Democrats and tax increases until the high property taxes and cost of living pushed him out. However, he is now going to be voting for the entire platform of Democrats and raising property taxes in North Carolina, his new state, and this is perhaps one of the biggest threats to our country.

These liberals are like disease-spreading cockroaches that go from area to area, dropping their liberalized contaminated larvae upon conservative states until their new homes become like the high-taxed cesspools they fled. As an example, take a look at Texas, a deep red state, and then look at Houston and Dallas, two of their once conservative cities which have now become Democrat hellholes because of the influx of liberals from California and other blue states.

4. Section eight vouchers are given to blacks: This has been going on for quite some time and really increased during Obama's tenure and his greatly expanded welfare rolls. Ever since African slaves were bought to these shores, they have truly been the pack mules of the Democrat Party, and it is no different here. Today white liberals make an enormous effort to get black and Hispanic welfare-dependent women onto the section eight rolls and provide them with vouchers to move into suburban areas.

Two things happen immediately with this strategy; almost the very instant these blacks and Hispanics move into conservative areas, crime goes up, and the districts flip to Democrat because law-abiding conservative whites and blacks move out to avoid the incivility, drug dealing, and trash strewn about in the streets by these new "residents." Then, mission accomplished, these areas are now solid Democrat voting hellholes.

5. Voter fraud, stuff the ballot box: If you look at the 2018 midterm elections, there are clues as to how Democrats, in the future, look to win seats in Congress by using fraudulent voter activity. After running for the Senate seat in Florida, Republican Rick Scott led Democrat Bill Nelson by 12,000 votes, and the election was called, yet Democrats suddenly and mysteriously found more ballots that were mailed in and the election had to be held up because *"every voice needed to be heard."*

In the governor's race in Florida, Republican Ron Desantis was leading Democrat socialist Andrew Gillum by about 35,000 votes, and the race was all but over. Gillum conceded, and then suddenly the Democrats again mysteriously "found" more ballots and Gillum rescinded his concession because *"every voice needed to be heard."*

In the governor's race in Georgia, Republican Brian Kemp whipped the hell out of Obama's and Oprah's darling Democrat Stacey Abrams by over 60,000 votes, yet suddenly the Democrat Party, you guessed it, found more ballots and wanted to hold the election up because *"every voice needed to be heard."*

In that race, sore at their lost, Democrats would also inject racism into the election as the cause of their somewhat obese candidate's defeat. Even old long-in-the-tooth black, uh, "reverend" overseer Al Sharpton himself weighed in, opining that this was just like blacks being lynched, or something to that effect.

In each of the 2018 midterm elections, all of the votes suddenly "found" were ballots supposedly cast for Democrats. *Even though they had lost every race, these cases were only test runs for Democrats, they were probing the election system and seeing how long the voting process could be held up while padding the ballot boxes with illegal votes and duplicate votes, seeing just how far they could go and if unsuccessful, to see what could be tweaked for them to be successful in future races.*

Now, over in the Senate race in Arizona, Democrat Krysten Senima won her race, beating Republican Martha McSally. This came about after McSally had been up by 12,000 votes near the close of the election. In this particular case, the Democrats gained victory because illegals there were much more emboldened, and encouraged to vote by open borders activists. There were even videos circulating around with liberal Democrat volunteers, on camera, urging illegal aliens to get out and vote, because "every voice needed to be heard."

6. Democrats are against voter Id reform: Just recently, liberal Democrats were yelling about Russian interference and election meddling in the 2016 election and even started up a two-year "Russian" investigation to supposedly "look" into the matter. Yet, in 2018, when President Trump set up a Voting Fraud Commission and asked his panel to look at each state's voting system and records to determine if there had indeed been voter fraud, the Democrats balked at the idea. And although they had been the ones screaming that election meddling had occurred, the Democrat Party quickly cried foul and refused to comply with Trump's request to investigate this "election meddling," even hiring lawyers and filing many lawsuits so they wouldn't have to.

Trump had called their bluff and Democrats had promptly retreated, knowing that many of their voters, in every election for decades now, have indeed been illegals and the dead. So no, it is not Russia, nor some social media "website" Americans should worry about, that's the shiny object Democrats are holding up to distract us from the real election meddling which is the millions of illegals now voting with impunity in elections all across our country.

But Democrats aren't finished just yet; currently, they are seeking ways to accelerate the spread of illegals across this nation and onto the voting rolls of every state. Keep watching because, if left unchecked, you will see where it will come to fruition that Republicans will never win another race, and open borders will reign, resulting in the whole of America becoming like Democrat inner cities. Hello, Honduras west!

7. Media and Hollywood influence: What passes for mainstream journalism nowadays is just opinion-laden gossip, innuendo, and supposition by liberal Democrat activists masquerading as hard-hitting "news" anchors and pundits. Also, I believe that the mainstream media is one of the most existential threats we face in the country right now and that networks like NBC, CNN, ABC, MSNBC, CBS and just about all of the liberal outlets and "papers" such as the Washington Post and NY Times, are all lying bastards set against this country's values and its citizens. These are operatives of the Democrat Party and traitors of the worst kind to our Republic. I sincerely believe that these "journalists" have given liberal Democrats all the cover needed, at every turn, to topple our nation by continually lying, suppressing, and omitting the truth in their broadcasts.

Before my awakening, I had always blindly, and naively, believed that the media was the fourth estate that would hold politicians accountable. But what happens when most of the press is in bed with one party and against the people of this nation, against Americans? The result is what you see playing out today within most of the "news" outlets, which is now just an extension of the Democrat Party. There is no accountability in most of the media for the crimes and corruption of liberal Democrats. Anti-American "journalists" are all on board with the liberal agenda, and we now have a media-driven, two-tiered justice system where the Democrat Party can do whatever they want with impunity. This takeover of most of the media by white liberals have greatly influenced the bulk of our dumbed-down populace, thus the negative focus on all things Republican.

So, going forward, pay very close attention to all these "news" networks and their broadcasts. Even when smiling "anchors" mention the weather, take it with a grain of salt because they are liars through and through; don't ever expect to hear the truth. Also, look at the sitcoms being produced nowadays, we are now, especially our youth, being inundated with homosexuality, gender fluidness, transgenderism, and immorality the likes of which we have never seen before.

A lot of these perverted and deviant behaviors are becoming normalized in our society while we sleep, snug and content in the technological and slickly produced cocoon of inclusiveness, tolerance, diversity, and equality Democrats have gotten the majority of Americans to buy into.

8. Welfare dependency and healthcare: If liberal Democrats can control these two footstools of our society, they know that they can then effectively chart their own political course because these are the biggest one-two enticement punch for the recruitment of black and illegal alien voters. If you look at the 2018 mid-term election, even though it was the Democrat Congress enacted Obamacare failure in 2009 which turned our healthcare system into a nightmare, liberal Democrats still ran on getting healthcare "fixed" and were highly successful in duping low-info and needy voters again, and winning back the house.

Obamacare is a shell game in which most Americans fail to understand that of the 20 million people enrolled in their "affordable" health plans, about 14 million were already on Medicaid before this law was even passed. So, in essence, the bulk of these "signups," from the beginning, were already welfare deadbeats, unemployed, and on the government dole, and probably for quite some time.

The remaining enrollees in Obamacare are mostly sick and elderly, and this is why the individual mandate was put in place, to force healthy people to pay for this middle-class draining monstrosity. However, this plan would backfire as millions opted to pay the penalty, to the tune of about $4 billion annually, instead of signing up and forking over outrageous premiums to the government for redistribution of their hard earned money to support generational deadbeats.

There is a recent study out that 63% of non-citizens are on some sort of government assistance and after being in this country ten years or more, over 70% are still on welfare and in the taxpayers pocket. So, no, illegal "immigrants" are not coming over to work and pick apples like Democrats have been continuously proclaiming for decades. *I mean, 22 million illegals in this country plucking fruit? There ain't that many damn apples, oranges, grapes, nectarines, figs or plums in America to pick.*

As a nation, we need to collectively turn the liberal media propaganda off, get off our iPhones, and back to reality. We need to learn the truth about what is really happening to our country, or life, as we know it in this country, will be all but over.

As we examine the above list of weapons that the Democrat Party utilizes, I will still argue that the common thread linking them all together is the emotional thrust of the black community. All of the things Democrats have been able to achieve, politically, for decades couldn't have happened without the support of plantation blacks. It is their 90% plus voting in every election since the 1960s, and electing Democrats, that has given this party the political might that liberals are now wielding as a sledgehammer to take America apart piece by piece.

So, this is it, we're at a precipice where this nation is in danger of being utterly destroyed from the inside out by the Democrat Party while most everyone mulls around like docile sheep grazing in their own little patch of grass, uncaring, and unconcerned with the direction of the country we call home. With that being said, I have laid out the two sides, and this is our war now. Democrats, for political power, are hell-bent on flooding our country with people from Guatemala, Mexico, and Honduras. These people are coming from violent, impoverished countries with different cultures and behaviors, and when their numbers are the majority, what then?

We must decide now, just what we want our country to look like in ten years, so choose carefully, the environment in which you would like your children and grandchildren to grow up in. The choice Americans make today will determine if future generations will have safe schools, safe neighborhoods, secure borders, free speech, the right to bear arms and to have all of their God-given Constitutional rights still intact within the next ten years.

It's time to choose a side, ***Americans or Democrats.*** It's just that simple, we are at critical mass. White liberals, with the aid of their media cohorts, are now employing their deceptive political correctness ideology to have all Americans involuntarily complicit in their takeover of this country. Democrats now utilize a most potent and formidable weapon called "Pretendism," which creates the lockstep, mindless zombies that, today, we often see all around us, glassy-eyed and content in their iPhone ignorance.

This brings us to the unvarnished truth of where we are right now as a nation.

Would you know more? Of course, you would, so go ahead, turn the page.

Chapter Twenty-Seven

Land Of Pretendism

Isaiah 5:20 "Woe unto them that call evil good, and good evil; that put darkness for light, and light for darkness; that put bitter for sweet, and sweet for bitter!"

Today, the descendants of African Slaves are still the pack mules for the Democrat Party, politically exploited to carry out their socialist, anti-American agenda. But where does this use of blacks by their white liberal masters leads us, and what is the end-game for our country? Well look about you, we are now witnessing what Democrats have had in store for this country for decades; to flip this country and its Christian foundation upside down and control the population by whatever means necessary.

With the extensive use of the black community, "pretendism" has been introduced to our nation, and is now forcing Americans to buy into the weaponized and deceptive philosophy of inclusiveness, tolerance, diversity, and equality on a massive and unprecedented scale.

This ideology has permeated the country and taken over our learning institutions, most of the media, various government agencies, our judicial system, the workplace, and just about every aspect of our lives. I am gonna go through the litany of wickedness and lies that we must now pretend to be wholesome and the truth, even to the detriment of our values, our principles, and way of life.

But first, let me say that I am black and conservative, and have fled the Democrat plantation. I am no longer a "pretender," and therefore I am hated by liberal Democrats who are pretenders. We patriotic "non-pretenders," along with President Trump, are now currently under siege by the enemies of this country, as I outlined in the previous chapter.

With that being said, welcome to the new America! You have just stepped into our country's new, and dangerously progressive, era of unicorns and special rainbows where inclusiveness, tolerance, diversity and equality rules, and citizens are told what to believe by the liberal-controlled media, Hollywood celebrities, academia, and slick politicians, even if it defies reality.

In the violent world of Democrats that we now live in, everything will be ok if we just follow the basic rules our enemies have laid out:

* *We now must pretend that a man who decides to take female hormones, throw on a wig, skirt, and lipstick, is then suddenly a woman. We must pretend that a woman who chooses to cut her hair short, take male hormones, and throw on male clothing is now suddenly a man.*

*We must pretend that there is no epidemic of black on black genocide, and no rampant drug dealing in black communities and we must pretend that all blacks are just peace-loving, barbecuing people who wouldn't harm a soul.

*We must pretend that violent and destructive leftist Democrat groups like Antifa and Black Lives Matter, while rioting and destroying property, are benevolent, anti-fascist groups that are just looking to "protect" Americans from the almost non-existent "KKK" and alleged "white supremacists."

*We must pretend Planned Parenthood is not a baby-butchering enterprise funded by bloodthirsty Democrats; instead we must pretend it is a loving and caring "family-planning" organization.

*We must pretend that abortion is not about the killing and dismembering of an unborn child, but instead believe that the killing of innocent children is merely a "woman's choice and right."

We must pretend that there are no corrupt Democrats and no deep-state operatives hard at work against our country; instead we must believe that the ones in opposition to the destruction of our country are somehow the ones corrupt.

We must pretend that no crimes are being committed by illegal aliens and believe that they are all just persecution-fleeing, asylum-seeking, burrito–eating, indigent, and harmless people. We must also pretend that the vast majority of the 22 million illegal aliens in this country are just hard-working folks, picking apples and oranges, and not on welfare and aggressively voting for Democrats in our elections.

We must pretend that the liberal mainstream media is full of honest, truth-seeking journalists, and not believe that they are all lying serpents in bed with anti-American Democrats and seeking to destroy our Constitution, freedoms, and suppress our rights.

We must pretend that Islam is a "peaceful" religion, even though there hasn't been any real peace in any Muslim country for thousands of years and that they have killed over 270 million people in their 1400 year existence.

We must pretend that a $15-an-hour minimum wage mandate is the silver bullet that will thrust the working poor up and into prosperity, and not the business killing, job-killing proposition it really is.

We must pretend that Hollywood is full of brilliant "actors" and" artists" practicing their "worthy craft" for public admiration, consumption, and enjoyment, and not believe that it is a cesspool of cocaine-sniffing, pedophile degenerates.

We must pretend that ISIS and MS-13 are not brutal gangs butchering Christians, gays, and innocent people, but simply milk-and-cookies-eating, leave-it-to-beaver, misguided, and thrill-seeking juvenile Muslim and Hispanic youths.

405

*We must pretend that governmental agencies like the FBI, CIA, and Justice Department aren't the deep state it is, and that it hasn't been infiltrated by anti-American leftists and Rinos. We must instead believe that these are just hard working "federal employees," government officials that are just looking out for America's best interest.

*We must now, all of a sudden, pretend that there are 82 genders, even though there has been only two since the beginning of mankind. We must also pretend that awkward-looking women commentators on manly sports shows are experts in the field, and not believe that they are just the product of forced diversity.

*We must also pretend that "Obamacare" is the healthcare panacea that we all longed for, and not the unaffordable, middle-class killing, wealth redistribution albatross that it really is.

** We must pretend that all religions are the same and that Jesus is a liar: **John 14:6:** Jesus saith unto him, "I am the way, the truth, and the life: no man cometh unto the Father, but by me."*

*We must pretend that Democrats never enslaved blacks and believe in the parties "switched" myth. And we must also pretend that these are not the same Democrats of the 1600s, 1700s, 1800s, and 1900s, who, for over 200 years, enslaved, lynched, bred and sold, and whipped blacks while denying them freedom, land ownership, education, and every other civil right in this nation.

I am gonna stop here, but there's probably much more "pretending" each one of us can think of because this list is ever expanding. Again, there is a common thread to all of this "pretendism" and "groupthink" that Americans are currently being wedged into. The ongoing exploitation of blacks has been the behind the scenes "dark" power making all of this liberal-induced insanity possible, all because of the omnipotent "parties switched" myth that the majority of the black community still trust and believe in. So, let's revisit this switch thing, just for a moment.

Chapter Twenty-Eight

Parties Switched?

Now, I am not gonna waste too much time going over this nonsense again, because if you have read my book up to this point, you should know the truth by now. I mean, people would have to be really thick in the noggin, almost retarded, to still believe that Republicans fought Democrats over black rights for over 200 years and then one day just up and switched.

But let me see if I can conjure up the scene if the parties did "switch." Republicans, along with Dr. Martin Luther King Jr, battled violent Democrats in 1964 and won, freeing blacks, again. And right after the Civil rights bill was passed, Republicans somehow, inexplicably, said: *"Hey, we fought for blacks, and over 300,000 of us died in a brutal civil war against Democrats. We also fought against the Jim Crow laws, black codes and segregation Democrats imposed upon blacks in the deep south and got all of the civil rights and freedoms passed that blacks enjoy today. So now, uh, let's just become Democrats for no particular reason. Yeah, that's it, let's become Democrats today, we now hate blacks!"*

Makes absolutely no sense, at all. Is ya head spinning yet? In other words, If Republicans supposedly switched in the 1960s, why were they still fighting for blacks in the 1960s? Here is something else even more profound; if the parties did indeed change in the 1960s as liberals claim, you gotta ask yourself, *why was it that this "switch" only occurred after Democrats lost their restrictions on blacks in the south in 1964? Then ask yourself another question, what would be the reason for a switch? Why would Republicans want to take on the Democrats' 200 plus years of black enslavement?*

As I previously noted, and to further debunk this "switched" theory, we must also remember that according to a Tuskegee study, between 1865 and 1968, there were over 4000 lynchings by Democrats, killing roughly 3000 blacks and over 1200 white Republicans assisting them. The curious thing here is that all of these lynchings mysteriously ceased shortly after the Democrat Party's Jim Crow Laws and segregation were effectively ended by the 1964 Civil Rights Act, and after Republicans and Dr. Martin Luther King Jr had stripped Democrats of their control over blacks in the south. *Let that run through your cerebral cortex for a minute.*

I recall some time ago, speaking with a low-intellect "brother" about the history of the Democrat Party and laid out a timeline of slavery. I then went over what black slaves had endured for generations at the hands of Democrats. I told him about blacks being enslaved, families separated, black males being forced into homosexual acts, blacks not being able to own land and being held back from getting an education, and treated as subhumans. I also made it known that this treatment went on for *HUNDREDS OF YEARS UNDER DEMOCRATS.*

After I was finished, he just stared at me incredulously and like most blacks, completely disregarded all of this factual and documented evidence of centuries of Democrat atrocities against blacks I had just gone through. He just kept staring as if in a trance and finally stated with conviction: *"The parties switched in the 1960s, Democrats are Republicans, and Republicans are Democrats now."*

This fool was crazy, he had unwittingly defended the Democrat Party and their centuries of atrocities and enslavement against his own people. Ignorant white liberals and uninformed emotional blacks, like this brother, will forever regurgitate the switched parties myth, never bothering to examine their irrational and illogical conclusions or even crack open a history book to expose the many contradictions of the alternate Democrat-created reality they live in.

I'm gonna take this to the bridge now, and give everyone something to think about. To further illustrate the idiocy of this "parties switched myth," we only need to look at the black community to prove the fallacy of this foolishness. *During the 1600s, 1700s, and*

1800s, the majority of blacks was enslaved by Democrats and were given food, housing, and medical care while being denied education and living on plantations ruled by violence.

Now today, in the 1900s and 2000s, a majority of blacks are still being controlled by Democrats on inner city plantations where they are mostly uneducated and given food, housing, and medical care while living amid chaos and violence.

So again, the parties never switched, and this is borne out by the black community itself. Just think, in between all of this consistency of blacks being enslaved and mostly under the Democrat Party's heel from the 1800s to the 2000s, how can anyone believe that the parties somehow switched without ever removing the majority of blacks from the control of Democrats?! Remember, up to 70% of blacks went over to the Democrat Party in the 1930s, and if the parties had switched in the 1960s, the majority of blacks would be Republicans at this point.

This is logic 101 and rationale at work, but never mind because, sadly, the damage is done, and most low-intellect plantation blacks will go to their graves believing in the "switched" hoax. I will leave that here, there's nothing further to be said on this subject.

Onward we go, I guess.

Chapter Twenty-Nine

Tale of two Muellers

You know, at one point, I wasn't gonna put this chapter in this book, but I felt that this tidbit was just too fascinating not to. So, I'm gonna go back again, for just a minute here, on how and why President Trump is being attacked at every turn by the Democrat Party and their media cohorts.

As I alluded to earlier, Trump's reaching out to the black community and opposing open borders and illegal immigration, are the main reasons behind the coup d'état that was orchestrated by Democrats and carried out by Robert Mueller, their special counselor. The black community, which the Democrat Party desperately needs, at all costs, to keep suppressed, underfoot, and controlled politically is perhaps the biggest reason though. We must remember that Lincoln, King, and Kennedy were all killed trying to help blacks break away from the Democrat plantation.

Let me give you something really chilling to think about here. President Trump and his policies are creating a modern-day Black Wall Street in this nation. As they did in the 1800s when they used the Klu Klux Klan to crush Black Wall Street, recently, Democrats employed Robert Mueller, their special counsel overseer, to try and stop Trump and by extension, destroy any and all black progress his policies are currently creating.

As of this writing, it appears that old Mueller's manufactured "investigation" is over, with nothing to show after two years. However, *Courtesy of War History Online,* this attempt by Democrats to weaponize and manipulate our government agencies, and political system is eerily similar to what the Nazis did in the 1930s by deploying Heinrich Mueller, the head of the Gestapo Secret Police, to control and exterminate Jews.

Then, Henrich Mueller was used by the Nazi Party to effectively crush Hitler's political adversaries in much the same way Robert Mueller was used for two years by the Democrat Party to try to bring down a Republican president.

It was said that Henrich Mueller approached his tasks with fanatical zeal and dogged dedication in his quest to annihilate the Nazi Party's political foes and suppress Jews. This is strikingly similar to Robert Mueller's dogged determination to stop Trump and the Republicans, and block the black community's progress.

Under Heinrich Mueller, the Nazis took control of the Jews, and with Robert Mueller, the Democrat Party is trying to remain in control of the black community, their power base.

In the 1930s, Heinrich Mueller was involved in espionage and counter-espionage and was known to have distributed false information to the Soviet Intelligence Service. Today, this is strikingly similar in that Robert Mueller had used a fabricated dossier by the Democrat Party and rogue FBI agents to investigate, create charges, and get indictments to try to topple Trump's presidency.

Also, like Heinrich Mueller's leaking and dissemination of false propaganda in the 1930s, Robert Mueller's manufactured and misleading information from the fake Russian dossier was also leaked to the Democrat-controlled media and disseminated to the American public.

I imagine that both Muellers, at the behest of the Nazi Party of the 1930s and Democrat Party of the 2000s, broke down doors in the dead of night to arrest and torture their political opponents into submission with threats of harm to them and their families.

*We must remember that Hitler and his Mueller in the 1930s used mistruths and misdirection to achieve and maintain power, and to implement policies of the Nazi party, just like the Democrat Party and their Mueller today.

*The website *"The Holocaust Explained"* explains how the Nazi Party went from a small, violent party to dominating politics in Germany, just like the evolution of the Democrat Party from the 1800s to today.

*Hitler accomplished his political ascension by separating Germany into groups during the 1920s and 1930s and creating his own identity politics, much like Democrats today.

*The Nazi Party's rise to power would dovetail with the popularity of Hitler among the German youth, just like with millennials and Democrats today.

*Think about this, the Great Depression of 1929 in America deeply affected Germany as well and Hitler and the Nazi Party took advantage of this "crisis' by offering "help" to downtrodden German Citizens, just like the Democrats did with the New Deal and welfare.

*Hitler's Nazi Party, like the Democrat Party today, placed emphasis on controlling most of the media, along with wanting the citizenry disarmed.

*Both parties, early on, tried to take their respective countries by force, only to fail in their initial attempt but would ultimately regain power and rule by violence, deceit, and political subterfuge.

History shows that there are many similarities between Democrats, and Nazis, so much so that it is almost like they are one and the same party. And there are a lot more similarities between the two Muellers, Robert and Heinrich, which you can research for yourself. You know, if I didn't know any better, I would swear these two are related, but I'll let you be the judge of that.

That's all on this one. We 'll move on.

Chapter Thirty

My Case and Summation

O k, I am close to wrapping things up, and as you can see, I have laid out my case regarding the threads of deceit and exploitation of blacks by the Democrat Party, which began during slavery of the 1600s and is still ongoing today.

And although the black community has always been the source for the political power Democrats now have; all Americans are now being affected by the abuse of their political machinery. If we really take an in-depth look into the foundation, platform, and ideologies of both the Democrats and real Conservative Republicans, the differences are unmistakable and quite remarkable. Republicans believe in God and diplomacy and that everyone should have free speech and rights as guaranteed by our Constitution. While Democrats believe in political might, violence, manipulation and that their will is your will.

As I've mentioned repeatedly, the Democrat Party's usage of black overseers and plantation blacks, and their weaponized and all-encompassing ideology of inclusiveness, tolerance, diversity, and equality, is the means and conduit by which white liberals have introduced immorality, Godlessness, and lawlessness to our youth and society in general. It is also ironic, and telling, that these "loving" and "inclusive" Democrats not only deliberately excludes two important groups, Christians and conservatives, especially black ones, from their party, but absolutely hates everything they represent.

But why is there so much animosity towards these harmless groups? The reason being is that Christians and Conservatives are at the very heart of the moral fabric of this country and are the only stumbling blocks in the way of progressivism and the remaking of our society into an immoral, lawless, and chaotic utopia that Democrats desire. Sorta like a new Roman empire.

Let's take Christianity for example and go over exactly why this religion is considered such an anathema and threat to the Democrat Party. Contrary to the leftist colleges and universities' twisted re-counting of history, our nation was founded on Christian principles and by God-fearing men who prayed often. *Were our founding fathers perfect? No, because man isn't perfect.* However, in the founding of this country, these inspired men would install Biblical principles and values which would inform our rights and morality as a people and create societal boundaries, and producing the proper and sound environment to raise generations of children who would learn of God and of prayer.

Our Bible-based founding principles would also make this country the most compassionate and charitable nation on earth. Therein lies the issue, these Christian values are in direct conflict with the Democrat Party's secular ideology and platform, and today are under constant assault by their wholly anti-God agenda. You see, for white liberals to have all things immoral become part of their Godless mainstream culture and to be viewed as normal in this country, Christianity and all of its tenets would have to be suppressed or abolished entirely.

This is why you see the recent assaults on Christian bakers by radical homosexuals and gay rights activists who are pushing to remove God and prayers from this nation. Currently, there is an accelerated movement by Democrats to advocate for and promote gender fluidity and transgenderism in a lot of the curriculum in schools across the country.

The reason why this assault on morality in this nation is happening at such an alarming pace is that ever since the 1990s, as I detailed earlier, the gay community have stealthily infiltrated all areas of power and influence within our country. These homosexuals now hold powerful and influential positions in our nation's corridors of power, such as Congressmen and Congresswomen, Senators, multibillionaire CEOs, judges, school teachers, professors, heads of universities and colleges, along with many other prominent positions embedded within the mainstream media and Hollywood. *Why do you think that, even though the gay community only make up about 4%, if that, of our population, most sitcoms and dramas on TV today always seem to have a homosexual or transgender character in a starring role?*

Also, just to reiterate, radical Muslims, a violent group that absolutely abhors homosexuality is also, strangely, under the Democrat's same umbrella of inclusiveness, tolerance, diversity, and equality. This inclusion would seem, on the surface, to make for strange bedfellows and pose a massive conflict with gays within the party, but remember this saying: *"The enemy of my enemy is my friend."* Muslims are sucking it up, for now, only because they hate Christianity even more than they hate gays, and if they had to feign love for the homosexual community for a short while to achieve the goal of seeing Christian values all but erased from America, so be it.

This unseemly partnership of homosexuals and Muslims working together in "brotherhood" comes as a result of a shared and mutual goal of ultimately destroying the one thing which stands as the sole impediment hindering the progression of both groups. However, if Democrats were ever successful in having the Bible and its teachings entirely removed from America and Islam indeed rises, Muslims will, at some point, turn upon homosexuals just as they now do in Muslim countries, for the two cannot ever coexist in peace.

And if this situation were to ever come about, white liberal Democrats would view the deaths of these gays as sacrifices, collateral damage, a small price to pay to achieve their ultimate goal of removing the moral restrictions of Christianity.

Strangely, unlike radical Muslims, conservative straight white men are excluded from the Democrats' inclusiveness blanket because they are descendants of the architects of this Christian based foundation and still live by biblical values and principles. Their ancestors are the white pioneers of the capitalist system we have in place today, and ones who have made this nation the best on earth. Nonetheless, liberals and deranged feminists have carefully crafted the illusion that all conservative white men are evil, even as they enjoy the fruits and comforts that these same Caucasian entrepreneurs have created.

Today's Democrats see a pathway of gaining control of the wealthiest nation on earth by demonizing and bringing down this demographic, which entails flooding the country with brown-skinned, welfare dependent, and eager Democrat voters. And if they were ever to be successful in their endeavor to gain complete control of our political system, an oligarchy would be formed consisting of the few select and very wealthy Democrat powerbrokers.

Think about the imagery of billionaire tech giants and other Democrat billionaire celebrities roosting at the very top of the political food chain and ruling America and its citizens. There are already, today, liberal Democrat billionaires like Tom Steyer, Mark Zuckerberg, Bill Gates, Warren Buffet, George Soros, Jeff Bezos, and many other Silicon Valley billionaires and wealthy celebrities who fancy themselves the upper crust of society.

These elitists have placed themselves upon a pedestal and have an aching desire to be admired as Gods and want lower class Americans to worship them, to be in awe of their wealth and power. They, along with most celebrities, desire and need worshippers and followers who cannot attain what they have attained, or do the things that they can, or own what they can own.

Just watch any awards show, watch the pompous and arrogant white liberal Democrats parading around in their finery and debauchery, and you will quickly grasp what I am referring to. They are all wealthy leftists, elites, with armed security and high walls around their homes, who have poured billions into Democrat races and into illegal migration, fully supporting every detrimental and immoral social cause against this country.

Again, the only firewall stopping them all is Conservatives and Christians and their belief in God, limited government, an intact nuclear family, hard work, and education. Coincidentally, these core principles are also the building blocks and pillars of our society which has made our nation the most incredible, morally successful, capitalist experiment ever created, in history.

With that being said, the Bible and its teachings have provided generations of American youths with the moral foundation and compass to guide them into productive and lawful adulthood. The backbone of any thriving society and, undoubtedly, the mainstay and bedrock upon which ours and any other country's has flourished is an intact family consisting of sound, God-fearing, male, and female parents. Nonetheless, the Democrat Party's continued assaults and destruction of the nuclear family has been devastating to our country and is no more pronounced than in the black community.

As I stated previously, there was a time when over 80% of black families were intact and were very spiritual; I mean really God-fearing religious people. The Democrats' war on Christianity and conservatism and the family unit has decimated these black families and turned them away from the one true God.

The plan was to purposely deconstruct and then reconstruct American families, primarily black. This is why the Defense of Marriage Act, which stated that marriage is between a man and woman, was attacked so viciously and finally defeated by Obama and liberal Democrats, to remove all of the meaning from this venerable institution.

Once the law was struck down, it opened the door for liberal Democrats to further demean and diminish the teachings of the Bible and God's intentions for male and female, thus, blurring the lines as to what or who could constitute a "marriage" It is not inconceivable that now under our new open society rules bought about by this change, that one day polygamy, bestiality, and even pedophilia could gain traction under Democrats in Congress. This is not to say that these things will ever happen, but without any conclusive definition of marriage anymore, I wouldn't bet the farm against it.

Liberals could and probably most certainly will, under their inclusiveness, tolerance, equality and diversity platform, usher all of these things into our mainstream society without most dumbed-down Americans even blinking an eye.

For blacks and most Americans, when it comes to spirituality, it has been a simple equation really: *"More God, less crime, less God, more crime."*

Just think, the black community, for a lowly monthly stipend and welfare table scraps have aided and abetted white liberal Democrats in plundering and pilfering their cache of hard-fought civil rights capital, all to be exploited for causes such as homosexuality and transgenderism.

417

When Republicans freed blacks in 1865 and gave them full rights in 1964, I don't think these God-fearing white men, nor Dr. King for that matter, could have ever envisioned the disastrous results that we are now seeing today among blacks.

Right now, I wanna take a little time and, again, go over the three pivotal points in the history of our nation, which we previously explored when our community had the opportunity to be entirely free and independent but were denied each and every time by Democrats.

1. *Democrats assassinated Abraham Lincoln* *to stop Reconstruction and Black Wall Street in 1865. He was killed because he bought freedom and autonomy for blacks under his presidency. For the first time, former black slaves had tasted the sweet wine of true equality and were building their own businesses and obtaining wealth, until Democrats loosed the KKK on'em.*

2. *Democrats killed John F Kennedy in 1963.* *Although he was a Democrat, this president leaned conservative and was all in for civil rights for blacks. His fatal error came in 1963 when he forced then Democrat Governor of Alabama, George Wallace, to integrate schools in the south. He would be assassinated later that same year in Dallas Texas by Democrats.*

3. *Democrats killed Dr. Martin Luther King Jr in 1968.* *Again, to stop black progression, Democrats killed King and installed their own black "Reverend" leaders in his place to make sure that no other black influence would rise up to try to free blacks from their plantations ever again.*

Even with all of these wasted chances, I genuinely believe that it's not over just yet for the downtrodden black community. I believe that God is giving blacks one last hurrah with Donald J Trump, our 45th president. I will repeat it again; Trump is restoring blue-collar manufacturing and factory jobs for blacks. He is removing illegal aliens from the country who were siphoning off the jobs that the black community have, for decades, depended on to support their families. He's funding historically black colleges and has invested millions in training minorities for skilled and well-paying jobs.

Trump has also earmarked billions for the revitalization of the Democrat-decimated inner cities. He is protecting Christians from the Democrat Party's anti-God onslaught and holding Bible meetings at the Whitehouse. Trump's policies have had a ripple effect, not only for blacks but for all Americans of all stripes. The economy is once again blue-collar worker friendly and good jobs are plentiful for the black community and all Americans.

Every citizen in this nation needs to look and see what God has wrought through Trump, our Deliverer. The black community has been drowning for decades, crying out for help, and God has heeded their calls on several occasions. He has sent the boat of deliverance and salvation three times to their aid since the 1800s. I believe that President Trump is God's fourth attempt to deliver the black community. There will come a time when he will send no more boats, and no more Deliverers.

Turn the page.

Chapter Thirty-One

Altar Call

Well, we've come to the end of my book, and as you can see, this has been my walkaway experience. I have found true freedom, now that I've escaped the Democrat plantation. At this time, I wanna thank each and every one of you for riding along with me on my journey and sharing in my thoughts. And, I want everyone to be aware that it's not just the black community that is being exploited and manipulated. All Americans, regardless of race, are very much in danger from the existential threat posed by liberal Democrats and their weaponized "pretendism."

Everyone must wake up, and now, to what's happening to our beautiful country before it is too late. The violent, win at all costs Democrat Party has never been about uplifting anyone and has always sought to bring all of America down to the level, and conditions, of the crime-ridden, drug-infested inner cities they currently preside over.

For total dominance, it is the Democrat Party's mission to create white plantations as well, starting with the easily swayed millennials. Americans need to wake up and take a quick look around, many white youths today are adopting the same attitudes, behaviors, and disregard for the law as most in the black community. So, an urgent message to whites; there is still time to heed my words, but the window is closing, and fast. Save yourselves, your communities, and children before it's too late, leave the Democrat Party post haste.

Unfortunately, at this point, I feel that it is much too late for the majority of the black community, most of my people are too far gone. Nonetheless, I am not giving up just yet, and at this time, in a last-ditch appeal, I wanna do like the pastors of the true church of the living God and give an altar call to my wayward and downtrodden brothers and sisters still living in Democrat inner cities, frustrated and filled with hopelessness:

"My brothers and sisters, our ancestors have been enslaved, beaten, lynched, and held back from owning land and attaining education by Democrats for centuries. And we've suffered as Democrats sicced dogs and turned water hoses on our black forebearers in the 1950s and 1960s, and killed our civil rights leaders.

"My brothers and sisters, you've been down in the gutters of despair and hopelessness for quite some time now. You've suffered from poor schools, gang violence, drugs and poverty in your communities long enough and you've heard the empty promises of liberal Democrats forever. And believing in their lies, you have voted faithfully for their party for decades.

Now after over fifty years of being black hamsters on the Democrat Plantation's wheel of exploitation, you still have nothing of substance to show for it except broken families and broken communities where fatherless children are shooting each over drugs and sneakers in the streets.

How long can our community take the wanton and senseless bloodshed of our youth? Brothers and sisters, there have been times when you've had just one can of beans left in your cabinet. You had fallen on your knees praying to God, whom the majority of you in the black community have turned their backs on, to give you the strength to find a means to support and feed your families.

Times have been rough, and some of you have turned to wrongdoing on occasion to make ends meet when they couldn't quite seem to come together on their own. My brothers and sisters, I stand before you today to tell you to let not your heart be troubled, that real hope has come to us. God has sent us his messenger, a deliverer, and builder to redeem our wretched communities if only we can just look past the color of his skin and search his heart and soul.

I know that for some of you, this is the most difficult thing to do because of how you've been conditioned and what you have been taught by the Democrat Party and their lying media. We, the black community, have been given light to remove the veil of darkness and ignorance from our eyes. We now have among us someone to lead us away from the unfulfilled and directionless wandering our community has endured for decades. But how can this savior, this Deliverer that God has sent to us, grasp your hands when they are clenched and balled tightly into fists? How can we be pulled up and out of bondage if we will not grab ahold of the conservative rope of freedom and financial independence?

Brothers and sisters, our window of enlightenment and fulfillment is now. So tonight, I'm asking all of you, will you take a stand with me? Will you throw off those repressive Democrat shackles of hate, ignorance, stagnation, and racial divisiveness, and turn to God's precious light of hope and salvation?

Will you come tonight and join with the rest of us as we seek that which is holy, righteous, and colorblind? Won't you do this now when the time is nigh? Brothers and sisters come with me to a better tomorrow, one in which your real potential is unlocked, and you can finally breathe free, partaking of all this land has to offer.

Will you take this opportunity that now presents itself and awaits you? Will you take the path prepareth unto you to restore your manhood, your womanhood, your communities, and your neighborhoods? Will you commit to rebuilding the black family, and restoring your faith and belief in God?

Won't you take a chance tonight to see what God has wrought? You have free will, and can stay content on the Democrat party's plantation, subsisting on their welfare scraps, subservient, and living in adverse conditions, or you can finally experience what Lincoln promised, true freedom and equality for all Americans, regardless of race, creed, or color.

Will you be the men and women that God always intended? Brothers and sisters, I ask you now with all sincerity, will you once again stand on the side that fought for your freedoms and rights and come on over to the truth. Will you come on over to the Republican Party?

After all, what have you got to lose?"

Conservative Resources and
Acknowledgements of Inspiration:

◆◆◆

Breitbart
Washington Examiner
PragerU
Truenews.org
Thomas Sowell
Jordan Peterson
Dailey Caller
Conservative Tribune

Dinesh D'Souza
Larry Elder
Jesse Lee Peterson
American Renaissance
Conservative Youtubers
Colin Flaherty
Daily Caller
Patriot Academy

Afterthought:

A t the start of this book I asked these fundamental questions, and will now do so again:

Germans banned the Nazi party's name because of the atrocities committed against millions of Jews, why hasn't America banned the Democrat name for the atrocities committed against millions of blacks?

And since all of the horrific acts of slavery and violence against blacks were done by Democrats before the supposedly "switch" of the 1960s, isn't the lynchings, whippings, separation of families, selling and breeding of blacks during the 200 plus years of slavery all fall under the Democrat Party's mantle?

Most importantly, knowing this, why would any American today wear the Democrat name like a badge of honor?

* *Just who are these people today still proudly calling themselves Democrats, and just how did it come about that this name got cleaned up after being associated with centuries of black enslavement? Shouldn't anyone calling themselves a Democrat be branded racists for associating with a party that enslaved, beat, and lynched blacks for such a long period?*

Lastly, why do the majority of blacks today call themselves Democrats and fiercely defend the enslavers of their ancestors?

I firmly believe that neither the Democrat Party, nor its name, should exist in our nation, and any traces be removed from our society entirely. With that said, I really thought about my values, and asked myself, why did I ever align myself with the Democrat Party? *I am not homosexual, I am not transgender, I am not welfare dependent, I am not a radical Muslim, I am not an illegal alien, I am not Godless, I am against abortions. I love my country, I love our constitution, I love the first amendment, I love the second amendment, I love my flag, I love my freedom, I love my country, and I love the lord, whom I thank every day for giving me clarity.* I am no longer a plantation black, and it feels beautiful.

◆◆◆

Right now, in our divisive and chaotic society, the shiny object is all things Trump, but his presidency is just the 45th, which means that there will possibly be a 46th, a 47th, and others after him if our country hasn't entirely failed by then.

Trump's presidency is but a ship passing in the night, unloading its America-First cargo for four, maybe eight years at most. However, there are those entrenched politicians who have been in office ten, twenty, thirty, and forty years who still will be there in our government after he leaves office.

Some of these long in the tooth, corrupt politicians have seen many administrations come and go, and over decades have become multimillionaires after receiving payouts and kickbacks from lobbyists and special interest groups. This corruption has continued, unabated, administration after administration with no end in sight.

There is now a two-tiered governmental system at work, and the president really does not control much of anything at this point, his power has been usurped by deep state politicians and federal agencies that have their own agenda.

Before Trump, we had staggering Illegal immigration, planes flown into buildings by radical Muslims, blacks killing each other like dogs in the streets, welfare dependency, job-killing anti-American globalists, racial tension, cops targeted, Christians targeted, etc.

After Trump, many of these same things will remain, and the next shiny object attempting to disrupt this status quo will be dealt with as he has. So, today, while Democrats, some who've been in office since the 1970s, want you to focus on all things Trump, the passing ship, they are the ones, who, after his administration, Americans must contend with or see this nation fail.

Since the founding of this country, Democrats has always been our enemies. Like it or not, the war is upon us. Take care, be cautious, and Godspeed.

"It is the duty of nations as well...And to recognize the sublime truth announced in the Holy Scriptures and proven by all history that those nations only are blessed whose God is the Lord [Psalm 33:12]. But we have forgotten God. We have forgotten the gracious hand which preserved us in peace and multiplied and enriched and strengthened us, and we have vainly imagined in the deceitfulness of our hearts that all these blessings were produced by some superior wisdom and virtue of our own. Intoxicated with unbroken success, we have become too self-sufficient to feel the necessity of redeeming and preserving grace – too proud to pray to the God that made us.
...*Lincoln....during the Civil War.

Made in the USA
Columbia, SC
24 June 2020